World business cycles

Editorial information compiled by The Economist

ISBN 0 85058 057 9

Published by
The Economist Newspaper Limited
25 St James's Street
London
England SW1A 1HG

Manufactured in the United Kingdom

Printed by
Page Bros (Norwich) Limited
Norwich
Norfolk

Bound by
Norton Bridge Bookbinders Limited
Hitchin
Hertfordshire

Distributed exclusively in North America by
Gale Research Company
Book Tower
Detroit
Michigan 48226
USA

Introduction

This book provides a broad look at world business cycles, and includes detailed information for 84 countries on gross domestic product and other series of interest, where available during the period 1950–80; also for 34 commodities on world production and a representative price, again for 1950–80.

Also included is a long-term view of gross domestic product, and other series of interest, for the United Kingdom and United States during the period from the 1850s to 1980. The Economist Commodity Price Index is included for 1860 to 1980 as a guide to changes in commodity prices generally.

The book attempts to define the problem of business cycles, and not to suggest a method of avoiding them and the unemployment they create. However. while defining the problem certain relationships become apparent which can be a guide to the future understanding of these fluctuations.

The volume is divided into four main sections: world business cycles 1950–80, taking a broad look at main items of economic interest; a long-term view, taking a look at various items of economic interest for the period 1850–1980; countries 1950–80, which includes detailed figures for 84 countries; and commodities 1950–80, which includes detailed figures for 34 commodities.

Points to note in using the information provided are:

1. *The terms expansion and recession* In this book, attention is focused on the percentage changes from year to year, and so on the various periods of expansion and recession rather than on the particular 'peak' or 'trough' of any cycle. Expansion is a clear and unemotive word, while recession can be used to cover periods of falling production; the line between recession and 'depression' is not defined. Here, recession means a period of negative growth, and also a period of comparatively low growth; 'comparatively' in this sense means low in relation to the rates of growth before and after the period concerned. No firm rule has been applied in allocating the term recession to various periods in the world and long-term view sections; the term 'mini-recession' has been used where a period does not include actual falls in product (negative growth), and where growth, while low in relation to the periods before and after, is still at a comparatively high rate. The definition of recessions in terms of actual years varies according to source, and the years specified here, based on the figures shown in the tables, may vary from those specified in other references; definition in years can also lead to differences, where a period of expansion ends about the centre of a year, and a recession starts in the same year.

2. *Series used* For definitions of the various series used see the Technical appendix; in general, gross domestic product, etc, are in quantity terms (at constant prices), and financial series are in value terms. Figures refer to calendar years (unless otherwise stated), except for money stock and international reserves which refer to the level at the end of the calendar year.

3. *Indexes* Figures have usually been standardised by showing them as index numbers, so that comparisons may be made more easily between countries. Further, indexes are shown with 1970 = 100, so that the amount of growth from 1970 to, say, 1980 is immediately apparent, and the earlier years also show the overall amount of growth from any year on a comparable basis for different items. For example, looking at the 1950 figure shows where the largest amount of growth to 1970 (smallest 1950 figure) has been.

4. *Charts* All charts have the same scale for showing the % change over year, which is the basis of virtually all charts (also see the Technical appendix concerning this measure). This means that the amount of fluctuation is comparable between all charts in the book, although, in the long-term view section, the different time scales mean that the steepness of a fluctuation is not comparable with those of charts in other sections, all based on a time scale of 1950–80. Comparing the amounts of fluctuation for different countries, items and commodities indicates which fluctuate the most; in general greater fluctuation means greater risk (higher 'volatility'), but it can also mean greater opportunity with regard to share prices and commodity prices.

5. *Accuracy* This book concentrates on broad rather than detailed movements; however, figures are shown to the number of decimal places justified in general by the underlying series. Figures for the main index have in some cases been rounded accordingly, while the % change over year, based on the original data before adjusting to a rounded index basis, may be more accurate than is apparent from the % change calculated from the index as shown in the tables. Where there has been a break in the original series used, earlier figures have been linked to the later to form a consistent series. Adjustments have been made to series to ensure as far as possible accuracy in the year-to-year change, rather than in the longer view; hence the series shown here will not necessarily agree with other series which take a look at isolated years over a long-term, perhaps based on information from censuses. Latest figures are in some cases provisional, and figures for the early fifties have in some cases been estimated. The degree of accuracy may vary over time.

Every care has been taken in the compilation of the information in this book, but no responsibility can be accepted for the accuracy of the data presented.

The main sources for information have been the United Nations, in particular publications of the International Monetary Fund and the International Labour Organisation, Organisation for Economic Co-operation and Development, 'National Income, Expenditure and Output of the United Kingdom 1855–1965' by C H Feinstein and 'Historical Statistics of the United States' (US Department of Commerce). British official statistics are reprinted by kind permission of the Controller of HM Stationery Office. All sources are gratefully acknowledged.

Contents

World business cycles
1950–80

Summary 1950–80

1. The main periods of expansion in the world were 1950–53, 1955–57, 1959–73 and 1976–79.

2. Main world recessions were in 1954, 1958, 1974–75 and 1980.

3. Mini-recessions, mainly in Europe, interrupted the 1950–53 expansion in 1952 and the 1976–79 expansion in 1977.

4. The long period of general expansion from 1959 to 1973 was interrupted by a number of mini-recessions, notably 1960–61, 1964–65, 1967, 1970 and 1972. This period, mainly of the sixties, was one of good growth, and generally falling commodity prices.

Mini-recessions tended to be concentrated on commodity-producing countries, affecting by falling prices.

5. Commodity prices, after rising to 1951 on the impact of the Korean war, fell generally until 1962, recovering to the 1951 level only by 1969 in sterling terms.

6. The rise in commodity prices from 1971, following the suspension of the gold convertibility of the dollar in 1971, was similar in broad outline to that associated with the Korean war; the 1974–75 recession followed the sharp rise in crude oil prices in 1973–74.

Gross domestic product

Fluctuations in the quantity of gross domestic product are shown in the following chart for the world, United States and United Kingdom; the chart shows the % change over the year to isolate the amount of fluctuation (also see the Technical appendix, pages 190–191). Figures for the world are included in the table below; figures for the United States are on page 145, and for the United Kingdom on page 139.

The main periods of expansion for world gross domestic product were 1950–53, 1955–57, 1959–73 and 1976–79, with main recessions in 1954, 1958, 1974–75 and 1980. These four recessions were those in which most main industrial countries participated; there were, in addition, a number of mini-recessions, where the rate of expansion was low for a number of countries but was not of sufficient

magnitude or did not occur in enough large countries, to influence markedly the world picture. These were for 1952, which occurred mainly in Europe, 1960–61, 1964–65, 1967, 1970, 1972 and 1977.

The main periods of expansion for the United States were 1950–53, 1955–57, 1959–69 (with mini-recessions in 1960–61 and 1967), 1971–73 and 1976–79, with main recessions in 1954, 1958, 1970, 1974–75 and 1980. Generally as for the world picture, but with a more severe recession in 1970. For the United Kingdom, the main periods of expansion were 1950–51, 1953–57, 1959–61, 1963–68, 1970–73 and 1976–79, with main recessions in 1952, 1958, 1962, 1969, 1974–75 and 1980 and mini-recessions in 1966 and 1977. Generally as for the United States, but with recession in 1952 instead of 1954, 1962 instead of 1960–61 and 1969 instead of 1970.

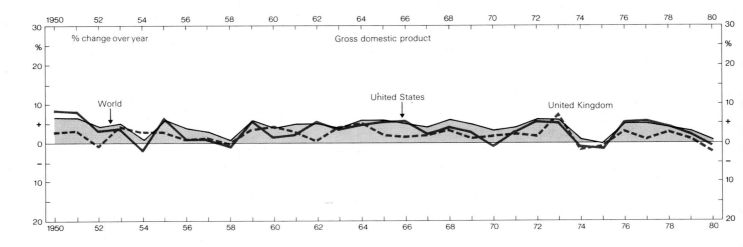

World gross domestic product

	Index 1970 = 100	% change over year		Index 1970 = 100	% change over year		Index 1970 = 100	% change over year		Index 1970 = 100	% change over year
1950	42	7	1958	56	1	1966	84	5	1974	118	1
1951	44	7	1959	60	6	1967	87	4	1975	118	0
1952	46	4	1960	62	4	1968	92	6	1976	124	5
1953	48	5	1961	65	5	1969	97	5	1977	130	5
1954	49	1	1962	68	5	1970	100	3	1978	135	4
1955	52	6	1963	71	4	1971	104	4	1979	139	3
1956	54	4	1964	75	6	1972	110	6	1980	140	1
1957	55	3	1965	79	6	1973	117	6			

Following is a broad summary of the countries affected by each of the recessions identified; the allocation to a particular recession is based only roughly on the year specified – it may have begun for any particular country in the preceding or following year. Further, a classification is made according to the general magnitude of the recession for each country; while a recession is a mini-recession from a world viewpoint, it may be either a main recession or a mini-recession from a country's point of view. As mentioned in the introduction, no firm definition of 'recession' is adopted; classification depends on whether the rate of growth is low in relation to those around it – although a negative rate of growth usually means that

there has been a main recession.

The classification is based mainly on the changes in gross domestic product, as shown for each country included in the countries section. Also included here is information on changes in commodity prices, since these can be related to recessions for some countries; recession for commodities means a main fall in the price. Detailed information on price changes is included in the commodities section.

It may be noted that 1980, the last year included here, in many cases marks the beginning of a longer recession.

Recessions summary

1952 recession Main recession: Argentina, Australia, Austria, Belgium, Denmark, France, Greece, Iceland, Israel, Luxembourg, Netherlands, Panama, Paraguay, Portugal, Sri Lanka, Sweden, Switzerland, United Kingdom; beef, copra, cotton, jute, lead, maize, manganese, palm oil, rubber, silver, sugar, tea, tin, tobacco, wool, zinc.
Mini-recession: Barbados, Chile, Costa Rica, Guatemala, Italy, Jamaica, Japan; coal, cocoa, groundnuts.

1954 recession Main recession: Bolivia, Brazil, Burma, Canada, Denmark, Dominican Republic, Finland, Guatemala, Haiti, Honduras, Mexico, Morocco, Peru, Thailand, Turkey, United States; butter, coal, coffee, groundnuts, iron ore, jute, maize, manganese, rice, soyabeans, tea, tin, wheat, wool.
Mini-recession: Cyprus, Ecuador, Ireland, Italy, Japan, Norway; bananas, beef, cocoa, copper, copra, newsprint.

1958 recession Main recession: Argentina, Barbados, Belgium, Bolivia, Brazil, Burma, Canada, Chile, Colombia, Costa Rica, Cyprus, Dominican Republic, Finland, France, Haiti, Iceland, Ireland, Jamaica, Luxembourg, Morocco, Netherlands, Nicaragua, Panama, Paraguay, Peru, Portugal, South Africa, Spain, Switzerland, Syria, Thailand, United Kingdom, United States, Uruguay, Venezuela, Zambia; aluminium, bananas, beef, butter, coal, coffee, copper, cotton, crude oil, groundnuts, iron ore, jute, lamb, lead, maize, manganese, palm oil, phosphate rock, rice, rubber, soyabeans, sugar, tea, tin, wheat, wool, zinc.
Mini-recession: Australia, Denmark, Ecuador, El Salvador, West Germany, Israel, Japan, Malawi, Malta, New Zealand, Norway, Philippines, Sweden, Trinidad and Tobago; newsprint, silver.

1960–61 recession (also includes 1962) Main recession: Argentina, Burma, Bolivia, Costa Rica, Cyprus, Greece, Guyana, Haiti, Honduras, Jamaica, Malta, Morocco, Nigeria, United Kingdom, Uruguay, Zambia; aluminium, bananas, beef, butter, cocoa, coffee, copper, copra, crude oil, groundnuts, iron ore, jute, lamb, lead, maize, newsprint, palm oil, phosphate rock, rubber, soyabeans, sugar, tea, zinc.
Mini-recession: Australia, Austria, Canada, Denmark, Ecuador, Guatemala, Iceland, Israel, Japan, South Korea, Luxembourg, Mexico, Netherlands, New Zealand, Philippines, Sri Lanka, Thailand, Trinidad and Tobago, Tunisia, Turkey, United States; coal, manganese, nickel, tin, tobacco, wool.

1964–65 recession (also includes 1963) Main recession: Barbados, Brazil, Burma, Cyprus, Dominican Republic, Ecuador, Haiti, India, Indonesia, Jugoslavia, Malawi, Morocco, Singapore, Sri Lanka, Syria; bananas, coal, cocoa, coffee, cotton, crude oil, manganese, rice, sugar, tobacco, wheat, wool.
Mini-recession: Colombia, Egypt, Ireland, Italy, Japan, Kenya, Panama, Philippines, Trinidad and Tobago, Turkey; newsprint, tea.

1967 recession Main recession: Burma, Egypt, West Germany, Ghana, Haiti, Iceland, Iraq, Israel, Luxembourg, Malawi, New Zealand, Nigeria, Pakistan, Paraguay, Peru, Singapore, Syria, Tunisia, Uruguay, Zaire, Zambia; bananas, beef, buffer, coffee, copper, copra, cotton, groundnuts, iron ore, jute, lamb, lead, maize, manganese, palm oil, phosphate rock, rubber, soyabeans, tea, tin, wheat, wool, zinc.
Mini-recession: Argentina, Australia, Austria, Canada, Chile, Denmark, Dominican Republic, Guyana, Jamaica, Malaysia, Netherlands, Nicaragua, Norway, Sweden, Switzerland, United Kingdom, United States, Venezuela.

1970 recession Main recession: Honduras, Jamaica, Liberia, Libya, Pakistan, Sri Lanka, Sweden, Syria, Tanzania, Trinidad and Tobago, United States, Zambia; bananas, beef, cocoa, coffee, copper, copra, cotton, crude oil, gold, iron ore, jute, lead, phosphate rock, rice, rubber, silver, sugar, tin, tobacco, wool.
Mini-recession: Malawi, Malaysia, Malta, Morocco, New Zealand, Nicaragua, Norway, Philippines, Portugal, Saudi Arabia, Spain, Thailand, Uganda, United Kingdom; lamb.

1972 recession (includes 1973) Main recession: Burma, Chile, Egypt, Ghana, Guyana, Haiti, India, Jamaica, Liberia, Syria, Tunisia, Uganda, Uruguay, Zaire, Zambia; aluminium, butter, copra, jute, palm oil.
Mini-recession: Argentina, Libya, Morocco, Nicaragua, South Africa, Venezuela; maize, tea.

1974–75 recession Main recession: Argentina, Australia, Austria, Barbados, Belgium, Canada, Chile, Cyprus, Denmark, Ethiopia, Finland, France, West Germany, Ghana, Greece, Guatemala, Haiti, Honduras, Iceland, India, Ireland, Italy, Jamaica, Japan, Kenya, Liberia, Luxembourg, Malawi, Malaysia, Netherlands, New Zealand, Panama, Papua New Guinea, Portugal, Singapore, South Africa, Spain, Sri Lanka, Surinam, Switzerland, Taiwan, Tanzania, Trinidad and Tobago, Uganda, United Kingdom, United States, Zaire, Zambia; beef, cocoa, copper, copra, cotton, gold, groundnuts, jute, lamb, maize, palm oil, phosphate rock, rice, rubber, silver, soyabeans, sugar, tin, wheat, wool, zinc.
Mini-recession: Colombia, Costa Rica, Fiji, Indonesia, Iran, Libya, Mexico, Nicaragua, Nigeria, Pakistan, Peru, Saudi Arabia; butter, lead.

1977 recession Main recession: Argentina, Australia, Ethiopia, Guyana, Haiti, Iran, Israel, Nicaragua, Peru, Sweden, Syria, Uganda, Uruguay, Zaire, Zambia; coal, cocoa, coffee, copper, cotton, iron ore, maize, nickel, phosphate rock, rice, sugar, tea, zinc.
Mini-recession: Austria, Belgium, Brazil, Denmark, Dominican Republic, France, Indonesia, Italy, Luxembourg, Morocco, Pakistan, Portugal, Saudi Arabia, Switzerland, Tunisia, United Kingdom; beef, manganese, soyabeans.

1980 recession Main recession: Bolivia, Canada, Denmark, El Salvador, France, West Germany, Greece, Guyana, Honduras, India, Ireland, Jamaica, South Korea, Liberia, Luxembourg, Malawi, Netherlands, New Zealand, Pakistan, Papua New Guinea, Spain, Surinam, Turkey, United Kingdom, United States, Venezuela, Zambia; cocoa, copra, groundnuts, jute, lead, palm oil.
Mini-recession: Colombia, Costa Rica, Iceland, Israel, Japan, Sweden, Taiwan, Tanzania.

Consumers expenditure

The following chart shows the % change for each year in the quantity of consumers expenditure, for the world, United States and United Kingdom. Figures for the world are included overleaf, for the United States on page 145, and for the United Kingdom on page 139.

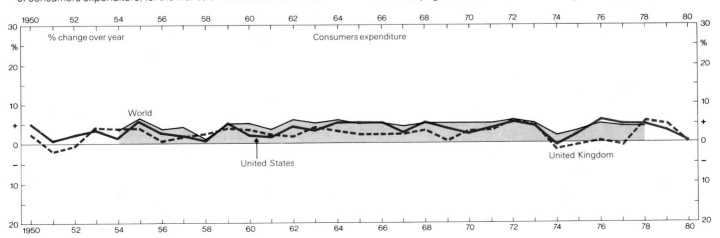

World consumers expenditure

	Index 1970 = 100	% change over year		Index 1970 = 100	% change over year		Index 1970 = 100	% change over year		Index 1970 = 100	% change over year
1950	na	na	1958	57	1	1966	83	5	1974	119	2
1951	na	na	1959	60	5	1967	87	4	1975	122	3
1952	na	na	1960	63	5	1968	91	5	1976	128	5
1953	47	na	1961	65	3	1969	96	5	1977	133	4
1954	49	3	1962	68	6	1970	100	5	1978	138	4
1955	53	7	1963	72	5	1971	105	5	1979	na	na
1956	54	3	1964	76	6	1972	111	6	1980	na	na
1957	56	4	1965	80	5	1973	117	5			

For the time covered, the main periods of expansion for world consumers expenditure were 1955–57, 1959–60, 1962–73 and 1976–78, with comparatively low growth in 1954, 1958, 1961 and 1974–75. In general the pattern is the same as for gross domestic product, although growth of consumers expenditure has been more stable, a rather higher rate of growth being maintained during recession.

The main periods of expansion for United States consumers expenditure were in 1950, 1952–53, 1955, 1959, 1962–66, 1968–69, 1971–73 and 1976–78; there were periods of low growth in 1951, the time of the Korean war, and in the recessions of 1954, 1958,

1960–61, 1967, 1970, 1974–75 and 1980. The rate of growth began to fall in 1979 towards the 1980 recession. The pattern was broadly the same as for gross domestic product, except for 1951.

For the United Kingdom, the main periods of expansion in consumers expenditure were 1950, 1953–55, 1959–60, 1963–64, 1966–68, 1970–73 and 1978–79; there were periods of low growth or a fall in consumers expenditure for 1951–52, 1956, 1965, 1969, 1974–77 and 1980. These were mainly at times of general recession, although consumers expenditure fell before the 1958 recession, increasing gradually through that recession, and there was virtually no increase at all throughout 1974–77.

Government expenditure

The following chart shows the % change for each year in the quantity of government expenditure, for the world, United States and United Kingdom. Figures for the world are shown on the facing page, for the United States on page 145, and for the United Kingdom on page 139.

For the time covered, the main periods of expansion for world government expenditure were 1957, 1961–63, 1965–68 and 1972–78, with a fall in 1954–55, and low growth for the periods 1958–60, 1964 and 1969–71. The fall in 1954–55 was associated with the end of the Korean war, concerning which more detail is included below. World government expenditure was comparatively low in the

major 1958 recession, but increased slightly in the 1974–75 major recession indicating some attempt to counter the fall in demand.

For the United States, the main periods of expansion in government expenditure were 1951–53, 1957–58, 1961–62 and 1965–68, with lower rates of increase for 1974–75, 1977–78 and 1980, very small increases for 1950, 1956, 1959–60, 1972–73, 1976 and 1979 and falls for 1954–55 and 1969–71. The sharp rise for 1951–52 was mainly due to the impact of the Korean war, which began June 1950, and continued in part after the cease-fire of July 1951 until the signing of an armistice in July 1953. Between 1950 and 1952 Federal defence

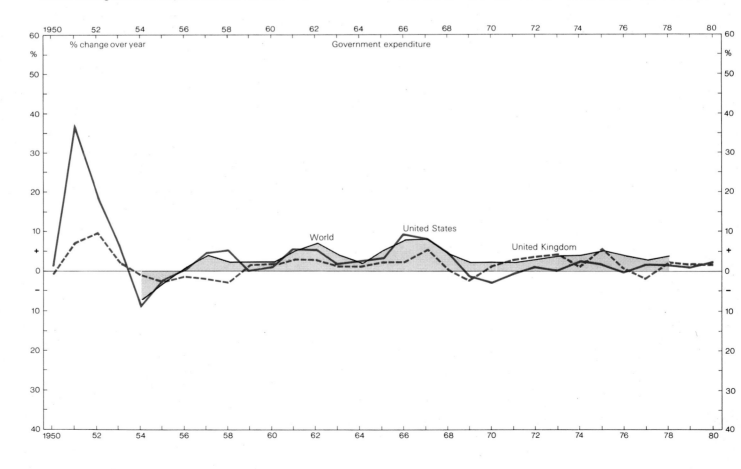

World government expenditure

Year	Index 1970 = 100	% change over year	Year	Index 1970 = 100	% change over year	Year	Index 1970 = 100	% change over year	Year	Index 1970 = 100	% change over year
1950	na	na	1958	60	2	1966	85	8	1974	113	4
1951	na	na	1959	62	2	1967	92	8	1975	119	5
1952	na	na	1960	63	2	1968	96	4	1976	124	4
1953	62	na	1961	66	5	1969	98	2	1977	127	3
1954	57	−7	1962	71	7	1970	100	2	1978	132	4
1955	56	−3	1963	74	4	1971	102	2	1979	na	na
1956	57	1	1964	75	2	1972	105	3	1980	na	na
1957	59	4	1965	79	5	1973	109	4			

spending increased by $ 32 billion per year (current prices) out of a total rise for government expenditure of $ 37 billion per year. After reaching a peak in 1953, US defence spending fell back from $ 49 billion for that year (current prices) to $ 39 billion for 1955. The 1961–62 expansion was the time of the Kennedy administration, and can partly be associated with the development of space flights which continued throughout the sixties to put a man on the moon in 1969. The 1965–68 expansion can partly be associated with the Vietnam war; Federal defence expenditure rose between 1965 and 1968 by $ 28 billion per year (current prices) out of a total increase of $ 63 billion.

For the United Kingdom, the main periods of expansion in government expenditure were 1951–53, 1961–62, 1965–67, 1971–73, 1975 and 1978–80; there were falls in government expenditure or low rates of increase for 1950, 1954–60 (especially 1955–58), 1963–64, 1968–70, 1974 and 1976–77. Government expenditure had fallen in the recessions of 1958 and 1969, but there was a boost in 1975 to counter the 1974–75 recession which followed the sharp rise in the crude oil price. For the period 1978–80, the rates of increase in government expenditure were virtually the same in the United Kingdom as in the United States.

Fixed investment

The chart below shows the % change for each year in the quantity of fixed investment, for the world, United States and United Kingdom. Figures for the world are in the table below, for the United States on page 145, and for the United Kingdom on page 139.

For the time covered, the main periods of expansion for world fixed investment were 1954–57, 1959–73 (with mini-recessions in 1967 and 1970) and 1976–78. The amount of world investment confirms that the worst recession of the three decades covered was in 1974–75, with 1958 the other recession in which fixed investment fell.

For the United States, the main periods of expansion in fixed investment were 1950, 1953, 1955, 1959, 1962–66, 1968–69, 1971–73 and 1976–79, with falls or a low rate of increase for 1951–52, 1954, 1957–58, 1960–61, 1967, 1970, 1974–75 and 1980. As is usual, the amount of fluctuation for fixed investment was greater than that for

gross domestic product, being about double the rate; for example, over the period 1976–78 the rate of increase for gross domestic product was about 5% per year, whereas for fixed investment it averaged 10% per year. The fall for fixed investment in 1951–52 was partly the counterpart of the rise in defence expenditure; there was at that time a recession for both fixed investment and consumers expenditure while government expenditure increased. The period of the mid-sixties was a time of strong investment.

For the United Kingdom, the main periods of expansion in fixed investment were 1950, 1953–57, 1959–61, 1964–65, 1967–68, 1970–71, 1973 and 1978, with falls or a low rate of growth for 1951–52, 1958, 1962–63, 1969, 1972, 1974–77 and 1979–80. Investment growth was at a high level in most of the fifties and sixties, but low in the seventies – it had not regained the actual level of 1973 by 1980.

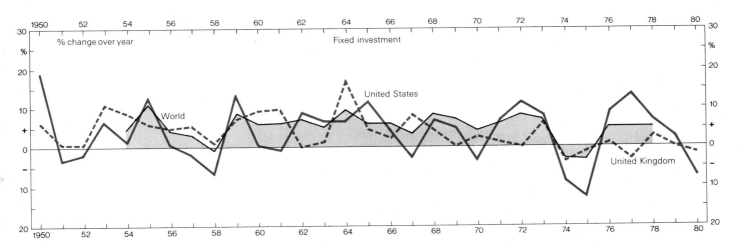

World fixed investment

Year	Index 1970 = 100	% change over year	Year	Index 1970 = 100	% change over year	Year	Index 1970 = 100	% change over year	Year	Index 1970 = 100	% change over year
1950	na	na	1958	48	−1	1966	80	6	1974	118	−3
1951	na	na	1959	52	8	1967	83	3	1975	114	−3
1952	na	na	1960	55	6	1968	90	8	1976	120	5
1953	39	na	1961	58	6	1969	96	7	1977	125	5
1954	41	5	1962	62	7	1970	100	4	1978	132	5
1955	45	11	1963	65	5	1971	106	6	1979	na	na
1956	47	4	1964	71	9	1972	114	8	1980	na	na
1957	48	3	1965	76	6	1973	122	7			

Exports

The following chart shows the % change for each year in the quantity of exports, for the world, United States and United Kingdom. Figures for the world are in the table below, for the United States on page 146, and for the United Kingdom on page 140.

The main periods of expansion for world exports were 1950–51, 1953–57, 1959–73 and 1976–79. Main recessions for exports were in 1952, 1958 and 1974, while there were rather lower rates of increase, interrupting the long 1959–73 expansion, in 1961–62, 1967 and 1971; there was a low rate of increase for 1980. The 1952 recession is associated with the European recession of that year, rather than the 1954 US recession, which was mainly due to the end of the Korean war. The long 1959–73 expansion covers the main period of EEC growth in the original six countries which formed the EEC in 1958 (the United Kingdom joined in 1973).

For the United States, the main periods of expansion in exports were 1951, 1954–57, 1960, 1962–64, 1966–70, 1972–74 and 1978–80, with falls or low rates of increase for 1950, 1952–53, 1958–59, 1961, 1965, 1971 and 1975–77. The most important recessions in US exports were for 1952–53 and 1958, and the strongest periods of expansion in 1954–57, 1966–70 and 1972–74.

For the United Kingdom, the main periods of expansion in exports were 1950, 1953–56, 1959–61, 1963–66, 1968–69, 1971, 1973–74 and 1976–77. There were falls or low rates of increase for 1951–52, 1957–58, 1962, 1967, 1970, 1972 and 1975; for 1978–80 there was a steady but low rate of growth. The comparatively steady rate of expansion over the period 1959–66, averaging about 4% per year, was at about half the level for world exports, which increased at an average of about 8% per year over that period.

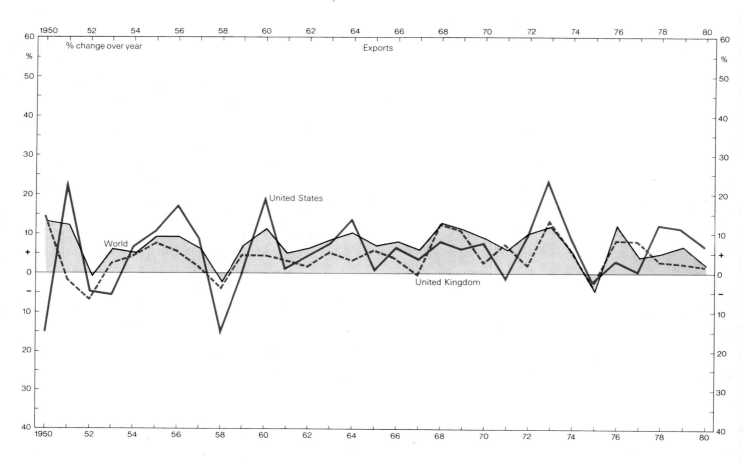

World exports

	Index 1970 = 100	% change over year		Index 1970 = 100	% change over year		Index 1970 = 100	% change over year		Index 1970 = 100	% change over year
1950	26	13	1958	39	−2	1966	70	8	1974	138	5
1951	29	12	1959	42	7	1967	74	6	1975	131	−5
1952	28	−1	1960	46	11	1968	83	13	1976	147	12
1953	30	6	1961	48	5	1969	92	11	1977	152	4
1954	32	5	1962	51	6	1970	100	9	1978	160	5
1955	34	9	1963	55	8	1971	106	6	1979	172	7
1956	37	9	1964	60	10	1972	117	10	1980	176	2
1957	40	6	1965	65	7	1973	131	12			

Unemployment

The most important social reason for studying business cycles is to attempt the removal of the amount of unemployment created during recessions. Despite this, statistical information on unemployment is not well defined and not consistently available. Wherever possible, the numbers of people unemployed have been included for each country in the countries section, when a consistent series of information has been available. The chart on the facing page shows

the % change in the numbers of people unemployed for three main countries, a world series not being available. Figures for the United States are shown on page 146, for the United Kingdom on page 140, and for Japan on page 88.

For the United States, the main reductions of unemployment were in 1950–53 (especially 1951), 1955–56, 1959, 1962, 1964–66, 1968,

1972–73 and 1976–79, generally coinciding with main periods of expansion in gross domestic product. Main increases in unemployment were in 1954, 1958, 1961, 1970–71, 1974–75 and 1980, generally coinciding with recessions in the United States; the 1967 recession had little impact on unemployment. There was a relatively steady fall from the 1961 peak of 4 714 000 unemployed to 2 832 000 people unemployed in 1969, before the 1970 recession.

For the United Kingdom, the main reductions in unemployment were in 1951, 1954–55, 1960–61, 1964–65 and 1973, with some reduction in 1979; whereas for the United States reductions occurred when expansion was under way, for the United Kingdom reductions tended to be made only once a period of expansion had been under way for some time – reductions were made only when the economy was approaching highest production. Main increases in unemployment for the United Kingdom were in 1952, 1957–58, 1962–63, 1967, 1971–72, 1975–76 and 1980, generally coincident with recessions, but with a tendency for unemployment to increase for a longer period than the recession in the general level of the economy had lasted.

For Japan, the main reductions in unemployment were in 1951, 1953, 1956–57, 1960–64, 1967–69, 1973 and 1979–80, in general coinciding with the later stages of expansion in gross domestic product in Japan, which themselves were similar to the periods of expansion in the United States. Main increases in unemployment were in 1950, 1952, 1954–55, 1958–59, 1965–66, 1970–72, 1974–76 and 1978; these increases, as in the United Kingdom, tended to occur both during and just after recessions.

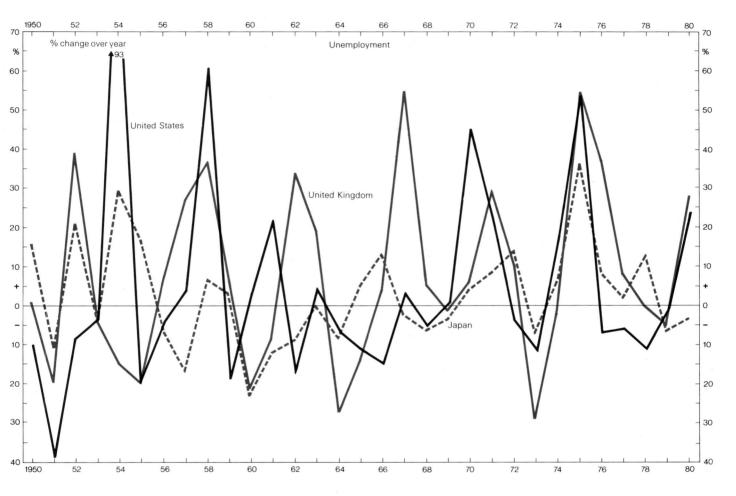

Looking at the period as a whole, unemployment in Japan has changed little, by comparison with the United Kingdom where there has been a marked increase. This is shown for these and other countries for which suitable information is available in the following table. This indicates rates of unemployment, being the numbers unemployed as a percentage of the total working population. Rates are shown for some significant years in the period. There was a significant increase in the rate of unemployment for most countries following the sharp rise in crude oil prices in 1974.

% rates of unemployment

	1950	1953	1958	1965	1969	1971	1973	1975	1980
Austria	6.2	9.0	5.1	2.7	2.8	2.1	1.6	2.0	1.9
Belgium	na	na	3.5	1.5	2.3	2.2	2.8	5.1	9.0
Canada	3.6	3.0	7.0	3.9	4.7	6.4	5.6	6.9	7.5
Denmark	3.6	3.8	3.9	0.8	1.6	1.6	1.1	6.0	6.9
Germany, West	11.3	8.4	3.8	0.6	0.9	0.8	1.2	4.7	3.8
Ireland	na	9.6	8.6	5.6	6.4	7.2	7.2	12.2	10.3
Japan	1.2	1.1	1.4	0.8	1.1	1.2	1.3	1.9	2.0
Korea, South	na	na	na	7.4	4.8	4.5	4.0	4.1	5.2
Netherlands	na	na	na	na	1.3	1.6	2.8	5.0	5.8
New Zealand	0.01	0.01	0.1	0.1	0.3	0.3	0.2	0.4	2.9
Spain	1.5	1.0	0.7	1.2	1.3	1.5	1.1	1.9	9.7
Sweden	na	na	2.5	1.2	1.9	2.5	2.5	1.6	2.0
United Kingdom	1.6	1.7	2.0	1.4	2.4	3.4	2.6	3.9	6.8
United States	5.3	2.9	6.8	4.5	3.5	5.9	4.9	8.5	7.1

Industrial production

The following chart shows the % change for each year in the quantity of industrial production, for the world, United States and United Kingdom. Figures for the world are shown in the table below, for the United States on page 147, and for the United Kingdom on page 141.

The main periods of expansion for world industrial production were 1950–52, 1955–57, 1959–73, and 1976–79. There were main recessions in 1953–54, 1958, 1974–75 and 1980, with mini-recessions interrupting the long 1959–73 expansion in 1967 and 1970–71, and a further mini-recession in 1978. These movements were similar to those for gross domestic product, but with an earlier downturn into the 1954 recession. The amount of fluctuation was rather greater than for gross domestic product, ranging from −3% to 11% compared with a range from 0% to 7%; that is, a total range of 14% for industrial production, compared with 7% for gross domestic product.

For the United States, the main periods of expansion in industrial production were 1950–53, 1955–56, 1959, 1962–66, 1968–69, 1972–73 and 1976–79, with falls or low rates of increase for 1954, 1957–58, 1960–61, 1967, 1970–71, 1974–75 and 1980. The 1957–58 and 1974–75 recessions were clearly the main recessions, and the pattern for the complete cycles was similar; that is, the period 1954–58 showed roughly the same amount of expansion and recession as did the period 1970–75.

For the United Kingdom, the main periods of expansion in industrial production were 1950–51, 1953–55, 1959–60, 1963–65, 1968–69, 1972–73 and 1976–79, with falls or low rates of increase for 1952, 1956–58, 1961–62, 1966–67, 1970–71, 1974–75 and 1980. Recessions for industrial production were in general similar to those for gross domestic product, although low growth of industrial production preceded the main recession of 1958, and followed the recession of 1969.

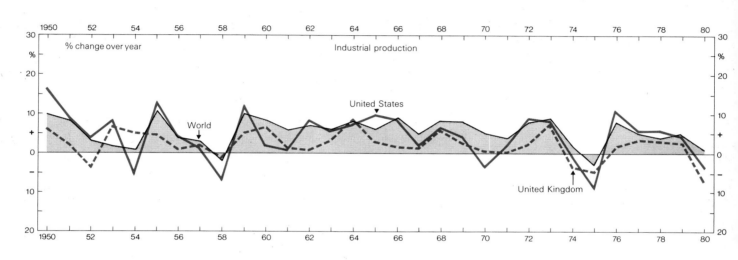

World industrial production

	Index 1970 = 100	% change over year		Index 1970 = 100	% change over year		Index 1970 = 100	% change over year		Index 1970 = 100	% change over year
1950	33	10	1958	44	−2	1966	79	9	1974	125	2
1951	35	8	1959	48	10	1967	82	5	1975	121	−3
1952	36	3	1960	52	8	1968	89	8	1976	131	8
1953	37	2	1961	55	6	1969	96	8	1977	137	5
1954	38	1	1962	59	7	1970	100	5	1978	142	4
1955	42	11	1963	63	6	1971	104	4	1979	149	.5
1956	44	4	1964	68	8	1972	112	8	1980	150	1
1957	45	3	1965	72	6	1973	122	9			

Steel and passenger car production

The charts on the facing page show the % change in the quantity of steel produced, and in the number of passenger cars produced, for the world, United States and United Kingdom. Figures for the world are shown on page 16 following, for the United States on page 147 for steel and 148 for passenger cars, and for the United Kingdom on page 141 for steel and 142 for passenger cars.

The main periods of expansion for world steel production were 1950–51, 1953, 1955–57, 1959–70 (with mini-recessions in 1961–62 and 1966–67), 1972–74, 1976 (recovery) and 1978–79, with recessions mainly affecting production for 1952, 1954, 1958, 1971, 1975, 1977 and 1980. The main periods of expansion for world passenger car production were 1950, 1953, 1955, 1957 (recovery), 1959–60, 1962–65, 1968–69, 1971–73 and 1976–78, with recessions affecting production for 1951–52, 1954, 1956, 1958, 1961, 1967, 1970, 1974–75 and 1979–80.

For the United States, the main periods of expansion for steel production were 1950–51, 1953, 1955, 1959–60, 1963–65, 1968–69, 1972–73, 1976 and 1978, with main falls in production for 1952, 1954, 1958, 1967, 1970–71, 1974–75 and 1980. For passenger cars, the main periods of expansion were 1950, 1953, 1955, 1959–60,

1962–63, 1965, 1968, 1971–73 and 1976–77, with production falling in 1951–52, 1954, 1956, 1958, 1961, 1966–67, 1969–70, 1974–75 and 1978–80.

For the United Kingdom, the main periods of expansion for steel production were 1950, 1952–57, 1959–60, 1963–65, 1968–70, 1972–73, 1976 and 1979, with main falls in production for 1951, 1958, 1961–62, 1966, 1971, 1974–75, 1977 and 1980 (this last year was also affected by a steel strike). For passenger cars, the main periods of expansion were 1950, 1953–55, 1957–60, 1962–64, 1968 and 1971–72, with production falling in 1951–52, 1956, 1961, 1965–67, 1969–70, 1973–75 and 1977–80.

For both steel and passenger cars, international products, the pattern for the world and the two main countries shown is similar; the direct link between the two products (the passenger car industry being a main user of steel) also leads to roughly similar fluctuations.

Steel and passenger car production

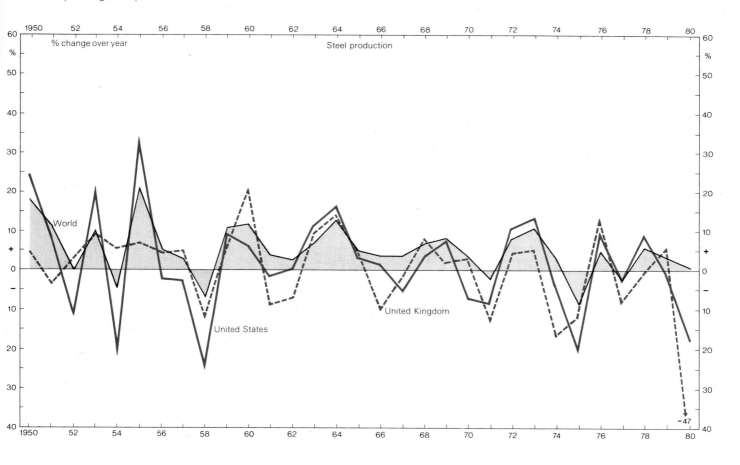

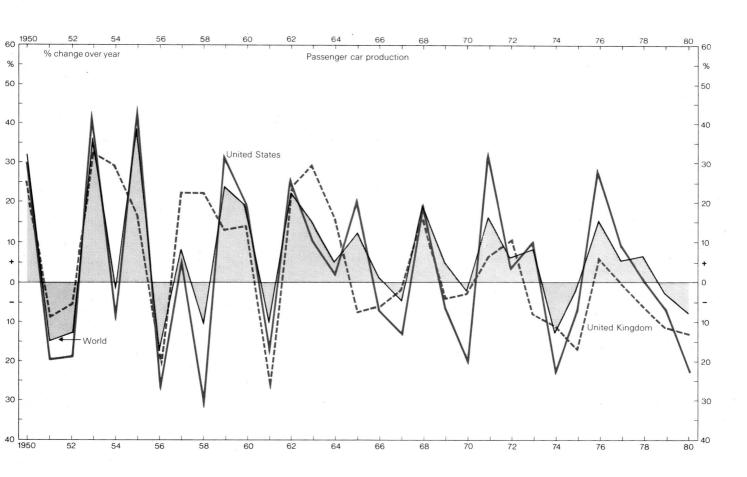

World steel production

	Index 1970 = 100	% change over year		Index 1970 = 100	% change over year		Index 1970 = 100	% change over year		Index 1970 = 100	% change over year
1950	32	18	1958	46	−7	1966	80	4	1974	120	3
1951	35	11	1959	51	11	1967	83	4	1975	110	−9
1952	35	0	1960	57	12	1968	89	7	1976	115	5
1953	39	10	1961	59	4	1969	96	8	1977	113	−2
1954	37	−5	1962	61	3	1970	100	4	1978	120	6
1955	45	21	1963	65	7	1971	98	−2	1979	125	4
1956	47	5	1964	74	13	1972	106	8	1980	126	1
1957	49	3	1965	77	5	1973	117	11			

World passenger car production

	Index 1970 = 100	% change over year		Index 1970 = 100	% change over year		Index 1970 = 100	% change over year		Index 1970 = 100	% change over year
1950	36	32	1958	39	−11	1966	86	1	1974	115	−13
1951	31	−15	1959	48	24	1967	81	−5	1975	112	−2
1952	27	−13	1960	57	19	1968	97	19	1976	129	15
1953	36	36	1961	52	−10	1969	102	5	1977	135	5
1954	36	−2	1962	63	22	1970	100	−2	1978	144	6
1955	49	38	1963	72	15	1971	116	16	1979	140	−3
1956	40	−18	1964	76	5	1972	123	6	1980	129	−8
1957	44	8	1965	85	12	1973	132	8			

Consumer prices

The chart below shows the % change for each year in consumer prices (or amount of inflation), for the world, United States and United Kingdom. Figures for the world are in the table below, for the United States on page 149, and for the United Kingdom on page 143.

World consumer prices rose mainly in 1951–52 and 1973–80, the former rise being mainly due to the Korean war, and the latest following the freeing of the gold price in 1971 and subsequent rise in commodity prices (concerning which see later, page 19). There was a gradually rising rate of increase from 1956 to 1972, with main increases in 1957–58, 1964–66 and 1970–71. During the 1973–80

rise there was some slowing down in the rate of increase for 1976–79.

For the United States, price rises followed a similar pattern, with main increases in 1951, 1973–75 and 1977–80, and other increases mainly for 1957–58 and 1969–70. For the United Kingdom, price rises were higher, with main rises in 1951–52, 1974–77 and 1979–80, and other increases mainly for 1955–58, 1961–62, 1964–66 and 1968–71. During the 1974–80 period of rising prices, the rate of increase for the United Kingdom was higher than that of the world in each year except 1978.

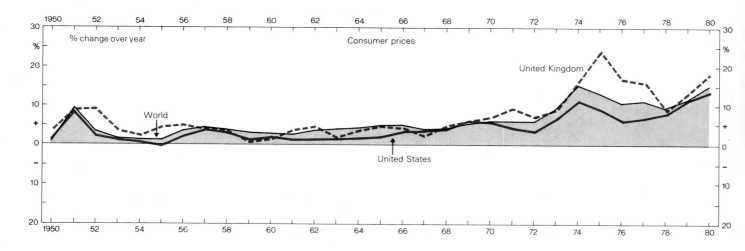

World consumer prices

	Index 1970 = 100	% change over year		Index 1970 = 100	% change over year		Index 1970 = 100	% change over year		Index 1970 = 100	% change over year
1950	46.3	0.3	1958	61.3	4.1	1966	82.6	5.1	1974	141.8	15.5
1951	50.6	9.4	1959	63.2	3.2	1967	86.0	4.1	1975	161.3	13.8
1952	52.6	3.8	1960	65.0	2.8	1968	89.7	4.3	1976	178.9	10.9
1953	53.4	1.5	1961	66.6	2.5	1969	94.4	5.2	1977	198.7	11.1
1954	54.0	1.2	1962	69.0	3.6	1970	100.0	6.0	1978	217.6	9.5
1955	54.5	0.9	1963	71.8	4.0	1971	106.0	6.0	1979	243.2	11.8
1956	56.5	3.6	1964	74.8	4.3	1972	112.1	5.8	1980	280.0	15.1
1957	58.9	4.3	1965	78.5	5.0	1973	122.7	9.5			

Share prices

The chart below shows the % change in share prices for three main countries, a world series not being available. Figures for the United States are shown on page 150, for the United Kingdom on page 144, and for Japan on page 89.

For the United States, share prices rose mainly in 1950–52, 1954–56, 1958–59, 1961, 1963–65, 1967–68, 1971–72, 1975–76 and 1979–80, with falls in 1957, 1960, 1962, 1966, 1969–70, 1973–74 and 1977–78. In general share prices have tended to fall at the beginning of the recession as defined in quantity terms – for example, in 1957 for the 1958 recession and 1973–74 for the 1974–75 recession.

For the United Kingdom, share prices rose mainly in 1950–51, 1953–55, 1959–60, 1963–64, 1967–68, 1971–72 and 1975–78, with

falls in 1952, 1956, 1958, 1962, 1965–66, 1969–70, 1973–74 and 1979–80. As for the United States, there has been some tendency for share prices to move before the quantity changes, for example in 1973–74 for the 1974–75 recession and 1979–80 for the 1980 recession.

For Japan, share prices rose mainly in 1951–53, 1955–57, 1959–61, 1963 (recovery), 1966 (recovery), 1968–73 (especially 1969 and 1972–73) and 1976–79; there were main falls in 1950, 1954, 1962, 1964–65 and 1974. There has been a tendency for share prices in Japan to follow those of the United States, with a delay of about one year; for example, a main rise in 1972–73 compared with 1971–72 for the United States.

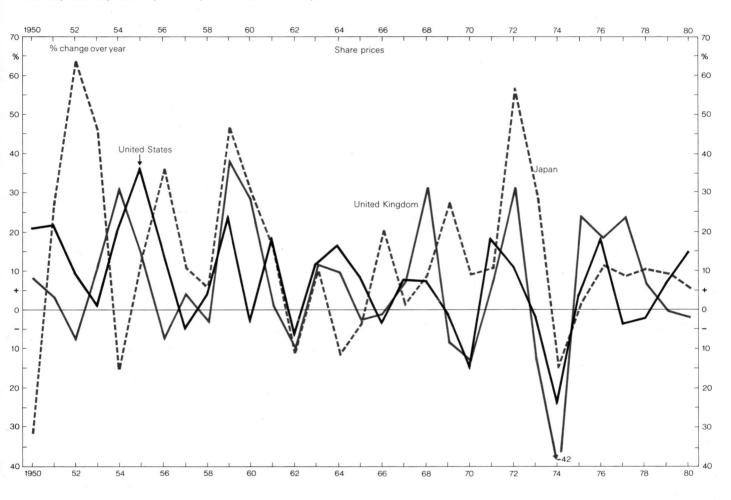

International reserves

A chart is included overleaf of the % change in the value of international reserves in dollar terms, for the world, United States and United Kingdom. Figures for the world are shown overleaf, for the United States on page 150, and for the United Kingdom on page 144.

The main periods of increase for world international reserves were 1950, 1953–54, 1956, 1960–61, 1963–65, 1968, 1970–72, 1974, 1976–77 and 1979–80, the increases for 1970–72 and 1974–80 being especially large. World international reserves fell or increased comparatively slowly for 1951–52, 1955, 1957–59, 1962, 1966–67, 1969 and 1973. The large increase over 1970–72 was partly due to the introduction of SDRs in 1970; the actual total level of SDRs was roughly constant from 1972 to 1978, increasing sharply again in 1979. The pattern is not directly affected by the change in the price of gold from 1971, as gold is valued at a constant price of SDR 35 per ounce

for the valuation of international reserves used here.

For the United States, international reserves rose mainly in 1952, 1956–57, 1968–69, 1974–77 and 1980, with falls in 1950, 1953–55, 1958–67, 1970–73 and 1978. The long period during which there was a fall in reserves, from 1958 to 1967, coincided with the long period of good growth for the economy.

For the United Kingdom, international reserves rose mainly in 1950, 1953–54, 1958, 1960, 1965, 1970–71, 1977 and 1979–80, with falls in 1951–52, 1955–57, 1959, 1961–64, 1967–68, 1972, 1975–76 and 1978. In the fifties and sixties, before devaluation of the pound in 1967, a fall in reserves usually preceded a recession, which was partly induced to maintain the level of reserves.

International reserves

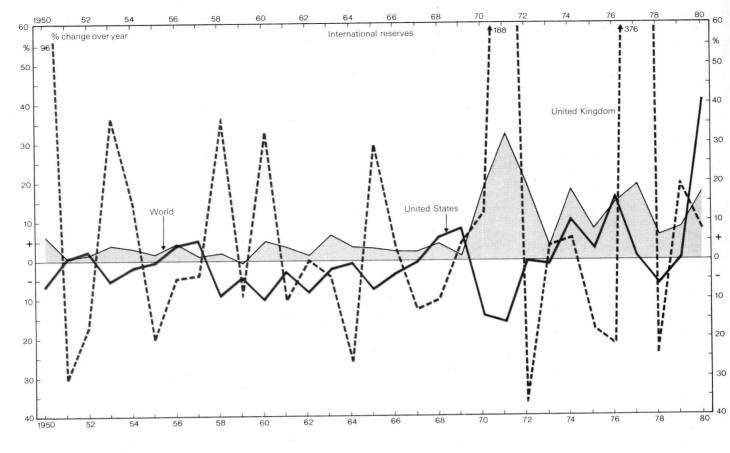

World international reserves

	Index 1970 = 100	% change over year		Index 1970 = 100	% change over year		Index 1970 = 100	% change over year		Index 1970 = 100	% change over year
1950	51.8	6.0	1958	61.6	1.8	1966	78.1	2.3	1974	192.8	18.0
1951	52.2	0.7	1959	61.2	−0.6	1967	79.9	2.4	1975	208.4	8.1
1952	52.8	1.2	1960	64.3	5.0	1968	83.4	4.4	1976	238.2	14.3
1953	54.8	3.8	1961	66.5	3.4	1969	84.4	1.2	1977	283.4	19.0
1954	56.7	3.3	1962	67.4	1.3	1970	100.0	18.5	1978	301.8	6.5
1955	57.5	1.4	1963	71.7	6.4	1971	132.0	32.0	1979	327.2	8.4
1956	59.9	4.3	1964	74.1	3.4	1972	157.2	19.1	1980	382.5	16.9
1957	60.5	1.0	1965	76.3	3.0	1973	163.4	3.9			

Interest rates

The following chart shows the actual rate of interest for main countries, a world series not being available. Figures for the United States are shown on page 150, for the United Kingdom on page 144, and for Japan on page 89.

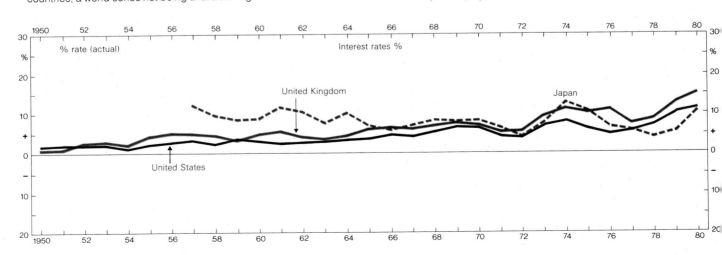

For the United States, the interest rate increased mainly in 1950–53, 1955–57, 1959, 1962–66, 1968–69, 1973–74 and 1978–80, with reductions in 1954, 1958, 1960–61, 1967, 1970–72 and 1975–76. Generally, in the fifties and sixties interest rates rose during expansion and were reduced during recession; for the seventies, with a greater rise in prices, there has been a tendency for reductions to be made late in a recession rather than as it occurs.

For the United Kingdom, the interest rate increased mainly in 1952, 1955–56, 1960–61, 1964–66, 1968–69, 1973–74, 1976 and 1978–80, with main falls in 1954, 1959, 1962–63, 1967, 1970–71, 1975 and 1977. Until the mid-sixties, the falls in interest rate in the United Kingdom were generally made at the end of recessions; from 1963, the interest rate in the United Kingdom has moved roughly in line with

that of the United States, slightly above it until 1973 and significantly above it for 1974–80.

For Japan, over the time covered, the interest rate increased mainly in 1961, 1964, 1967–68, 1970, 1973–74 and 1979–80, with main falls in 1958–59, 1962–63, 1965–66, 1971–72 and 1975–78. The interest rate has been at a high level throughout the time covered, being around 10% in the early sixties and also in 1980; by contrast, interest rates for the United States and United Kingdom have increased throughout these decades from a low starting level. Reductions in interest rates tended to occur at the end of recessions, and from 1970 the rate has moved roughly in line with that of the United States, although about one year behind – for example, mainly in 1976 rather than mainly in 1975 as for the United States.

Commodity prices

The chart below shows the % change for each year in commodity prices generally, as represented by The Economist Commodity Price Index (sterling basis), in the gold price (London dollar price from 1963, dollar price before) and in the crude oil price (dollar price). Figures for The Economist index are shown, with 1975 = 100 (the current base), in a table overleaf, and also, with 1970 = 100, in a long-term view on page 29. Figures for the gold price are shown on page 167 and for the crude oil price on page 166.

Commodity prices generally, as shown by the index (which excludes gold and crude oil prices), rose mainly in 1950–51, 1954 (recovery), 1963–66, 1968–70, 1972–74, 1976–77 and 1979–80, with falls in 1952–53, 1955–59, 1961–62, 1967, 1971, 1975 and 1978. The 1950 sterling index rise was substantially due to the September 1949 sterling devaluation of 44%.

The gold price (a London price), fixed in the United States until convertibility of the dollar was suspended in 1971, rose mainly in 1971–74 and 1977–80; there had been a temporary rise in the London price during 1968–69, following devaluation of the £ sterling. The main fall was in 1976, following the 1974–75 recession and the

fall for commodity prices in 1975. The rise in gold price from 1971 to 1973 preceded the rise in general commodity prices.

The crude oil price was comparatively stable over the period 1950–70, although with falls in the price for 1950, 1957–64 and 1968–69. There were high increases in price during 1971–73, preceding the very large increase in 1974, and substantial increases again in 1979–80. The crude oil price had fallen from 1950 to 1970 by 24%, compared with a rise in general commodity prices of 29% in sterling terms (10% in dollar terms); the 1971–73 increase in the price of crude oil did not make up for the amount by which the oil price had fallen behind, and was followed by the 1974 increase which more than made up for the previous relative fall.

The general pattern of timing can be said to be as follows. The rise in commodity prices from 1972 followed the freeing of the gold price in 1971 and its subsequent rise. The rise in the gold price, and the rise in commodity prices, helped to cause a sharp rise in the price of crude oil which was in part a recovery from the relative falls of the fifties and sixties.

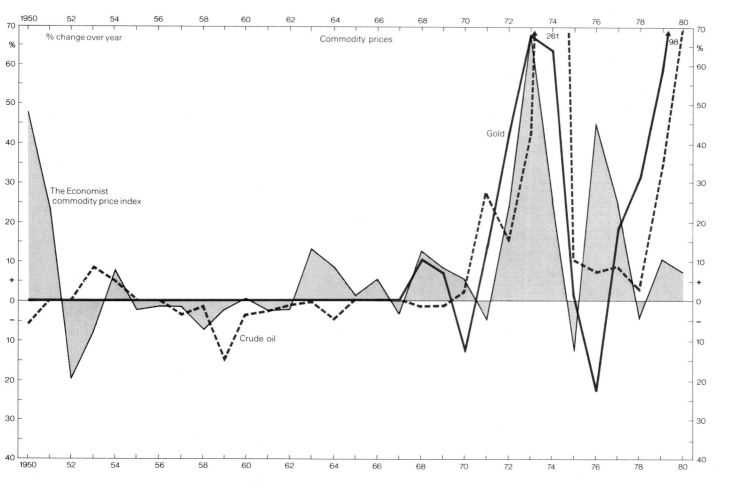

Commodity prices

The chart below shows the % change for each year in the price of iron ore and the price of lead (dollar prices); The Economist Commodity Price Index, discussed on the previous page, is also included for reference, and a table of that index follows the chart. Figures for the iron ore price are shown on page 169 and for the lead price on page 172.

The price of iron ore increased mainly in 1950–52, 1955–57, 1961, 1970, 1973–75 and 1979–80, with falls mainly in 1953–54, 1958–59, 1962–63, 1966–69, 1971–72 and 1976–78. The price movements were sometimes rather behind the movements in commodity prices

generally; for example, a fall in 1953–54 rather than 1952–53, a rise in 1973 rather than 1972, and a fall in 1976 rather than in 1975.

The price of lead increased mainly in 1951, 1954–56, 1963–65, 1969–70, 1972–74 and 1977–79, with falls in 1950, 1952–53, 1957–58, 1960–62, 1966–68, 1971, 1975 and 1980. The falls in price were generally at times of recession in main countries of the world, with a tendency for the lead price to fall at an early stage of recession, notably in 1957 and 1980.

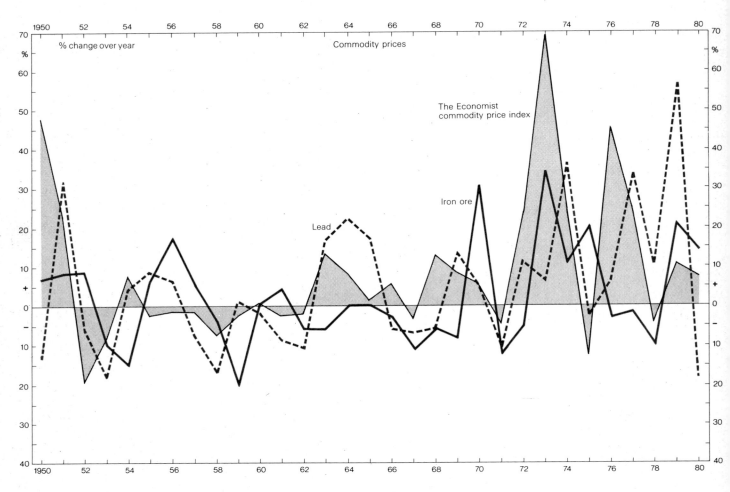

The Economist Commodity Price Index (sterling basis)

	Index 1975 = 100	% change over year		Index 1975 = 100	% change over year		Index 1975 = 100	% change over year		Index 1975 = 100	% change over year
1950	35.8	47.6	1958	30.7	−7.5	1966	37.1	5.1	1974	114.1	24.7
1951	44.0	22.9	1959	29.9	−2.6	1967	35.8	−3.5	1975	100.0	−12.4
1952	35.5	−19.3	1960	30.0	0.3	1968	40.4	12.8	1976	145.2	45.2
1953	32.6	−8.2	1961	29.1	−3.0	1969	43.9	8.7	1977	180.8	24.5
1954	35.1	7.7	1962	28.5	−2.1	1970	46.2	5.2	1978	172.4	−4.6
1955	34.3	−2.3	1963	32.3	13.3	1971	43.9	−5.0	1979	190.4	10.4
1956	33.8	−1.5	1964	34.9	8.0	1972	54.4	23.9	1980	204.8	7.6
1957	33.2	−1.8	1965	35.3	1.1	1973	91.5	68.2			

A long-term view

UK gross domestic product

The main periods of expansion in UK gross domestic product on a long-term view were 1849–57, 1859–66, 1887–91, 1894–99, 1909–13, 1922–25, 1933–41, 1948–51, 1953–57, 1959–73 (with mini-recessions in 1962 and 1969) and 1976–79; there were main recessions in 1867–69, 1872–73, 1878–79, 1884–86, 1892–93, 1907–08, 1918–21, 1930–32, 1952, 1958, 1974–75 and 1980.

The following table sets out the detailed periods, as based on the movements of gross domestic product, supplemented by other general information:

Expansion	Recession
1849–57 (gold discovery in California 1848 and Australia 1851)	1858
1859–66 (1862–63 mini-recession)	1867–69 (1868 mini-expansion)
1870–71 (Franco-Prussian war)	1872–73
1874–77 (slow)	1878–79
1880 (mini)	1881 (mini)
1882–83	1884–86
1887–91 (1890 mini-recession)	1892–93
1894–99 (1897 mini-recession)	1900–03 (1901 mini-expansion)

Expansion	Recession
1904–06 (slow)	1907–08
1909–13 (1912 mini-recession)	1914 (mini)
1915 (1914–18 world war)	1916–18 (world war)
	1919–21 (post-war)
1922–25	1926
1927–29	1930–32
1933–41 (1938 mini-recession, 1939 world war began)	1942–45 (world war)
	1946–47 (post-war)
1948–51	1952
1953–57	1958
1959–61	1962 (mini)
1963–68	1969 (mini)
1970–73	1974–75
1976–79 (1977 mini-recession)	1980

In the detailed table the period of 1959 to 1973 is shown in three parts; on a long-term view, the whole of the sixties could be regarded as a period of expansion.

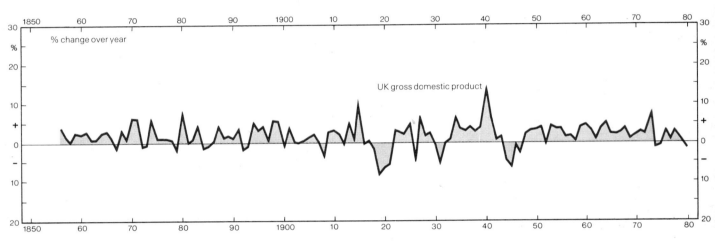

	Index 1970 = 100	% change over year		Index 1970 = 100	% change over year		Index 1970 = 100	% change over year		Index 1970 = 100	% change over year
1850	na	na	1883	22.3	4.4	1916	40.9	−0.1	1949	55.7	3.0
1851	na	na	1884	22.1	−1.0	1917	41.1	0.5	1950	57.4	3.1
1852	na	na	1885	21.9	−0.6	1918	40.4	−1.8	1951	59.5	3.6
1853	na	na	1886	22.1	0.6	1919	36.9	−8.7	1952	59.4	−0.2
1854	na	na	1887	23.1	4.6	1920	34.4	−6.7	1953	62.1	4.6
1855	12.7	na	1888	23.5	1.6	1921	32.4	−5.8	1954	64.5	3.8
1856	13.2	4.0	1889	23.9	1.9	1922	33.5	3.5	1955	67.0	3.8
1857	13.4	1.8	1890	24.2	1.1	1923	34.6	3.1	1956	68.1	1.7
1858	13.5	0.3	1891	25.1	3.7	1924	35.6	3.0	1957	69.4	1.9
1859	13.8	2.6	1892	24.6	−1.9	1925	37.4	5.0	1958	69.5	0.1
1860	14.1	2.2	1893	24.4	−0.6	1926	35.6	−4.6	1959	72.2	4.0
1861	14.5	2.7	1894	25.7	5.4	1927	38.1	7.0	1960	75.6	4.7
1862	14.6	0.8	1895	26.5	2.9	1928	38.8	1.7	1961	78.1	3.3
1863	14.7	0.8	1896	27.7	4.7	1929	39.7	2.4	1962	78.8	0.9
1864	15.1	2.6	1897	27.8	0.2	1930	39.6	−0.1	1963	82.0	4.1
1865	15.6	3.1	1898	29.4	5.7	1931	37.6	−5.1	1964	86.3	5.3
1866	15.8	1.5	1899	31.0	5.5	1932	37.7	0.3	1965	88.4	2.4
1867	15.7	−1.0	1900	30.5	−1.6	1933	38.2	1.1	1966	90.2	2.1
1868	16.2	3.2	1901	31.7	3.9	1934	40.7	6.8	1967	92.6	2.6
1869	16.3	0.7	1902	31.9	0.4	1935	42.3	3.8	1968	96.4	4.2
1870	17.3	6.2	1903	31.9	0.0	1936	43.6	3.1	1969	97.8	1.4
1871	18.4	6.2	1904	32.1	0.6	1937	45.5	4.3	1970	100.0	2.2
1872	18.2	−0.8	1905	32.6	1.7	1938	46.8	3.0	1971	102.7	2.7
1873	18.2	−0.4	1906	33.3	2.2	1939	48.6	3.9	1972	105.1	2.3
1874	19.2	5.8	1907	33.4	0.2	1940	55.7	14.4	1973	112.9	7.5
1875	19.5	1.2	1908	32.2	−3.5	1941	59.0	6.0	1974	111.8	−1.0
1876	19.7	1.1	1909	33.3	3.3	1942	59.6	1.0	1975	111.2	−0.5
1877	19.9	1.0	1910	34.4	3.5	1943	60.7	1.8	1976	115.3	3.6
1878	20.0	0.5	1911	35.2	2.3	1944	57.9	−4.5	1977	116.7	1.3
1879	19.6	−2.1	1912	35.1	−0.3	1945	54.4	−6.2	1978	120.6	3.3
1880	21.1	7.9	1913	37.0	5.2	1946	54.1	−0.6	1979	122.3	1.4
1881	21.1	−0.2	1914	37.2	0.8	1947	52.7	−2.4	1980	120.6	−1.4
1882	21.4	1.5	1915	41.0	10.1	1948	54.1	2.6			

UK fixed investment

The periods of expansion and recession for fixed investment were similar in general to those for gross domestic product, although with rather longer recession times, and with greater amounts of fluctuation. Main periods of expansion were 1858–65, 1870–72, 1874–76, 1883, 1888–92, 1894–99, 1901–03, 1913, 1919–21 (post-war recovery), 1923–25, 1927, 1933–37, 1945–50 (post-war recovery), 1953–57, 1959–61, 1964–68, 1970, 1973 and 1978; main recessions were in 1857, 1866–69, 1873, 1877–82, 1884–87, 1893, 1904–08, 1911–12, 1915–18 (world war), 1922, 1926, 1931–32, 1939–44 (world war), 1951–52, 1958, 1962–63, 1974–77 and 1979–80.

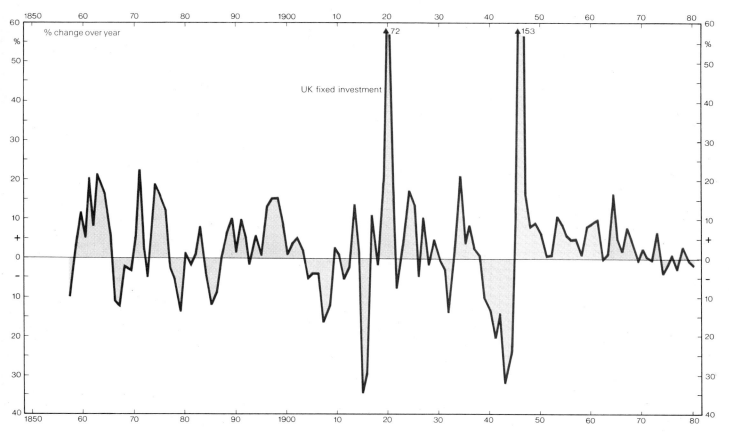

% change over year

UK fixed investment

Year	Index 1970 = 100	% change over year	Year	Index 1970 =100	% change over year	Year	Index 1970 = 100	% change over year	Year	Index 1970 = 100	% change over year
1850	na	na	1883	9.2	8	1916	6.5	−29	1949	34.1	9
1851	na	na	1884	8.8	−4	1917	7.2	11	1950	36.1	6
1852	na	na	1885	7.8	−12	1918	7.1	−1	1951	36.4	1
1853	na	na	1886	7.1	−9	1919	8.6	20	1952	36.6	1
1854	na	na	1887	7.1	0	1920	14.7	72	1953	40.6	11
1855	na	na	1888	7.6	6	1921	16.9	15	1954	44.2	9
1856	3.5	na	1889	8.3	10	1922	15.5	−8	1955	46.8	6
1857	3.2	−10	1890	8.5	2	1923	16.0	3	1956	49.0	5
1858	3.3	3	1891	9.4	10	1924	18.6	17	1957	51.7	5
1859	3.6	11	1892	9.8	5	1925	21.3	14	1958	52.1	1
1860	3.8	5	1893	9.7	−1	1926	20.6	−3	1959	56.1	8
1861	4.5	20	1894	10.3	6	1927	22.9	11	1960	61.2	9
1862	4.9	8	1895	10.4	1	1928	22.7	−1	1961	67.2	10
1863	5.9	21	1896	11.8	13	1929	23.9	5	1962	67.3	0
1864	6.9	16	1897	13.5	15	1930	24.0	0	1963	68.2	1
1865	7.2	5	1898	15.5	15	1931	23.5	−2	1964	79.6	17
1866	6.4	−11	1899	16.9	9	1932	20.5	−13	1965	83.5	5
1867	5.7	−12	1900	17.1	1	1933	21.2	3	1966	85.5	2
1868	5.6	−2	1901	17.8	4	1934	25.8	22	1967	92.8	8
1869	5.4	−3	1902	18.6	5	1935	26.8	4	1968	97.0	5
1870	5.7	5	1903	19.1	2	1936	29.3	9	1969	97.4	0
1871	7.0	23	1904	18.0	−5	1937	30.3	3	1970	100.0	3
1872	7.1	2	1905	17.3	−4	1938	30.7	1	1971	101.5	1
1873	6.8	−5	1906	16.6	−4	1939	27.5	−10	1972	101.9	0
1874	8.1	19	1907	13.9	−16	1940	23.8	−13	1973	108.9	7
1875	9.4	16	1908	12.2	−12	1941	19.2	−20	1974	105.7	−3
1876	10.5	12	1909	12.5	3	1942	16.6	−14	1975	104.9	−1
1877	10.3	−2	1910	12.7	1	1943	11.4	−31	1976	106.1	1
1878	9.8	−5	1911	12.1	−5	1944	8.8	−23	1977	103.6	−2
1879	8.4	−14	1912	11.8	−2	1945	9.8	12	1978	107.1	3
1880	8.5	1	1913	13.5	14	1946	24.9	153	1979	107.4	0
1881	8.4	−1	1914	13.7	1	1947	29.0	17	1980	106.7	−1
1882	8.5	1	1915	9.1	−34	1948	31.3	8			

US gross domestic product

The main series of US gross domestic product is available only from 1919; the series used here has been estimated before then by linking the series of gross national product for 1889–1919, and the series of industrial production for 1860–89 to indicate timing. This would tend to overstate the amount of fluctuation for 1860–89; for example, over 1897–1902 industrial production averaged 9% per year expansion compared with 6% per year for gross national product.

With that reservation, the main periods of expansion in US gross domestic product on a long-term view were 1863–64, 1866–72, 1877–83, 1886–92, 1897–1903, 1905–07, 1909–13, 1916–18, 1922–26, 1929, 1934–37, 1939–44, 1948–53, 1955–57, 1959–69, 1971–73 and 1976–79; there were main recessions in 1862, 1865, 1873–76, 1884–85, 1893–94, 1908, 1914–15, 1919–21, 1930–33, 1938, 1945–47, 1954, 1958, 1970, 1974–75 and 1980.

The following table sets out the detailed periods:

Expansion	Recession
1863–64	1865 (civil war 1861–65)
1866–72 (1870 mini-recession)	1873–76
1877–83	1884–85

Expansion	Recession
1886–92	1893–94
1895 (mini)	1896 (mini)
1897–1903 (1902 mini-recession)	1904
1905–07	1908
1909–13	1914–15
1916–18	1919–21 (post-war)
1922–26	1927–28
1929	1930–33
1934–37	1938
1939–44	1945–47 (post-war)
1948–53	1954
1955–57	1958
1959	1960–61 (mini)
1962–66	1967 (mini)
1968–69	1970
1971–73	1974–75
1976–79	1980

From the expansion ending in 1883, movements in the United States have corresponded very roughly with those of the United Kingdom.

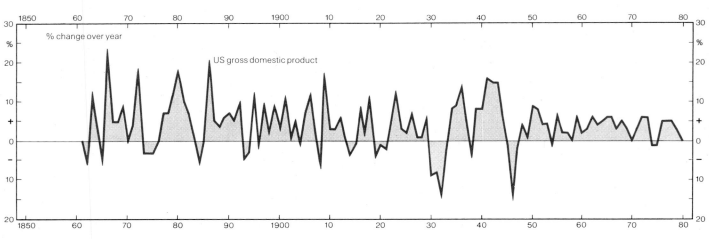

US gross domestic product

Year	Index 1970 = 100	% change over year	Year	Index 1970 =100	% change over year	Year	Index 1970 = 100	% change over year	Year	Index 1970 = 100	% change over year
1850	na	na	1883	5.2	2	1916	18.9	8	1949	45.4	1
1851	na	na	1884	4.9	−6	1917	19.0	1	1950	49.4	9
1852	na	na	1885	4.9	0	1918	21.4	12	1951	53.4	8
1853	na	na	1886	6.0	21	1919	20.6	−4	1952	55.4	4
1854	na	na	1887	6.3	5	1920	20.4	−1	1953	57.5	4
1855	na	na	1888	6.5	3	1921	20.0	−2	1954	56.8	−1
1856	na	na	1889	6.9	6	1922	21.0	5	1955	60.6	7
1857	na	na	1890	7.4	7	1923	23.8	13	1956	61.9	2
1858	na	na	1891	7.8	5	1924	24.5	3	1957	62.9	2
1859	na	na	1892	8.5	10	1925	25.1	2	1958	62.8	0
1860	1.7	na	1893	8.1	−5	1926	26.8	7	1959	66.5	6
1861	1.7	0	1894	7.9	−3	1927	27.0	1	1960	67.9	2
1862	1.6	−6	1895	8.8	12	1928	27.3	1	1961	69.7	3
1863	1.8	13	1896	8.6	−2	1929	29.0	6	1962	73.7	6
1864	1.9	6	1897	9.4	9	1930	26.2	−9	1963	76.6	4
1865	1.8	−6	1898	9.7	2	1931	24.2	−8	1964	80.6	5
1866	2.2	24	1899	10.5	9	1932	20.9	−14	1965	85.5	6
1867	2.3	5	1900	10.8	3	1933	20.4	−2	1966	90.7	6
1868	2.4	5	1901	12.1	11	1934	22.1	8	1967	93.2	3
1869	2.6	9	1902	12.2	1	1935	24.0	9	1968	97.4	5
1870	2.6	0	1903	12.8	5	1936	27.3	14	1969	100.2	3
1871	2.7	4	1904	12.6	−1	1937	28.6	5	1970	100.0	0
1872	3.2	19	1905	13.5	7	1938	27.4	−4	1971	103.3	3
1873	3.1	−3	1906	15.1	12	1939	29.5	8	1972	109.0	6
1874	3.0	−3	1907	15.4	2	1940	31.8	8	1973	115.1	6
1875	2.9	−3	1908	14.1	−8	1941	37.0	16	1974	114.2	−1
1876	2.9	0	1909	16.4	17	1942	42.7	15	1975	113.2	−1
1877	3.1	7	1910	16.9	3	1943	49.2	15	1976	119.2	5
1878	3.3	7	1911	17.3	3	1944	52.7	7	1977	125.7	5
1879	3.8	12	1912	18.3	6	1945	51.9	−1	1978	131.5	5
1880	4.4	17	1913	18.5	1	1946	44.2	−15	1979	135.1	3
1881	4.8	10	1914	17.7	−4	1947	43.4	−2	1980	134.8	0
1882	5.1	7	1915	17.5	−1	1948	45.2	4			

US steel production

Steel production on a large scale began in the 1860s, and expanded in general at a high rate until 1882; thereafter main periods of expansion were 1885–87, 1889–90, 1892, 1895, 1897–99, 1901–02, 1905–06, 1909–10, 1912, 1915–17, 1920 (recovery), 1922–23 (recovery), 1925–26, 1928–29, 1933–37, 1939–41, 1947–48.

1950–51, 1953, 1955, 1959–60, 1963–65, 1968–69 and 1972–73. Main falls were in 1883–84, 1888, 1891, 1893, 1896, 1908, 1911, 1914, 1919, 1921, 1924, 1927, 1930–32, 1938, 1945–46, 1949, 1952, 1954, 1958, 1967, 1970–71, 1974–75 and 1980.

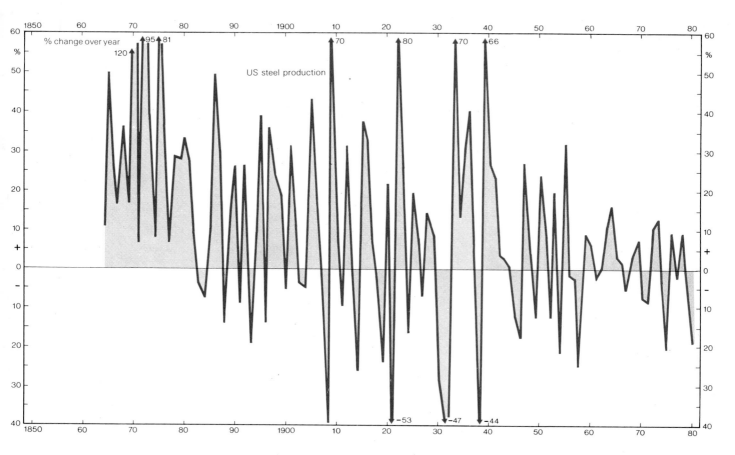

	Index 1970 = 100	% change over year		Index 1970 = 100	% change over year		Index 1970 = 100	% change over year		Index 1970 = 100	% change over year
1850	na	na	1883	1.42	−3.7	1916	35.58	33.0	1949	59.29	−12.0
1851	na	na	1884	1.32	−7.3	1917	37.86	6.4	1950	73.63	24.2
1852	na	na	1885	1.46	10.4	1918	37.27	−1.6	1951	79.99	8.6
1853	na	na	1886	2.18	49.7	1919	28.97	−22.3	1952	70.84	−11.4
1854	na	na	1887	2.84	30.1	1920	35.12	21.2	1953	84.87	19.8
1855	na	na	1888	2.46	−13.3	1921	16.45	−53.1	1954	67.15	−20.9
1856	na	na	1889	2.88	16.9	1922	29.61	80.0	1955	88.99	32.5
1857	na	na	1890	3.63	26.3	1923	37.27	25.9	1956	87.61	−1.6
1858	na	na	1891	3.31	−9.0	1924	31.51	−15.4	1957	85.71	−2.2
1859	na	na	1892	4.18	26.3	1925	37.79	19.9	1958	64.83	−24.4
1860	na	na	1893	3.40	−18.6	1926	40.23	6.4	1959	71.05	9.6
1861	na	na	1894	3.73	9.6	1927	37.47	−6.9	1960	75.49	6.2
1862	na	na	1895	5.16	38.5	1928	43.05	14.9	1961	74.53	−1.3
1863	0.007	na	1896	4.45	−13.8	1929	46.95	9.0	1962	74.77	0.3
1864	0.008	11.1	1897	6.04	35.7	1930	33.91	−27.8	1963	83.08	11.1
1865	0.011	50.0	1898	7.52	24.5	1931	21.75	−35.8	1964	96.63	16.3
1866	0.014	26.7	1899	8.93	18.7	1932	11.50	−47.1	1965	99.96	3.5
1867	0.017	15.8	1900	8.54	−4.4	1933	19.56	70.1	1966	101.97	2.0
1868	0.023	36.4	1901	11.24	31.7	1934	22.19	13.4	1967	96.73	−5.1
1869	0.027	16.7	1902	12.47	10.9	1935	29.03	30.8	1968	99.96	3.3
1870	0.059	120.0	1903	12.06	−3.3	1936	40.68	40.1	1969	107.41	7.5
1871	0.062	6.5	1904	11.56	−4.2	1937	43.07	5.9	1970	100.00	−6.9
1872	0.12	95.1	1905	16.64	43.9	1938	24.14	−43.9	1971	91.58	−8.4
1873	0.17	39.4	1906	19.35	16.3	1939	40.15	66.3	1972	101.31	10.6
1874	0.18	8.5	1907	19.29	−0.3	1940	50.93	26.9	1973	114.66	13.2
1875	0.33	80.6	1908	11.70	−39.4	1941	62.99	23.7	1974	110.80	−3.4
1876	0.45	36.6	1909	19.94	70.4	1942	65.42	3.9	1975	88.69	−20.0
1877	0.49	6.9	1910	21.54	8.1	1943	67.55	3.3	1976	97.28	9.7
1878	0.62	28.5	1911	19.72	−8.4	1944	68.16	0.9	1977	95.30	−2.0
1879	0.80	27.8	1912	25.91	31.4	1945	60.60	−11.1	1978	104.19	9.3
1880	1.06	33.3	1913	25.92	0.0	1946	50.64	−16.4	1979	103.67	−0.5
1881	1.35	27.3	1914	19.47	−24.9	1947	64.55	27.5	1980	85.04	−18.0
1882	1.48	9.3	1915	26.75	37.4	1948	67.40	4.4			

US lead price

The price of lead in the United States rose mainly in 1853–55, 1862–64, 1879–80, 1885–86, 1890, 1897–99, 1905–06, 1915–17, 1920, 1922–25, 1933 (recovery), 1936–37, 1939–42, 1946–48, 1951, 1954–56, 1963–65, 1969–70, 1972–74 and 1977–79. Main falls in the price were in 1856–59, 1861, 1865, 1867–71, 1874–75, 1877–78, 1883–84, 1887–89, 1891–96, 1902, 1907–08, 1914, 1918–19, 1921, 1926–28, 1930–32, 1938, 1949–50, 1952–53, 1957–58, 1960–62, 1966–68, 1971, 1975 and 1980. The total fall from 1864 to 1896 was 58%.

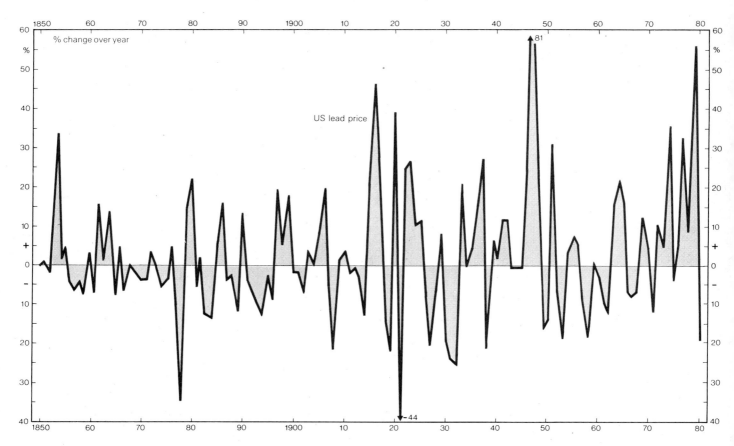

	Index 1970 = 100	% change over year		Index 1970 =100	% change over year		Index 1970 = 100	% change over year		Index 1970 = 100	% change over year
1850	31	0	1883	28	−12	1916	44	46	1949	98	−15
1851	31	1	1884	24	−13	1917	56	28	1950	85	−13
1852	31	−1	1885	25	6	1918	48	−14	1951	111	32
1853	41	34	1886	30	17	1919	37	−22	1952	105	−6
1854	42	2	1887	29	−3	1920	51	39	1953	86	−18
1855	44	5	1888	28	−2	1921	29	−44	1954	90	4
1856	42	−4	1889	25	−11	1922	36	25	1955	96	8
1857	39	−6	1890	29	14	1923	46	27	1956	102	6
1858	38	−4	1891	28	−3	1924	51	11	1957	93	−8
1859	35	−7	1892	26	−6	1925	57	12	1958	77	−17
1860	36	3	1893	24	−9	1926	54	−7	1959	78	1
1861	33	−7	1894	21	−12	1927	43	−20	1960	76	−2
1862	39	16	1895	21	−2	1928	40	−7	1961	69	−9
1863	40	2	1896	19	−8	1929	44	8	1962	61	−11
1864	45	14	1897	23	20	1930	35	−19	1963	71	16
1865	42	−7	1898	24	6	1931	27	−23	1964	87	22
1866	44	5	1899	28	18	1932	20	−25	1965	102	17
1867	41	−6	1900	28	−1	1933	25	22	1966	96	−6
1868	41	0	1901	28	−1	1934	25	0	1967	89	−7
1869	41	−1	1902	26	−6	1935	26	5	1968	84	−6
1870	40	−3	1903	27	4	1936	30	16	1969	95	13
1871	39	−3	1904	28	1	1937	38	28	1970	100	5
1872	40	4	1905	30	9	1938	30	−21	1971	89	−11
1873	40	0	1906	36	20	1939	32	7	1972	98	11
1874	38	−5	1907	34	−5	1940	33	3	1973	105	6
1875	37	−3	1908	27	−21	1941	37	12	1974	142	36
1876	39	5	1909	27	2	1942	41	12	1975	138	−3
1877	35	−10	1910	29	4	1943	41	0	1976	147	6
1878	23	−34	1911	28	−1	1944	41	0	1977	196	33
1879	26	15	1912	29	0	1945	41	0	1978	215	10
1880	32	22	1913	28	−2	1946	52	25	1979	338	57
1881	31	−5	1914	25	−12	1947	93	81	1980	277	−18
1882	31	2	1915	30	21	1948	115	23			

US consumer prices

Consumer prices in the United States rose mainly in 1850–51, 1853, 1855–57, 1861–65, 1881–82, 1888, 1899–1903, 1906–07, 1910, 1912, 1916–20, 1925 (recovery), 1934–35 (recovery), 1941–43, 1946–48, 1951–52, 1957–58, 1968–71 and 1973–80. Main falls in prices were in 1858–60, 1867–71, 1873, 1875–77, 1883–85, 1891,

1893–94, 1908, 1913, 1921–22, 1927–28, 1930–33, 1938–39 and 1949. The major increase in prices of 63% for 1861–66 was followed by an overall fall of 29% between 1866 and 1894.

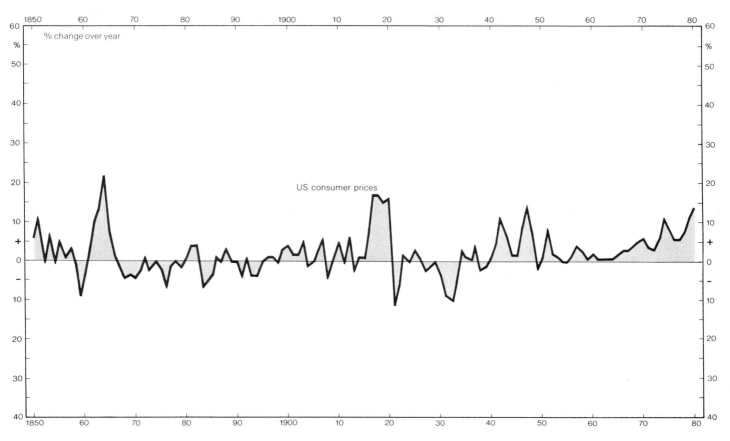

	Index 1970 = 100	% change over year		Index 1970 = 100	% change over year		Index 1970 = 100	% change over year		Index 1970 = 100	% change over year
1850	14	6	1883	21	−6	1916	28	8	1949	61	−1
1851	15	11	1884	20	−5	1917	33	17	1950	62	1
1852	15	0	1885	19	−3	1918	39	17	1951	67	8
1853	16	7	1886	19	1	1919	45	15	1952	68	2
1854	16	0	1887	19	0	1920	52	16	1953	69	1
1855	17	5	1888	20	3	1921	46	−11	1954	69	0
1856	17	1	1889	20	0	1922	43	−6	1955	69	0
1857	18	3	1890	20	0	1923	44	2	1956	70	1
1858	18	−1	1891	19	−3	1924	44	0	1957	72	4
1859	16	−9	1892	20	1	1925	45	3	1958	74	3
1860	16	−3	1893	19	−3	1926	46	1	1959	75	1
1861	16	3	1894	19	−3	1927	45	−2	1960	76	2
1862	18	10	1895	19	0	1928	44	−1	1961	77	1
1863	20	13	1896	19	1	1929	44	0	1962	78	1
1864	24	22	1897	19	1	1930	43	−3	1963	79	1
1865	26	7	1898	19	0	1931	39	−9	1964	80	1
1866	26	1	1899	20	3	1932	35	−10	1965	81	2
1867	26	−1	1900	20	4	1933	33	−5	1966	84	3
1868	25	−4	1901	21	2	1934	34	3	1967	86	3
1869	24	−3	1902	21	2	1935	35	2	1968	90	4
1870	23	−4	1903	22	5	1936	36	1	1969	94	5
1871	23	−2	1904	22	−1	1937	37	4	1970	100	6
1872	23	1	1905	22	0	1938	36	−2	1971	104	4
1873	22	−2	1906	23	3	1939	36	−1	1972	108	3
1874	22	0	1907	24	6	1940	36	1	1973	114	6
1875	22	−2	1908	23	−4	1941	38	5	1974	127	11
1876	21	−6	1909	23	0	1942	42	11	1975	139	9
1877	20	−1	1910	25	5	1943	45	6	1976	147	6
1878	20	0	1911	25	0	1944	45	2	1977	156	6
1879	20	−1	1912	26	6	1945	46	2	1978	168	8
1880	20	1	1913	26	−2	1946	50	9	1979	187	11
1881	21	4	1914	26	1	1947	58	14	1980	212	14
1882	22	4	1915	26	1	1948	62	8			

US share prices

Share prices in the United States rose mainly in 1878–81, 1886–87, 1892, 1897–99, 1901–02, 1905–06, 1909, 1916, 1919, 1922, 1924–29, 1933–36, 1943–46, 1950–52, 1954–56, 1958–59, 1961, 1963–65, 1967–68, 1971–72, 1975–76 and 1979–80. Main falls in share prices were in 1873–77, 1882–85, 1888, 1891, 1893–94, 1896, 1903, 1907, 1913–14, 1917–18, 1920–21, 1930–32, 1938, 1940–42, 1947, 1957, 1960, 1962, 1966, 1970, 1974 and 1977–78. The total fall in share prices from 1872 to 1896 was 16%; the rise from 1921 to 1929 was 279%.

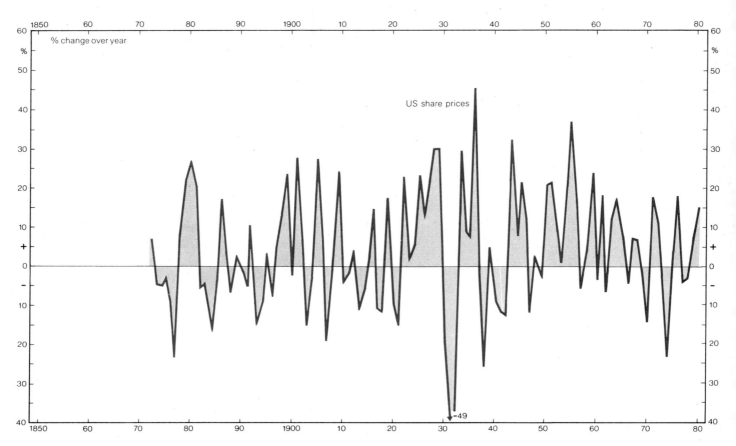

	Index 1970 = 100	% change over year		Index 1970 = 100	% change over year		Index 1970 = 100	% change over year		Index 1970 = 100	% change over year
1850	na	na	1883	6.77	−4.6	1916	11.38	14.0	1949	18.30	−1.9
1851	na	na	1884	5.70	−15.8	1917	10.21	−10.2	1950	22.11	20.8
1852	na	na	1885	5.53	−3.0	1918	9.06	−11.3	1951	26.84	21.4
1853	na	na	1886	6.44	16.5	1919	10.55	16.4	1952	29.44	9.7
1854	na	na	1887	6.65	3.2	1920	9.59	−9.1	1953	29.72	0.9
1855	na	na	1888	6.25	−6.0	1921	8.24	−14.0	1954	35.68	20.1
1856	na	na	1889	6.39	2.3	1922	10.11	22.6	1955	48.65	36.4
1857	na	na	1890	6.33	−0.9	1923	10.30	1.9	1956	56.02	15.1
1858	na	na	1891	6.04	−4.6	1924	10.87	5.6	1957	53.33	−4.8
1859	na	na	1892	6.67	10.3	1925	13.40	23.2	1958	55.56	4.2
1860	na	na	1893	5.74	−13.9	1926	15.13	12.9	1959	68.95	24.1
1861	na	na	1894	5.28	−8.2	1927	18.43	21.8	1960	67.11	−2.7
1862	na	na	1895	5.44	3.2	1928	23.97	30.1	1961	79.63	18.7
1863	na	na	1896	5.08	−6.6	1929	31.27	30.4	1962	74.96	−5.9
1864	na	na	1897	5.35	5.2	1930	25.27	−19.2	1963	83.96	12.0
1865	na	na	1898	6.07	13.5	1931	16.41	−35.0	1964	97.78	16.5
1866	na	na	1899	7.56	24.6	1932	8.33	−49.3	1965	105.95	8.4
1867	na	na	1900	7.39	−2.2	1933	10.77	29.3	1966	102.45	−3.3
1868	na	na	1901	9.42	27.5	1934	11.82	9.8	1967	110.47	7.8
1869	na	na	1902	10.12	7.4	1935	12.74	7.7	1968	118.60	7.4
1870	na	na	1903	8.66	−14.4	1936	18.59	45.9	1969	117.57	−0.9
1871	5.64	na	1904	8.47	−2.2	1937	18.52	−0.4	1970	100.00	−14.9
1872	6.04	7.2	1905	10.80	27.5	1938	13.81	−25.4	1971	118.11	18.1
1873	5.77	−4.6	1906	11.58	7.2	1939	14.49	5.0	1972	131.22	11.1
1874	5.49	−4.8	1907	9.42	−18.7	1940	13.24	−8.6	1973	129.09	−1.6
1875	5.35	−2.6	1908	9.35	−0.8	1941	11.80	−10.9	1974	99.56	−22.9
1876	4.88	−8.8	1909	11.67	24.8	1942	10.42	−11.7	1975	103.53	4.0
1877	3.77	−22.7	1910	11.24	−3.7	1943	13.82	32.6	1976	122.58	18.4
1878	4.06	7.6	1911	11.10	−1.2	1944	14.98	8.4	1977	118.00	−3.7
1879	4.95	21.9	1912	11.45	3.1	1945	18.22	21.6	1978	115.38	−2.2
1880	6.26	26.5	1913	10.23	−10.7	1946	20.52	12.7	1979	123.78	7.3
1881	7.51	20.0	1914	9.71	−5.1	1947	18.23	−11.2	1980	142.73	15.3
1882	7.09	−5.6	1915	9.99	2.8	1948	18.66	2.4			

Commodity prices

The chart and figures in the table below, discussed overleaf, are for The Economist Commodity Price Index, sterling basis, with 1970 = 100.

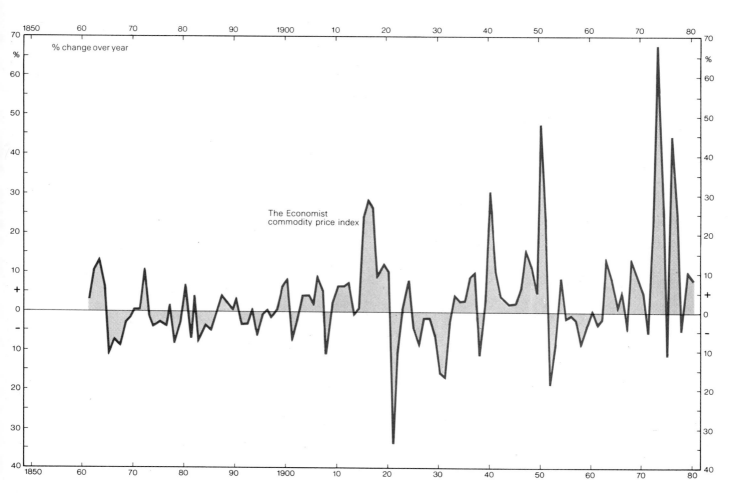

	Index 1970 =100	% change over year		Index 1970 =100	% change over year		Index 1970 =100	% change over year		Index 1970 =100	% change over year
1850	na	na	1883	17.4	−7	1916	33.5	28	1949	52.5	5
1851	na	na	1884	16.8	−4	1917	42.3	26	1950	77.5	48
1852	na	na	1885	15.9	−5	1918	46.0	9	1951	95.2	23
1853	na	na	1886	15.9	0	1919	51.7	12	1952	76.8	−19
1854	na	na	1887	16.6	4	1920	56.8	10	1953	70.6	−8
1855	na	na	1888	16.9	2	1921	38.0	−33	1954	76.0	8
1856	na	na	1889	16.9	0	1922	33.9	−11	1955	74.2	−2
1857	na	na	1890	17.4	3	1923	33.9	0	1956	73.2	−1
1858	na	na	1891	16.9	−3	1924	36.4	8	1957	71.9	−2
1859	na	na	1892	16.4	−3	1925	34.9	−4	1958	66.5	−8
1860	21.2	na	1893	16.4	0	1926	31.6	−9	1959	64.7	−3
1861	21.9	3	1894	15.4	−6	1927	31.0	−2	1960	64.9	0
1862	24.1	10	1895	15.2	−1	1928	30.3	−2	1961	63.0	−3
1863	27.4	13	1896	15.2	0	1929	28.6	−6	1962	61.7	−2
1864	29.1	6	1897	14.9	−2	1930	23.9	−16	1963	69.9	13
1865	26.0	−11	1898	14.9	0	1931	19.8	−17	1964	75.5	8
1866	24.1	−7	1899	15.7	6	1932	19.2	−3	1965	76.4	1
1867	21.9	−9	1900	16.9	8	1933	19.8	4	1966	80.3	5
1868	21.2	−3	1901	15.7	−7	1934	20.5	3	1967	77.5	−4
1869	20.9	−2	1902	15.4	−2	1935	21.2	3	1968	87.4	13
1870	20.9	0	1903	16.1	4	1936	23.1	9	1969	95.0	9
1871	20.9	0	1904	16.8	4	1937	25.3	10	1970	100.0	5
1872	23.1	11	1905	17.1	2	1938	22.4	−11	1971	95.0	−5
1873	22.8	−1	1906	18.6	9	1939	23.1	3	1972	117.7	24
1874	21.9	−4	1907	19.5	5	1940	29.9	30	1973	198.1	68
1875	21.2	−3	1908	17.3	−11	1941	33.0	10	1974	247.0	25
1876	20.4	−4	1909	17.6	2	1942	34.4	4	1975	216.5	−12
1877	20.5	1	1910	18.6	6	1943	35.4	3	1976	314.3	45
1878	18.8	−8	1911	19.7	6	1944	36.3	2	1977	391.3	25
1879	18.3	−3	1912	21.0	7	1945	36.9	2	1978	373.2	−5
1880	19.3	6	1913	20.9	−1	1946	39.3	6	1979	412.1	10
1881	18.1	−6	1914	21.0	1	1947	45.3	15	1980	443.3	8
1882	18.8	4	1915	26.2	24	1948	50.1	11			

Commodity prices

The Economist index (overleaf) is a general index of commodity prices, and excludes gold and crude oil prices. Commodity prices as shown by the index rose mainly in 1861–64, 1872, 1880 (recovery), 1887–88, 1890, 1899–1900, 1903–07, 1909–12, 1915–20, 1924, 1933–37 (recovery), 1940–41, 1946–48, 1950–51, 1954 (recovery), 1963–66, 1968–70, 1972–74, 1976–77 and 1979–80. Main falls in commodity prices were in 1865–69, 1873–76, 1878–79, 1881, 1883–85, 1891–92, 1894–95, 1897, 1901–02, 1908, 1921–22, 1925–26, 1929–32, 1938, 1952–53, 1955–59, 1961–62, 1967, 1971, 1975 and 1978.

The total fall in sterling commodity prices from 1864 to 1897 was 49%. That time, in the second half of the 1800s, was a period of falling prices generally. A summary of the amount of fall for various prices is as follows:

	% fall from mid 1860s to mid 1890s
The Economist index	49
US lead price	58
US copper price	80
US consumer prices	29
US share prices	16[a]

[a] From early 1870s

This fall happened at a time when world markets and production were increasing rapidly; UK gross domestic product increased about 110%, and US industrial product increased about 350%. Transport costs were lowered and commodity supplies increased.

Periods of large rises in commodity prices have generally been associated with increases in gold production or the gold price (through the impact on the money stock), or with wars (through the creation of extra demand at a time when supply is likely to be restricted). The chart which is included below shows the five periods of major rise in commodity prices which have occurred within the time under review; these have been shown in the same chart to indicate the broad similarity between the initial impact on prices, and the subsequent lower rate of increases. The chart is based on % changes for The Economist index, as shown overleaf.

The period of rises beginning in 1861 can be regarded as following from the increase in gold production arising from the discoveries of gold in California (1848) and Australia (1851); US gold production increased from 43 000 troy ounces in 1847 to 2 419 000 troy ounces in 1850, remaining at about 2½ million troy ounces throughout the 1850s and 1860s. The period of rises beginning 1914, 1939 and 1949 can be associated with the first world war, second world war and Korean war respectively; the latter period was also substantially affected (in sterling terms) by the 1949 sterling devaluation. The period of rises beginning 1971 can be associated with the freeing of the gold price by the United States in 1971.

The amount and pattern of fluctuation has been broadly similar for the five periods. In particular, the period beginning in 1971 is similar to that beginning 1861 in its dependence on gold, and, more recently, the period beginning with the Korean war.

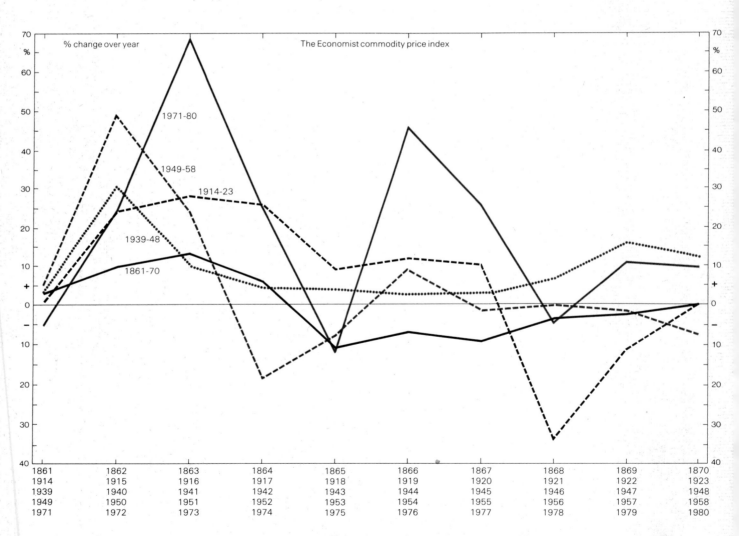

Argentina

The main periods of expansion in gross domestic product were 1951, 1953–55, 1958, 1960–61, 1965–66, 1968–70, 1973–74, 1977 and 1979; there were falls in growth or a low growth rate in 1952, 1956–57, 1959, 1962–64, 1967, 1972, 1975–76, 1978 and 1980. Exports increased mainly in 1951, 1953, 1962–63, 1965–66, 1969–70,

1972–74, 1976–77 and 1979; main falls were in 1951–52, 1954–55, 1961, 1967–68, 1971, 1975 and 1980. Unemployment, for the time covered, increased mainly in 1966–67, 1970–72 and 1976, and fell mainly in 1968–69, 1973–75, 1977 and 1979. Consumer prices increased mainly in 1959, 1972–73 and 1975–80.

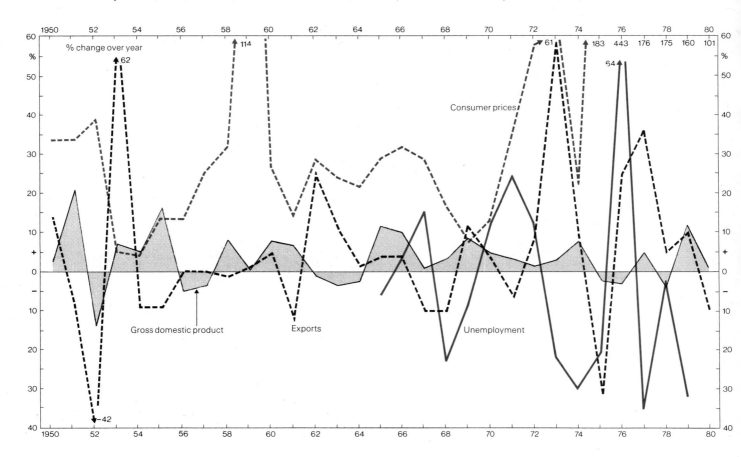

	Gross domestic product		Exports		Unemployment		Consumer prices		
	Index 1970 = 100	% change over year	Index 1970 = 100	% change over year	Number (000)	% change over year	Index 1970 = 100	% change over year	
1950	48.1	2.5	107	14	na	na	1.3	33	1950
1951	57.9	20.4	98	−8	na	na	1.7	33	1951
1952	49.7	−14.1	57	−42	na	na	2.4	38	1952
1953	53.1	6.9	92	62	na	na	2.5	5	1953
1954	55.9	5.1	84	−9	na	na	2.6	4	1954
1955	64.7	15.8	76	−9	na	na	2.9	13	1955
1956	61.3	−5.3	76	0	na	na	3.3	13	1956
1957	59.3	−3.3	76	0	na	na	4.1	25	1957
1958	64.0	8.0	75	−1	na	na	5.4	32	1958
1959	64.0	0.0	76	1	na	na	11.5	114	1959
1960	68.8	7.4	80	5	na	na	14.6	27	1960
1961	73.6	6.9	71	−12	na	na	16.6	14	1961
1962	72.9	−0.9	88	25	na	na	21.2	28	1962
1963	70.2	−3.7	98	11	na	na	26.3	24	1963
1964	68.5	−2.4	100	2	177.6	na	32.1	22	1964
1965	76.5	11.7	104	4	167.4	−5.7	41.3	29	1965
1966	84.2	10.1	107	4	172.7	3.2	54.5	32	1966
1967	84.8	0.8	96	−10	198.7	15.1	70.5	29	1967
1968	87.7	3.4	86	−10	153.3	−22.8	81.8	16	1968
1969	95.5	8.9	96	12	140.3	−8.5	88.2	8	1969
1970	100.0	4.8	100	4	158.0	12.6	100.0	13	1970
1971	103.6	3.6	94	−6	196.5	24.4	134.8	35	1971
1972	105.3	1.6	102	8	221.5	12.7	213.5	58	1972
1973	108.9	3.4	161	58	173.0	−21.9	344.3	61	1973
1974	117.3	7.7	175	9	121.2	−29.9	425.0	23	1974
1975	114.8	−2.1	120	−31	97.0	−20.0	1201.9	183	1975
1976	111.1	−3.2	151	25	159.1	64.0	6526.3	443	1976
1977	116.7	5.0	204	36	103.3	−35.1	18028.5	176	1977
1978	112.3	−3.8	215	5	101.6	−1.6	49650.5	175	1978
1979	125.8	12.1	235	10	69.5	−31.6	128855.7	160	1979
1980	127.0	0.9	213	−10	na	na	258697.0	101	1980

Australia

The main periods of expansion in gross domestic product were 1950–51, 1954–56, 1959–61, 1963–65, 1967–74, 1976–77 and 1979–80; there was a fall or low growth for 1952–53, 1957–58, 1962, 1966, 1975 and 1978. Consumers expenditure increased mainly in 1950, 1954–56, 1958–60, 1963–65, 1967–74 and 1979–80, following generally the same pattern as gross domestic product. Government expenditure increased mainly in 1950–52, 1955–56, 1959, 1965–68, 1970–71 and 1974–79, with main falls in 1954 and 1960. Fixed investment increased mainly in 1950–51, 1954–56, 1958–61, 1963–66, 1968–71, 1974, 1976 and 1979.

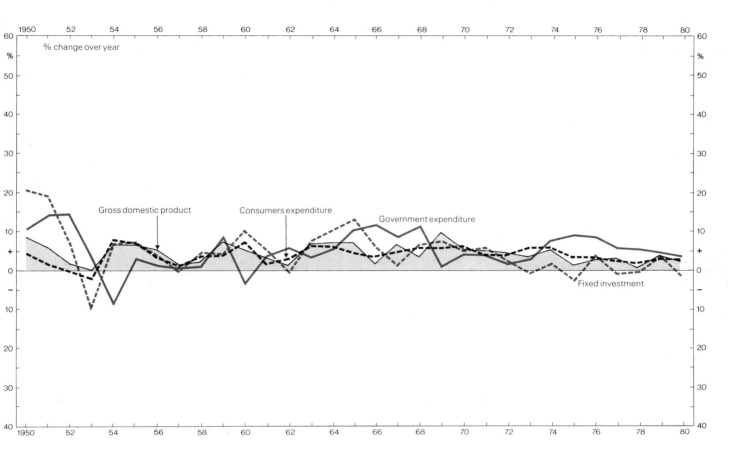

	Gross domestic product[a]		Consumers expenditure[a]		Government expenditure[a]		Fixed investment[a]		
	Index 1970 = 100	% change over year	Index 1970 = 100	% change over year	Index 1970 = 100	% change over year	Index 1970 = 100	% change over year	
1950	39.8	8.0	48.2	4.0	38.3	10.9	32.6	20.9	1950
1951	42.1	5.9	48.8	1.3	43.7	14.1	38.9	19.4	1951
1952	43.0	2.0	48.5	−0.5	50.1	14.6	41.6	7.1	1952
1953	42.9	−0.2	47.4	−2.3	52.3	4.3	37.6	−9.6	1953
1954	45.6	6.4	50.7	7.1	48.0	−8.2	40.4	7.3	1954
1955	48.4	6.0	54.0	6.6	49.3	2.8	43.4	7.4	1955
1956	50.8	5.0	55.8	3.2	50.3	1.9	45.2	4.2	1956
1957	51.8	1.9	56.3	0.9	50.6	0.6	45.3	0.3	1957
1958	52.9	2.2	58.1	3.3	51.0	0.9	47.4	4.7	1958
1959	56.8	7.4	60.0	3.2	55.3	8.3	49.6	4.5	1959
1960	59.8	5.4	64.1	6.9	53.6	−3.0	54.7	10.4	1960
1961	61.9	3.5	65.3	1.9	55.7	3.9	57.7	5.4	1961
1962	62.6	1.2	67.0	2.6	58.8	5.6	57.6	−0.1	1962
1963	66.9	6.8	71.1	6.2	60.8	3.4	62.0	7.6	1963
1964	71.7	7.1	75.5	6.1	64.1	5.4	68.2	10.1	1964
1965	76.8	7.2	79.0	4.7	70.8	10.4	77.1	13.1	1965
1966	78.4	2.1	81.4	3.0	79.2	11.9	82.0	6.3	1966
1967	83.5	6.5	85.3	4.8	85.8	8.3	83.4	1.7	1967
1968	86.4	3.5	89.8	5.4	95.2	10.9	88.5	6.1	1968
1969	94.7	9.5	94.6	5.3	95.9	0.7	95.1	7.5	1969
1970	100.0	5.6	100.0	5.7	100.0	4.3	100.0	5.1	1970
1971	105.1	5.1	104.0	4.0	104.0	4.0	105.5	5.5	1971
1972	109.9	4.5	108.3	4.1	105.7	1.6	107.9	2.3	1972
1973	113.8	3.6	114.3	5.5	108.5	2.7	107.1	−0.7	1973
1974	119.6	5.1	120.4	5.4	116.6	7.5	109.1	1.9	1974
1975	121.6	1.7	124.1	3.1	126.4	8.4	106.7	−2.2	1975
1976	124.8	2.6	127.8	2.9	136.8	8.2	109.8	3.0	1976
1977	128.8	3.2	130.8	2.4	144.3	5.4	108.9	−0.8	1977
1978	129.2	0.3	132.9	1.6	151.5	5.0	108.3	−0.5	1978
1979	134.3	3.9	136.5	2.7	157.6	4.1	111.4	2.8	1979
1980	137.2	2.2	139.7	2.3	161.6	2.5	109.9	−1.3	1980

[a]Years ending June 30th

33

Australia

Exports increased mainly in 1953, 1956–57, 1959, 1961, 1963, 1967–72, 1975–76 and 1979; main falls were in 1951–52, 1954, 1958, 1960 and 1974, with a negligible rate of growth in 1977–78 and 1980. Imports increased mainly in 1950–51, 1954–55, 1958–60, 1962–65, 1967–68, 1970, 1973–74 and 1976, with a comparatively stable rate of growth for 1978–80; main falls were in 1952–53, 1956–57, 1961, 1966, 1971–72 and 1975. Unemployment, for the time covered, increased mainly in 1966–67, 1971–72, 1974–75 and 1977–78; main falls were in 1965, 1970 and 1973. Consumer prices increased mainly in 1950–52, 1956 and 1971–80.

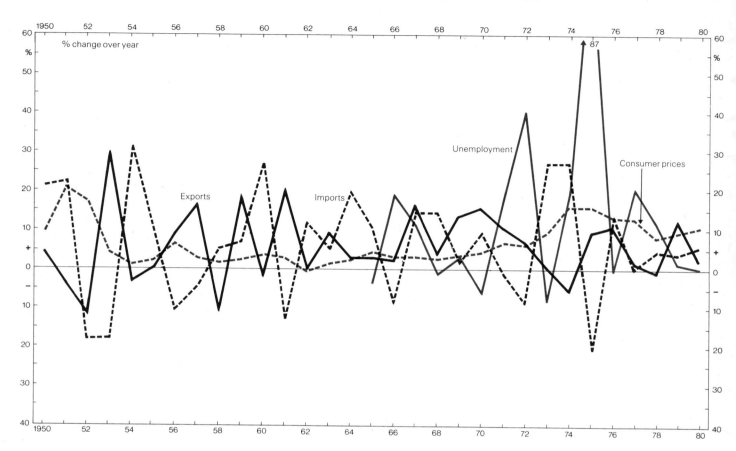

	Exports		Imports		Unemployment		Consumer prices		
	Index 1970 = 100	% change over year	Index 1970 = 100	% change over year	Number (000)	% change over year	Index 1970 = 100	% change over year	
1950	33	4	39	21	na	na	44.7	9.2	1950
1951	32	−4	47	22	na	na	53.7	20.1	1951
1952	28	−12	39	−18	na	na	62.8	17.0	1952
1953	36	29	32	−18	na	na	65.4	4.1	1953
1954	35	−3	42	31	na	na	65.9	0.8	1954
1955	35	0	46	10	na	na	67.2	2.0	1955
1956	38	9	41	−11	na	na	71.4	6.2	1956
1957	44	16	39	−5	na	na	73.2	2.5	1957
1958	39	−11	41	5	na	na	74.2	1.4	1958
1959	46	18	44	7	na	na	75.6	1.9	1959
1960	45	−2	56	27	na	na	78.4	3.7	1960
1961	54	20	49	−13	na	na	80.4	2.6	1961
1962	54	0	55	12	na	na	80.1	−0.4	1962
1963	59	9	58	5	na	na	80.6	0.6	1963
1964	61	3	69	19	76.8	na	82.5	2.4	1964
1965	63	3	76	10	73.6	−4	85.8	4.0	1965
1966	64	2	69	−9	86.7	18	88.3	2.9	1966
1967	74	16	79	14	95.9	11	91.1	3.2	1967
1968	77	4	90	14	94.4	−2	93.6	2.7	1968
1969	87	13	92	2	97.0	3	96.2	2.8	1969
1970	100	15	100	9	90.6	−7	100.0	4.0	1970
1971	110	10	98	−2	107.3	18	106.1	6.1	1971
1972	118	7	89	−9	150.1	40	112.4	5.9	1972
1973	118	0	113	27	136.3	−9	122.9	9.3	1973
1974	111	−6	144	27	161.6	19	141.5	15.1	1974
1975	121	9	114	−21	302.5	87	162.8	15.1	1975
1976	133	10	129	13	298.1	−1	184.8	13.5	1976
1977	134	1	129	0	358.0	20	207.6	12.3	1977
1978	133	−1	135	4	402.1	12	224.0	7.9	1978
1979	149	12	139	3	404.7	1	244.4	9.1	1979
1980	151	2	146	5	405.6	0	269.3	10.2	1980

Australia

Share prices increased mainly in 1950–51, 1954–55, 1957–60, 1963–64, 1967–69, 1972, 1976 and 1978–80; main falls were in 1952, 1961, 1965, 1970–71, 1973–75 and 1977. Money stock increased mainly in 1950–51, 1953, 1957, 1959, 1963–64, 1966–69, 1972–73, 1975 and 1978–80. International reserves increased mainly in 1950, 1953, 1956–57, 1959, 1961, 1963, 1966, 1970–72 and 1980; there were substantial falls in 1951–52, 1954–55, 1958, 1960, 1965, 1967, 1969, 1973–75, 1977 and 1979. Interest rates increased mainly in 1952–53, 1955–56, 1960–61, 1964–65, 1968–70, 1973–74, 1977 and 1979–80.

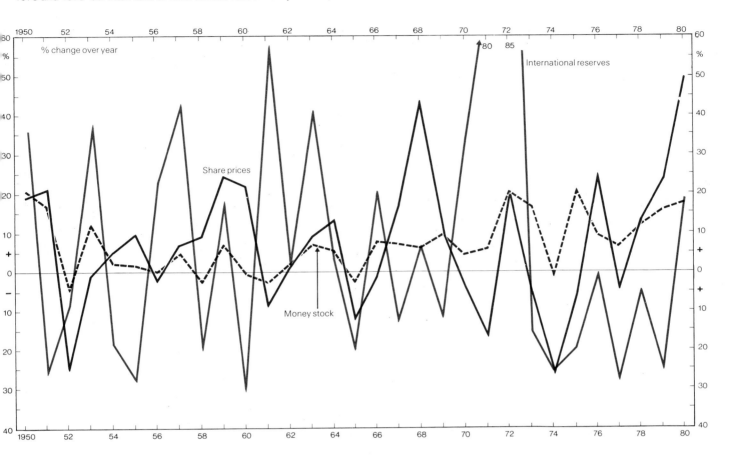

	Share prices		Money stock		International reserves		Interest rate[a]		
	Index 1970 = 100	% change over year	Index 1970 = 100	% change over year	Index 1970 = 100	% change over year	%	Change over year[b]	
1950	32	19	45.1	20.5	82.9	35.7	1.95	−0.04	1950
1951	38	21	52.6	16.6	60.4	−27.2	2.01	0.06	1951
1952	29	−25	50.7	−3.6	54.3	−10.0	2.49	0.48	1952
1953	28	−1	57.0	12.4	73.5	35.2	3.07	0.58	1953
1954	30	5	58.5	2.5	58.8	−20.0	3.34	0.27	1954
1955	33	10	59.8	2.3	41.3	−29.7	3.79	0.45	1955
1956	32	−2	59.8	0.0	50.4	22.0	4.71	0.92	1956
1957	34	7	62.8	4.9	71.1	41.0	4.57	−0.14	1957
1958	37	9	61.3	−2.4	55.8	−21.5	4.29	−0.28	1958
1959	46	24	65.7	7.2	64.7	16.1	3.99	−0.30	1959
1960	56	22	65.2	−0.7	43.9	−32.2	4.39	0.40	1960
1961	52	−8	63.5	−2.6	68.4	55.9	4.99	0.60	1961
1962	52	1	64.7	2.0	69.0	0.9	4.29	−0.70	1962
1963	57	9	69.5	7.3	96.5	39.9	3.82	−0.47	1963
1964	64	13	73.3	5.5	99.2	2.8	4.12	0.30	1964
1965	57	−12	71.7	−2.1	77.8	−21.6	4.85	0.73	1965
1966	56	−1	77.2	7.6	92.6	19.1	4.92	0.07	1966
1967	66	17	82.5	6.9	80.6	−13.0	4.55	−0.37	1967
1968	95	43	87.2	5.7	85.2	5.7	4.81	0.26	1968
1969	104	10	95.6	9.5	74.5	−12.6	5.25	0.44	1969
1970	100	−4	100.0	4.6	100.0	34.3	6.26	1.01	1970
1971	83	−17	105.6	5.6	180.4	80.4	6.14	−0.12	1971
1972	100	20	126.7	20.0	334.1	85.2	4.91	−1.23	1972
1973	94	−6	146.7	15.8	279.0	−16.5	6.30	1.39	1973
1974	69	−26	145.2	−1.0	206.0	−26.2	9.33	3.03	1974
1975	65	−6	179.1	23.3	164.3	−20.2	8.46	−0.87	1975
1976	81	24	195.2	9.0	161.1	−1.9	8.69	0.23	1976
1977	77	−4	208.2	6.7	115.9	−28.1	9.74	1.05	1977
1978	88	13	233.3	12.0	109.6	−5.4	8.80	−0.94	1978
1979	108	23	269.2	15.4	80.3	−26.8	9.62	0.82	1979
1980	161	49	316.1	17.5	94.7	18.0	11.50	1.88	1980

[a]Government bond yield (short-term) [b]In percentage points

Austria

The main periods of expansion in gross domestic product were 1950, 1954–57, 1960–61, 1963–66, 1968–74, 1976–77 and 1979–80; there was a fall in product or low growth rate for 1951–52, 1958–59, 1962, 1967, 1975 and 1978. Consumers expenditure increased at a comparatively stable rate, with dips in the growth rate mainly in 1951 and 1978. Fixed investment increases were mainly in 1950–51, 1954–55, 1959–61, 1964–66, 1970–72, 1976–80 (with a dip in 1978), generally as for gross domestic product (although with greater fluctuations). Unemployment increased mainly in 1950, 1952–53, 1958, 1962–63, 1967–68, 1975 and 1978.

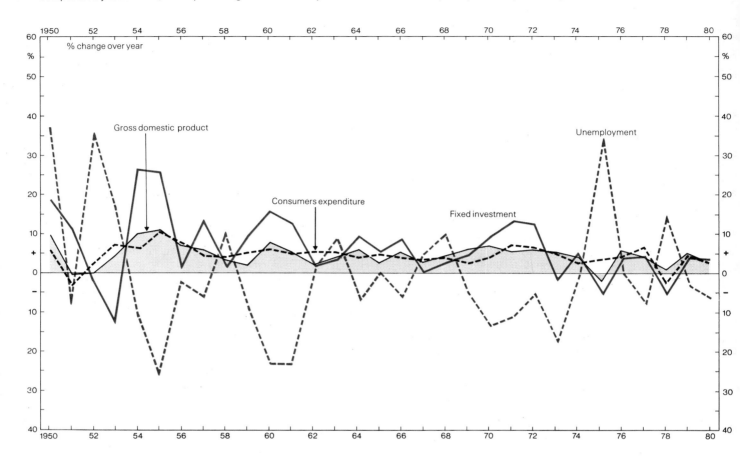

	Gross domestic product		Consumers expenditure		Fixed investment		Unemployment		
	Index 1970 = 100	% change over year	Index 1970 = 100	% change over year	Index 1970 = 100	% change over year	Number (000)	% change over year	
1950	37.5	9.9	39.6	5.8	25.1	18.7	124.2	37	1950
1951	37.5	−0.1	38.5	−2.8	28.0	11.3	115.6	−7	1951
1952	37.5	0.0	39.5	2.5	27.4	−2.0	156.2	35	1952
1953	39.1	4.4	42.4	7.4	23.9	−12.7	182.8	17	1953
1954	43.1	10.2	45.1	6.5	30.2	26.1	163.0	−11	1954
1955	47.9	11.1	49.9	10.5	37.8	25.5	120.1	−26	1955
1956	51.2	6.9	53.7	7.6	38.5	1.7	117.2	−2	1956
1957	54.3	6.1	56.2	4.6	43.5	13.2	109.7	−6	1957
1958	56.3	3.7	58.4	4.1	44.2	1.6	120.2	10	1958
1959	57.9	2.8	61.4	5.1	48.5	9.8	109.2	−9	1959
1960	62.7	8.2	65.2	6.2	56.2	15.7	83.7	−23	1960
1961	66.2	5.6	68.6	5.1	63.2	12.6	64.6	−23	1961
1962	67.9	2.6	72.3	5.4	65.0	2.7	65.8	2	1962
1963	70.7	4.2	76.1	5.4	67.2	3.4	71.8	9	1963
1964	75.1	6.2	79.2	4.1	73.7	9.6	66.9	−7	1964
1965	77.3	2.9	83.2	5.0	77.5	5.2	66.6	0	1965
1966	81.6	5.6	86.7	4.2	84.3	8.9	62.5	−6	1966
1967	84.1	3.0	89.8	3.5	84.4	0.1	65.7	5	1967
1968	87.8	4.5	93.3	3.9	86.8	2.9	72.0	10	1968
1969	93.4	6.3	96.0	2.9	91.1	4.9	68.2	−5	1969
1970	100.0	7.1	100.0	4.2	100.0	9.8	59.4	−13	1970
1971	105.6	5.6	107.3	7.3	113.3	13.3	52.9	−11	1971
1972	112.0	6.0	114.4	6.6	127.2	12.3	50.0	−5	1972
1973	117.9	5.3	120.4	5.2	125.6	−1.3	41.3	−17	1973
1974	122.9	4.3	123.7	2.8	132.6	5.5	41.3	0	1974
1975	120.8	−1.7	128.0	3.5	126.3	−4.7	55.5	34	1975
1976	127.8	5.8	133.7	4.4	131.6	4.2	55.3	0	1976
1977	133.4	4.4	142.8	6.8	137.8	4.7	51.2	−7	1977
1978	134.8	1.0	139.6	−2.2	131.3	−4.7	58.6	14	1978
1979	141.6	5.1	146.1	4.7	136.8	4.2	56.7	−3	1979
1980	146.0	3.1	150.6	3.1	142.4	4.0	53.2	−6	1980

Austria

The rate of increase in consumer prices was comparatively stable throughout, with main increases in 1950–52, 1973–76 and 1980. Share prices increased mainly in 1951–52, 1954–56, 1959–61, 1969–73 (although quiet for 1971) and 1979–80; main falls were in 1950, 1957–58, 1963–68, 1974 and 1977–78. Money stock increased mainly in 1950–51, 1954, 1958–59, 1961–65, 1971–72, 1975–76, 1978 and 1980. The interest rate, for the time covered, increased mainly in 1973–74 and 1980, with main reductions in 1976 and 1978.

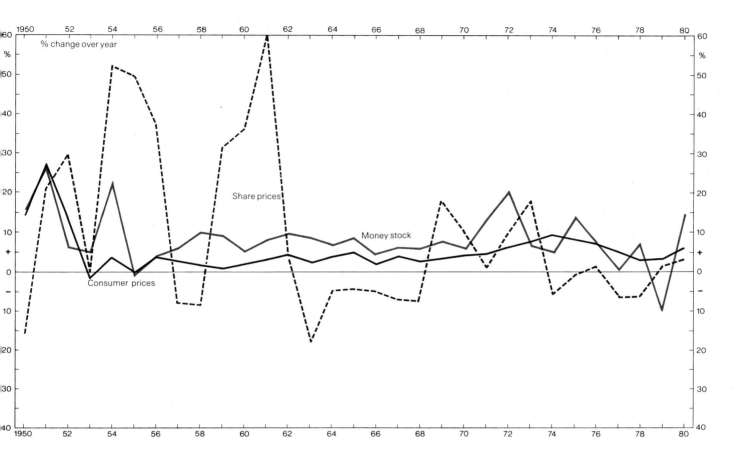

	Consumer prices		Share prices		Money stock		Interest rate[a]		
	Index 1970 = 100	% change over year	Index 1970 = 100	% change over year	Index 1970 = 100	% change over year	%	Change over year[b]	
1950	42.4	14.6	9.9	−15.8	19.7	15.9	na	na	1950
1951	54.1	27.5	12.0	21.2	24.9	26.3	na	na	1951
1952	61.3	13.4	15.5	29.9	26.5	6.3	na	na	1952
1953	60.5	−1.4	15.5	0.0	27.8	5.2	na	na	1953
1954	62.7	3.8	23.7	52.4	34.1	22.4	na	na	1954
1955	62.7	0.0	35.5	50.0	34.0	−0.4	na	na	1955
1956	65.1	3.9	49.0	37.8	35.5	4.6	na	na	1956
1957	67.0	2.8	45.1	−7.8	37.8	6.3	na	na	1957
1958	68.3	1.9	41.4	−8.2	41.7	10.3	na	na	1958
1959	69.0	1.0	54.6	31.8	45.6	9.4	na	na	1959
1960	70.4	2.1	74.5	36.3	48.0	5.4	na	na	1960
1961	72.8	3.4	119.4	60.3	52.1	8.6	na	na	1961
1962	76.0	4.3	124.3	4.1	57.4	10.0	na	na	1962
1963	78.1	2.8	102.3	−17.7	62.4	8.8	na	na	1963
1964	81.2	4.0	97.4	−4.8	66.9	7.2	na	na	1964
1965	85.2	4.9	93.2	−4.3	73.0	9.1	6.52	na	1965
1966	87.1	2.2	88.7	−4.9	76.7	5.0	6.93	0.41	1966
1967	90.5	3.9	82.7	−6.7	81.7	6.5	7.24	0.31	1967
1968	92.9	2.7	76.7	−7.3	86.8	6.3	7.74	0.50	1968
1969	95.9	3.2	90.8	18.3	93.9	8.2	7.52	−0.22	1969
1970	100.0	4.3	100.0	10.2	100.0	6.5	7.82	0.30	1970
1971	104.7	4.7	101.2	1.2	113.9	13.9	7.71	−0.11	1971
1972	111.2	6.2	111.2	9.9	137.8	21.0	7.37	−0.34	1972
1973	119.8	7.7	131.3	18.1	148.1	7.5	8.25	0.88	1973
1974	131.2	9.5	124.2	−5.4	156.5	5.7	9.74	1.49	1974
1975	142.2	8.5	123.3	−0.7	178.9	14.3	9.61	−0.13	1975
1976	152.6	7.3	124.9	1.3	193.9	8.3	8.75	−0.86	1976
1977	161.0	5.5	116.9	−6.4	196.6	1.4	8.74	−0.01	1977
1978	166.9	3.6	109.5	−6.3	212.9	8.3	8.21	−0.53	1978
1979	173.0	3.7	111.5	1.8	193.7	−9.0	7.96	−0.25	1979
1980	183.9	6.3	115.2	3.3	224.0	15.6	9.24	1.28	1980

[a]Government bond yield   [b]In percentage points

Barbados

The main periods of expansion in gross domestic product were 1951, 1953, 1956–57, 1961, 1963, 1967–70, 1972–73 and 1976–80; main falls occurred in 1958, 1964, 1971 and 1974–75. Exports increased mainly in 1950–52, 1957, 1959, 1961–63, 1965–66, 1972–75, 1978 and 1980, with main falls in 1954–56, 1958, 1960, 1964, 1968–69 and

1976. Consumer prices, over the time covered, increased mainly in 1971, 1973–75 and 1979–80, with comparatively stable but fairly substantial rates of increase for other years. The interest rate, over the time covered, increased mainly in 1968–70, 1973–74 and 1980, with main falls in 1972 and 1975–76.

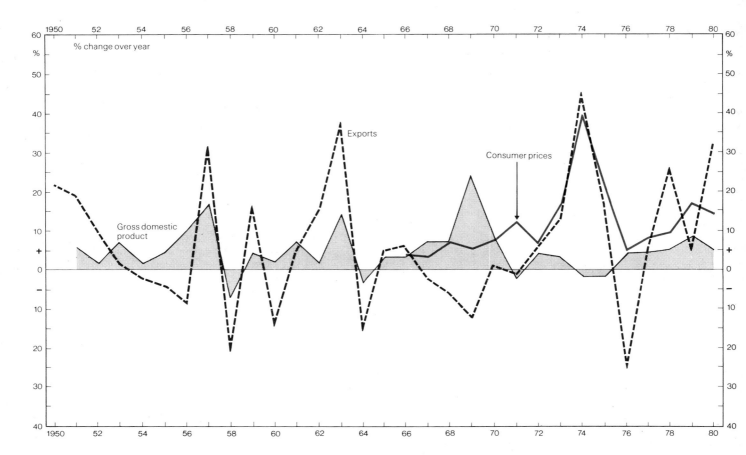

	Gross domestic product		Exports		Consumer prices		Interest rate		
	Index 1970 = 100	% change over year	Index 1970 = 100	% change over year	Index 1970 = 100	% change over year	%	Change over year[a]	
1950	32	na	66	22	na	na	na	na	1950
1951	34	6	78	19	na	na	na	na	1951
1952	35	2	86	10	na	na	na	na	1952
1953	37	7	88	2	na	na	na	na	1953
1954	38	2	86	−2	na	na	na	na	1954
1955	39	4	83	−4	na	na	na	na	1955
1956	43	10	76	−8	na	na	na	na	1956
1957	51	17	100	31	na	na	na	na	1957
1958	47	−7	79	−20	na	na	na	na	1958
1959	49	4	92	16	na	na	na	na	1959
1960	50	2	79	−14	na	na	na	na	1960
1961	54	7	83	5	na	na	na	na	1961
1962	55	2	95	15	na	na	na	na	1962
1963	63	14	130	37	na	na	na	na	1963
1964	61	−3	111	−15	na	na	na	na	1964
1965	63	3	117	5	76.1	na	na	na	1965
1966	65	3	123	6	79.1	4.0	na	na	1966
1967	70	7	121	−2	81.9	3.6	5.35	na	1967
1968	74	7	113	−6	88.0	7.4	5.83	0.48	1968
1969	92	24	99	−12	92.7	5.3	6.12	0.29	1969
1970	100	8	100	1	100.0	7.8	7.01	0.89	1970
1971	98	−2	99	−1	112.4	12.4	7.17	0.16	1971
1972	102	4	103	5	120.2	6.9	5.95	−1.22	1972
1973	105	3	117	13	140.4	16.8	6.57	0.62	1973
1974	103	−2	170	45	195.1	39.0	8.96	2.39	1974
1975	100	−2	197	16	234.7	20.3	5.67	−3.29	1975
1976	105	4	148	−25	246.5	5.0	4.44	−1.23	1976
1977	109	4	156	5	266.9	8.3	4.63	0.19	1977
1978	114	5	195	25	292.3	9.5	4.82	0.19	1978
1979	123	8	204	5	342.0	17.0	4.88	0.06	1979
1980	129	5	270	32	391.3	14.4	5.63	0.75	1980

[a]In percentage points

Belgium

The main periods of expansion in gross domestic product were 1950–51, 1953–56, 1959–74 (with some slackening of growth in 1963, 1966 and 1971), 1976 and 1978–79; main periods of low growth were 1952, 1957–58, 1975 and 1977. Consumers expenditure increased at a comparatively stable rate throughout the period, with lower growth in 1951–53, 1956–59, 1961, 1975 and 1977–78. Government expenditure increased mainly in 1950–53, 1958–60, 1962–63 and 1978, with a period of steady growth over 1964–77. Fixed investment increased mainly in 1950, 1953–56, 1959–62, 1964–66, 1969–70, 1972–74 and 1980, with main falls in 1951 and 1957–58.

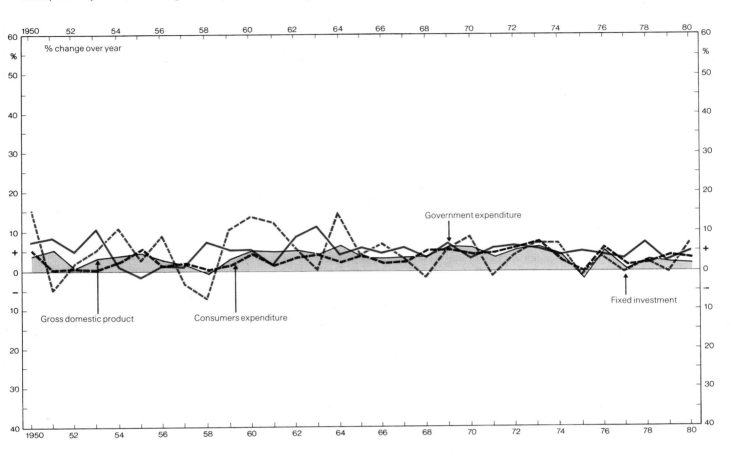

	Gross domestic product		Consumers expenditure		Government expenditure		Fixed investment		
	Index 1970 = 100	% change over year	Index 1970 = 100	% change over year	Index 1970 = 100	% change over year	Index 1970 = 100	% change over year	
1950	44.9	4.1	55.7	5.3	37.7	7.8	38.7	15.5	1950
1951	47.4	5.4	56.0	0.4	40.9	8.5	37.1	−4.3	1951
1952	48.0	1.2	56.4	0.9	43.0	5.1	37.9	2.3	1952
1953	49.8	3.9	56.6	0.3	47.9	11.5	39.8	5.1	1953
1954	51.9	4.1	58.2	2.8	48.6	1.4	44.3	11.2	1954
1955	54.4	4.8	61.7	5.9	47.9	−1.4	45.6	3.0	1955
1956	55.9	2.9	62.8	1.9	48.7	1.6	49.7	9.0	1956
1957	57.0	1.9	64.4	2.5	49.2	1.1	48.2	−3.1	1957
1958	56.9	−0.2	64.8	0.6	52.9	7.6	44.9	−6.7	1958
1959	58.7	3.2	66.0	2.0	55.7	5.2	49.7	10.7	1959
1960	61.8	5.4	69.3	4.9	58.7	5.4	56.7	14.0	1960
1961	64.9	5.0	70.4	1.6	59.8	1.9	63.7	12.4	1961
1962	68.3	5.2	73.2	3.9	65.0	8.6	67.5	5.9	1962
1963	71.3	4.4	76.4	4.4	72.5	11.6	67.6	0.1	1963
1964	76.2	7.0	78.4	2.6	75.5	4.2	77.5	14.7	1964
1965	79.0	3.6	81.8	4.3	79.7	5.5	80.7	4.1	1965
1966	81.5	3.2	84.0	2.7	83.5	4.7	86.2	6.8	1966
1967	84.6	3.9	86.3	2.8	88.2	5.7	88.7	2.9	1967
1968	88.2	4.2	90.9	5.3	91.3	3.5	87.6	−1.3	1968
1969	94.0	6.6	95.8	5.4	97.0	6.3	92.2	5.3	1969
1970	100.0	6.4	100.0	4.4	100.0	3.1	100.0	8.4	1970
1971	103.9	3.9	104.8	4.8	105.5	5.5	98.5	−1.5	1971
1972	109.3	5.3	111.0	5.9	111.8	5.9	101.7	3.3	1972
1973	116.1	6.2	119.7	7.8	117.6	5.2	108.6	6.8	1973
1974	121.3	4.5	123.3	3.0	121.6	3.4	116.2	7.0	1974
1975	119.0	−1.9	123.9	0.5	127.4	4.8	114.3	−1.6	1975
1976	125.2	5.3	130.5	5.4	132.2	3.8	118.0	3.2	1976
1977	126.2	0.8	133.0	1.9	136.1	3.0	117.5	−0.4	1977
1978	130.0	3.0	136.3	2.5	145.2	6.7	119.9	2.1	1978
1979	133.0	2.4	142.7	4.7	148.8	2.5	119.1	−0.7	1979
1980	135.6	2.0	147.5	3.4	155.6	4.6	126.3	6.1	1980

Belgium

Exports increased mainly in 1950–51, 1953–56, 1959–60, 1962–65, 1968–73 and 1976, with main falls in 1952, 1957 and 1975 and steady but low expansion over 1977–80. Imports followed a similar pattern, with main expansion in 1950–51, 1953–56, 1959–60, 1962–66, 1968–73, 1976 and 1979, and main periods of low growth or falls in imports for 1952, 1958 and 1975. Unemployment increased mainly in 1952, 1958–59, 1965–68, 1972, 1974–77 and 1980; main reductions in unemployment were in 1950–51, 1954–57, 1960–64 and 1969–70. Consumer prices were comparatively stable throughout most of the period, with main increases in 1951, 1972–77 and 1980.

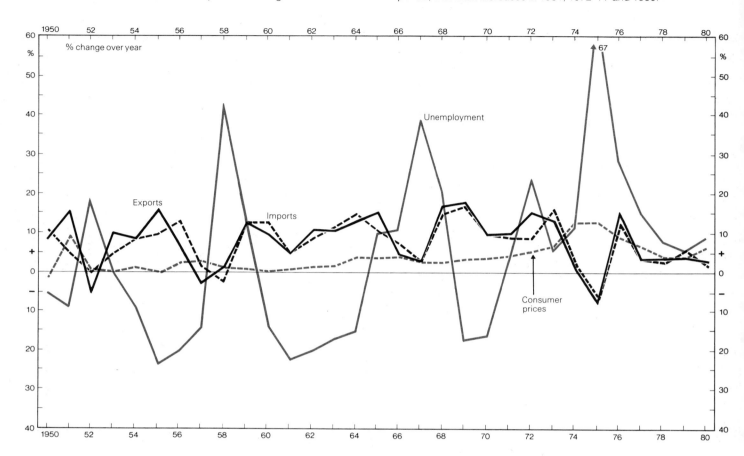

	Exports		Imports		Unemployment		Consumer prices		
	Index 1970 = 100	% change over year	Index 1970 = 100	% change over year	Number (000)	% change over year	Index 1970 = 100	% change over year	
1950	18	9	20	11	177	−5	61.5	−1.0	1950
1951	21	16	21	5	163	−8	67.3	9.5	1951
1952	20	−5	21	0	195	19	67.8	0.7	1952
1953	22	10	22	5	194	0	67.6	−0.3	1953
1954	23	9	24	9	178	−9	68.4	1.2	1954
1955	27	16	26	10	136	−23	68.1	−0.4	1955
1956	29	7	29	13	109	−20	70.0	2.8	1956
1957	29	−2	30	2	94	−14	72.2	3.1	1957
1958	29	2	29	−2	134	43	73.2	1.4	1958
1959	33	13	33	13	152	14	74.1	1.2	1959
1960	36	10	37	13	131	−14	74.3	0.3	1960
1961	38	5	39	5	102	−22	75.0	0.9	1961
1962	42	11	43	9	82	−20	76.1	1.5	1962
1963	47	11	48	12	68	−17	77.7	2.1	1963
1964	53	13	55	15	58	−15	81.0	4.2	1964
1965	61	15	61	11	64	10	84.2	4.0	1965
1966	64	5	66	8	71	11	87.8	4.3	1966
1967	66	3	68	3	98	39	90.3	2.8	1967
1968	77	17	78	15	118	20	92.8	2.8	1968
1969	91	18	91	17	98	−17	96.2	3.7	1969
1970	100	10	100	10	82	−16	100.0	4.0	1970
1971	110	10	109	9	84	3	104.3	4.3	1971
1972	126	15	119	9	105	24	110.0	5.5	1972
1973	142	13	138	16	111	6	117.7	7.0	1973
1974	143	1	141	2	124	12	132.6	12.7	1974
1975	133	−7	133	−6	208	67	149.5	12.7	1975
1976	153	15	150	13	267	28	163.3	9.2	1976
1977	160	4	156	4	308	15	174.8	7.1	1977
1978	166	4	161	3	333	8	182.7	4.5	1978
1979	173	4	170	6	352	6	190.8	4.4	1979
1980	178	3	173	2	382	9	203.5	6.7	1980

Belgium

Share prices increased mainly in 1950–52, 1954–56, 1959, 1961, 1964, 1968–69, 1971–73 and 1978–79; main falls were in 1953, 1958, 1962–63, 1965–67, 1970, 1974–77 and 1980. Money stock increased at a comparatively stable rate over the period to 1968, although with some slowing down in the rate in 1956–57 and 1960; after a fall in

1969 there was a high rate of increase over 1970–78. International reserves rose mainly in 1951, 1955, 1958, 1960–61, 1963–64, 1967, 1969–73, 1975 and 1979–80, with falls in 1950, 1954, 1957, 1959, 1962, 1968, 1976 and 1978. The interest rate increased mainly in 1960, 1964, 1966, 1969–70, 1973–74, 1976 and 1979–80.

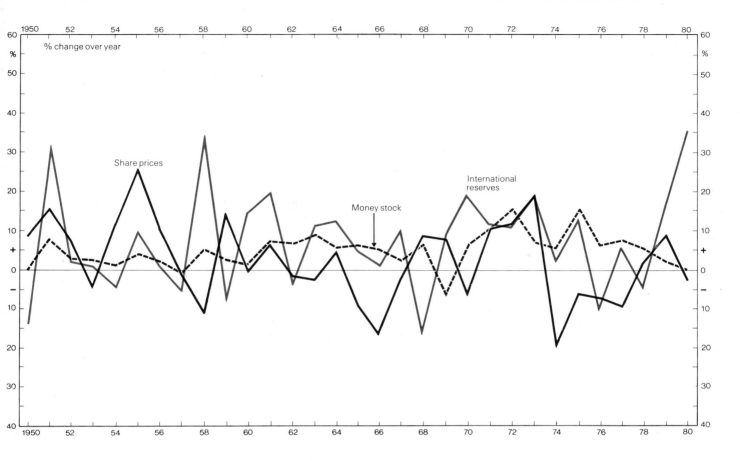

	Share prices		Money stock		International reserves		Interest rate		
	Index 1970 = 100	% change over year	Index 1970 = 100	% change over year	Index 1970 = 100	% change over year	%	Change over year[a]	
1950	57	9	41.3	0.1	27	−13	1.25	0.00	1950
1951	66	16	44.6	8.1	35	31	1.25	0.00	1951
1952	72	8	46.2	3.5	36	2	1.25	0.00	1952
1953	69	−4	47.7	3.3	36	1	1.25	0.00	1953
1954	77	12	48.6	1.8	35	−4	1.25	0.00	1954
1955	97	26	50.9	4.8	38	10	1.35	0.10	1955
1956	108	11	52.4	2.9	39	1	1.58	0.23	1956
1957	107	−1	52.4	−0.1	37	−5	1.77	0.19	1957
1958	95	−11	55.4	5.8	50	34	1.41	−0.36	1958
1959	108	14	57.2	3.2	46	−7	1.14	−0.27	1959
1960	108	0	58.3	1.9	53	15	2.82	1.68	1960
1961	116	7	62.8	7.7	64	20	2.56	−0.26	1961
1962	115	−1	67.3	7.2	62	−3	2.14	−0.42	1962
1963	113	−2	73.8	9.7	69	12	2.31	0.17	1963
1964	119	5	78.7	6.5	78	13	3.35	1.04	1964
1965	110	−8	84.3	7.1	82	5	3.17	−0.18	1965
1966	92	−16	89.8	6.6	83	1	3.88	0.71	1966
1967	90	−2	92.7	3.2	91	10	3.19	−0.69	1967
1968	98	9	99.4	7.2	77	−16	2.84	−0.35	1968
1969	106	8	93.5	−6.0	84	9	5.40	2.56	1969
1970	100	−6	100.0	7.0	100	19	6.25	0.85	1970
1971	111	11	111.2	11.2	112	12	3.70	−2.55	1971
1972	124	12	128.1	15.2	125	11	2.48	−1.22	1972
1973	147	19	137.6	7.5	148	19	4.81	2.33	1973
1974	120	−18	146.2	6.2	153	3	9.25	4.44	1974
1975	113	−6	169.1	15.7	174	13	4.63	−4.62	1975
1976	105	−7	180.9	7.0	157	−10	8.31	3.68	1976
1977	96	−9	196.0	8.3	167	6	5.49	−2.82	1977
1978	98	2	207.5	5.9	159	−4	5.23	−0.26	1978
1979	107	9	212.7	2.5	186	17	7.97	2.74	1979
1980	105	−2	213.2	0.3	254	36	11.22	3.25	1980

[a]In percentage points

41

Bolivia

The main periods of expansion in gross domestic product were 1951–52, 1954–55, 1958, 1960, and a long period of relatively stable expansion from 1963 to 1976; there were falls or a slackening in growth for 1953, 1956–57, 1959, 1961–62 and 1979–80. Fixed investment increased, over the time covered, mainly in 1960, 1962, 1967–68, 1970–72 and 1974–78, with a fall or slackening rate mainly in 1961, 1966, 1969, 1973, 1977 and 1980. Exports increased mainly in 1951, 1959, 1963–64, 1966–67, 1971–72 and 1976. Consumer prices increased substantially in 1953–57, and thereafter increased mainly in 1959–60, 1973–74 and 1979–80.

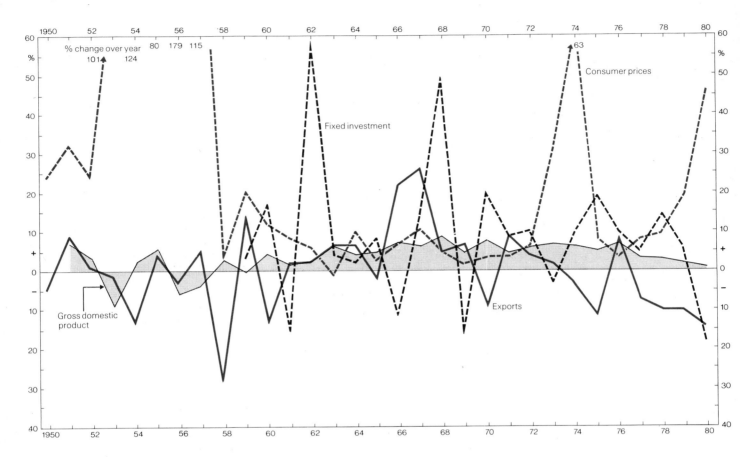

	Gross domestic product		Fixed investment		Exports		Consumer prices		
	Index 1970 = 100	% change over year	Index 1970 = 100	% change over year	Index 1970 = 100	% change over year	Index 1970 = 100	% change over year	
1950	57.2	na	na	na	77	−5	0.53	24	1950
1951	61.2	7.0	na	na	84	9	0.70	32	1951
1952	63.1	3.0	na	na	85	1	0.87	24	1952
1953	57.1	−9.5	na	na	84	−1	1.75	101	1953
1954	58.3	2.1	na	na	73	−13	3.92	124	1954
1955	61.4	5.3	na	na	76	4	7.06	80	1955
1956	57.7	−5.9	na	na	74	−3	19.67	179	1956
1957	55.8	−3.3	na	na	78	5	42.33	115	1957
1958	57.2	2.4	36	na	56	−28	43.64	3	1958
1959	57.0	−0.3	37	3	63	13	52.50	20	1959
1960	59.4	4.3	43	17	55	−13	58.55	12	1960
1961	60.2	1.3	36	−16	56	2	62.98	8	1961
1962	61.7	2.4	57	59	57	2	66.68	6	1962
1963	65.8	6.8	60	4	61	7	66.21	−1	1963
1964	68.4	4.0	61	2	65	7	72.95	10	1964
1965	71.8	4.9	66	8	64	−2	75.04	3	1965
1966	77.0	7.2	59	−11	78	22	80.26	7	1966
1967	81.8	6.3	67	14	98	26	89.25	11	1967
1968	88.7	8.4	99	48	103	5	94.14	5	1968
1969	92.7	4.6	83	−16	110	7	96.23	2	1969
1970	100.0	7.8	100	20	100	−9	100.00	4	1970
1971	104.9	4.9	109	9	109	9	103.61	4	1971
1972	111.0	5.8	120	10	113	4	110.35	7	1972
1973	118.5	6.8	117	−3	115	2	145.18	32	1973
1974	125.8	6.1	129	10	112	−3	236.28	63	1974
1975	132.2	5.1	154	19	100	−11	255.13	8	1975
1976	141.2	6.8	168	10	108	8	266.61	4	1976
1977	146.0	3.4	176	5	100	−7	288.20	8	1977
1978	150.5	3.1	200	14	90	−10	318.06	10	1978
1979	153.6	2.0	213	6	81	−10	380.82	20	1979
1980	154.9	0.8	176	−18	70	−14	560.67	47	1980

Brazil

The main periods of expansion for gross domestic product were 1950–52, 1954–55, 1957–61 and 1968–1974, with substantial growth also in 1964–67 and 1976–80; growth slackened only slightly in 1953, 1956 and 1963. Exports increased mainly in 1951, 1953, 1955–56, 1959, 1963, 1965–66, 1968–69, 1972–73 and 1978–80, with falls in 1950, 1952, 1954, 1957–58, 1964 and 1967. Consumer prices increased at very high rates over the period from 1952, with especially high increases for 1961–66 and 1974–80. The interest rate, for the time covered, was also at a high level, with reductions for 1971–73 and 1979, and a sharp increase in 1976.

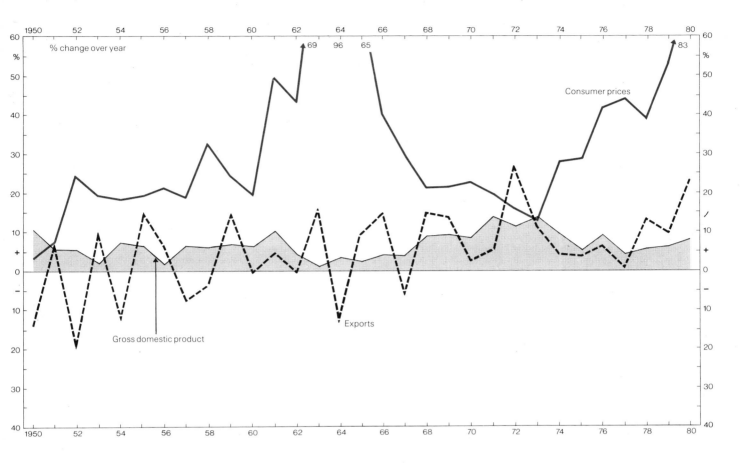

	Gross domestic product		Exports		Consumer prices		Interest rate		
	Index 1970 = 100	% change over year	Index 1970 = 100	% change over year	Index 1970 = 100	% change over year	%	Change over year[a]	
1950	31.8	11.0	56	−13	0.4	4	na	na	1950
1951	33.7	5.9	59	7	0.4	8	na	na	1951
1952	35.7	5.9	49	−18	0.5	25	na	na	1952
1953	36.7	2.6	54	10	0.6	20	na	na	1953
1954	39.5	7.7	47	−13	0.7	19	na	na	1954
1955	42.2	6.8	54	15	0.9	20	na	na	1955
1956	43.0	1.9	58	7	1.1	22	na	na	1956
1957	45.9	6.9	54	−7	1.3	19	na	na	1957
1958	49.0	6.6	52	−4	1.7	33	na	na	1958
1959	52.6	7.3	60	15	2.1	25	na	na	1959
1960	56.1	6.7	60	0	2.5	20	na	na	1960
1961	61.9	10.5	63	5	3.8	50	na	na	1961
1962	64.8	4.6	63	0	5.5	44	na	na	1962
1963	65.7	1.3	73	16	9.2	69	na	na	1963
1964	68.3	3.9	62	−15	18.1	96	na	na	1964
1965	70.2	2.8	68	10	29.8	65	na	na	1965
1966	73.5	4.7	78	15	42.0	41	na	na	1966
1967	76.9	4.6	74	−5	54.6	30	na	na	1967
1968	83.8	9.0	85	15	66.8	22	na	na	1968
1969	91.9	9.6	97	14	81.5	22	na	na	1969
1970	100.0	8.8	100	3	100.0	23	18.48	na	1970
1971	113.3	13.3	106	6	120.2	20	18.02	−0.46	1971
1972	126.6	11.7	135	27	139.9	16	15.90	−2.12	1972
1973	144.2	13.9	151	12	157.6	13	13.83	−2.07	1973
1974	158.3	9.8	158	5	201.3	28	15.79	1.96	1974
1975	167.3	5.7	165	4	259.7	29	18.33	2.54	1975
1976	182.3	9.0	176	7	368.7	42	30.19	11.86	1976
1977	190.8	4.7	177	1	530.0	44	32.23	2.04	1977
1978	202.3	6.0	200	13	735.1	39	34.46	2.23	1978
1979	215.3	6.4	219	10	1 122.3	53	32.62	−1.84	1979
1980	232.5	8.0	269	23	2 051.8	83	33.03	0.41	1980

[a] In percentage points

Burma

The main periods of expansion in gross domestic product were 1951–52, 1955, 1957, 1959–60, 1962–63, 1965, 1968–69 and 1973–80; falls, or a low growth rate, occurred in 1954, 1956, 1958, 1961, 1964, 1966–67 and 1972. Exports increased mainly in 1951–52, 1954–56, 1959, 1962, 1969–71, 1976 and 1979, with main falls in 1950, 1953, 1957–58, 1961, 1964–68, 1972–74 and 1978. Unemployment, for the time covered, increased mainly in 1967, 1971–73 and 1976–78, with further substantial increases in 1979–80. Consumer prices increased mainly in 1955–57, 1960, 1965–66, 1972–76 and 1979.

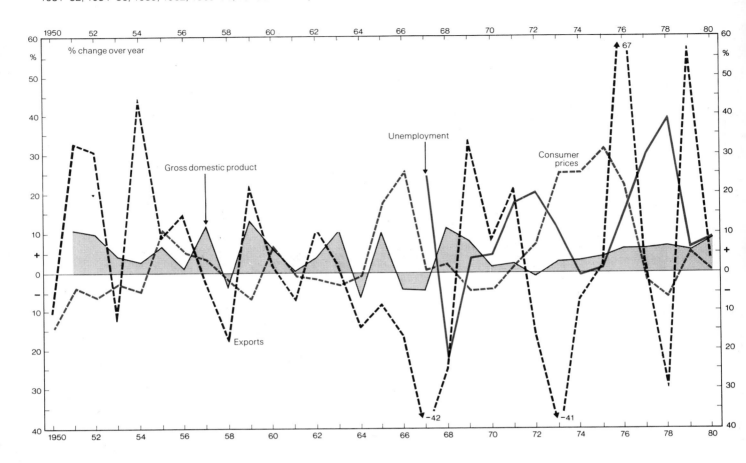

	Gross domestic product[a]		Exports		Unemployment		Consumer prices		
	Index 1970 = 100	% change over year	Index 1970 = 100	% change over year	Number (000)	% change over year	Index 1970 = 100	% change over year	
1950	40.4	na	80	−10	na	na	75.0	−13.4	1950
1951	44.6	10.4	107	33	na	na	72.2	−3.7	1951
1952	49.1	10.0	141	31	na	na	68.0	−5.9	1952
1953	51.3	4.6	124	−12	na	na	66.4	−2.4	1953
1954	52.8	2.9	179	44	na	na	63.4	−4.5	1954
1955	56.6	7.2	195	9	na	na	70.4	11.0	1955
1956	57.4	1.3	224	15	na	na	74.3	5.5	1956
1957	64.5	12.4	219	−2	na	na	76.7	3.2	1957
1958	62.2	−3.6	181	−17	na	na	74.9	−2.3	1958
1959	70.2	13.0	221	22	na	na	69.9	−6.7	1959
1960	74.6	6.3	226	2	na	na	75.1	7.4	1960
1961	75.0	0.5	211	−7	na	na	74.9	−0.3	1961
1962	78.3	4.3	233	11	na	na	73.7	−1.6	1962
1963	87.0	11.1	239	2	na	na	71.8	−2.6	1963
1964	81.7	−6.1	206	−14	na	na	71.4	−0.6	1964
1965	89.9	10.1	190	−8	na	na	84.1	17.8	1965
1966	86.1	−4.3	159	−16	115.8	na	105.5	25.4	1966
1967	82.2	−4.5	93	−42	144.6	24.9	106.4	0.9	1967
1968	91.5	11.3	69	−25	113.4	−21.6	108.9	2.3	1968
1969	98.8	8.0	92	34	117.8	3.9	104.2	−4.3	1969
1970	100.0	1.3	100	8	123.6	4.9	100.0	−4.0	1970
1971	102.4	2.4	121	21	145.6	17.8	102.1	2.1	1971
1972	101.5	−1.0	101	−16	175.0	20.2	109.9	7.6	1972
1973	104.1	2.6	60	−41	194.1	10.9	137.7	25.3	1973
1974	106.9	2.7	56	−7	193.9	−0.1	172.4	25.2	1974
1975	111.3	4.1	57	2	197.3	1.8	226.8	31.6	1975
1976	118.1	6.1	95	67	227.7	15.4	277.6	22.4	1976
1977	125.1	5.9	98	3	296.8	30.3	274.4	−1.1	1977
1978	133.3	6.5	70	−29	415.0	39.8	257.9	−6.0	1978
1979	140.4	5.4	110	57	445.0	7.2	272.4	5.6	1979
1980	152.1	8.3	114	4	486.0	9.2	274.0	0.6	1980

[a]Years beginning April 1st

Canada

The main periods of expansion in gross domestic product were 1950–53, 1955–56, 1959, 1962–66, 1968–69, 1971–74, 1976 and 1978–79; there were falls or a low growth rate for 1954, 1957–58, 1960–61, 1967, 1970, 1975, 1977 and 1980. Consumers expenditure expanded throughout at a generally stable rate, with main increases in 1950, 1952–53, 1955–56, 1964–69 and 1971–76. Government expenditure increased mainly in 1951–52, 1955–56, 1958, 1961–62, 1965–75 (with some slackening for 1969 and 1972) and 1977. Fixed investment increased mainly in 1952–53, 1955–57, 1962–66, 1969, 1971–75 and 1979–80; main falls were in 1958–61, 1967 and 1977.

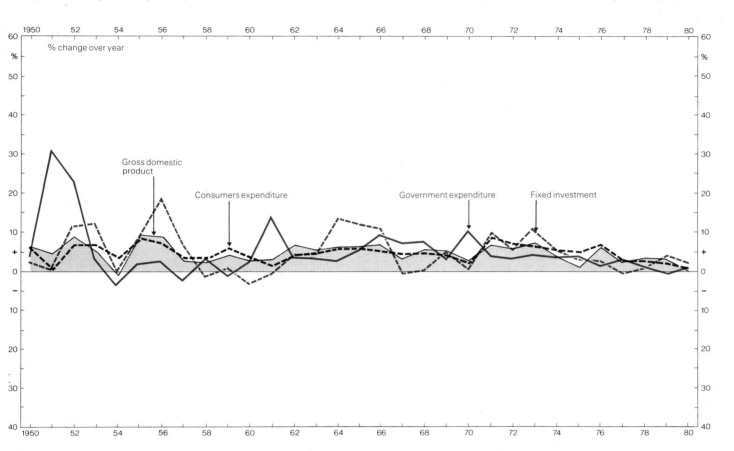

	Gross domestic product		Consumers expenditure		Government expenditure		Fixed investment		
	Index 1970 = 100	% change over year	Index 1970 = 100	% change over year	Index 1970 = 100	% change over year	Index 1970 = 100	% change over year	
1950	38.3	6.3	39.6	6.2	30.3	4.1	37.3	2.6	1950
1951	40.0	4.5	39.8	0.6	39.6	30.6	37.4	0.4	1951
1952	43.5	8.7	42.6	7.0	48.8	23.2	41.7	11.7	1952
1953	45.6	5.0	45.6	6.9	50.4	3.1	46.9	12.3	1953
1954	45.1	−1.1	47.2	3.7	48.4	−3.8	46.9	0.0	1954
1955	49.4	9.5	51.3	8.6	49.5	2.1	51.2	9.3	1955
1956	53.7	8.6	55.2	7.5	50.7	2.6	60.6	18.3	1956
1957	55.0	2.6	57.2	3.7	49.8	−1.8	64.9	7.1	1957
1958	56.2	2.1	59.3	3.6	51.4	3.1	64.1	−1.1	1958
1959	58.4	4.0	62.6	5.6	50.9	−0.9	64.5	0.5	1959
1960	60.1	2.8	64.7	3.4	52.2	2.5	62.4	−3.3	1960
1961	61.9	3.1	65.5	1.2	59.4	13.8	62.1	−0.4	1961
1962	66.1	6.8	68.4	4.5	61.8	4.0	64.9	4.5	1962
1963	69.8	5.5	71.8	4.9	64.1	3.7	67.9	4.6	1963
1964	74.2	6.4	76.1	6.1	65.9	2.8	77.0	13.3	1964
1965	79.2	6.8	80.8	6.1	69.3	5.2	86.0	11.8	1965
1966	84.8	7.0	85.0	5.2	75.8	9.3	95.3	10.8	1966
1967	87.7	3.4	89.0	4.7	81.3	7.2	94.9	−0.4	1967
1968	92.6	5.6	93.4	4.9	87.4	7.6	95.0	0.1	1968
1969	97.4	5.2	97.7	4.6	90.6	3.7	99.7	4.9	1969
1970	100.0	2.6	100.0	2.3	100.0	10.3	100.0	0.3	1970
1971	107.0	7.0	108.0	8.0	104.1	4.1	110.0	10.0	1971
1972	113.2	5.8	116.0	7.4	107.3	3.0	116.1	5.6	1972
1973	121.7	7.5	124.1	7.0	112.2	4.5	129.0	11.1	1973
1974	126.1	3.5	130.8	5.4	116.6	4.0	135.9	5.4	1974
1975	127.5	1.1	137.3	5.0	121.3	4.0	141.0	3.8	1975
1976	134.9	5.8	146.3	6.6	123.0	1.4	144.9	2.8	1976
1977	138.1	2.4	150.1	2.6	127.1	3.3	144.2	−0.5	1977
1978	143.2	3.6	154.4	2.9	128.1	0.8	144.5	0.2	1978
1979	147.3	2.9	157.5	2.0	127.0	−0.9	150.7	4.3	1979
1980	147.4	0.0	158.9	0.9	127.9	0.7	154.1	2.2	1980

Canada

Exports increased mainly in 1951–52, 1955–56, 1959–61, 1963–64, 1966–73 and 1976–78; main falls or periods of low growth were 1953–54, 1957–58, 1965, 1974–75 and 1979–80. Imports increased mainly in 1950–53, 1955–56, 1959, 1964–69, 1971–74, 1976 and 1978–79, with falls in 1954, 1957–58, 1960, 1970, 1975 and 1980.

Unemployment increased mainly in 1950, 1952, 1954, 1957–58, 1960, 1967–68, 1970–71 and 1975–78; main reductions occurred in 1951, 1956, 1959, 1962–66, 1973 and 1979. Consumer prices were comparatively stable in the 1950s and 1960s (although with a high rate in 1951), with high increases over 1973–80.

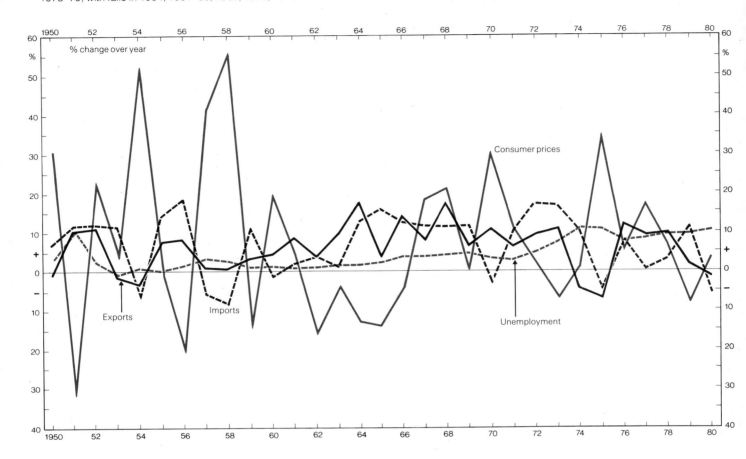

	Exports		Imports		Unemployment		Consumer prices		
	Index 1970 = 100	% change over year	Index 1970 = 100	% change over year	Number (000)	% change over year	Index 1970 = 100	% change over year	
1950	26.3	−0.4	28.7	7.0	183	31	61.4	3.1	1950
1951	29.0	10.3	31.9	11.5	124	−32	67.8	10.4	1951
1952	32.3	11.2	35.7	11.8	153	23	69.5	2.5	1952
1953	31.8	−1.5	39.7	11.2	160	5	68.9	−0.9	1953
1954	30.8	−3.1	37.1	−6.5	244	52	69.3	0.6	1954
1955	33.2	7.8	42.3	14.0	241	−1	69.5	0.3	1955
1956	36.0	8.4	50.0	18.2	194	−20	70.5	1.4	1956
1957	36.4	1.1	47.3	−5.4	274	41	72.7	3.1	1957
1958	36.6	0.5	43.5	−8.0	425	55	74.6	2.6	1958
1959	37.7	3.0	48.4	11.3	366	−14	75.4	1.1	1959
1960	39.4	4.5	47.7	−1.4	439	20	76.4	1.3	1960
1961	42.8	8.6	48.7	2.1	458	4	77.1	0.9	1961
1962	44.4	3.7	50.5	3.7	384	−16	77.9	1.0	1962
1963	48.6	9.5	51.0	1.0	368	−4	79.3	1.8	1963
1964	57.1	17.5	57.6	12.9	319	−13	80.8	1.9	1964
1965	59.3	3.9	66.4	15.3	275	−14	82.7	2.4	1965
1966	67.3	13.5	74.6	12.3	263	−5	85.8	3.7	1966
1967	72.8	8.2	83.4	11.8	310	18	88.9	3.6	1967
1968	85.2	17.0	92.7	11.2	376	21	92.5	4.0	1968
1969	90.6	6.3	103.3	11.4	376	0	96.7	4.5	1969
1970	100.0	10.4	100.0	−3.2	487	30	100.0	3.4	1970
1971	106.2	6.2	110.1	10.1	543	11	102.8	2.8	1971
1972	116.2	9.4	128.7	16.9	553	2	107.7	4.8	1972
1973	128.6	10.7	149.4	16.1	512	−7	115.9	7.6	1973
1974	122.6	−4.7	164.3	10.0	515	1	128.5	10.9	1974
1975	113.9	−7.1	155.5	−5.4	690	34	142.3	10.7	1975
1976	127.5	11.9	167.8	7.9	727	5	153.0	7.5	1976
1977	139.0	9.0	168.6	0.5	850	17	165.2	8.0	1977
1978	152.7	9.9	174.0	3.2	911	7	180.0	9.0	1978
1979	155.5	1.8	193.3	11.1	838	−8	196.5	9.2	1979
1980	153.1	−1.5	182.4	−5.6	867	3	216.4	10.1	1980

Canada

Share prices increased markedly in 1950–51, 1954–56, 1959, 1961, 1964–65, 1972–73 and 1979–80; main falls were in 1953, 1957–58, 1960, 1962, 1966, 1970, 1974–75 and 1977. Money stock increased mainly in 1950–52, 1954–55, 1958, 1961, 1963–67, 1971–73, 1975, 1977–78 and 1980. International reserves increased especially in

1950, 1954, 1958, 1961–62, 1964–65, 1968, 1970–71 and 1976, with falls in 1953, 1955, 1957, 1959–60, 1966, 1973–75 and 1977–79. The interest rate increased mainly in 1953, 1956–57, 1959, 1962, 1966, 1968–69, 1973–74, 1976 and 1978–80, with reductions in 1954, 1958, 1960–61, 1963, 1967, 1970–71, 1975 and 1977.

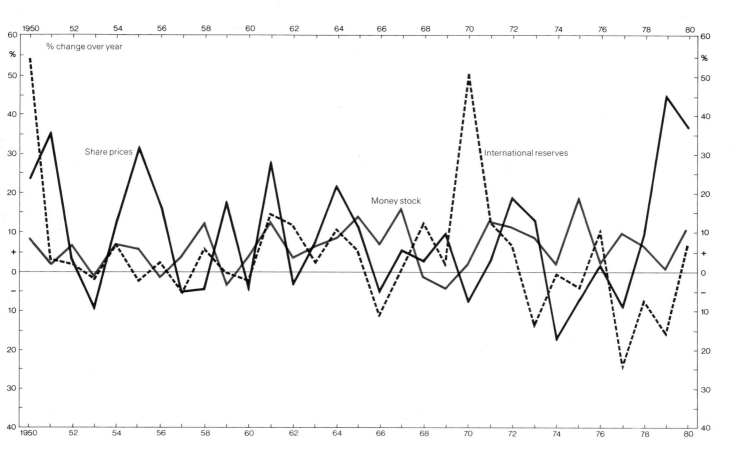

	Share prices		Money stock		International reserves		Interest rate		
	Index 1970 = 100	% change over year	Index 1970 = 100	% change over year	Index 1970 = 100	% change over year	%	Change over year[a]	
1950	24.2	23.6	37	9	39.4	54.1	0.55	0.06	1950
1951	32.7	35.1	38	2	40.7	3.3	0.79	0.24	1951
1952	33.7	3.0	40	7	41.5	2.0	1.07	0.28	1952
1953	30.6	−9.2	40	−1	40.8	−1.8	1.71	0.64	1953
1954	34.8	13.7	43	7	43.5	6.7	1.43	−0.28	1954
1955	45.7	31.3	45	6	42.6	−2.1	1.62	0.19	1955
1956	52.9	15.8	45	−1	43.7	2.5	2.93	1.31	1956
1957	50.2	−5.1	47	4	41.4	−5.2	3.76	0.83	1957
1958	47.9	−4.6	53	12	43.7	5.7	2.25	−1.51	1958
1959	56.4	17.7	51	−3	43.5	−0.4	4.81	2.56	1959
1960	53.8	−4.6	53	4	42.7	−1.9	3.20	−1.61	1960
1961	68.7	27.7	60	13	49.0	14.7	2.81	−0.39	1961
1962	66.3	−3.5	62	4	54.7	11.7	4.05	1.24	1962
1963	71.1	7.2	67	7	55.8	2.0	3.56	−0.49	1963
1964	86.5	21.7	73	9	61.8	10.6	3.75	0.19	1964
1965	96.1	11.1	83	14	64.9	5.1	3.99	0.24	1965
1966	91.4	−4.9	89	7	57.7	−11.0	4.99	1.00	1966
1967	96.5	5.6	103	16	58.1	0.6	4.64	−0.35	1967
1968	98.8	2.4	103	−1	65.1	12.1	6.27	1.63	1968
1969	108.5	9.8	98	−4	66.4	2.0	7.19	0.92	1969
1970	100.0	−7.8	100	2	100.0	50.6	5.99	−1.20	1970
1971	103.3	3.3	113	13	112.2	12.2	3.56	−2.43	1971
1972	122.7	18.8	127	12	119.1	6.1	3.56	0.00	1972
1973	138.5	12.9	138	9	102.2	−14.2	5.47	1.91	1973
1974	115.3	−16.8	140	2	101.7	−0.5	7.83	2.36	1974
1975	107.7	−6.6	167	19	97.2	−4.4	7.40	−0.43	1975
1976	109.5	1.7	169	2	107.5	10.6	8.87	1.47	1976
1977	99.6	−9.0	187	10	81.1	−24.6	7.33	−1.54	1977
1978	109.2	9.6	200	7	75.0	−7.5	8.67	1.34	1978
1979	158.2	44.9	203	1	63.1	−15.9	11.68	3.01	1979
1980	215.9	36.5	224	11	67.5	7.0	12.80	1.12	1980

[a]In percentage points

Chile

The main periods of expansion in gross domestic product were 1950, 1952–55, 1957–58, 1961–66, 1969–71, 1974 and 1977–80; there were falls or low growth in 1951, 1956, 1959–60, 1967–68, 1972–73 and 1975. Exports of copper increased mainly in 1950–52, 1954–57, 1959–63, 1966–67, 1969, 1973–74, 1976 and 1980, with falls especially in 1953, 1958, 1964–65, 1970–71, 1975 and 1978. Imports increased mainly in 1951, 1955, 1957, 1960–61, 1964, 1966, 1968, 1973–74 and 1977–80, with main falls in 1950, 1953–54, 1958, 1962–63, 1967 and 1975–76. Consumer prices increased at a high rate, especially for 1954–56, 1963–64 and 1972–78.

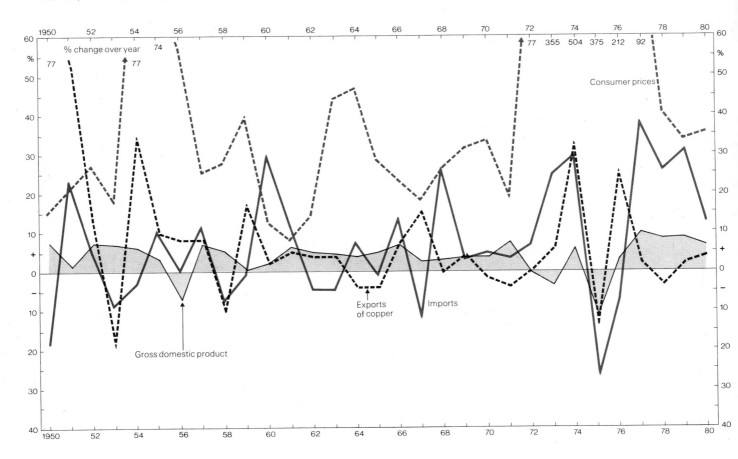

	Gross domestic product		Exports of copper		Imports		Consumer prices		
	Index 1970 = 100	% change over year	Index 1970 = 100	% change over year	Index 1970 = 100	% change over year	Index 1970 = 100	% change over year	
1950	47.0	7.3	30	77	43	−19	0.4	15	1950
1951	47.7	1.4	45	52	53	23	0.5	22	1951
1952	51.3	7.5	51	13	56	5	0.7	27	1952
1953	55.0	7.3	41	−19	51	−9	0.8	18	1953
1954	58.3	6.1	55	34	50	−3	1.4	77	1954
1955	60.3	3.4	61	10	55	10	2.5	74	1955
1956	56.2	−6.9	66	8	55	0	3.9	57	1956
1957	60.0	6.8	72	8	61	11	4.9	25	1957
1958	63.1	5.1	64	−10	56	−8	6.1	27	1958
1959	63.5	0.6	75	17	56	−1	8.5	39	1959
1960	64.8	2.0	77	2	72	29	9.5	12	1960
1961	68.8	6.2	81	5	80	11	10.3	8	1961
1962	72.2	5.0	84	4	76	−5	11.7	14	1962
1963	75.6	4.7	87	4	72	−5	16.8	44	1963
1964	78.8	4.2	84	−4	76	7	24.6	46	1964
1965	82.8	5.0	80	−4	75	−1	31.4	28	1965
1966	88.6	7.0	86	7	85	13	38.6	23	1966
1967	90.7	2.3	99	15	75	−12	45.7	18	1967
1968	93.3	2.9	99	0	94	25	57.7	26	1968
1969	96.5	3.5	102	4	96	3	75.4	31	1969
1970	100.0	3.6	100	−2	100	4	100	33	1970
1971	107.7	7.7	96	−4	103	3	119	19	1971
1972	107.6	−0.1	96	0	108	6	211	77	1972
1973	103.7	−3.6	102	6	134	24	959	355	1973
1974	109.6	5.7	135	32	173	29	5 797	504	1974
1975	97.2	−11.3	118	−13	127	−27	27 518	375	1975
1976	100.6	3.5	147	25	116	−8	85 801	212	1976
1977	110.5	9.9	151	2	159	37	164 695	92	1977
1978	119.6	8.2	146	−3	198	25	230 711	40	1978
1979	129.5	8.3	149	2	259	30	307 761	33	1979
1980	137.9	6.5	155	4	290	12	415 880	35	1980

Colombia

Gross domestic product increased at a comparatively stable rate throughout the period, although with some slackening of the growth rate in 1957–58, 1963, 1965, 1975 and 1980. Fixed investment increased mainly in 1952–55, 1959–61, 1964, 1966–71, 1973–74 and 1976–80, with falls in 1951, 1956–58, 1963, 1965, and 1972, and a slackening of growth in 1975–76. Consumer prices increased mainly in 1950–51, 1953–54, 1956–59, 1961, 1963–64, 1966–67 and 1969, thereafter increasing at a high rate over 1972–80. Share prices increased substantially in 1955–57, 1964, 1967–70 and 1976–79, with main falls in 1965–66, 1971–72, 1975 and 1980.

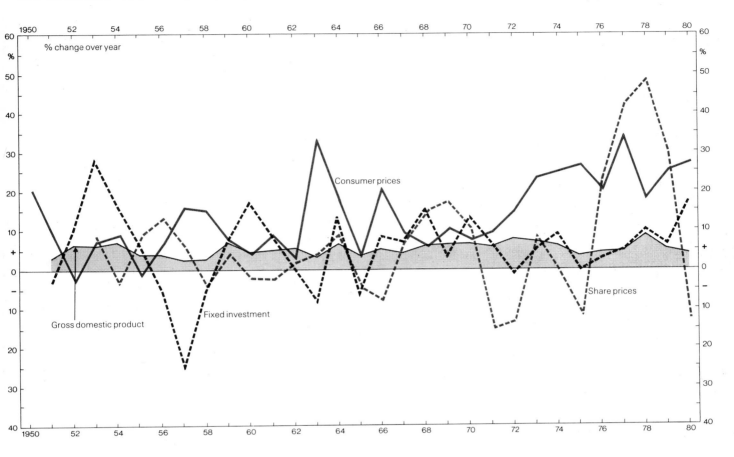

	Gross domestic product		Fixed investment		Consumer prices		Share prices		
	Index 1970 = 100	% change over year	Index 1970 = 100	% change over year	Index 1970 = 100	% change over year	Index 1970 = 100	% change over year	
1950	38.2	na	42	na	17.9	20.5	na	na	1950
1951	39.4	3.1	41	−3	19.6	9.1	na	na	1951
1952	41.9	6.3	45	10	19.1	−2.3	50.2	na	1952
1953	44.5	6.1	58	28	20.5	7.3	54.1	7.7	1953
1954	47.5	6.9	68	16	22.3	8.8	52.1	−3.7	1954
1955	49.4	3.9	72	6	22.1	−0.9	56.8	9.0	1955
1956	51.4	4.1	68	−5	23.5	6.3	64.3	13.2	1956
1957	52.5	2.2	51	−25	27.1	15.3	68.2	6.0	1957
1958	53.8	2.5	49	−5	31.1	14.8	64.9	−4.8	1958
1959	57.7	7.2	52	7	33.3	7.1	67.5	4.0	1959
1960	60.2	4.3	61	17	34.6	3.9	66.2	−2.0	1960
1961	63.2	5.1	66	8	37.6	8.7	64.6	−2.4	1961
1962	66.7	5.4	67	0	38.5	2.4	65.4	1.3	1962
1963	68.9	3.3	61	−8	50.9	32.2	67.7	3.4	1963
1964	73.1	6.2	69	13	59.8	17.5	73.4	8.5	1964
1965	75.7	3.6	65	−6	61.9	3.5	69.6	−5.1	1965
1966	79.8	5.4	70	8	74.2	19.9	64.2	−7.8	1966
1967	83.1	4.2	75	7	80.3	8.2	68.2	6.3	1967
1968	88.2	6.1	86	15	85.0	5.9	77.9	14.2	1968
1969	93.8	6.3	88	3	93.6	10.1	90.8	16.5	1969
1970	100.0	6.6	100	13	100.0	6.8	100.0	10.1	1970
1971	105.8	5.8	106	6	109.0	9.0	84.4	−15.6	1971
1972	114.0	7.8	105	−1	124.6	14.3	72.6	−14.0	1972
1973	122.1	7.1	110	5	153.0	22.8	78.0	7.4	1973
1974	129.5	6.0	120	9	190.3	24.4	77.6	−0.5	1974
1975	134.4	3.8	120	0	239.2	25.7	68.2	−12.0	1975
1976	140.6	4.6	124	3	287.5	20.2	83.9	23.0	1976
1977	147.4	4.9	130	5	382.7	33.1	118.9	41.7	1977
1978	160.6	9.0	143	10	450.7	17.7	175.9	47.9	1978
1979	168.8	5.1	152	6	562.1	24.7	227.7	29.5	1979
1980	175.5	4.0	178	17	711.1	26.5	196.7	−13.6	1980

Costa Rica

The main periods of expansion in gross domestic product were 1952–55, 1957, 1960, 1962, 1965–74 and 1976–79, with low or negative growth in 1951, 1956, 1958–59, 1961, 1975 and 1980. Fixed investment, for the time covered, increased mainly in 1961–62, 1965, 1967, 1969–71, 1973–74 and 1976–79; there were falls in 1964, 1975 and 1980. Consumer prices increased at a high rate over 1950–51, and thereafter increased at a comparatively stable rate until 1972, after when there were high increases in 1973–75 and 1979–80. Money stock increased mainly in 1951–54, 1957–59, 1962–63, 1967, 1969, 1971–78 and 1980.

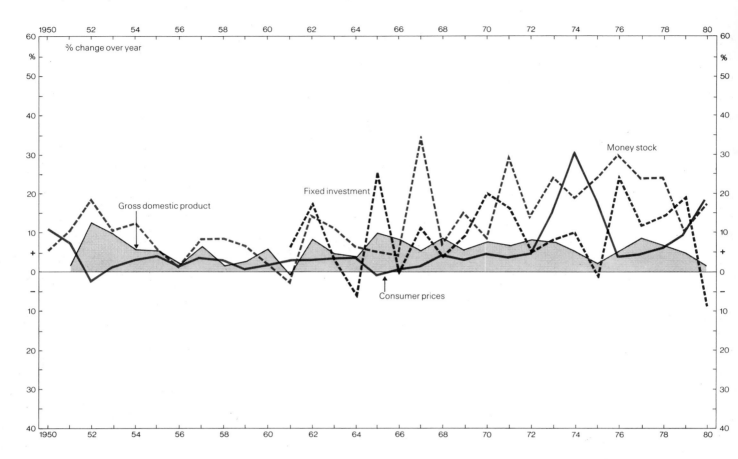

	Gross domestic product		Fixed investment		Consumer prices		Money stock		
	Index 1970 = 100	% change over year	Index 1970 = 100	% change over year	Index 1970 = 100	% change over year	Index 1970 = 100	% change over year	
1950	33.7	na	na	na	66.3	10.5	19	5	1950
1951	34.1	1.2	na	na	70.8	6.7	21	10	1951
1952	38.3	12.3	na	na	68.8	−2.8	24	18	1952
1953	42.0	9.8	na	na	69.2	0.6	27	10	1953
1954	44.3	5.4	na	na	71.0	2.6	30	12	1954
1955	46.6	5.2	na	na	73.6	3.7	31	5	1955
1956	47.5	2.0	na	na	74.3	1.0	31	1	1956
1957	50.4	6.1	na	na	76.5	3.0	34	8	1957
1958	51.2	1.6	na	na	78.6	2.7	37	8	1958
1959	52.5	2.4	na	na	78.8	0.3	39	6	1959
1960	55.5	5.8	45	na	79.4	0.8	39	1	1960
1961	55.0	−0.8	48	6	81.3	2.4	38	−3	1961
1962	59.5	8.1	56	17	83.5	2.7	44	14	1962
1963	62.4	4.8	57	3	86.0	3.0	49	11	1963
1964	64.9	4.1	54	−6	88.8	3.3	51	6	1964
1965	71.3	9.8	67	25	88.2	−0.7	54	5	1965
1966	76.9	7.9	66	0	88.4	0.2	56	4	1966
1967	81.3	5.7	74	11	89.4	1.1	75	34	1967
1968	88.2	8.5	76	4	93.0	4.0	81	7	1968
1969	93.0	5.5	83	9	95.6	2.8	92	15	1969
1970	100.0	7.5	100	20	100.0	4.6	100	8	1970
1971	106.8	6.8	116	16	103.1	3.1	129	29	1971
1972	115.5	8.2	122	5	107.8	4.6	147	14	1972
1973	124.4	7.7	132	8	124.2	15.2	183	24	1973
1974	131.3	5.5	145	10	161.6	30.1	218	19	1974
1975	134.1	2.1	143	−1	189.7	17.4	271	24	1975
1976	141.5	5.5	177	24	196.3	3.5	353	30	1976
1977	154.1	8.9	199	12	204.5	4.2	439	24	1977
1978	163.7	6.3	228	14	216.8	6.0	545	24	1978
1979	171.8	4.9	272	19	236.7	9.2	601	10	1979
1980	174.0	1.2	246	−9	279.6	18.1	704	17	1980

Cyprus

The main periods of expansion in gross domestic product were 1952–53, 1956–57, 1959, 1961, 1963, 1965–69, 1971–72 and 1976–79; there were main falls in 1958, 1960, 1964 and, especially, 1974–75 (affected by conflicts in 1974). Exports, for the time covered, increased mainly in 1957, 1959, 1962–63, 1965, 1967–68, 1971, 1973, 1976–77 and 1979–80, with main falls in 1958, 1961, 1964, 1974–75 and 1978. Imports increased mainly in 1950–51, 1954–57, 1959, 1962–63, 1965, 1967–69, 1972–73 and 1976–79. Consumer prices, after high increases in 1956–57, were comparatively stable until 1972; there were high increases in 1973–74 and 1977–80.

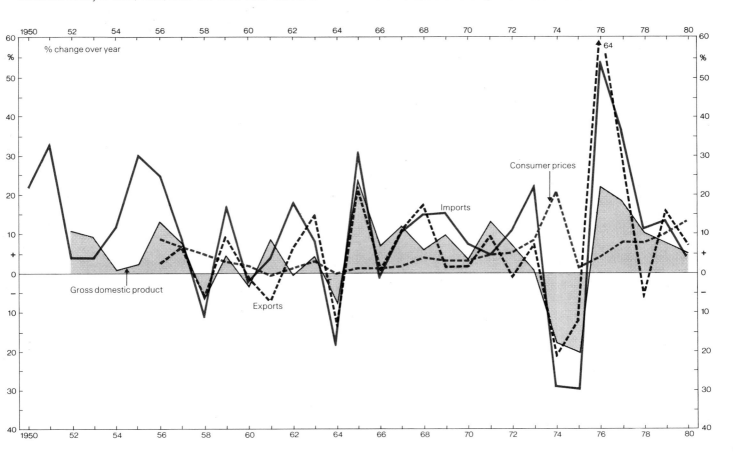

	Gross domestic product		Exports		Imports		Consumer prices		
	Index 1970 = 100	% change over year	Index 1970 = 100	% change over year	Index 1970 = 100	% change over year	Index 1970 = 100	% change over year	
1950	na	na	na	na	17.9	21.0	na	na	1950
1951	38.8	na	na	na	23.6	32.0	na	na	1951
1952	43.0	10.6	na	na	24.5	3.5	na	na	1952
1953	47.0	9.3	na	na	25.3	3.4	na	na	1953
1954	47.3	0.7	na	na	28.1	10.8	na	na	1954
1955	48.3	2.0	57.1	na	36.3	29.4	72.6	na	1955
1956	54.6	13.1	58.6	2.6	45.1	24.2	78.3	7.9	1956
1957	58.6	7.4	62.5	6.7	48.6	7.8	83.5	6.6	1957
1958	54.8	−6.6	58.5	−6.4	43.0	−11.5	87.2	4.4	1958
1959	57.3	4.7	63.9	9.2	49.7	15.6	89.0	2.1	1959
1960	55.3	−3.6	63.2	−1.1	48.0	−3.4	89.7	0.8	1960
1961	60.1	8.8	58.5	−7.4	49.5	3.1	89.1	−0.7	1961
1962	60.0	−0.3	62.1	6.2	58.0	17.2	89.2	0.1	1962
1963	62.5	4.2	71.3	14.8	62.4	7.6	91.1	2.1	1963
1964	57.3	−8.3	61.6	−13.6	50.2	−19.6	90.7	−0.4	1964
1965	71.0	23.9	75.0	21.8	65.4	30.3	91.0	0.3	1965
1966	75.4	6.2	75.3	0.4	64.7	−1.1	91.4	0.4	1966
1967	84.0	11.3	83.4	10.8	71.2	10.0	92.0	0.7	1967
1968	88.6	5.6	97.7	17.1	81.5	14.5	95.4	3.7	1968
1969	97.1	9.6	98.8	1.1	93.6	14.8	97.7	2.4	1969
1970	100.0	2.9	100.0	1.2	100.0	6.8	100.0	2.4	1970
1971	113.0	13.0	109.1	9.1	104.2	4.2	104.2	4.2	1971
1972	120.8	6.9	108.0	−1.0	114.9	10.3	109.2	4.8	1972
1973	121.0	0.2	115.7	7.1	139.4	21.3	117.7	7.8	1973
1974	99.0	−18.1	91.5	−20.9	97.7	−29.9	142.0	20.6	1974
1975	78.8	−20.5	81.1	−11.4	68.1	−30.3	143.2	0.8	1975
1976	95.5	21.2	132.9	63.9	104.7	53.7	148.8	3.9	1976
1977	112.6	18.0	170.0	27.9	142.2	35.8	159.7	7.3	1977
1978	123.9	10.0	160.5	−5.6	157.4	10.7	171.4	7.4	1978
1979	132.9	7.3	185.3	15.5	177.9	13.0	187.6	9.4	1979
1980	139.4	4.9	198.5	7.1	185.0	4.0	213.1	13.6	1980

Denmark

The main periods of expansion in gross domestic product were 1950, 1953–54, 1957–62, 1964–65, 1967–69, 1972–73, 1976 and 1979; periods of comparatively low growth occurred in 1951–52, 1955–56, 1963, 1966, 1970–71, 1974–75, 1977–78 and 1980. Consumers expenditure increased mainly in 1950, 1953–54, 1958–62, 1964–67, 1969, 1973, 1975–76 and 1979. Fixed investment increased mainly in 1950, 1952–54, 1956–62, 1964, 1967, 1969, 1972–73 and 1976, with falls in 1951, 1955, 1963, 1974–75, 1977 and 1979–80.
Unemployment increased mainly in 1951–52, 1955–56, 1963, 1968, 1971, 1974–75 and 1977–78.

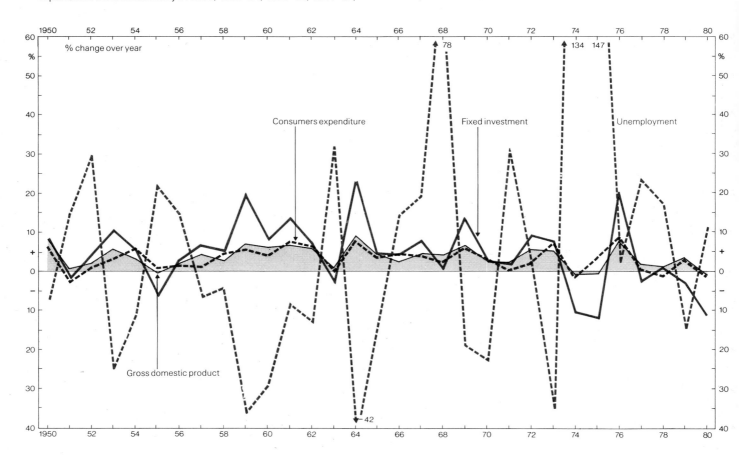

	Gross domestic product		Consumers expenditure		Fixed investment		Unemployment		
	Index 1970 = 100	% change over year	Index 1970 = 100	% change over year	Index 1970 = 100	% change over year	Number (000)	% change over year	
1950	45.6	8.3	51.3	6.0	28.4	8.8	57.8	−7	1950
1951	45.8	0.4	50.1	−2.4	28.2	−0.7	66.4	15	1951
1952	46.6	1.9	50.5	0.8	29.6	4.9	86.0	30	1952
1953	49.3	5.8	52.0	3.0	32.8	10.7	64.3	−25	1953
1954	51.0	3.5	55.0	5.7	34.6	5.7	57.0	−11	1954
1955	50.8	−0.4	55.1	0.2	32.6	−5.8	69.5	22	1955
1956	51.9	2.0	56.1	1.8	33.6	3.1	79.6	15	1956
1957	54.1	4.3	56.6	1.0	36.0	7.0	74.7	−6	1957
1958	55.6	2.8	59.3	4.7	37.9	5.4	72.1	−4	1958
1959	59.4	6.9	62.3	5.2	45.4	19.7	46.5	−36	1959
1960	63.0	5.9	65.0	4.2	49.3	8.7	33.1	−29	1960
1961	67.0	6.4	69.7	7.3	56.2	13.9	30.5	−8	1961
1962	70.8	5.7	73.8	5.9	59.9	6.7	26.4	−13	1962
1963	71.2	0.6	73.9	0.0	58.5	−2.4	34.8	32	1963
1964	77.8	9.3	79.7	7.8	72.2	23.5	20.1	−42	1964
1965	81.4	4.6	82.4	3.4	75.6	4.7	17.5	−13	1965
1966	83.6	2.7	85.9	4.3	78.8	4.3	19.9	14	1966
1967	87.5	4.6	89.5	4.2	84.8	7.7	23.7	19	1967
1968	91.2	4.2	91.5	2.3	85.5	0.8	42.1	78	1968
1969	97.5	6.9	97.3	6.4	97.3	13.8	33.9	−19	1969
1970	100.0	2.6	100.0	2.7	100.0	2.7	26.0	−23	1970
1971	102.4	2.4	100.2	0.2	101.8	1.8	34.0	31	1971
1972	108.0	5.4	102.2	2.0	111.1	9.2	34.8	2	1972
1973	113.6	5.2	109.6	7.2	119.3	7.3	22.6	−35	1973
1974	112.6	−0.9	108.2	−1.2	106.8	−10.5	52.9	134	1974
1975	112.0	−0.6	112.3	3.8	93.7	−12.2	130.6	147	1975
1976	120.8	7.9	122.2	8.8	112.5	20.0	133.2	2	1976
1977	123.0	1.8	122.6	0.4	109.8	−2.4	163.6	23	1977
1978	124.6	1.3	121.7	−0.8	110.9	1.1	190.7	17	1978
1979	129.0	3.5	125.3	3.0	107.6	−3.0	161.8	−15	1979
1980	128.7	−0.2	124.1	−1.0	95.5	−11.3	180.2	11	1980

Consumer prices increased mainly in 1950–51, 1955–56, 1961–63, 1966–68, with a comparatively stable rate over 1970–72 and a high rate over 1973–80. Share prices rose substantially in 1950, 1954–56, 1959–60, 1964, 1969, 1972–73 and 1975–76, with main falls in 1951–52, 1967, 1970–71, 1974 and 1978–80. Money stock increased

mainly in 1952–53, 1958–59, 1961–69, 1971–73, 1975 and 1978–80, with periods of steady increase in 1955–57 and 1976–77 and reductions only in 1950–51 and 1954. The interest rate, for the short time for which the short-term rate is available, rose in 1973–74, 1976–78 and 1980, with falls in 1975 and 1979.

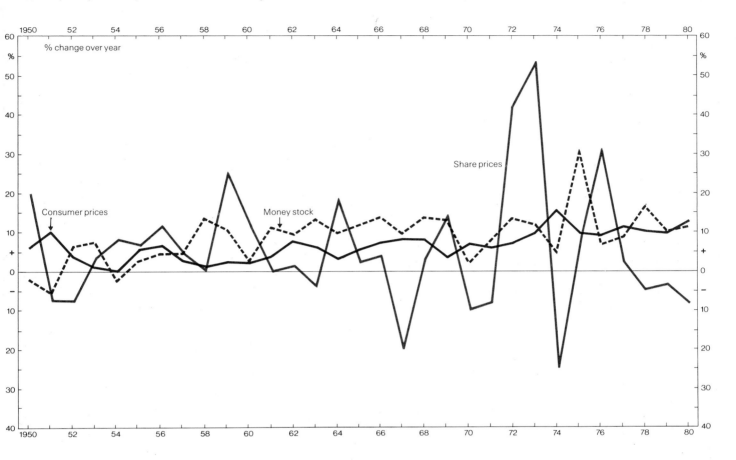

	Consumer prices		Share prices		Money stock		Interest rate		
	Index 1970 = 100	% change over year	Index 1970 = 100	% change over year	Index 1970 = 100	% change over year	%	Change over year[a]	
1950	41.2	6.0	56	20	23.8	−2.0	na	na	1950
1951	45.4	10.2	53	−7	22.5	−5.4	na	na	1951
1952	47.1	3.8	49	−7	23.9	6.3	na	na	1952
1953	47.5	0.8	51	4	25.7	7.6	na	na	1953
1954	47.5	0.0	55	8	25.2	−2.0	na	na	1954
1955	50.1	5.5	59	7	25.9	2.6	na	na	1955
1956	53.2	6.2	66	12	27.1	4.6	na	na	1956
1957	54.5	2.4	69	5	28.4	4.7	na	na	1957
1958	55.0	0.9	69	0	32.2	13.6	na	na	1958
1959	55.9	1.6	86	25	35.7	10.8	na	na	1959
1960	56.6	1.3	96	12	36.5	2.3	na	na	1960
1961	58.6	3.5	96	0	40.6	11.1	na	na	1961
1962	62.9	7.3	97	1	44.4	9.5	na	na	1962
1963	66.7	6.0	93	−4	50.5	13.6	na	na	1963
1964	68.8	3.1	110	18	55.4	9.8	na	na	1964
1965	72.5	5.4	112	2	61.8	11.4	na	na	1965
1966	77.6	7.0	117	4	70.4	13.9	na	na	1966
1967	83.9	8.1	94	−20	76.9	9.3	na	na	1967
1968	90.6	8.0	97	3	87.6	13.9	na	na	1968
1969	93.9	3.6	111	14	98.8	12.8	na	na	1969
1970	100.0	6.5	100	−10	100.0	1.3	na	na	1970
1971	105.8	5.8	92	−8	107.8	7.8	na	na	1971
1972	112.8	6.6	131	42	122.5	13.6	6.26	na	1972
1973	123.3	9.3	201	53	136.8	11.7	8.10	1.84	1973
1974	142.1	15.2	150	−25	143.3	4.7	13.34	5.24	1974
1975	155.8	9.6	164	9	186.6	30.3	6.47	−6.87	1975
1976	169.8	9.0	215	31	198.4	6.3	10.28	3.81	1976
1977	188.7	11.1	220	2	214.2	8.0	14.48	4.20	1977
1978	207.7	10.1	208	−5	248.6	16.0	15.42	0.94	1978
1979	227.6	9.6	200	−4	273.2	9.9	12.63	−2.79	1979
1980	255.7	12.3	184	−8	302.9	10.9	16.93	4.30	1980

[a]In percentage points

Dominican Republic

The main periods of expansion in gross domestic product were 1951–52, 1954–58, 1962–64, 1966–67, 1969–73, with a high stable rate over 1974–77; main falls or slackening of growth occurred in 1953, 1959–61, 1965, 1968 and 1978. Fixed investment increased mainly in 1951–52, 1955–56, 1962–64, 1966 (recovery from the sharp fall of 1965) and 1969–75; there were falls in 1953–54, 1959–61, 1965 and 1976. Exports increased mainly in 1952, 1955–56, 1960, 1967, 1970–71, 1976–77 and 1979, with substantial falls in 1961, 1965, 1975, 1978 and 1980. Consumer prices, comparatively stable, increased mainly in 1951, 1962–63, 1972–77 and 1979–80.

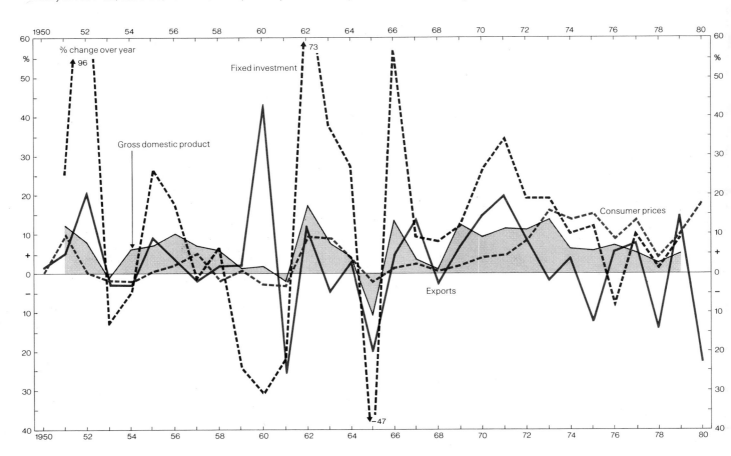

	Gross domestic product		Fixed investment		Exports		Consumer prices		
	Index 1970 = 100	% change over year	Index 1970 = 100	% change over year	Index 1970 = 100	% change over year	Index 1970 = 100	% change over year	
1950	36.2	na	19	na	61	1	77.7	0.0	1950
1951	40.6	11.9	24	25	64	5	85.1	9.5	1951
1952	43.8	7.9	47	96	76	20	85.1	0.0	1952
1953	43.2	−1.3	41	−13	74	−3	83.8	−1.5	1953
1954	45.8	5.8	39	−5	72	−3	82.2	−1.9	1954
1955	48.6	6.2	49	26	78	9	82.2	0.0	1955
1956	53.5	10.0	57	17	80	3	83.2	1.2	1956
1957	56.8	6.3	57	−1	79	−2	87.3	4.9	1957
1958	59.8	5.3	60	6	80	1	85.5	−2.1	1958
1959	60.2	0.7	45	−25	80	1	85.5	0.0	1959
1960	61.0	1.3	31	−31	115	43	82.4	−3.6	1960
1961	59.6	−2.2	24	−22	85	−26	79.1	−4.0	1961
1962	69.8	17.0	42	73	95	11	86.4	9.2	1962
1963	75.0	7.5	57	37	90	−5	93.8	8.6	1963
1964	78.1	4.1	73	27	92	2	95.8	2.1	1964
1965	69.6	−10.9	38	−47	73	−21	93.9	−2.0	1965
1966	78.7	13.1	60	57	76	4	94.2	0.3	1966
1967	81.4	3.4	65	9	86	13	95.4	1.3	1967
1968	81.8	0.5	71	8	83	−3	95.5	0.1	1968
1969	91.8	12.2	79	12	88	6	96.3	0.8	1969
1970	100.0	9.0	100	26	100	14	100.0	3.8	1970
1971	110.9	10.9	134	34	119	19	104.3	4.3	1971
1972	122.4	10.4	159	19	129	8	112.5	7.9	1972
1973	138.2	12.9	189	19	127	−2	129.5	15.1	1973
1974	146.5	6.0	207	10	131	3	146.5	13.1	1974
1975	154.1	5.2	232	12	114	−13	167.8	14.5	1975
1976	164.5	6.7	214	−8	120	5	180.9	7.8	1976
1977	172.6	5.0	235	10	128	7	204.2	12.9	1977
1978	176.4	2.2	238	1	108	−15	211.4	3.5	1978
1979	184.9	4.8	259	9	123	14	230.7	9.1	1979
1980	na	na	na	na	93	−24	269.5	16.8	1980

Ecuador

The main periods of expansion in gross domestic product were 1952, 1954, 1956–57, 1959–60, 1962–64, and a period of high growth over 1966 to 1980, with especially high growth for 1972–73; growth was low in 1955, 1958 and 1961, and there was a fall in 1965. Fixed investment increased mainly in 1951, 1953–54, 1959–60, 1967–71,

1973–75 and 1977. Exports increased mainly in 1950, 1952, 1954–55, 1959–60, 1962, 1965, 1967, 1970, 1972–73 and 1978, with main falls in 1961, 1966, 1969, 1974–75, 1977 and 1980. Money stock increased mainly in 1950, 1952, 1954, 1956, 1959–60, 1962–64, 1966–74, 1976–77 and 1979–80.

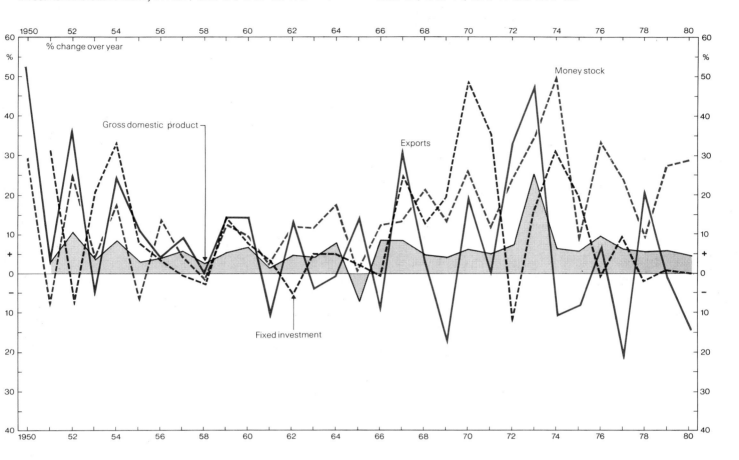

	Gross domestic product		Fixed investment		Exports		Money stock		
	Index 1970 = 100	% change over year	Index 1970 = 100	% change over year	Index 1970 = 100	% change over year	Index 1970 = 100	% change over year	
1950	41.6	na	15	na	28	52	15.2	28.8	1950
1951	42.7	2.8	19	31	29	3	14.1	−7.4	1951
1952	47.2	10.5	18	−8	39	36	17.6	24.4	1952
1953	48.7	3.2	22	21	37	−5	18.2	3.5	1953
1954	52.7	8.1	29	33	46	24	21.3	17.0	1954
1955	54.0	2.6	31	8	51	11	19.9	−6.3	1955
1956	56.0	3.6	32	3	53	4	22.7	13.8	1956
1957	58.9	5.3	32	−1	58	9	23.6	4.0	1957
1958	60.3	2.3	31	−3	58	0	23.4	−0.8	1958
1959	63.4	5.2	35	14	66	14	26.3	12.6	1959
1960	67.6	6.6	38	7	75	14	28.9	9.8	1960
1961	68.6	1.5	39	3	67	−11	29.7	2.7	1961
1962	71.7	4.5	36	−6	76	13	33.4	12.5	1962
1963	74.5	3.9	38	5	73	−4	37.4	12.0	1963
1964	80.3	7.8	40	5	72	−1	43.9	17.2	1964
1965	74.3	−7.5	41	2	82	14	44.6	1.7	1965
1966	80.3	8.0	41	−1	75	−9	50.4	13.0	1966
1967	86.7	7.9	51	24	98	31	57.4	14.0	1967
1968	90.7	4.7	57	13	101	3	69.7	21.3	1968
1969	94.4	4.0	68	19	84	−17	79.3	13.9	1969
1970	100.0	6.0	100	48	100	19	100.0	26.0	1970
1971	105.0	5.0	135	35	100	0	112.2	12.2	1971
1972	112.3	7.0	118	−12	133	33	139.9	24.7	1972
1973	140.7	25.3	137	16	195	47	188.7	34.9	1973
1974	149.8	6.4	179	31	173	−11	281.7	49.3	1974
1975	158.1	5.6	214	20	159	−8	306.3	8.8	1975
1976	172.7	9.2	212	−1	170	7	407.1	32.9	1976
1977	183.4	6.2	231	9	135	−21	504.3	23.9	1977
1978	193.5	5.5	227	−2	164	21	554.0	9.9	1978
1979	204.7	5.8	229	1	162	−1	705.0	27.3	1979
1980	214.2	4.6	229	0	140	−14	904.2	28.3	1980

Egypt

Over the time for which figures are available, from 1961, the main periods of expansion in gross domestic product were 1961–64, 1969, 1971–72 and 1975–79; the rate of increase slackered mainly in 1965, 1967–68, 1970 and 1973. For the time from 1961, fixed investment mainly increased in 1961–64, 1969, 1973–75 and 1978–79 with main falls in 1965, 1967–68 and 1976. Exports increased mainly in 1950–51, 1954, 1957, 1960, 1963, 1965, 1968–70, 1973–74, 1977 and 1979–80; exports fell mainly in 1952, 1955–56, 1961–62, 1972, 1975 and 1978. The main increases in money stock were in 1956, 1961, 1963–64, and the period 1972 to 1980.

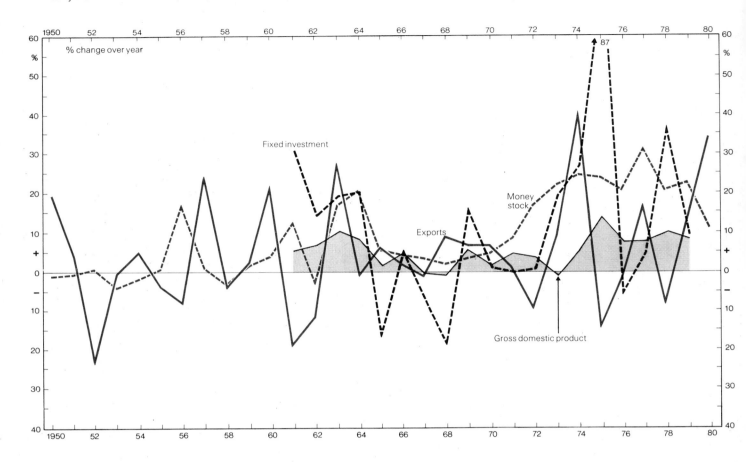

	Gross domestic product		Fixed investment		Exports		Money stock		
	Index 1970 = 100	% change over year	Index 1970 = 100	% change over year	Index 1970 = 100	% change over year	Index 1970 = 100	% change over year	
1950	na	na	na	na	77	19	46.5	−1.1	1950
1951	na	na	na	na	80	4	46.2	−0.8	1951
1952	na	na	na	na	62	−23	46.3	0.2	1952
1953	na	na	na	na	61	−1	44.3	−4.3	1953
1954	na	na	na	na	64	5	43.4	−2.0	1954
1955	na	na	na	na	61	−4	43.4	0.1	1955
1956	na	na	na	na	57	−8	50.7	16.7	1956
1957	na	na	na	na	70	23	50.9	0.4	1957
1958	na	na	na	na	67	−4	49.2	−3.4	1958
1959	na	na	na	na	68	2	49.8	1.2	1959
1960	65.4	na	61	na	83	22	51.7	3.9	1960
1961	68.8	5.3	79	31	68	−19	58.2	12.5	1961
1962	73.5	6.8	91	14	59	−12	56.5	−2.8	1962
1963	81.2	10.5	108	19	75	27	65.9	16.5	1963
1964	88.0	8.3	129	20	75	−1	79.3	20.4	1964
1965	89.7	2.0	108	−16	79	6	83.6	5.4	1965
1966	94.2	5.0	113	5	81	2	87.4	4.5	1966
1967	93.9	−0.3	106	−7	80	−1	90.3	3.4	1967
1968	93.1	−0.9	87	−18	87	9	92.2	2.1	1968
1969	98.2	5.5	99	15	93	7	95.3	3.4	1969
1970	100.0	1.8	100	1	100	7	100.0	4.9	1970
1971	104.9	4.9	100	0	101	1	108.1	8.1	1971
1972	108.9	3.9	101	1	92	−9	126.4	16.9	1972
1973	108.1	−0.8	120	19	100	9	153.9	21.8	1973
1974	113.6	5.1	152	27	141	41	192.0	24.7	1974
1975	129.1	13.7	286	87	121	−14	237.9	23.9	1975
1976	139.2	7.8	270	−5	119	−2	286.0	20.2	1976
1977	150.2	7.9	285	5	139	17	376.0	31.4	1977
1978	165.4	10.1	390	37	128	−8	453.9	20.7	1978
1979	179.7	8.7	424	9	144	13	556.2	22.5	1979
1980	na	na	na	na	194	34	620.7	11.6	1980

El Salvador

The main periods of expansion in gross domestic product were 1954–57, 1959–67 and 1971–78, with a period of steady growth over 1968–70; there was a slackening of growth in 1958, and the only main fall in product occurred in 1979–80. Fixed investment increased mainly in 1956–57, 1960, 1963–66, 1969–72, 1974–75 and 1977–78; main falls for fixed investment were in 1954, 1958–59, 1961, 1968, 1976 and 1979–80. Exports increased mainly in 1950–52, 1955–57, 1959, 1962, 1964–65, 1967–68, 1972, 1975 and 1979. Money stock increased mainly in 1950–54, 1956, 1963, 1972–76 and 1979, with a period of comparatively steady increase over 1964–71.

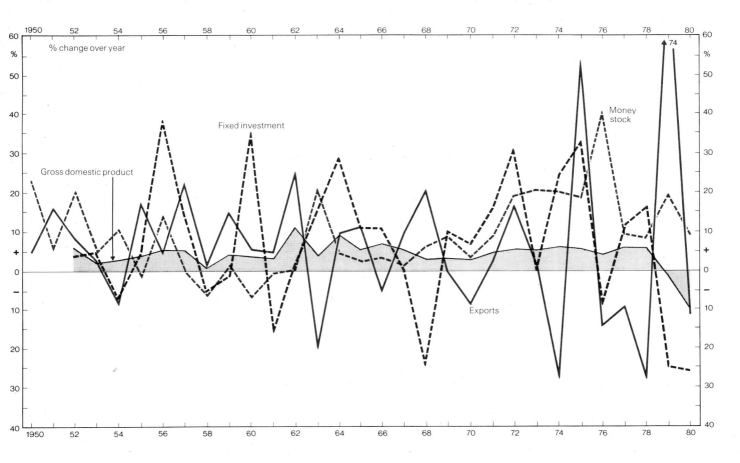

	Gross domestic product		Fixed investment		Exports		Money stock		
	Index 1970 = 100	% change over year	Index 1970 = 100	% change over year	Index 1970 = 100	% change over year	Index 1970 = 100	% change over year	
1950	na	na	na	na	29	5	40.6	23.4	1950
1951	40.0	na	33	na	34	16	43.0	5.8	1951
1952	42.5	6.4	34	4	37	8	51.7	20.2	1952
1953	43.6	2.6	36	5	38	3	54.2	.4.9	1953
1954	45.0	3.1	33	−7	35	−8	60.1	10.8	1954
1955	47.0	4.3	35	5	41	17	59.1	−1.6	1955
1956	49.8	6.0	48	38	43	5	67.8	14.7	1956
1957	52.6	5.6	55	15	53	23	67.9	0.1	1957
1958	53.1	1.1	53	−5	54	2	63.8	−6.0	1958
1959	55.5	4.5	52	−1	62	15	64.9	1.7	1959
1960	57.8	4.0	70	35	66	6	60.9	−6.2	1960
1961	59.8	3.5	60	−15	69	5	60.9	−0.1	1961
1962	67.0	11.9	61	2	86	25	60.9	0.1	1962
1963	69.8	4.3	70	15	70	−19	73.3	20.3	1963
1964	76.3	9.3	90	29	77	10	76.9	4.9	1964
1965	80.4	5.4	100	11	86	12	79.0	2.8	1965
1966	86.2	7.2	111	11	82	−5	81.7	3.5	1966
1967	90.9	5.4	111	0	90	10	83.4	2.0	1967
1968	93.9	3.2	85	−24	109	21	88.9	6.6	1968
1969	97.1	3.5	93	10	109	0	96.4	8.5	1969
1970	100.0	3.0	100	7	100	−8	100.0	3.7	1970
1971	104.8	4.8	116	16	103	3	108.9	8.9	1971
1972	110.5	5.5	152	31	121	17	129.9	19.3	1972
1973	116.1	5.1	152	0	124	2	156.7	20.7	1973
1974	123.6	6.4	188	24	91	−27	188.8	20.4	1974
1975	130.5	5.6	251	33	140	54	224.7	19.0	1975
1976	135.6	4.0	227	−9	120	−14	316.0	40.6	1976
1977	143.9	6.1	255	12	109	−9	347.0	9.8	1977
1978	152.5	6.0	296	16	80	−27	376.8	8.6	1978
1979	150.2	−1.5	223	−25	139	74	451.1	19.7	1979
1980	135.8	−9.6	165	−26	123	−11	494.9	9.7	1980

Ethiopia

Over the time for which figures are available, from 1961, there has been a comparatively steady rate of increase for gross domestic product during 1961–73, with subsequent falls in 1975 and 1977–79. Exports increased and fell for alternate years from 1951 to 1959; main increases thereafter were in 1961–63, 1965, 1968–69, 1971–73 and 1978–79, with main falls in 1966, 1970, 1974–75 and 1977. Imports increased mainly in 1950, 1952, 1954–55, 1957–65, 1968, 1970–71, 1974, 1976, 1978 and 1980. Money stock increased mainly in 1950–53, 1955–57, 1960–65, 1968–69, 1972–75 and 1977–80.

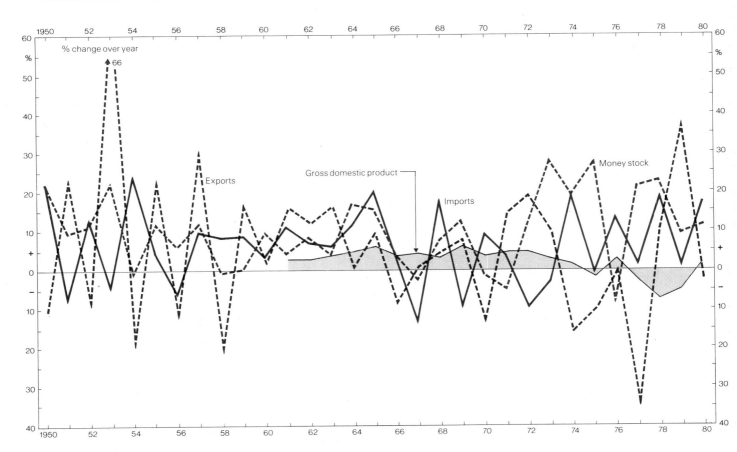

	Gross domestic product		Exports		Imports		Money stock		
	Index 1970 = 100	% change over year	Index 1970 = 100	% change over year	Index 1970 = 100	% change over year	Index 1970 = 100	% change over year	
1950	na	na	34.5	−10.3	33.1	22.8	23.5	21.8	1950
1951	na	na	42.6	23.4	30.7	−7.3	25.9	10.1	1951
1952	na	na	39.2	−8.1	34.7	13.2	28.9	11.6	1952
1953	na	na	64.9	65.6	33.3	−4.0	35.3	22.1	1953
1954	na	na	52.6	−19.0	41.4	24.2	35.0	−0.7	1954
1955	na	na	64.3	22.2	43.3	4.6	39.2	11.7	1955
1956	na	na	56.7	−11.8	40.7	−5.9	41.5	6.1	1956
1957	na	na	73.7	30.0	44.8	10.0	46.4	11.7	1957
1958	na	na	58.5	−20.6	48.8	8.8	46.2	−0.4	1958
1959	na	na	67.8	15.9	53.2	9.1	46.4	0.4	1959
1960	67.0	na	69.0	1.8	55.1	3.5	50.9	9.8	1960
1961	68.8	2.8	79.5	15.2	61.7	12.0	53.3	4.6	1961
1962	70.7	2.7	88.9	11.8	66.3	7.5	58.0	8.9	1962
1963	73.3	3.7	102.8	15.6	70.5	6.2	60.6	4.5	1963
1964	76.9	4.9	103.0	0.2	79.0	12.1	70.9	16.9	1964
1965	81.4	5.9	112.4	9.1	95.2	20.6	81.8	15.4	1965
1966	84.6	3.9	102.7	−8.6	98.8	3.8	85.0	3.9	1966
1967	88.4	4.5	103.4	0.7	85.6	−13.3	83.2	−2.1	1967
1968	91.0	3.0	108.2	4.6	101.0	18.0	89.7	7.8	1968
1969	96.5	6.0	116.0	7.2	91.6	−9.4	100.9	12.5	1969
1970	100.0	3.6	100.0	−13.8	100.0	9.2	100.0	−0.9	1970
1971	104.5	4.5	114.3	14.3	104.1	4.1	95.5	−4.5	1971
1972	109.5	4.8	135.3	18.4	93.9	−9.8	106.1	11.2	1972
1973	112.4	2.7	148.2	9.5	91.8	−2.2	136.2	28.3	1973
1974	114.1	1.4	123.4	−16.7	109.3	19.0	162.2	19.1	1974
1975	112.1	−1.7	110.7	−10.3	108.7	−0.5	206.3	27.2	1975
1976	115.1	2.7	110.1	−0.5	123.7	13.8	189.3	−8.3	1976
1977	112.3	−2.5	72.3	−34.4	126.2	2.0	230.1	21.6	1977
1978	104.0	−7.4	79.7	10.3	150.0	18.8	282.9	22.9	1978
1979	98.8	−5.0	108.3	35.8	151.6	1.1	310.1	9.6	1979
1980	100.4	1.7	105.7	−2.4	176.6	16.5	345.4	11.4	1980

Fiji

Over the period from 1966 to 1978, the main periods of expansion in gross domestic product were 1967–68, 1970–73 and 1977–78, with lower levels of growth in 1969 and 1974–76. Exports of sugar, for the time covered, increased mainly in 1962–64, 1967–68, 1970, 1977 and 1979–80; exports of sugar fell in 1965–66, 1969 and 1972–75.

Imports increased mainly in 1951–52, 1954–56, 1958, 1963–64, 1967–73, 1977 and 1979; there was a fall or slackening of growth in 1950, 1953, 1957, 1959–62, 1965–66, 1975–76, 1978 and 1980. The rate of increase of consumer prices was low in 1966–68, increased up to 1974, fell to 1978, and increased again in 1979–80.

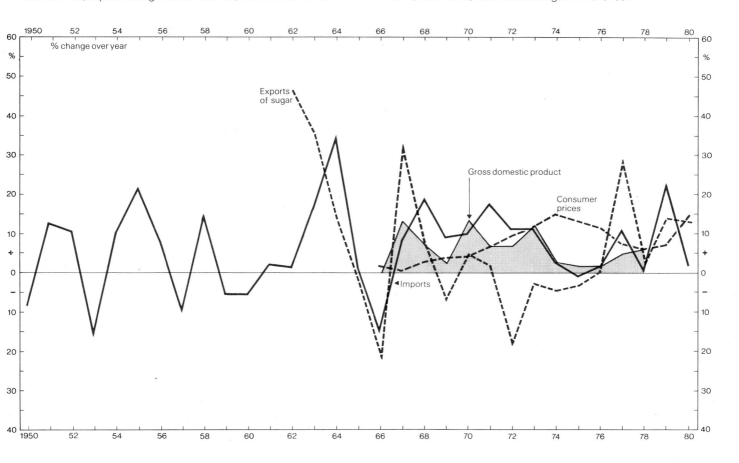

	Gross domestic product		Exports of sugar		Imports		Consumer prices		
	Index 1970 = 100	% change over year	Index 1970 = 100	% change over year	Index 1970 = 100	% change over year	Index 1970 = 100	% change over year	
1950	na	na	na	na	35	−9	na	na	1950
1951	na	na	na	na	39	12	na	na	1951
1952	na	na	na	na	43	10	na	na	1952
1953	na	na	na	na	36	−16	na	na	1953
1954	na	na	na	na	40	10	na	na	1954
1955	na	na	na	na	48	21	na	na	1955
1956	na	na	na	na	52	8	na	na	1956
1957	na	na	na	na	47	−10	na	na	1957
1958	na	na	na	na	53	14	na	na	1958
1959	na	na	na	na	50	−6	na	na	1959
1960	na	na	na	na	47	−6	na	na	1960
1961	na	na	40.9	na	48	2	na	na	1961
1962	na	na	59.7	46.2	49	1	na	na	1962
1963	na	na	81.1	35.7	57	16	na	na	1963
1964	na	na	93.0	14.7	76	34	na	na	1964
1965	71	na	91.1	−2.0	76	1	88.4	na	1965
1966	71	0	71.8	−21.2	65	−15	89.7	1.5	1966
1967	81	13	95.1	32.5	70	8	90.0	0.4	1967
1968	86	7	101.9	7.2	83	18	92.6	2.8	1968
1969	89	3	95.3	−6.5	91	9	96.0	3.6	1969
1970	100	13	100.0	4.9	100	10	100.0	4.2	1970
1971	107	7	101.8	1.8	117	17	106.6	6.6	1971
1972	115	7	83.6	−17.9	130	11	116.1	9.0	1972
1973	128	12	81.1	−3.0	144	11	129.2	11.3	1973
1974	131	3	77.4	−4.6	148	3	148.6	15.0	1974
1975	135	2	74.9	−3.3	146	−1	168.1	13.1	1975
1976	137	2	75.0	0.2	148	2	187.2	11.4	1976
1977	144	5	96.3	28.4	165	11	201.3	7.5	1977
1978	152	6	98.7	2.4	167	1	213.4	6.0	1978
1979	na	na	112.6	14.2	203	22	228.9	7.2	1979
1980	na	na	127.5	13.2	207	2	262.2	14.5	1980

Finland

The main periods of expansion in gross domestic product were 1950–52, 1954–55, 1959–61, 1964–65, 1969–70, 1972–73 and 1979–80, with lower expansion in 1962–63 and 1966–68; periods of low growth were in 1953, 1957–58, 1971 and 1975–77. Consumers expenditure moved in line with gross domestic product, with main increases in 1950–52, 1954–56, 1959–65, 1969–70, 1972–73 and 1978–80. Fixed investment increased mainly in 1950–56 (with a dip in the growth rate in 1953), 1958–61, 1964–66, 1969–70, 1972–75 and 1979–80. Unemployment, for the time covered, increased mainly in 1963, 1966–68, 1971–72 and 1975–78.

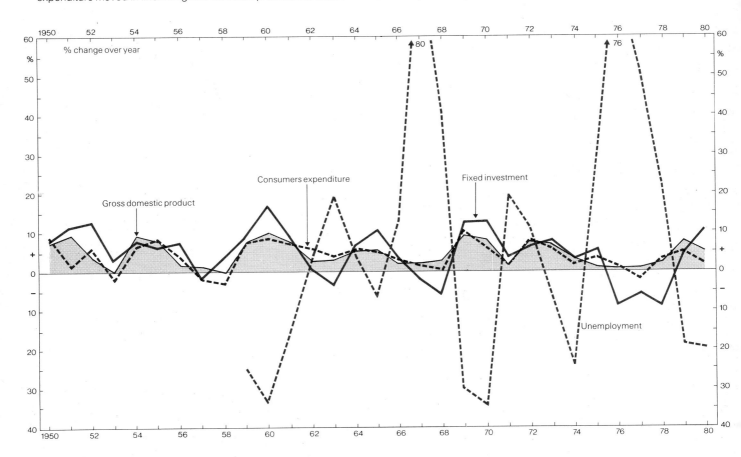

	Gross domestic product		Consumers expenditure		Fixed investment		Unemployment		
	Index 1970 = 100	% change over year	Index 1970 = 100	% change over year	Index 1970 = 100	% change over year	Number (000)	% change over year	
1950	38.5	7.3	43.2	8.4	31.1	7.9	na	na	1950
1951	42.1	9.3	44.1	1.9	34.7	11.7	na	na	1951
1952	43.6	3.4	46.8	6.2	39.1	12.8	na	na	1952
1953	43.6	0.1	45.9	−1.9	40.7	3.9	na	na	1953
1954	47.6	9.1	49.1	7.0	44.1	8.5	na	na	1954
1955	51.2	7.6	53.3	8.5	47.0	6.5	na	na	1955
1956	52.2	2.0	55.6	4.3	50.6	7.7	na	na	1956
1957	53.0	1.5	54.5	−1.9	49.7	−1.8	na	na	1957
1958	52.9	−0.1	53.1	−2.6	51.6	3.9	61	na	1958
1959	56.8	7.2	56.9	7.2	56.3	9.1	46	−25	1959
1960	62.4	9.9	61.6	8.2	65.7	16.7	31	−33	1960
1961	67.1	7.6	66.2	7.5	71.7	9.2	26	−16	1961
1962	68.9	2.7	70.1	5.8	71.9	0.3	27	4	1962
1963	71.2	3.3	73.0	4.2	69.3	−3.5	32	19	1963
1964	75.0	5.3	76.9	5.3	73.8	6.5	33	3	1964
1965	78.9	5.3	81.0	5.2	81.6	10.6	31	−6	1965
1966	80.6	2.1	83.2	2.7	84.5	3.5	35	13	1966
1967	82.5	2.3	85.0	2.2	83.0	−1.8	63	80	1967
1968	84.5	2.5	85.3	0.3	78.6	−5.3	89	41	1968
1969	92.7	9.6	94.1	10.4	88.5	12.6	62	−30	1969
1970	100.0	7.9	100.0	6.3	100.0	13.0	41	−34	1970
1971	101.8	1.8	101.8	1.8	104.3	4.3	49	20	1971
1972	109.5	7.5	109.7	7.7	111.2	6.6	55	12	1972
1973	116.7	6.5	116.2	5.9	120.2	8.1	51	−7	1973
1974	120.4	3.2	118.6	2.1	124.5	3.6	39	−24	1974
1975	121.1	0.6	122.4	3.1	131.6	5.7	51	31	1975
1976	121.4	0.3	123.5	0.9	120.1	−8.8	90	76	1976
1977	121.8	0.4	121.7	−1.4	113.6	−5.4	137	52	1977
1978	124.6	2.3	124.9	2.6	103.7	−8.7	169	23	1978
1979	133.6	7.2	131.2	5.0	108.3	4.5	139	−18	1979
1980	140.3	5.1	133.8	2.0	120.3	11.0	112	−19	1980

Finland

Exports increased mainly in 1950–51, 1953–55, 1959–60, 1968–70, 1972–73 and 1976–80, with a comparatively steady period of expansion over 1962–67; main falls were in 1952, 1971 and 1974–75. Consumer prices increased mainly in 1950–51, 1956–57, 1964, 1968, 1973–77 and 1980. Share prices increased mainly in 1950–51,

1953–56, 1959–60, 1963–64, 1968–73 (with a slackening in the rate of increase for 1970–71) and 1979–80; main falls were in 1952, 1957–58, 1965–67 and 1974–78, with a quiet period for 1961–62. Money stock increased mainly in 1950–51, 1953–56, 1958–59, 1961, 1963, 1968–75 and 1978–79.

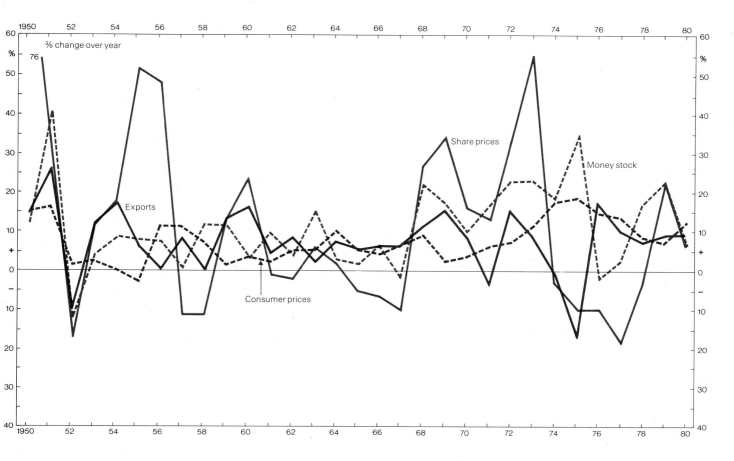

	Exports		Consumer prices		Share prices		Money stock		
	Index 1970 = 100	% change over year	Index 1970 = 100	% change over year	Index 1970 = 100	% change over year	Index 1970 = 100	% change over year	
1950	23	15	38	15	17	76	20.3	12.6	1950
1951	29	26	45	16	22	35	28.7	41.7	1951
1952	26	−10	45	1	19	−17	25.4	−11.4	1952
1953	29	12	46	2	21	12	26.5	4.3	1953
1954	34	17	46	0	25	18	28.9	9.1	1954
1955	36	6	45	−3	37	52	31.3	8.0	1955
1956	36	0	50	11	55	48	33.7	7.7	1956
1957	39	8	55	11	49	−11	34.0	0.9	1957
1958	39	0	59	7	44	−11	37.8	11.3	1958
1959	44	13	60	1	49	13	42.1	11.2	1959
1960	51	16	62	3	61	23	43.4	3.2	1960
1961	53	4	63	2	60	−1	47.8	10.0	1961
1962	57	8	66	5	59	−2	50.0	4.7	1962
1963	58	2	69	5	63	6	57.6	15.3	1963
1964	62	7	76	10	64	2	59.3	2.8	1964
1965	65	5	79	5	61	−5	60.5	2.1	1965
1966	69	6	82	4	57	−6	64.5	6.6	1966
1967	73	6	87	6	51	−10	63.4	−1.7	1967
1968	81	11	95	9	65	27	77.4	22.2	1968
1969	93	15	97	2	86	34	90.7	17.2	1969
1970	100	8	100	3	100	16	100.0	10.2	1970
1971	96	−4	106	6	113	13	116.8	16.8	1971
1972	110	15	114	7	151	33	144.0	23.2	1972
1973	119	8	127	11	234	55	177.5	23.3	1973
1974	118	−1	148	17	227	−3	210.9	18.8	1974
1975	98	−17	174	18	204	−10	283.7	34.5	1975
1976	115	17	199	14	183	−10	278.7	−1.7	1976
1977	126	10	224	13	150	−18	286.5	2.8	1977
1978	135	7	242	8	145	−3	333.7	16.5	1978
1979	148	9	260	7	178	22	408.9	22.5	1979
1980	162	9	290	12	189	6	434.8	6.3	1980

France

The main periods of expansion in gross domestic product were 1950–51, 1954–57, a comparatively stable period from 1960 to 1973, 1976 and 1978–79; lower growth occurred in 1952–53, 1958–59, 1974–75, 1977 and 1980. Consumers expenditure increased at a comparatively stable rate throughout the period, with lower growth mainly for 1958–59 and 1974–75. Government expenditure increased mainly in 1951–52, 1956–57, 1975–76 and 1978–80, with a comparatively stable growth period from 1961 to 1973. Fixed investment increased mainly in 1951, 1954–57, 1960–73, 1976 and 1979–80; main falls were in 1952, 1975 and 1977.

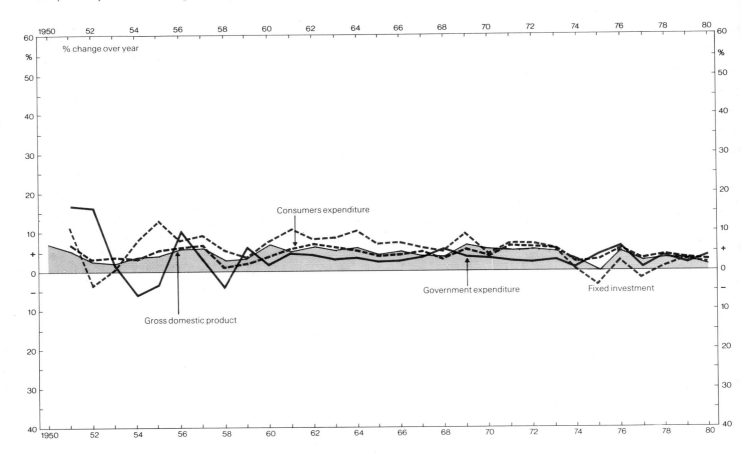

	Gross domestic product		Consumers expenditure		Government expenditure		Fixed investment		
	Index 1970 = 100	% change over year	Index 1970 = 100	% change over year	Index 1970 = 100	% change over year	Index 1970 = 100	% change over year	
1950	37.2	7.4	37.4	na	44.8	na	25.7	na	1950
1951	39.4	6.0	40.3	7.6	52.4	16.8	28.5	10.6	1951
1952	40.7	3.4	41.8	3.9	60.9	16.2	27.4	−3.6	1952
1953	41.8	2.5	43.7	4.4	62.1	2.1	27.6	0.5	1953
1954	43.5	4.2	45.3	3.8	58.5	−5.8	29.9	8.4	1954
1955	45.5	4.7	48.1	6.0	56.7	−3.1	33.8	13.0	1955
1956	48.2	5.9	51.0	6.2	62.7	10.5	36.7	8.5	1956
1957	51.1	6.0	54.6	6.9	64.8	3.3	40.2	9.5	1957
1958	52.6	2.9	55.3	1.2	62.0	−4.3	42.5	5.8	1958
1959	54.3	3.2	56.6	2.5	65.7	6.0	43.8	3.2	1959
1960	58.2	7.2	59.3	4.6	66.8	1.8	47.2	7.6	1960
1961	61.4	5.5	62.8	5.9	70.0	4.8	52.3	10.9	1961
1962	65.5	6.7	67.2	7.1	73.3	4.7	56.7	8.5	1962
1963	69.0	5.3	71.9	6.9	75.8	3.4	61.7	8.8	1963
1964	73.5	6.5	75.9	5.6	79.0	4.2	68.2	10.5	1964
1965	77.0	4.8	79.0	4.0	81.5	3.2	73.0	7.0	1965
1966	81.0	5.2	82.8	4.8	83.7	2.7	78.3	7.3	1966
1967	84.8	4.7	87.0	5.1	87.3	4.3	83.0	6.0	1967
1968	88.4	4.3	90.5	4.0	92.2	5.6	87.6	5.5	1968
1969	94.6	7.0	95.9	6.0	96.0	4.1	95.6	9.2	1969
1970	100.0	5.7	100.0	4.3	100.0	4.2	100.0	4.6	1970
1971	105.4	5.4	106.6	6.6	103.5	3.5	107.1	7.1	1971
1972	111.6	5.9	113.1	6.1	106.2	2.7	114.9	7.2	1972
1973	117.6	5.4	119.6	5.8	109.6	3.2	121.9	6.1	1973
1974	121.4	3.2	123.1	2.9	110.9	1.1	123.0	0.9	1974
1975	121.6	0.2	127.2	3.4	116.1	4.7	119.1	−3.2	1975
1976	127.9	5.2	134.4	5.6	123.3	6.2	123.5	3.7	1976
1977	131.5	2.8	138.4	3.0	125.1	1.4	121.7	−1.4	1977
1978	136.3	3.6	144.0	4.1	130.1	4.0	123.2	1.2	1978
1979	140.6	3.2	148.8	3.4	133.4	2.5	127.2	3.3	1979
1980	142.9	1.6	153.5	3.2	138.9	4.1	130.0	2.2	1980

France

Exports increased mainly in 1950–51, 1954–55, 1957–60, 1963–74 (with rather lower growth in 1966–67) and 1976–79; main falls were in 1952, 1956 and 1975, with a slackening of the growth rate in 1962 and 1980. Imports increased mainly in 1950–51, 1954–57, 1960–64, 1966–74 (with lower growth in 1970–71), 1976 and 1978–80.

Unemployment increased mainly in 1950, 1952–53, 1958–59, 1965–68, 1970–72 and 1974–75, with further substantial increases for 1976–80; main reductions in unemployment were in 1951, 1955–57, 1960–64 and 1969. Consumer prices increased mainly in 1950–52, 1958 and 1974–80.

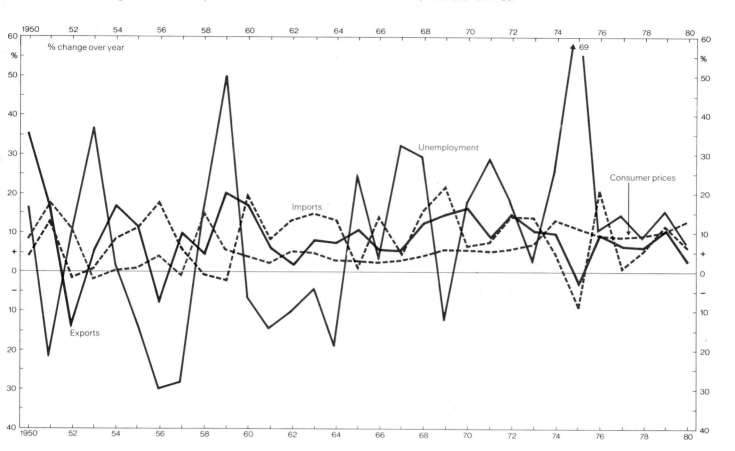

	Exports		Imports		Unemployment		Consumer prices		
	Index 1970 = 100	% change over year	Index 1970 = 100	% change over year	Number (000)	% change over year	Index 1970 = 100	% change over year	
1950	21.6	35.1	17.9	3.9	214	16.6	39.1	8.0	1950
1951	25.1	16.0	20.2	12.9	168	−21.5	46.0	17.6	1951
1952	21.6	−13.8	19.9	−1.3	184	9.7	51.5	12.0	1952
1953	22.7	5.1	20.0	0.5	252	36.6	50.5	−1.9	1953
1954	26.4	16.3	21.6	8.0	256	1.8	50.7	0.4	1954
1955	29.5	11.7	24.1	11.6	223	−13.0	51.2	1.0	1955
1956	27.2	−7.8	28.4	17.8	157	−29.8	53.4	4.3	1956
1957	29.9	9.9	30.1	6.0	112	−28.1	53.0	−0.7	1957
1958	31.3	4.7	29.9	−0.7	130	15.4	61.1	15.3	1958
1959	37.6	20.1	29.3	−2.0	195	50.1	64.6	5.7	1959
1960	43.8	16.5	35.0	19.5	183	−6.2	67.3	4.2	1960
1961	46.3	5.7	37.8	8.0	156	−14.6	68.9	2.4	1961
1962	46.9	1.3	42.9	13.5	141	−10.0	72.5	5.2	1962
1963	50.9	8.5	49.2	14.7	135	−4.0	76.2	5.1	1963
1964	54.5	7.1	55.8	13.4	110	−18.7	78.6	3.1	1964
1965	60.4	10.8	56.2	0.7	137	24.5	80.7	2.7	1965
1966	63.8	5.6	64.0	13.9	142	3.9	82.8	2.6	1966
1967	67.1	5.2	67.1	4.8	189	32.7	85.1	2.8	1967
1968	75.3	12.2	77.3	15.2	244	29.5	89.0	4.6	1968
1969	86.3	14.6	93.9	21.5	214	−12.1	94.4	6.1	1969
1970	100.0	15.9	100.0	6.5	252	17.5	100.0	5.9	1970
1971	108.4	8.4	107.6	7.6	325	29.0	105.5	5.5	1971
1972	123.8	14.2	122.7	14.0	383	17.9	112.0	6.2	1972
1973	136.5	10.3	139.4	13.6	394	2.7	120.2	7.3	1973
1974	149.4	9.5	145.4	4.3	498	26.4	136.7	13.7	1974
1975	144.1	−3.5	131.6	−9.5	840	68.7	152.8	11.8	1975
1976	157.2	9.1	159.0	20.8	933	11.2	167.5	9.6	1976
1977	167.6	6.6	160.3	0.8	1072	14.8	183.2	9.4	1977
1978	177.7	6.0	168.6	5.2	1167	8.9	199.9	9.1	1978
1979	195.5	10.1	188.2	11.6	1350	15.7	221.3	10.7	1979
1980	199.7	2.1	200.0	6.3	1451	7.5	250.7	13.3	1980

France

Share prices increased mainly in 1951–52, 1954–55, 1957, 1959–61, 1968–70, 1972–73 and 1978–80; main falls were in 1950, 1958, 1963–67, 1971, 1974 and 1977. Money stock increased mainly in 1950–56, 1959–63, 1970–75 and 1977–79; there was a fall in money stock in 1969, and the rate of increase slackened in 1957–58,

1964–67, 1973, 1976 and 1980. International reserves increased mainly in 1950, 1952–55, 1958–64, 1970–72, 1975 and 1978–80; main falls were in 1951, 1956–57, 1968–69, 1973 and 1976. The interest rate increased mainly in 1951–53, 1957–58, 1963–64, 1966–69, 1973–74, 1976–77 and 1979–80.

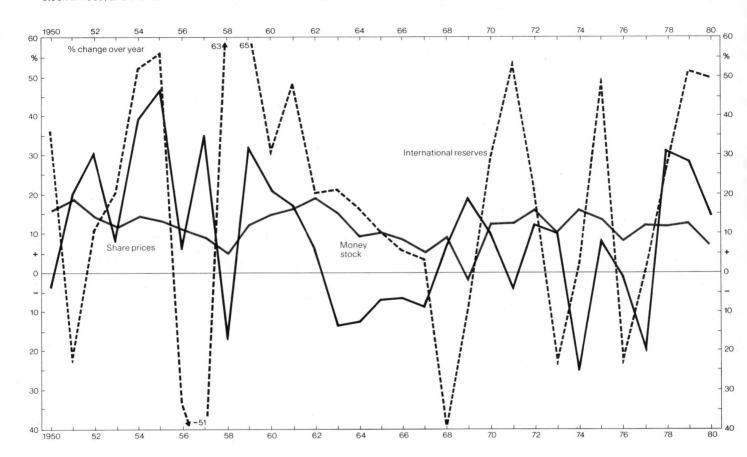

	Share prices		Money stock		International reserves		Interest rate		
	Index 1970 = 100	% change over year	Index 1970 = 100	% change over year	Index 1970 = 100	% change over year	%	Change over year[a]	
1950	14.6	−3.2	13.5	15.4	15.9	36.4	2.43	−0.09	1950
1951	17.6	20.3	15.9	18.1	12.4	−22.1	2.70	0.27	1951
1952	22.9	30.4	18.0	13.3	13.8	11.4	3.71	1.01	1952
1953	24.8	8.3	20.0	11.2	16.7	20.8	4.04	0.33	1953
1954	34.6	39.5	22.8	13.7	25.5	52.5	3.59	−0.45	1954
1955	50.8	46.8	25.7	12.7	39.8	56.2	3.16	−0.43	1955
1956	53.9	6.1	28.3	10.3	26.4	−33.6	3.19	0.03	1956
1957	72.7	34.9	30.7	8.4	13.0	−50.8	5.35	2.16	1957
1958	60.5	−16.8	32.1	4.5	21.2	62.8	6.49	1.14	1958
1959	79.9	32.1	35.7	11.4	35.0	65.3	4.07	−2.42	1959
1960	96.7	21.0	40.8	14.1	45.8	30.9	4.08	0.01	1960
1961	113.0	16.9	47.1	15.5	67.8	48.1	3.65	−0.43	1961
1962	119.4	5.7	55.7	18.2	81.6	20.3	3.61	−0.04	1962
1963	103.3	−13.5	63.8	14.5	99.0	21.2	3.98	0.37	1963
1964	90.6	−12.3	69.1	8.3	115.4	16.6	4.74	0.76	1964
1965	84.3	−7.0	75.6	9.4	127.9	10.8	4.21	−0.53	1965
1966	78.8	−6.5	81.4	7.8	135.7	6.1	4.78	0.57	1966
1967	71.8	−8.9	85.3	4.8	141.0	3.9	4.80	0.02	1967
1968	76.4	6.4	92.1	8.0	84.7	−39.9	6.15	1.35	1968
1969	90.9	19.0	89.8	−2.5	77.3	−8.8	8.96	2.81	1969
1970	100.0	10.0	100.0	11.4	100.0	29.4	8.68	−0.28	1970
1971	95.7	−4.3	111.8	11.8	153.3	53.3	5.84	−2.84	1971
1972	107.4	12.2	128.6	15.0	186.0	21.3	4.95	−0.89	1972
1973	118.5	10.3	141.0	9.7	142.5	−23.4	8.91	3.96	1973
1974	88.2	−25.6	162.5	15.2	145.7	2.2	12.91	4.00	1974
1975	95.5	8.3	182.9	12.6	216.9	48.8	7.92	−4.99	1975
1976	94.4	−1.1	196.6	7.5	168.8	−22.2	8.56	0.64	1976
1977	75.7	−19.8	218.9	11.4	169.2	0.2	9.07	0.51	1977
1978	99.0	30.8	243.2	11.1	215.6	27.4	7.98	−1.09	1978
1979	126.8	28.1	271.8	11.8	326.9	51.6	9.04	1.06	1979
1980	145.4	14.7	289.1	6.4	490.0	49.9	11.85	2.81	1980

[a]In percentage points

Germany, West

The main periods of expansion in gross domestic product were 1950–57, 1959–66 (although with a lower growth rate for 1961–63), 1968–73 and 1976–79; there was comparatively low growth in 1958, and a fall in growth or very low rate for 1967, 1974–75 and 1980. Consumers expenditure expanded at a high and generally stable rate for 1951–65, with further main expansion periods in 1968–72 and 1975–79. Government expenditure increased mainly in 1951–52, 1958–63, 1965–67, 1969–75 and 1978–80. Fixed investment increased mainly in 1951–56, 1959–61, 1964–65, 1968–72 and 1976–80; growth slackened in 1957, with falls in 1967 and 1974–75.

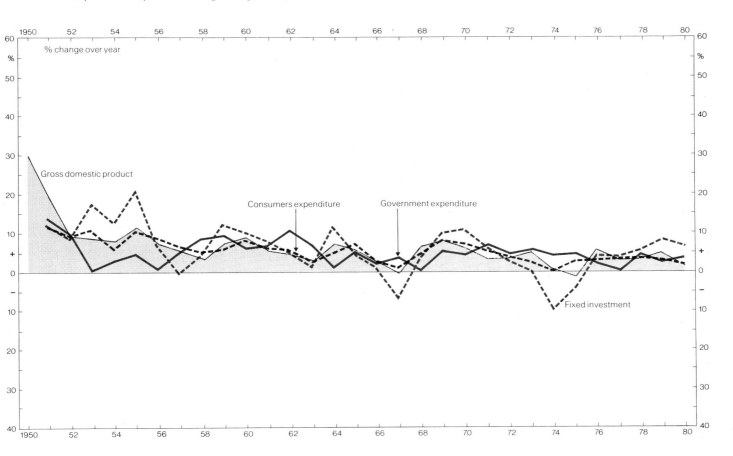

	Gross domestic product		Consumers expenditure		Government expenditure		Fixed investment		
	Index 1970 = 100	% change over year	Index 1970 = 100	% change over year	Index 1970 = 100	% change over year	Index 1970 = 100	% change over year	
1950	27.4	29.4	28.1	na	36.3	na	23.4	na	1950
1951	32.4	18.3	31.4	11.5	41.3	13.6	26.1	11.5	1951
1952	35.3	8.8	34.2	9.1	45.3	9.7	28.4	8.7	1952
1953	38.2	8.3	38.0	10.9	45.4	0.3	33.3	17.1	1953
1954	41.1	7.7	40.3	6.0	46.6	2.6	37.4	12.5	1954
1955	46.1	12.0	44.4	10.4	48.8	4.6	45.2	20.7	1955
1956	49.4	7.2	48.3	8.8	49.1	0.6	49.1	8.7	1956
1957	52.2	5.6	51.4	6.3	51.4	4.8	49.1	−0.1	1957
1958	54.0	3.5	53.9	5.0	55.7	8.3	51.1	4.2	1958
1959	58.0	7.4	57.0	5.7	60.7	9.0	57.1	11.8	1959
1960	63.2	8.9	61.6	8.0	64.3	6.0	62.9	10.1	1960
1961	66.4	5.1	65.3	6.0	68.5	6.5	67.4	7.1	1961
1962	69.3	4.4	68.8	5.4	75.6	10.4	70.4	4.6	1962
1963	71.4	3.0	70.8	2.9	80.7	6.7	71.3	1.2	1963
1964	76.2	6.7	74.4	5.0	81.6	1.1	79.3	11.3	1964
1965	80.5	5.6	79.5	6.9	85.8	5.1	83.2	4.8	1965
1966	82.5	2.5	81.8	2.9	87.8	2.4	84.2	1.2	1966
1967	82.3	−0.2	82.6	1.0	90.9	3.6	78.5	−6.8	1967
1968	87.5	6.3	86.4	4.5	91.0	0.1	81.6	4.0	1968
1969	94.4	7.8	93.2	7.9	95.6	5.1	90.2	10.5	1969
1970	100.0	6.0	100.0	7.3	100.0	4.6	100.0	10.8	1970
1971	103.2	3.2	105.2	5.2	106.3	6.3	106.4	6.4	1971
1972	107.0	3.7	109.4	4.0	111.3	4.6	110.1	3.5	1972
1973	112.2	4.9	112.2	2.5	117.3	5.5	110.4	0.2	1973
1974	112.8	0.5	112.6	0.3	122.4	4.3	99.4	−9.9	1974
1975	110.8	−1.8	116.1	3.1	127.9	4.5	95.2	−4.2	1975
1976	116.5	5.2	120.0	3.4	130.4	2.0	99.7	4.7	1976
1977	120.0	3.0	124.1	3.5	131.1	0.5	103.6	3.9	1977
1978	124.0	3.3	128.9	3.8	136.6	4.2	109.6	5.8	1978
1979	129.7	4.6	133.0	3.2	140.6	2.9	119.1	8.7	1979
1980	132.0	1.8	136.0	2.2	146.1	3.9	126.9	6.5	1980

Exports increased mainly in 1950–57, 1959–60, 1963–69, 1972–74 and 1976, with substantial growth also for the periods 1970–72 and 1977–80; there was a fall or slackening in growth for 1958, 1962 and 1975. Imports increased mainly in 1950, 1952–55, 1959–60, 1962, 1964–65, 1968–73, 1976 and 1978–79; imports fell in 1967 and 1974.

Unemployment increased mainly in 1950, 1958, 1963, 1966–67, 1971–75 and 1980; main reductions in unemployment were in 1951–57, 1959–62, 1964–65, 1968–70 and 1976–79. Consumer prices were comparatively stable throughout the period, with main increases in 1951, 1971–75 and 1979–80.

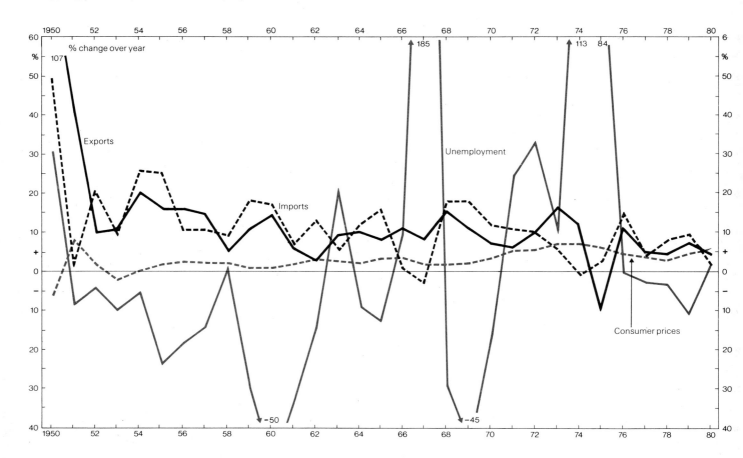

	Exports		Imports		Unemployment		Consumer prices		
	Index 1970 = 100	% change over year	Index 1970 = 100	% change over year	Number (000)	% change over year	Index 1970 = 100	% change over year	
1950	10.3	107	10.0	49	1 868.5	31.4	64.2	−6.3.	1950
1951	14.6	41	10.3	2	1 713.9	−8.3	69.2	7.8	1951
1952	16.1	10	12.4	21	1 651.9	−3.6	70.7	2.1	1952
1953	17.8	11	13.6	10	1 491.0	−9.7	69.4	−1.8	1953
1954	21.3	20	17.1	26	1 410.7	−5.4	69.6	0.3	1954
1955	24.7	16	21.3	25	1 073.6	−23.9	70.7	1.6	1955
1956	28.6	16	23.6	11	876.3	−18.4	72.5	2.5	1956
1957	32.5	14	26.3	11	753.7	−14.0	74.0	2.1	1957
1958	34.0	5	28.6	9	763.6	1.3	75.6	2.2	1958
1959	37.6	11	33.8	18	539.9	−29.3	76.4	1.1	1959
1960	43.0	14	39.4	17	270.7	−49.9	77.4	1.3	1960
1961	45.5	6	42.1	7	180.9	−33.2	79.2	2.3	1961
1962	47.0	3	47.6	13	154.6	−14.5	81.6	3.0	1962
1963	51.1	9	50.5	6	185.6	20.1	84.0	2.9	1963
1964	56.4	10	56.6	12	169.1	−8.9	85.9	2.3	1964
1965	60.9	8	65.6	16	147.4	−12.8	88.7	3.3	1965
1966	67.3	11	66.0	1	161.1	9.3	91.9	3.6	1966
1967	73.0	8	64.1	−3	459.5	185.2	93.4	1.6	1967
1968	83.7	15	75.5	18	323.5	−29.6	94.9	1.6	1968
1969	93.1	11	89.4	18	178.6	−44.8	96.7	1.9	1969
1970	100.0	7	100.0	12	148.8	−16.7	100.0	3.4	1970
1971	105.9	6	110.6	11	185.1	24.4	105.3	5.3	1971
1972	115.2	9	121.8	10	246.4	33.1	111.1	5.5	1972
1973	133.3	16	129.2	6	273.5	11.0	118.8	6.9	1973
1974	149.9	12	127.4	−1	582.6	113.0	127.1	7.0	1974
1975	134.3	−10	130.7	3	1 074.2	84.4	134.7	6.0	1975
1976	149.6	11	149.5	14	1 060.3	−1.3	140.5	4.3	1976
1977	157.7	5	155.0	4	1 030.0	−2.9	145.6	3.6	1977
1978	164.2	4	166.9	8	992.9	−3.6	149.7	2.8	1978
1979	175.9	7	181.8	9	876.1	−11.8	155.7	4.1	1979
1980	183.2	4	185.9	2	888.9	1.5	164.3	5.5	1980

Germany, West

Share prices increased mainly in 1951–52, 1955, 1958–60, 1964, 1968–69, 1972, 1975–76 and 1978; main falls were in 1953–54, 1956–57, 1962, 1965–66, 1970–71, 1973–74 and 1979–80. Money stock increased at a comparatively stable rate over 1950–65, with main increases in 1950, 1954, 1958–59 and 1961; thereafter main increases occurred in 1967–68, 1971–72, 1974–75 and 1977–78. International reserves increased over the period 1950–60, substantially early in the period, and thereafter increased mainly in 1963, 1968, 1970–73 and 1976–78. The interest rate increased mainly in 1951, 1956, 1960, 1963–66, 1969–70, 1973 and 1979–80.

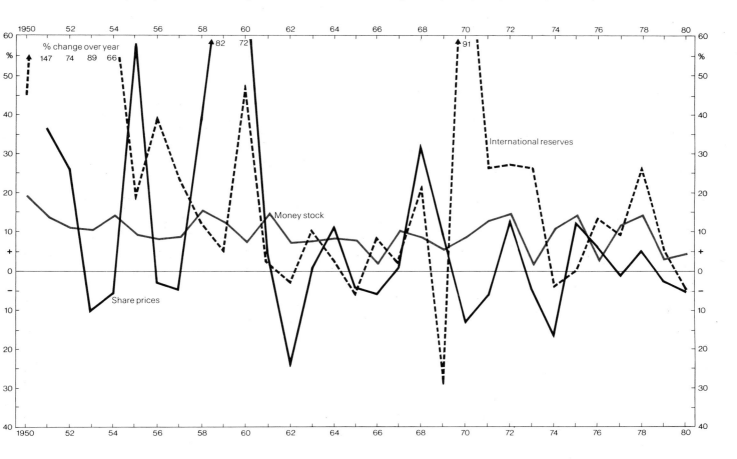

	Share prices		Money stock		International reserves		Interest rate		
	Index 1970 = 100	% change over year	Index 1970 = 100	% change over year	Index 1970 = 100	% change over year	%	Change over year[a]	
1950	11.0	na	16.8	18.3	1.1	45	4.3	na	1950
1951	15.0	36.2	19.1	13.7	2.7	147	6.0	1.7	1951
1952	19.0	26.6	21.2	10.9	4.7	74	5.1	−0.9	1952
1953	17.0	−10.5	23.3	10.3	8.9	89	3.6	−1.5	1953
1954	16.0	−5.9	26.6	14.0	14.7	66	2.9	−0.7	1954
1955	25.1	56.9	29.0	8.9	17.5	19	3.1	0.2	1955
1956	24.4	−2.8	31.3	7.8	24.4	39	4.7	1.6	1956
1957	23.2	−4.9	33.9	8.5	30.0	23	4.0	−0.7	1957
1958	32.2	38.8	39.1	15.2	33.5	12	3.1	−0.9	1958
1959	58.6	82.0	43.8	12.2	35.2	5	2.7	−0.4	1959
1960	100.9	72.2	47.0	7.2	51.7	47	4.6	1.9	1960
1961	105.0	4.1	53.8	14.5	52.6	2	2.9	−1.7	1961
1962	79.2	−24.6	57.5	6.8	51.1	−3	2.7	−0.2	1962
1963	80.0	1.0	61.6	7.2	56.2	10	3.0	0.3	1963
1964	88.7	10.9	66.9	8.5	57.9	3	3.3	0.3	1964
1965	84.6	−4.6	72.0	7.7	54.6	−6	4.1	0.8	1965
1966	79.5	−6.0	73.4	1.9	59.0	8	5.3	1.2	1966
1967	80.3	1.0	80.7	10.0	59.9	2	3.4	−1.9	1967
1968	105.5	31.4	87.5	8.3	73.1	22	2.6	−0.8	1968
1969	115.0	9.0	92.1	5.3	52.4	−28	4.8	2.2	1969
1970	100.0	−13.0	100.0	8.6	100.0	91	8.7	3.9	1970
1971	93.9	−6.1	112.8	12.8	126.3	26	6.1	−2.6	1971
1972	106.0	12.9	128.8	14.1	161.0	27	4.3	−1.8	1972
1973	100.8	−4.9	131.0	1.7	202.0	26	10.2	5.9	1973
1974	84.4	−16.3	145.0	10.7	194.4	−4	8.9	−1.3	1974
1975	95.0	12.6	165.7	14.3	194.8	0	4.4	−4.5	1975
1976	100.8	6.1	171.1	3.3	220.1	13	3.9	−0.5	1976
1977	99.6	−1.2	191.7	12.0	240.4	9	4.1	0.2	1977
1978	104.4	4.9	218.9	14.2	303.9	26	3.4	−0.7	1978
1979	101.0	−3.3	226.0	3.2	317.6	5	5.9	2.5	1979
1980	95.8	−5.2	234.9	4.0	301.1	−5	9.1	3.2	1980

[a]In percentage points

Ghana

Over the time for which figures are available, the main periods of expansion in gross domestic product were 1957–62, 1969–71 and 1973–74, with low growth in 1963–68 and low or negative growth in 1972 and 1975–77. Exports of cocoa increased mainly in 1953, 1956–57, 1959–61, 1965, 1970 and 1972–73, with falls in 1951–52,

1954–55, 1958, 1963–64, 1966–67, 1969, 1971 and 1974–77. Unemployment increased mainly in 1956–58, 1960–61, 1967, 1970–72, 1974–76, 1978 and 1980, with main reductions in 1955, 1964–65, 1969, 1973 and 1979. Consumer prices increased mainly in 1950–51, 1961–66, 1968–70 and at a very high rate in 1972–80.

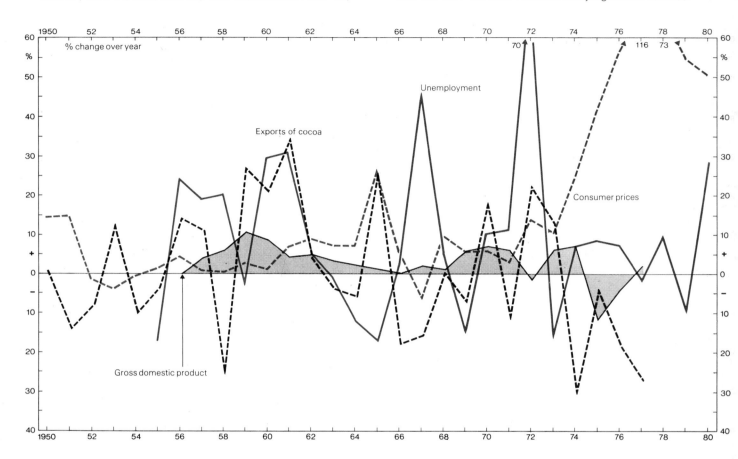

	Gross domestic product		Exports of cocoa		Unemployment		Consumer prices		
	Index 1970 = 100	% change over year	Index 1970 = 100	% change over year	Number (000)	% change over year	Index 1970 = 100	% change over year	
1950	na	na	74	1	na	na	41.8	14.6	1950
1951	na	na	63	−14	na	na	48.0	14.9	1951
1952	na	na	59	−8	na	na	47.3	−1.4	1952
1953	na	na	66	12	na	na	45.4	−4.0	1953
1954	na	na	59	−10	6.1	na	45.1	−0.7	1954
1955	57	na	57	−4	5.0	−17	45.5	0.9	1955
1956	56	0	65	14	6.3	24	47.3	4.0	1956
1957	59	4	72	11	7.5	19	47.6	0.6	1957
1958	62	6	54	−25	8.9	20	47.8	0.4	1958
1959	68	11	69	27	8.8	−2	48.9	2.3	1959
1960	74	8	84	21	11.3	29	49.4	1.0	1960
1961	76	4	112	34	14.7	31	52.7	6.7	1961
1962	80	5	117	4	15.5	5	57.3	8.7	1962
1963	83	3	112	−4	15.4	−1	61.4	7.2	1963
1964	84	2	106	−6	13.6	−12	65.8	7.2	1964
1965	86	1	133	25	11.3	−17	82.5	25.4	1965
1966	86	0	108	−18	11.5	2	86.9	5.3	1966
1967	87	2	91	−16	16.7	45	81.6	−6.1	1967
1968	88	1	91	0	17.6	5	89.1	9.2	1968
1969	94	6	85	−7	15.0	−15	94.3	5.8	1969
1970	100	7	100	18	16.5	10	100.0	6.0	1970
1971	106	6	89	−11	18.4	11	102.6	2.6	1971
1972	103	−2	109	22	31.2	70	116.4	13.5	1972
1973	109	6	123	13	26.3	−16	128.3	10.2	1973
1974	116	7	85	−30	28.3	7	159.4	24.2	1974
1975	102	−12	81	−5	30.5	8	225.0	41.2	1975
1976	98	−4	67	−18	32.7	7	351.2	56.1	1976
1977	100	2	49	−27	31.9	−2	760.1	116.4	1977
1978	na	na	na	na	34.8	9	1315.8	73.1	1978
1979	na	na	na	na	31.3	−10	2031.8	54.4	1979
1980	na	na	na	na	40.0	28	3049.6	50.1	1980

Greece

The main periods of expansion in gross domestic product were 1950–51, 1953, 1955–57, 1961, 1963–73, 1975–76 and 1978; there were very low rates of growth in 1952, 1962 and 1980, with a fall in 1974. Consumers expenditure expanded at a generally stable rate throughout the period 1951–80, with some slackening in 1959–60,

1974 and 1979. Government expenditure increased mainly in 1950–51, 1954–56, 1958, 1960–67 and 1969–79 (especially in 1974–75). Fixed investment increased mainly in 1950, 1955–56, 1958, 1960–62, 1964–65, 1968–69, 1971–73 and 1976–79, with falls in 1951–52, 1957, 1967, 1970, 1974 and 1980.

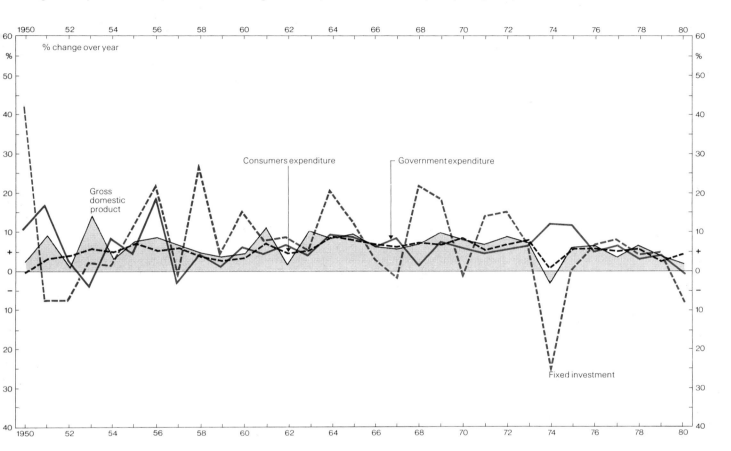

	Gross domestic product		Consumers expenditure		Government expenditure		Fixed investment		
	Index 1970 = 100	% change over year	Index 1970 = 100	% change over year	Index 1970 = 100	% change over year	Index 1970 = 100	% change over year	
1950	26.5	2.3	33.9	−0.3	32.7	10.5	23.0	43.5	1950
1951	28.9	8.8	34.8	2.8	38.0	16.3	21.4	−7.2	1951
1952	29.1	0.7	36.0	3.4	39.0	2.6	19.8	−7.4	1952
1953	33.1	13.7	38.0	5.5	37.4	−4.1	20.2	1.9	1953
1954	34.1	3.1	39.9	4.9	40.5	8.3	20.4	1.0	1954
1955	36.7	7.6	42.7	7.2	42.2	4.0	22.6	10.8	1955
1956	39.8	8.5	44.9	5.1	49.9	18.3	27.4	21.6	1956
1957	42.4	6.5	47.6	5.9	48.4	−2.9	27.1	−1.4	1957
1958	44.4	4.6	49.3	3.7	50.6	4.5	34.2	26.4	1958
1959	46.0	3.7	50.8	2.9	51.2	1.1	35.8	4.5	1959
1960	48.0	4.3	52.4	3.2	54.3	6.1	41.2	15.3	1960
1961	53.3	11.1	55.9	6.8	56.7	4.4	44.5	8.1	1961
1962	54.1	1.5	58.3	4.3	60.5	6.7	48.3	8.4	1962
1963	59.6	10.1	61.3	5.1	63.0	4.2	50.9	5.5	1963
1964	64.5	8.3	66.7	8.8	68.9	9.3	61.5	20.7	1964
1965	70.6	9.4	71.8	7.7	75.1	9.0	69.3	12.8	1965
1966	74.9	6.1	76.6	6.8	79.8	6.3	71.6	3.2	1966
1967	79.0	5.5	81.4	6.2	86.5	8.5	70.4	−1.6	1967
1968	84.3	6.7	87.0	6.9	87.7	1.3	85.5	21.4	1968
1969	92.6	9.9	92.4	6.2	94.4	7.7	101.4	18.6	1969
1970	100.0	8.0	100.0	8.3	100.0	5.9	100.0	−1.4	1970
1971	107.1	7.1	105.5	5.5	104.9	4.9	114.0	14.0	1971
1972	116.6	8.9	112.9	7.0	110.9	5.7	131.6	15.4	1972
1973	125.2	7.3	121.6	7.8	118.4	6.8	141.6	7.7	1973
1974	120.6	−3.6	122.4	0.6	132.7	12.1	105.4	−25.6	1974
1975	127.9	6.1	129.4	5.7	148.6	11.9	105.7	0.2	1975
1976	136.1	6.4	136.7	5.6	156.2	5.1	112.9	6.8	1976
1977	140.7	3.4	143.8	5.1	166.4	6.5	121.6	7.8	1977
1978	149.5	6.2	151.6	5.4	172.2	3.5	127.4	4.7	1978
1979	155.2	3.8	155.4	2.5	180.2	4.6	133.6	4.9	1979
1980	157.7	1.6	161.8	4.1	179.8	−0.2	122.5	−8.3	1980

Greece

Exports increased mainly in 1952–55, 1957–58, 1961–62, 1964–67, 1969–70, 1972–76, 1978 and 1980; there were falls in 1956, 1959, 1968 and 1977. Imports increased mainly in 1954–58, 1960–65, 1968–73 (with rather lower growth in 1970–71), 1976–77 and 1979; there were falls or a slackening of growth in 1952–53, 1959, 1966–67,

1974–75, 1978 and 1980. Consumer prices increased mainly in 1950–51, 1953–55, 1966 and at a very high rate for 1973–80; there was a comparatively stable period for consumer prices from 1956 to 1972. Money stock increased mainly in 1950–51, 1953–55, 1957, 1959–67 and 1970–80, with substantial growth for other years.

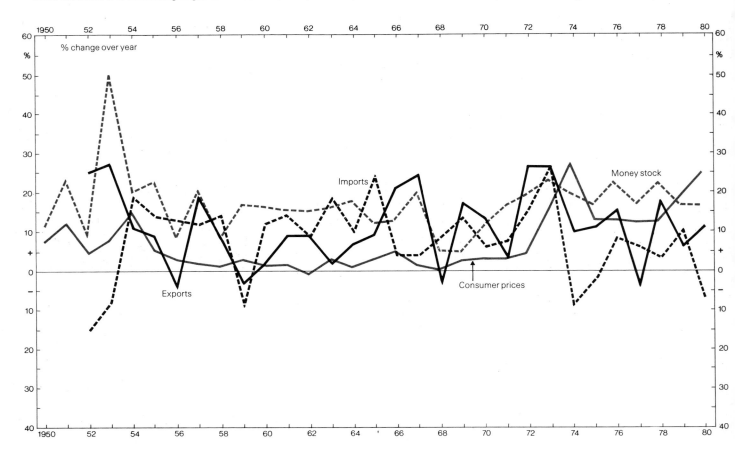

	Exports		Imports		Consumer prices		Money stock		
	Index 1970 = 100	% change over year	Index 1970 = 100	% change over year	Index 1970 = 100	% change over year	Index 1970 = 100	% change over year	
1950	na	na	na	na	46.2	7.9	4.8	11.9	1950
1951	16	na	23	na	52.0	12.5	6.0	23.5	1951
1952	20	25	19	−15	54.7	5.2	6.6	9.8	1952
1953	25	27	18	−8	59.5	8.8	9.9	50.3	1953
1954	28	11	21	19	68.5	15.1	11.9	20.6	1954
1955	30	9	24	14	72.4	5.7	14.7	23.4	1955
1956	29	−4	27	13	75.1	3.7	16.0	9.2	1956
1957	34	19	31	12	76.8	2.3	19.3	20.7	1957
1958	37	8	35	14	77.9	1.4	21.0	8.4	1958
1959	36	−3	32	−9	80.2	3.0	24.5	17.0	1959
1960	37	2	36	12	81.5	1.6	28.6	16.4	1960
1961	40	9	41	14	82.9	1.7	33.1	15.8	1961
1962	44	9	44	9	82.7	−0.2	38.1	15.3	1962
1963	44	2	52	18	85.1	2.9	44.3	16.2	1963
1964	48	7	58	10	85.8	0.8	52.6	18.7	1964
1965	52	9	71	24	88.4	3.0	59.2	12.6	1965
1966	63	21	74	4	92.9	5.1	67.1	13.2	1966
1967	78	24	77	4	94.4	1.6	80.6	20.2	1967
1968	75	−3	83	8	94.8	0.4	85.1	5.5	1968
1969	88	17	94	13	97.1	2.4	89.5	5.2	1969
1970	100	13	100	6	100.0	3.0	100.0	11.7	1970
1971	103	3	107	7	103.0	3.0	116.6	16.6	1971
1972	130	26	123	15	107.5	4.4	139.0	19.2	1972
1973	163	26	155	26	124.2	15.5	171.5	23.4	1973
1974	180	10	141	−9	157.6	26.9	205.5	19.8	1974
1975	199	11	138	−2	178.7	13.4	239.2	16.4	1975
1976	230	15	149	8	202.5	13.3	292.3	22.2	1976
1977	222	−4	158	6	227.1	12.2	341.7	16.9	1977
1978	259	17	163	3	255.5	12.5	417.9	22.3	1978
1979	275	6	180	10	304.1	19.0	486.2	16.3	1979
1980	305	11	167	−7	379.7	24.9	565.5	16.3	1980

Guatemala

Gross domestic product increased at a comparatively steady rate throughout the period, with rather higher rates of growth for 1956–57, 1963, 1968, 1970–74 and 1976–77, and lower rates in 1950–51, 1954–55, 1960 and 1975. Fixed investment increased mainly in 1950–51, 1953, 1955–56, 1963–65, 1967–68, 1971, 1973 and 1975–78; main falls were in 1952, 1958–60, 1962 and 1979–80. Exports of coffee increased mainly in 1952, 1955–56, 1958–59, 1962–63, 1965–66, 1968–69, 1971–72, 1974–75, 1977 and 1979. Consumer prices were comparatively stable for 1952–72, after a high rate of increase for 1950–51; they rose at a high rate for 1973–80.

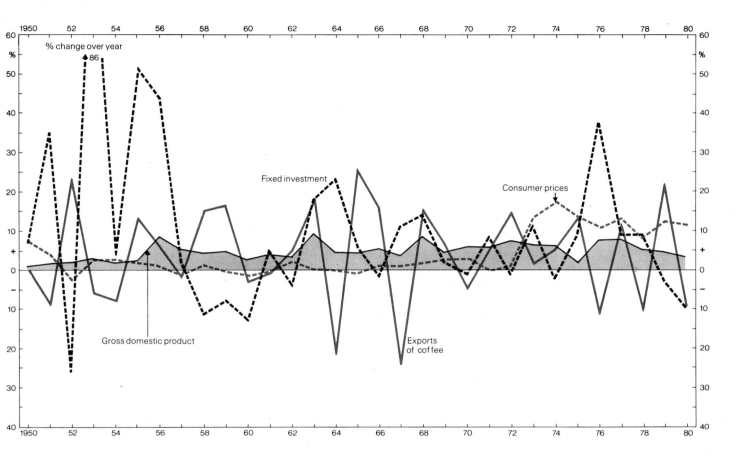

	Gross domestic product		Fixed investment		Exports of coffee		Consumer prices		
	Index 1970 = 100	% change over year	Index 1970 = 100	% change over year	Index 1970 = 100	% change over year	Index 1970 = 100	% change over year	
1950	40.3	0.9	17	7	57	0	84.4	7.1	1950
1951	40.9	1.4	23	35	52	−9	88.2	4.4	1951
1952	41.7	2.1	17	−26	64	23	86.3	−2.1	1952
1953	43.2	3.6	32	86	60	−6	88.9	3.0	1953
1954	44.1	1.9	33	4	55	−8	91.3	2.7	1954
1955	45.1	2.5	49	51	62	13	92.9	1.8	1955
1956	49.2	9.1	71	44	66	6	93.7	0.9	1956
1957	52.0	5.6	72	2	65	−2	92.7	−1.1	1957
1958	54.5	4.7	64	−11	75	15	93.7	1.1	1958
1959	57.1	4.9	59	−8	87	16	93.3	−0.4	1959
1960	58.5	2.5	51	−13	84	−3	92.2	−1.2	1960
1961	61.1	4.3	54	5	83	−1	91.7	−0.5	1961
1962	63.2	3.5	52	−4	87	5	93.6	2.1	1962
1963	69.2	9.5	61	18	103	18	93.7	0.1	1963
1964	72.4	4.6	75	23	80	−22	93.5	−0.2	1964
1965	75.6	4.4	80	6	100	25	92.8	−0.7	1965
1966	79.8	5.5	79	−1	115	15	93.4	0.6	1966
1967	83.0	4.1	88	11	86	−25	93.9	0.5	1967
1968	90.3	8.8	100	14	99	15	95.6	1.8	1968
1969	94.6	4.7	101	2	105	6	97.7	2.2	1969
1970	100.0	5.7	100	−1	100	−5	100.0	2.4	1970
1971	105.6	5.6	108	8	105	5	99.5	−0.5	1971
1972	113.3	7.3	108	−1	120	14	100.1	0.6	1972
1973	121.0	6.8	120	11	121	1	113.9	13.8	1973
1974	128.7	6.4	118	−2	127	5	132.7	16.5	1974
1975	131.2	2.0	129	9	143	13	150.1	13.1	1975
1976	140.9	7.4	177	37	126	−12	166.2	10.7	1976
1977	151.9	7.8	194	9	140	11	187.0	12.6	1977
1978	159.5	5.0	211	9	124	−11	201.9	7.9	1978
1979	167.1	4.7	205	−3	150	21	225.2	11.5	1979
1980	172.9	3.5	185	−10	136	−10	249.3	10.7	1980

Guyana

Over the time for which figures are available, the main periods of expansion for gross domestic product were 1961, 1964–65, 1967 1969–71 and 1973–76; there were falls or low growth rates for 1962–63, 1966, 1968, 1972 and 1977–80. Exports, for the time covered, increased mainly in 1962, 1965–67, 1969, 1971, 1974–75 and 1978, with main falls in 1961, 1963, 1972–73, 1976–77 and 1979–80. Unemployment increased mainly in 1956–58, 1961–62, 1964–65, 1975 and 1979, with reductions in 1955, 1959–60, 1963, 1966–74 and 1976–78. Consumer prices were comparatively stable over 1957–71, with high increases for 1972–80.

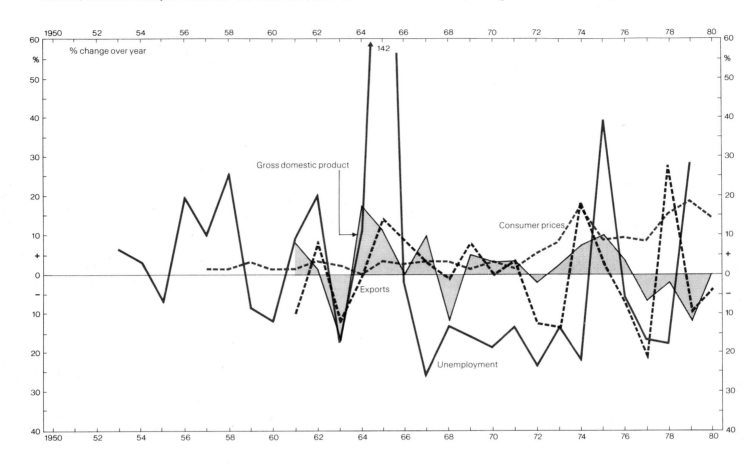

	Gross domestic product		Exports		Unemployment[a]		Consumer prices		
	Index 1970 = 100	% change over year	Index 1970 = 100	% change over year	Number (000)	% change over year	Index 1970 = 100	% change over year	
1950	na	na	na	na	1.59	44	na	na	1950
1951	na	na	na	na	na	na	na	na	1951
1952	na	na	na	na	3.20	na	na	na	1952
1953	na	na	na	na	3.39	6	na	na	1953
1954	na	na	na	na	3.49	3	na	na	1954
1955	na	na	na	na	3.25	−7	na	na	1955
1956	na	na	na	na	3.87	19	76	na	1956
1957	na	na	na	na	4.27	10	77	1	1957
1958	na	na	na	na	5.33	25	78	1	1958
1959	na	na	na	na	4.84	−9	80	3	1959
1960	81	na	85	na	4.24	−12	80	1	1960
1961	88	8	77	−10	4.62	9	81	1	1961
1962	89	1	83	8	5.55	20	84	3	1962
1963	73	−17	73	−12	4.60	−17	85	2	1963
1964	86	17	73	0	5.09	11	86	0	1964
1965	95	11	83	14	12.34	142	88	3	1965
1966	95	0	91	9	12.06	−2	90	2	1966
1967	105	10	94	3	8.94	−26	93	3	1967
1968	92	−12	93	−1	7.65	−14	95	3	1968
1969	97	5	100	8	6.40	−16	97	1	1969
1970	100	3	100	0	5.18	−19	100	3	1970
1971	103	3	103	3	4.45	−14	101	1	1971
1972	101	−2	90	−13	3.39	−24	106	5	1972
1973	103	2	77	−14	2.90	−14	114	8	1973
1974	110	7	91	18	2.27	−22	134	17	1974
1975	121	10	93	2	3.16	39	145	8	1975
1976	125	3	85	−8	2.97	−6	158	9	1976
1977	116	−7	68	−21	2.46	−17	171	8	1977
1978	113	−2	86	27	2.00	−18	197	15	1978
1979	100	−12	78	−10	2.56	28	232	18	1979
1980	100	0	75	−4	na	na	264	14	1980

[a]Georgetown, New Amsterdam and Anna Regina districts only

Haiti

The main periods of expansion in gross domestic product were 1951–52, 1954, 1956, 1958, 1962, 1968–69, 1971, 1973–74, 1976 and 1978–80; falls or low growth occurred in 1953, 1955, 1957, 1959, 1961, 1963–64, 1966–67, 1970, 1972, 1975 and 1977. Exports of coffee increased mainly in 1951–52, 1954, 1956, 1958, 1960, 1962, 1969, 1971, 1976, 1978 and 1980 with falls mainly in alternate years 1953 to 1961, 1963–64, 1966–68, 1970, 1972, 1977 and 1979. Consumer prices increased mainly in 1954, 1964, 1966, 1971, 1973–77 and 1979–80. Money stock increased mainly in 1951–52, 1954, 1956, 1961–63, 1967–73 and 1975–80.

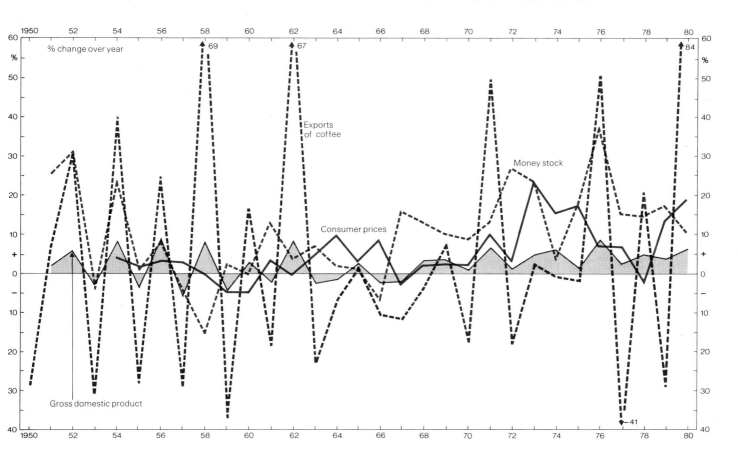

	Gross domestic product[a]		Exports of coffee		Consumer prices		Money stock		
	Index 1970 = 100	% change over year	Index 1970 = 100	% change over year	Index 1970 = 100	% change over year	Index 1970 = 100	% change over year	
1950	81.0	na	152	−29	na	na	31.5	na	1950
1951	82.2	1.5	163	7	na	na	39.5	25.1	1951
1952	86.9	5.7	211	30	na	na	51.6	30.7	1952
1953	84.1	−3.2	145	−31	74.9	na	49.5	−4.0	1953
1954	91.0	8.1	201	39	78.2	4.4	61.3	23.7	1954
1955	87.3	−4.0	144	−28	79.4	1.5	61.8	0.9	1955
1956	95.0	8.7	178	24	82.3	3.7	66.6	7.7	1956
1957	89.3	−6.0	126	−29	84.2	2.3	63.7	−4.3	1957
1958	96.4	7.9	213	69	84.0	−0.2	53.8	−15.5	1958
1959	91.9	−4.7	134	−37	80.0	−4.8	54.8	1.8	1959
1960	94.2	2.6	155	16	76.0	−5.0	54.7	−0.1	1960
1961	92.0	−2.4	126	−19	78.8	3.7	61.9	13.1	1961
1962	99.7	8.4	211	67	78.4	−0.5	64.3	3.8	1962
1963	96.7	−2.9	161	−24	81.7	4.2	68.6	6.7	1963
1964	95.2	−1.6	150	−7	89.3	9.3	69.5	1.4	1964
1965	97.2	2.1	152	1	91.3	2.2	70.0	0.7	1965
1966	94.8	−2.6	135	−11	98.9	8.3	64.6	−7.6	1966
1967	92.8	−2.1	119	−12	96.0	−2.9	74.6	15.4	1967
1968	95.7	3.2	114	−4	97.3	1.4	83.9	12.5	1968
1969	99.3	3.8	122	7	98.7	1.4	92.1	9.7	1969
1970	100.0	0.7	100	−18	100.0	1.3	100.0	8.5	1970
1971	106.5	6.5	149	49	109.5	9.5	112.6	12.6	1971
1972	107.5	1.0	122	−18	113.1	3.3	142.3	26.4	1972
1973	112.6	4.8	124	2	138.8	22.7	174.6	22.7	1973
1974	119.1	5.8	123	−1	159.5	14.9	179.6	2.9	1974
1975	120.4	1.1	120	−2	186.3	16.8	211.2	17.6	1975
1976	130.6	8.4	180	50	199.3	7.0	288.4	36.5	1976
1977	133.0	1.9	107	−41	212.4	6.5	330.1	14.5	1977
1978	139.2	4.7	128	20	206.8	−2.6	376.6	14.1	1978
1979	144.2	3.6	91	−29	233.6	13.0	440.5	17.0	1979
1980	152.4	5.7	168	84	275.4	17.9	485.2	10.1	1980

[a]Years ending September 30th

Honduras

The main periods of expansion in gross domestic product were 1951–53, 1955–58, 1962–68, 1970–73 and 1976–79; there was a fall or slackening of growth in 1954, 1960, 1969, 1974–75 and 1980. Fixed investment increased mainly in 1951–53, 1955–57, 1960, 1962–63, 1965–68, 1970, 1973 and 1975–79, with falls in 1954,

1958–59, 1961 and 1971–72. Exports, for the time covered, increased mainly in 1961, 1963–68, 1971, 1973, 1976 and 1978–79, with falls in 1962, 1969–70, 1972, 1974–75 and 1980. Consumer prices increased mainly in 1950–51, 1954–55, 1963–65, 1972–75 and 1977–80, with especially high rates in 1974 and 1979–80.

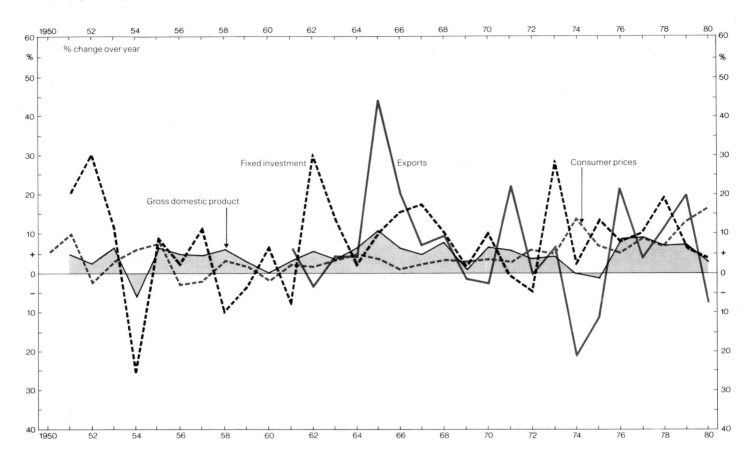

	Gross domestic product		Fixed investment		Exports		Consumer prices		
	Index 1970 = 100	% change over year	Index 1970 = 100	% change over year	Index 1970 = 100	% change over year	Index 1970 = 100	% change over year	
1950	45.8	na	28	na	na	na	67	5.1	1950
1951	47.8	4.4	34	20	na	na	73	9.8	1951
1952	48.8	2.1	44	30	na	na	72	−2.2	1952
1953	51.7	6.0	48	11	na	na	73	2.3	1953
1954	48.5	−6.2	36	−26	na	na	77	5.6	1954
1955	51.4	6.0	39	9	na	na	83	7.5	1955
1956	53.7	4.4	40	2	na	na	81	−3.1	1956
1957	56.0	4.3	44	11	na	na	79	−2.1	1957
1958	59.1	5.5	39	−10	na	na	81	2.7	1958
1959	60.4	2.3	38	−4	na	na	82	1.1	1959
1960	60.4	−0.1	40	6	47	na	80	−1.8	1960
1961	62.0	2.7	37	−8	50	6	82	1.6	1961
1962	65.2	5.1	48	30	48	−4	83	1.1	1962
1963	67.3	3.3	54	13	50	4	85	3.0	1963
1964	71.3	5.9	55	2	52	4	89	4.6	1964
1965	78.7	10.3	61	10	75	44	92	3.1	1965
1966	83.3	5.9	70	15	89	20	92	0.2	1966
1967	87.2	4.6	82	17	96	7	93	1.2	1967
1968	93.5	7.3	90	10	104	9	95	2.6	1968
1969	93.8	0.3	91	1	103	−2	97	1.8	1969
1970	100.0	6.6	100	10	100	−3	100	2.9	1970
1971	105.4	5.4	99	−1	122	22	102	2.3	1971
1972	108.7	3.1	94	−5	121	−1	108	5.2	1972
1973	112.8	3.8	120	28	128	6	112	4.6	1973
1974	112.5	−0.3	123	2	100	−22	128	13.5	1974
1975	110.6	−1.7	139	13	88	−12	136	6.3	1975
1976	119.9	8.4	150	8	106	21	142	4.8	1976
1977	130.3	8.7	164	10	110	3	154	8.4	1977
1978	138.8	6.5	195	19	122	11	164	6.2	1978
1979	148.0	6.6	206	6	145	19	184	12.5	1979
1980	151.9	2.6	212	3	133	−8	213	15.6	1980

Iceland

The main periods of expansion in gross domestic product were 1953–55, 1958–60, 1962–66, 1970–73 and 1976–78; there were falls or a slackening of growth in 1950–52, 1956–57, 1961, 1967–68, 1975 and 1979–80. Fixed investment increased mainly in 1953–55, 1959–60, 1962–64, 1966–67, 1970–71, 1973–74, 1977 and 1980,

with main falls in 1958, 1961, 1968–69, 1975 and 1978. Exports increased mainly in 1951, 1953–54, 1956, 1960, 1962–66, 1969–70, 1972–73 and 1975–79, with substantial falls in 1952, 1967–68, 1971 and 1974. Unemployment, for the time covered, fell in 1970–73, 1976–77 and 1980, increasing in 1975 and 1978–79.

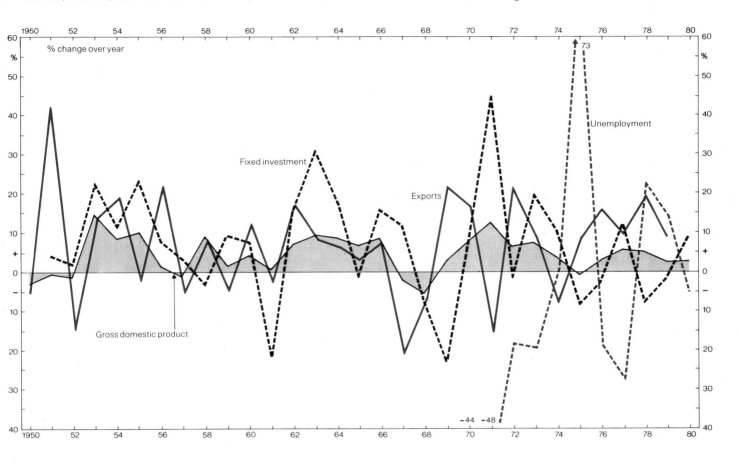

	Gross domestic product		Fixed investment		Exports		Unemployment		
	Index 1970 = 100	% change over year	Index 1970 = 100	% change over year	Index 1970 = 100	% change over year	Number (000)	% change over year	
1950	41.3	−2.8	33.2	na	30	−5	na	na	1950
1951	41.1	−0.7	34.7	4.7	44	43	na	na	1951
1952	40.7	−1.0	35.3	1.5	37	−15	na	na	1952
1953	46.7	14.8	43.1	22.3	42	14	na	na	1953
1954	50.6	8.4	48.3	12.0	50	19	na	na	1954
1955	55.8	10.3	59.6	23.5	49	−2	na	na	1955
1956	56.7	1.6	64.2	7.7	60	22	na	na	1956
1957	56.1	−1.0	66.6	3.6	57	−5	na	na	1957
1958	61.3	9.2	64.0	−3.8	62	9	na	na	1958
1959	62.5	2.0	69.9	9.3	59	−5	na	na	1959
1960	65.2	4.3	75.0	7.3	66	12	na	na	1960
1961	65.6	0.7	58.8	−21.6	65	−2	na	na	1961
1962	70.6	7.5	67.9	15.4	76	17	na	na	1962
1963	77.2	9.4	88.7	30.6	82	8	na	na	1963
1964	83.8	8.5	103.9	17.2	87	6	na	na	1964
1965	89.4	6.6	102.8	−1.0	90	3	na	na	1965
1966	97.0	8.5	119.1	15.8	96	7	na	na	1966
1967	95.4	−1.7	133.2	11.8	76	−21	na	na	1967
1968	90.0	−5.7	121.9	−8.4	71	−7	na	na	1968
1969	92.8	3.1	92.8	−23.9	86	21	1.95	na	1969
1970	100.0	7.8	100.0	7.8	100	16	1.10	−44	1970
1971	112.7	12.7	144.7	44.7	84	−16	0.57	−48	1971
1972	120.0	6.5	143.3	−1.0	102	21	0.46	−19	1972
1973	129.5	7.9	171.3	19.5	110	8	0.37	−20	1973
1974	134.7	4.0	189.1	10.4	101	−8	0.37	0	1974
1975	134.1	−0.5	173.0	−8.5	109	8	0.64	73	1975
1976	138.8	3.5	168.7	−2.5	125	15	0.51	−20	1976
1977	146.9	5.8	188.6	11.8	136	9	0.36	−28	1977
1978	154.6	5.2	174.6	−7.5	160	18	0.45	22	1978
1979	158.5	2.6	172.6	−1.1	173	8	0.50	13	1979
1980	162.9	2.8	188.1	9.0	na	na	0.47	−6	1980

India

Over the time for which figures are available, the main periods of expansion in gross domestic product were 1961–64, 1967–71, 1973–75 and 1977–78; there were falls or low growth in 1965–66, 1972, 1976 and 1979. Exports increased mainly in 1950, 1953–55, 1957, 1959, 1961–64, 1968 and alternate years 1970 to 1976, with falls in 1951–52, 1956, 1958, 1960, 1965, 1967, 1969 and 1977–78. Unemployment increased throughout the period 1950 to 1963, especially in 1953–54, 1958–59 and 1963; thereafter there were main increases in 1969–73 and 1978–80. Share prices increased mainly in 1950–51, 1954–55, 1959–60, 1969–70, 1973–74, 1976 and 1978–80.

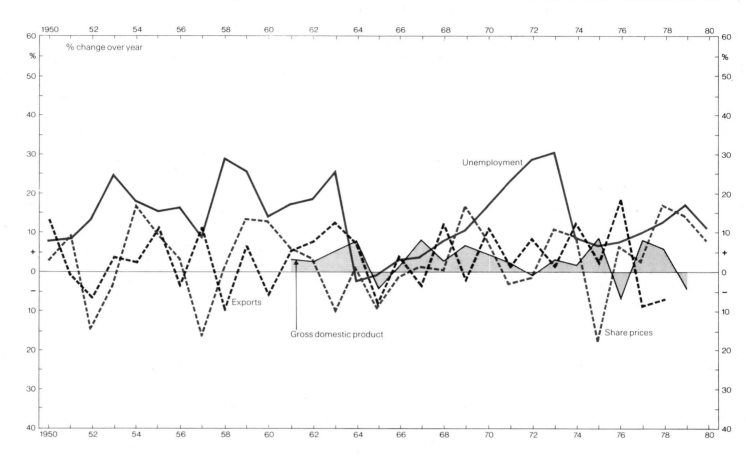

	Gross domestic product[a]		Exports		Unemployment		Share prices		
	Index 1970 = 100	% change over year	Index 1970 = 100	% change over year	Number (000)	% change over year	Index 1970 = 100	% change over year	
1950	na	na	64	13	314	7.3	70.7	2.5	1950
1951	na	na	64	−1	338	7.7	76.7	8.5	1951
1952	na	na	59	−7	384	13.5	65.1	−15.1	1952
1953	na	na	61	3	478	24.4	62.9	−3.4	1953
1954	na	na	62	2	562	17.7	73.2	16.4	1954
1955	na	na	69	11	647	15.1	80.0	9.3	1955
1956	na	na	66	−4	749	15.8	82.9	3.6	1956
1957	na	na	73	11	816	9.0	69.6	−16.0	1957
1958	na	na	66	−10	1049	28.5	69.9	0.4	1958
1959	na	na	70	6	1314	25.3	78.9	12.9	1959
1960	69.5	na	66	−6	1502	14.3	88.9	12.7	1960
1961	71.9	3.5	69	5	1754	16.8	94.1	5.8	1961
1962	73.9	2.7	74	7	2081	18.7	97.3	3.4	1962
1963	77.8	5.3	83	12	2605	25.2	87.4	−10.2	1963
1964	83.8	7.6	89	7	2542	−2.4	87.9	0.6	1964
1965	80.1	−4.3	82	−8	2527	−0.6	79.7	−9.3	1965
1966	81.0	1.1	85	4	2610	3.3	78.6	−1.4	1966
1967	87.7	8.2	82	−4	2706	3.7	79.2	0.8	1967
1968	90.1	2.8	92	12	2903	7.3	79.3	0.1	1968
1969	95.9	6.4	90	−2	3204	10.4	92.4	16.5	1969
1970	100.0	4.3	100	11	3726	16.3	100.0	8.2	1970
1971	102.3	2.3	101	1	4602	23.5	96.7	−3.3	1971
1972	101.6	−0.7	109	8	5928	28.8	95.1	−1.7	1972
1973	105.2	3.6	110	1	7714	30.1	105.0	10.4	1973
1974	106.8	1.5	123	12	8378	8.6	114.3	8.9	1974
1975	115.9	8.5	125	2	8918	6.4	94.1	−17.7	1975
1976	107.8	−7.0	148	18	9563	7.2	100.1	6.4	1976
1977	116.9	8.4	134	−9	10513	9.9	102.7	2.5	1977
1978	123.7	5.9	125	−7	11837	12.6	119.3	16.2	1978
1979	118.1	−4.5	na	na	13794	16.5	136.5	14.4	1979
1980	na	na	na	na	15317	11.0	147.4	7.9	1980

[a]Years beginning April 1st

Indonesia

Over the time for which figures are available, from 1961, the main periods of expansion in gross domestic product were 1961–62, 1964, and the full period 1968–80; there was a fall in 1963 and nil growth in 1965. Production of crude oil increased mainly in 1950–53, 1957, 1959–62, 1967–70, 1972–73 and 1976–77, with falls in 1963, 1966,

1975 and 1978–79. Exports, for the time covered, increased mainly in 1961, 1964–65, 1967–68, 1970–73 and 1976–78, with falls in 1962–63, 1966, 1969 and 1979–80. Consumer prices generally increased at a high rate throughout 1959–70 and 1973–80, with especially high increases for 1962–68.

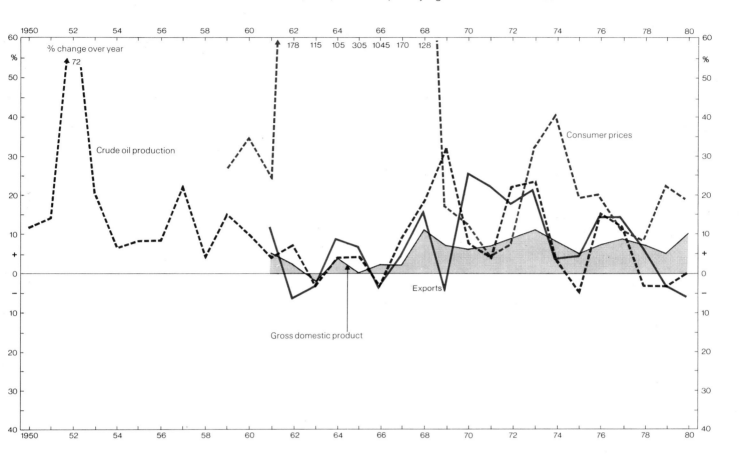

	Gross domestic product		Crude oil production		Exports		Consumer prices		
	Index 1970 = 100	% change over year	Index 1970 = 100	% change over year	Index 1970 = 100	% change over year	Index 1970 = 100	% change over year	
1950	na	na	10	12	na	na	na	na	1950
1951	na	na	12	14	na	na	na	na	1951
1952	na	na	20	72	na	na	na	na	1952
1953	na	na	24	20	na	na	na	na	1953
1954	na	na	25	6	na	na	na	na	1954
1955	na	na	28	8	na	na	na	na	1955
1956	na	na	30	8	na	na	na	na	1956
1957	na	na	36	22	na	na	na	na	1957
1958	na	na	38	4	na	na	0.01	na	1958
1959	na	na	44	15	na	na	0.01	26	1959
1960	69	na	48	10	65	na	0.02	34	1960
1961	73	5	50	4	72	11	0.02	24	1961
1962	74	2	54	7	67	−7	0.06	178	1962
1963	73	−2	52	−3	64	−4	0.13	115	1963
1964	75	4	54	4	69	8	0.27	105	1964
1965	75	0	56	4	73	6	1.09	305	1965
1966	77	2	55	−3	70	−4	12.5	1 045	1966
1967	79	2	60	9	73	4	33.7	170	1967
1968	88	11	70	18	84	15	77.0	128	1968
1969	94	7	93	32	80	−5	89.0	16	1969
1970	100	6	100	7	100	25	100.0	12	1970
1971	107	7	104	4	122	22	104.0	4	1971
1972	117	9	127	22	143	17	111.0	7	1972
1973	130	11	157	23	173	21	146.0	32	1973
1974	140	8	161	3	179	3	205.0	40	1974
1975	147	5	153	−5	186	4	244.0	19	1975
1976	157	7	176	15	212	14	292.3	20	1976
1977	171	9	197	12	242	14	324.8	11	1977
1978	183	7	191	−3	257	6	351.1	8	1978
1979	193	5	186	−3	249	−3	428.0	22	1979
1980	211	10	185	0	234	−6	507.3	19	1980

Iran

Over the time for which figures are available, 1960–77, the main periods of expansion in gross domestic product were 1965–69, 1971–73 and 1976, with stable growth in other years except for 1975 and 1977. Exports of crude oil increased mainly in 1950, 1954–59, 1961–73 and 1976, with falls in 1951–52, 1960, 1975 and 1977–80.

Consumer prices increased mainly in 1952–53, 1956–57, 1959–60, and, after a stable period for 1961–71, increased at a high rate from 1973 to 1980. International reserves increased mainly in 1955–57, 1961, 1963, 1965–67, 1971–75, 1977 and 1979, with falls in 1950–52, 1959–60, 1964, 1968, 1970 and 1978.

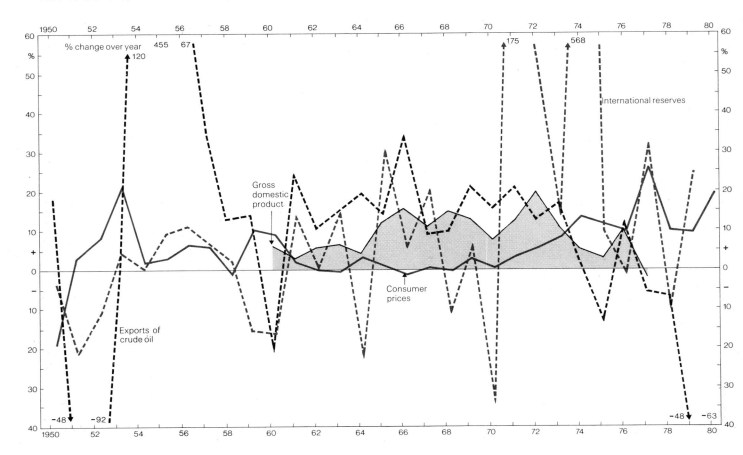

	Gross domestic product[a]		Exports of crude oil		Consumer prices		International reserves		
	Index 1970 = 100	% change over year	Index 1970 = 100	% change over year	Index 1970 = 100	% change over year	Index 1970 = 100	% change over year	
1950	na	na	18.2	18	41.5	−18.2	120	−3	1950
1951	na	na	9.5	−48	43.2	4.2	95	−21	1951
1952	na	na	0.7	−92	47.0	8.7	85	−11	1952
1953	na	na	0.7	0	57.2	21.7	89	5	1953
1954	na	na	1.6	120	58.6	2.4	89	1	1954
1955	na	na	9.0	455	60.6	3.4	99	10	1955
1956	na	na	15.0	67	65.0	7.3	110	12	1956
1957	na	na	20.3	35	69.2	6.5	118	7	1957
1958	na	na	22.9	13	69.0	−0.3	122	3	1958
1959	38.0	na	26.0	14	76.7	11.2	104	−15	1959
1960	40.4	6.4	20.5	−21	84.4	10.0	88	−16	1960
1961	41.7	3.2	25.5	24	87.0	3.1	100	14	1961
1962	44.3	6.3	28.4	11	87.6	0.7	101	1	1962
1963	47.2	6.6	32.6	15	87.8	0.2	116	15	1963
1964	49.4	4.6	38.8	19	91.3	4.0	92	−21	1964
1965	55.5	12.3	44.3	14	93.2	2.1	121	31	1965
1966	64.2	15.7	59.5	34	92.9	−0.3	129	7	1966
1967	71.4	11.3	65.0	9	94.4	1.6	156	21	1967
1968	82.1	15.0	71.3	10	94.9	0.5	140	−10	1968
1969	92.8	13.0	86.2	21	98.4	3.7	149	7	1969
1970	100.0	7.8	100.0	16	100.0	1.6	100	−33	1970
1971	112.6	12.6	120.7	21	104.2	4.2	275	175	1971
1972	135.0	19.9	136.5	13	111.0	6.5	425	55	1972
1973	150.4	11.4	159.7	17	121.9	9.8	493	16	1973
1974	158.5	5.4	162.5	2	139.2	14.2	3 292	568	1974
1975	162.9	2.8	141.4	−13	157.0	12.8	3 654	11	1975
1976	180.3	10.7	157.8	12	174.7	11.3	3 655	0	1976
1977	176.5	−2.1	147.6	−6	222.5	27.3	4 855	33	1977
1978	na	na	136.6	−7	248.4	11.6	4 484	−8	1978
1979	na	na	70.4	−48	274.4	10.5	5 616	25	1979
1980	na	na	26.2	−63	331.3	20.7	na	na	1980

[a]Years beginning March 21st

78

Iraq

Over the time for which figures are available, 1966–78, the main periods of expansion in gross domestic product were 1966, 1968 and 1973–78, with stable growth in other years except for 1967. Exports of crude oil increased mainly in 1950–55, 1958–60, 1963–66, 1968, 1971, 1973, 1975–76 and 1978–79, with falls in 1956–57, 1967, 1972,

1974, 1977 and 1980. Consumer prices increased mainly in 1951–52, 1956–57, and, after a comparatively stable period for 1960–73, increased at a high rate for 1974–77. International reserves increased mainly in 1950, 1952–56, 1958–59, 1963, 1966–68, 1971–74 and 1976–77, with main falls in 1957, 1960–62, 1964–65 and 1975.

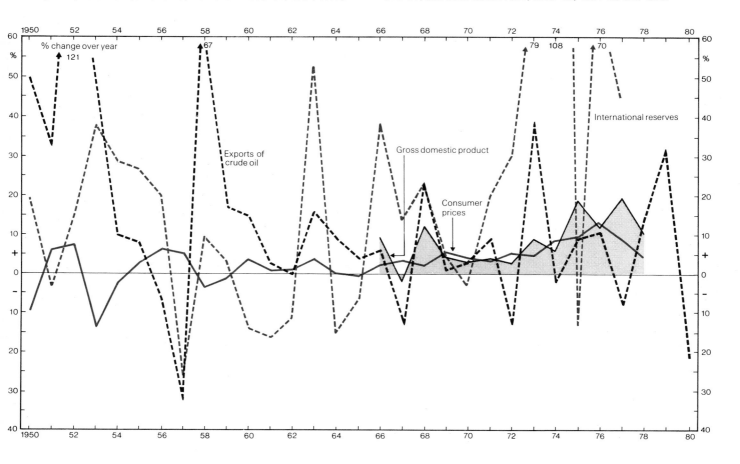

	Gross domestic product		Exports of crude oil		Consumer prices		International reserves		
	Index 1970 = 100	% change over year	Index 1970 = 100	% change over year	Index 1970 = 100	% change over year	Index 1970 = 100	% change over year	
1950	na	na	8	50	71.4	−9.1	25	19	1950
1951	na	na	11	33	76.1	6.6	25	−3	1951
1952	na	na	24	121	82.1	7.8	28	15	1952
1953	na	na	37	51	71.4	−13.0	39	38	1953
1954	na	na	40	10	69.9	−2.1	50	29	1954
1955	na	na	44	8	72.0	3.0	64	27	1955
1956	na	na	40	−7	76.7	6.5	77	20	1956
1957	na	na	28	−32	80.6	5.1	57	−26	1957
1958	na	na	46	67	78.0	−3.2	63	10	1958
1959	na	na	54	17	77.0	−1.3	65	3	1959
1960	na	na	62	15	79.6	3.4	56	−14	1960
1961	na	na	64	3	80.4	1.0	47	−16	1961
1962	na	na	64	0	81.4	1.2	42	−11	1962
1963	na	na	74	16	84.6	3.9	64	53	1963
1964	na	na	81	9	84.6	0.0	54	−15	1964
1965	76.7	na	84	4	84.2	−0.5	51	−6	1965
1966	84.3	9.9	89	6	85.9	2.0	70	38	1966
1967	82.4	−2.2	78	−12	88.7	3.3	80	14	1967
1968	92.6	12.3	96	23	90.7	2.3	98	23	1968
1969	97.0	4.8	97	1	95.8	5.6	103	5	1969
1970	100.0	3.1	100	3	100.0	4.4	100	−3	1970
1971	104.4	4.4	109	9	103.6	3.6	120	20	1971
1972	107.4	2.9	95	−13	109.0	5.2	156	30	1972
1973	117.2	9.1	131	38	114.3	4.9	279	79	1973
1974	124.4	6.1	128	−2	123.8	8.3	579	108	1974
1975	147.8	18.8	139	9	135.5	9.5	504	−13	1975
1976	165.4	11.9	154	11	152.8	12.8	857	70	1976
1977	197.9	19.6	142	−8	166.8	9.1	1247	45	1977
1978	218.0	10.2	161	14	174.5	4.6	na	na	1978
1979	na	na	213	32	na	na	na	na	1979
1980	na	na	165	−22	na	na	na	na	1980

Ireland

The main periods of expansion in gross domestic product were 1950–53, 1955, 1959–64, 1967–69, 1972–73 and 1977–78; there were falls or a low rate of growth in 1954, 1956–58, 1965–66, 1970–71, 1975–76 and 1979–80. Consumers expenditure increased mainly in 1950, 1953, 1955, 1960–64, 1967–69, 1972–73 and 1977–79, with falls in 1952, 1956–57 and 1975. Fixed investment increased mainly in 1950–51, 1954–55, 1959–65, 1967–69, 1971–73 and 1976–79; there were falls in 1952–53, 1956–58, 1966, 1974–75 and 1980. Exports increased mainly in 1950, 1952–53, 1957, 1960–61, 1963–64, 1966–68, 1970–75 and 1977–80.

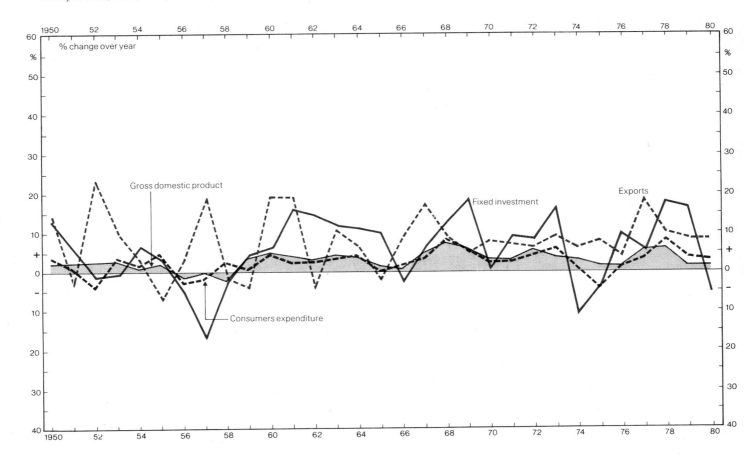

	Gross domestic product		Consumers expenditure		Fixed investment		Exports		
	Index 1970 = 100	% change over year	Index 1970 = 100	% change over year	Index 1970 = 100	% change over year	Index 1970 = 100	% change over year	
1950	55.4	2.1	62.0	3.7	39.7	12.8	28	14	1950
1951	56.7	2.4	62.8	1.4	42.0	5.7	27	−3	1951
1952	58.2	2.6	60.4	−3.9	41.5	−1.1	33	23	1952
1953	59.7	2.7	62.4	3.4	41.3	−0.5	36	10	1953
1954	60.3	1.0	63.4	1.5	44.2	7.0	38	3	1954
1955	61.8	2.5	66.5	5.0	45.9	3.8	35	−7	1955
1956	61.0	−1.3	64.8	−2.6	43.3	−5.6	36	3	1956
1957	61.0	−0.1	63.6	−1.8	36.1	−16.7	43	19	1957
1958	59.7	−2.1	65.4	2.8	35.2	−2.5	42	−2	1958
1959	62.2	4.1	66.1	1.0	36.9	4.9	40	−4	1959
1960	65.6	5.6	69.3	5.0	39.4	6.7	48	19	1960
1961	68.7	4.7	71.3	2.8	45.7	15.9	57	19	1961
1962	71.3	3.7	73.8	3.6	52.4	14.8	55	−4	1962
1963	74.7	4.8	76.9	4.1	58.7	12.0	60	11	1963
1964	77.8	4.2	80.2	4.3	65.5	11.6	65	7	1964
1965	79.4	2.0	80.5	0.4	72.0	10.0	64	−2	1965
1966	80.2	1.0	81.8	1.7	69.9	−2.9	69	8	1966
1967	84.3	5.1	84.6	3.4	74.5	6.5	81	17	1967
1968	91.1	8.1	91.9	8.5	84.2	13.1	88	9	1968
1969	96.6	6.1	97.2	5.7	99.7	18.3	92	5	1969
1970	100.0	3.5	100.0	2.9	100.0	0.3	100	8	1970
1971	103.4	3.4	103.2	3.2	108.8	8.8	107	7	1971
1972	109.6	6.0	107.9	4.5	117.4	7.9	114	6	1972
1973	114.2	4.2	114.7	6.4	136.4	16.2	125	9	1973
1974	118.4	3.7	116.9	1.9	120.6	−11.6	131	6	1974
1975	121.0	2.2	112.1	−4.1	115.3	−4.4	142	8	1975
1976	123.4	2.0	114.3	2.0	126.8	10.0	147	4	1976
1977	130.6	5.8	118.7	3.9	134.1	5.7	173	18	1977
1978	138.8	6.3	129.2	8.8	157.9	17.8	191	10	1978
1979	141.5	1.9	133.8	3.6	183.7	16.3	207	8	1979
1980	144.1	1.9	137.9	3.0	173.4	−5.6	224	8	1980

Ireland

Unemployment increased mainly in 1956–57, 1963, 1966–67, 1970–72, 1974–76 and 1980, and fell in 1954–55, 1958–61, 1964, 1969, 1973 and 1977–79. Consumer prices increased at a comparatively high rate over 1951–53, then increased at a stable rate until 1968 with lower rates in 1954–55 and 1959–60; there was a high rate of increase for 1969–80, with some slackening in 1978. Share prices increased mainly in 1954–55, 1959–64, 1968, 1972–73 and 1977–79, with falls especially in 1952–53, 1956–57, 1965–66, 1970–71 and 1974. The interest rate, for the time covered, increased in 1973–74, 1976 and 1978–80, with falls in 1972, 1975 and 1977.

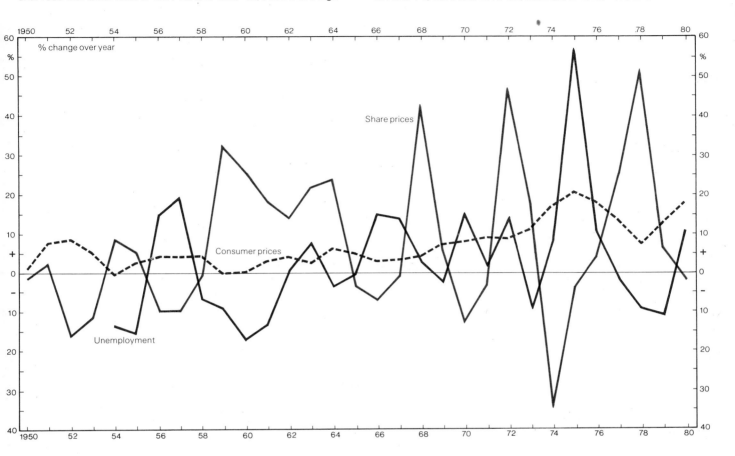

	Unemployment		Consumer prices		Share prices		Interest rate		
	Number (000)	% change over year	Index 1970 = 100	% change over year	Index 1970 = 100	% change over year	%	Change over year[a]	
1950	na	na	43.4	1.0	33.3	−1.4	na	na	1950
1951	na	na	46.8	7.9	34.2	2.6	na	na	1951
1952	na	na	51.1	9.1	28.8	−15.8	na	na	1952
1953	41.6	na	53.8	5.3	25.6	−11.1	na	na	1953
1954	36.1	−13	53.8	0.0	27.9	9.0	na	na	1954
1955	30.8	−15	55.2	2.6	29.5	5.7	na	na	1955
1956	35.4	15	57.5	4.2	26.7	−9.5	na	na	1956
1957	42.1	19	59.9	4.2	24.2	−9.4	na	na	1957
1958	39.1	−7	62.6	4.5	24.2	0.0	na	na	1958
1959	35.7	−9	62.6	0.0	32.1	32.6	na	na	1959
1960	29.6	−17	62.8	0.3	40.4	25.9	na	na	1960
1961	25.8	−13	64.6	2.9	47.9	18.6	na	na	1961
1962	26.2	1	67.3	4.2	54.8	14.4	na	na	1962
1963	28.4	8	69.0	2.5	66.9	22.1	na	na	1963
1964	27.5	−3	73.6	6.7	83.3	24.5	na	na	1964
1965	27.5	0	77.3	5.0	81.0	−2.8	na	na	1965
1966	31.8	15	79.6	3.0	75.6	−6.7	na	na	1966
1967	36.2	14	82.2	3.3	75.4	−0.3	na	na	1967
1968	37.3	3	86.0	4.6	107.5	42.6	na	na	1968
1969	36.1	−3	92.4	7.4	113.7	5.8	na	na	1969
1970	41.6	15	100.0	8.2	100.0	−12.0	na	na	1970
1971	42.4	2	108.9	8.9	97.0	−3.0	5.87	na	1971
1972	48.2	14	118.4	8.7	142.7	47.1	5.76	−0.11	1972
1973	44.0	−9	131.8	11.3	168.6	18.1	10.04	4.28	1973
1974	48.1	9	154.2	17.0	113.2	−32.9	11.31	1.27	1974
1975	75.4	57	186.4	20.9	109.3	−3.4	9.97	−1.34	1975
1976	83.5	11	220.0	18.0	114.2	4.5	10.83	0.86	1976
1977	81.9	−2	250.0	13.6	143.4	25.6	7.73	−3.10	1977
1978	74.7	−9	269.0	7.6	217.1	51.4	8.42	0.69	1978
1979	66.4	−11	304.6	13.2	232.3	7.0	13.47	5.05	1979
1980	73.7	11	360.1	18.2	228.4	−1.6	15.37	1.90	1980

[a] In percentage points

Israel

The main periods of expansion in gross domestic product were 1951, 1954–65 and 1968–72, followed by lower growth for 1973–74 and 1978–79, and very low growth in 1976–77 and 1980; gross domestic product fell in 1952–53 and there was low growth in 1966–67. Fixed investment increased mainly in 1951–57, 1961–62, 1964, 1968–73

and 1978–79, with falls in 1966–67 and 1974–77. Exports increased mainly in 1951, 1953–54, 1956–57, 1959–63, 1965–72, 1974, 1976–77 and 1980, with falls in 1952, 1955 and 1973. Share prices rose mainly in 1951, 1953–54, 1959–61, 1963, 1972–73 and 1975–80, with falls in 1955–58, 1964–67, 1970 and 1974.

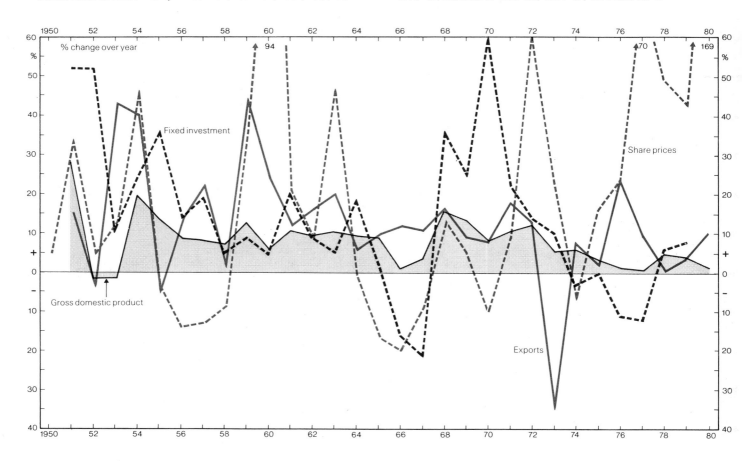

	Gross domestic product		Fixed investment		Exports		Share prices		
	Index 1970 = 100	% change over year	Index 1970 = 100	% change over year	Index 1970 = 100	% change over year	Index 1970 = 100	% change over year	
1950	16.0	na	5	na	6	na	20.5	5	1950
1951	20.6	28.8	7	52	7	15	27.2	33	1951
1952	20.3	−1.6	11	52	7	−3	28.5	5	1952
1953	20.0	−1.4	12	11	10	43	32.3	13	1953
1954	23.9	19.5	15	24	13	40	47.1	46	1954
1955	27.1	13.6	21	36	13	−5	45.2	−4	1955
1956	29.5	9.0	23	14	14	14	38.9	−14	1956
1957	32.1	8.8	28	19	18	22	33.7	−13	1957
1958	34.5	7.2	29	5	18	2	30.8	−9	1958
1959	38.9	12.7	32	9	26	44	42.3	37	1959
1960	41.4	6.6	33	5	32	24	82.2	94	1960
1961	45.9	10.9	40	20	36	12	99.1	21	1961
1962	50.5	9.9	44	9	42	16	107.7	9	1962
1963	55.8	10.5	46	5	50	20	157.6	46	1963
1964	61.3	9.8	55	18	53	6	155.3	−1	1964
1965	66.8	9.1	56	2	59	10	128.2	−17	1965
1966	67.7	1.4	47	−16	66	12	103.2	−20	1966
1967	70.2	3.7	37	−21	73	11	94.0	−9	1967
1968	81.4	15.9	50	36	85	16	105.8	13	1968
1969	92.3	13.4	63	25	93	9	110.8	5	1969
1970	100.0	8.3	100	59	100	8	100.0	−10	1970
1971	110.7	10.7	122	22	118	18	109.5	9	1971
1972	124.1	12.1	138	14	132	12	175.2	60	1972
1973	131.0	5.5	152	10	86	−35	214.2	22	1973
1974	138.6	5.8	148	−3	92	7	199.0	−7	1974
1975	143.4	3.4	147	0	94	2	230.0	16	1975
1976	145.3	1.4	131	−11	116	23	282.9	23	1976
1977	146.1	0.6	116	−12	126	9	481.2	70	1977
1978	153.3	4.9	123	6	126	0	716.0	49	1978
1979	159.8	4.2	133	8	130	3	1 023.5	43	1979
1980	162.7	1.8	na	na	143	10	2 748.7	169	1980

Italy

Gross domestic product increased at a comparatively high and stable rate over the period 1950 to 1970, although with lower growth in 1952, 1954 and 1964–65; thereafter the main periods of expansion were 1972–74, 1976 and 1979–80, with low or negative growth in 1971, 1975 and 1977–78. Consumers expenditure also increased at a steady rate from 1951 until 1970, with some slackening in 1954 and 1964–65, thereafter increasing mainly in 1972–73, 1976 and 1979–80. Government expenditure increased at a stable rate throughout after a high rate for 1951. Fixed investment increased mainly in 1951–57, 1959–63, 1967–69, 1973–74 and 1979–80.

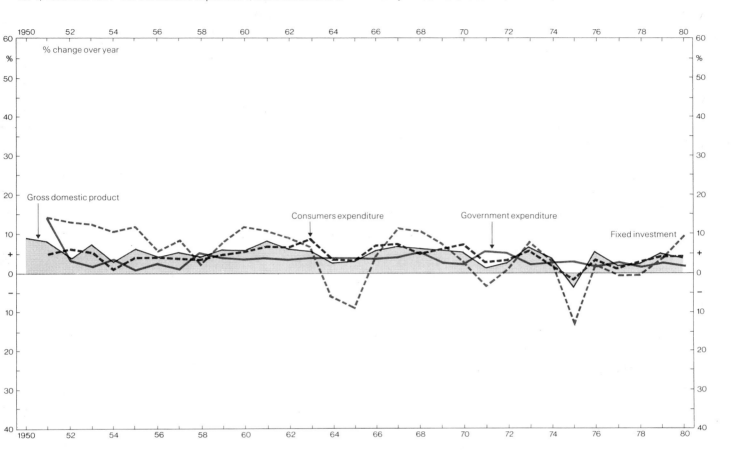

	Gross domestic product		Consumers expenditure		Government expenditure		Fixed investment		
	Index 1970 = 100	% change over year	Index 1970 = 100	% change over year	Index 1970 = 100	% change over year	Index 1970 = 100	% change over year	
1950	32.6	9.6	33.7	na	43.5	na	22.7	na	1950
1951	35.3	8.5	35.5	5.1	49.8	14.6	26.0	14.7	1951
1952	36.9	4.4	37.8	6.6	51.9	4.2	29.6	14.1	1952
1953	39.7	7.5	40.1	6.2	53.1	2.2	33.5	13.1	1953
1954	41.1	3.6	40.7	1.5	55.3	4.3	37.3	11.4	1954
1955	43.8	6.7	42.5	4.3	56.3	1.7	42.0	12.3	1955
1956	45.9	4.7	44.5	4.7	58.2	3.4	44.7	6.6	1956
1957	48.3	5.3	46.3	4.1	59.2	1.7	48.8	9.0	1957
1958	50.7	4.8	48.2	4.0	62.4	5.5	50.1	2.6	1958
1959	54.0	6.5	50.6	5.0	65.2	4.4	54.4	8.7	1959
1960	57.4	6.3	53.7	6.1	67.8	4.0	61.1	12.3	1960
1961	62.1	8.2	57.7	7.5	70.8	4.4	68.1	11.6	1961
1962	66.0	6.2	61.8	7.1	73.5	3.9	74.8	9.8	1962
1963	69.7	5.6	67.5	9.3	76.7	4.3	80.8	8.1	1963
1964	71.6	2.8	69.8	3.3	79.9	4.2	76.1	−5.8	1964
1965	73.9	3.3	72.0	3.3	83.1	4.0	69.7	−8.4	1965
1966	78.4	6.0	77.2	7.2	86.4	4.0	72.8	4.3	1966
1967	84.0	7.2	82.9	7.4	90.2	4.4	81.3	11.7	1967
1968	89.5	6.5	87.2	5.2	94.8	5.2	90.1	10.8	1968
1969	95.0	6.1	92.9	6.6	97.5	2.8	97.1	7.8	1969
1970	100.0	5.3	100.0	7.6	100.0	2.6	100.0	3.0	1970
1971	101.6	1.6	102.9	2.9	105.7	5.7	96.8	−3.2	1971
1972	104.9	3.2	106.4	3.4	111.3	5.3	97.7	0.9	1972
1973	112.3	7.0	112.7	5.9	114.0	2.4	105.2	7.7	1973
1974	116.9	4.1	115.7	2.6	117.2	2.8	108.7	3.3	1974
1975	112.7	−3.6	113.8	−1.6	121.0	3.2	94.9	−12.7	1975
1976	119.3	5.9	117.8	3.4	123.6	2.2	97.1	2.3	1976
1977	121.6	1.9	119.4	1.4	127.1	2.8	96.8	−0.4	1977
1978	124.7	2.6	122.5	2.6	129.4	1.9	96.7	−0.1	1978
1979	130.9	5.0	128.4	4.8	133.0	2.7	101.1	4.5	1979
1980	136.0	4.0	134.0	4.4	135.7	2.0	111.1	10.0	1980

Exports increased mainly in 1950–51, 1954–57, 1959–62, 1964–66, 1968–72, 1974 and 1976–79; there was a fall or slackening of growth in 1952, 1958, 1963, 1967, 1973, 1975 and 1980. Imports increased mainly in 1950–53; 1955–57, 1959–63, 1966–67, 1969–70, 1972–73, 1976 and 1978–79; imports fell in 1958, 1964, 1974–75 and 1977.

Unemployment increased mainly in 1951–53, 1956, 1964–66, 1972, 1975–77 and 1979; main reductions in unemployment were in 1950, 1955, 1957–63, 1967, 1969–70 and 1974. Consumer prices were comparatively stable until 1969, except for high increases in 1951 and 1962–65; they increased markedly over 1973–80.

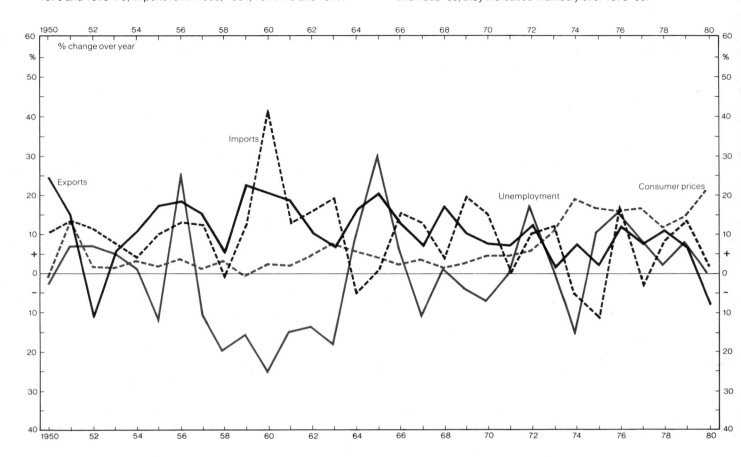

	Exports		Imports		Unemployment		Consumer prices		
	Index 1970 = 100	% change over year	Index 1970 = 100	% change over year	Number (000)	% change over year	Index 1970 = 100	% change over year	
1950	9.8	24.7	10.9	10.7	2538	−3	50.6	−1.0	1950
1951	11.2	15.1	12.4	13.2	2705	7	56.9	12.5	1951
1952	10.1	−10.1	13.8	11.7	2907	7	57.9	1.8	1952
1953	10.7	5.9	15.0	8.7	3060	5	58.8	1.6	1953
1954	11.9	11.2	15.7	4.7	3079	1	60.5	2.9	1954
1955	14.0	17.6	17.3	10.2	2702	−12	61.9	2.3	1955
1956	16.6	18.6	19.6	13.3	3369	25	64.0	3.4	1956
1957	19.1	15.1	22.1	12.8	2997	−11	64.8	1.2	1957
1958	20.2	5.8	22.0	−0.5	2412	−20	66.7	2.9	1958
1959	24.8	22.8	24.8	12.7	2038	−16	66.3	−0.6	1959
1960	29.9	20.6	35.2	41.9	1525	−25	67.9	2.4	1960
1961	35.5	18.7	39.8	13.1	1295	−15	69.3	2.1	1961
1962	39.2	10.4	46.3	16.3	1115	−14	72.5	4.6	1962
1963	41.9	6.9	55.3	19.4	919	−18	78.0	7.6	1963
1964	48.7	16.2	52.6	−4.9	1002	9	82.6	5.9	1964
1965	58.7	20.5	53.2	1.1	1303	30	86.3	4.5	1965
1966	66.2	12.8	61.3	15.2	1385	6	88.3	2.3	1966
1967	71.1	7.4	69.4	13.2	1239	−11	91.6	3.7	1967
1968	83.6	17.6	72.3	4.2	1248	1	92.8	1.3	1968
1969	92.5	10.6	86.5	19.6	1195	−4	95.3	2.7	1969
1970	100.0	8.1	100.0	15.6	1111	−7	100.0	4.9	1970
1971	107.6	7.6	100.4	0.4	1109	0	104.8	4.8	1971
1972	120.6	12.1	110.6	10.2	1297	17	110.8	5.7	1972
1973	122.9	1.9	123.9	12.0	1305	1	122.8	10.8	1973
1974	132.0	7.4	117.1	−5.5	1113	−15	146.3	19.1	1974
1975	135.0	2.3	103.8	−11.4	1230	11	171.1	17.0	1975
1976	151.3	12.1	122.1	17.6	1426	16	199.8	16.8	1976
1977	163.4	7.9	118.6	−2.8	1545	8	233.9	17.0	1977
1978	182.0	11.4	129.0	8.7	1571	2	262.3	12.1	1978
1979	194.9	7.1	146.3	13.4	1698	8	301.0	14.7	1979
1980	179.6	−7.9	149.2	2.0	1698	0	364.8	21.2	1980

Italy

Share prices increased mainly in 1951–55, 1957, 1959–61, 1966, 1969, 1973 and 1979–80; there were falls in 1950, 1956, 1962–65, 1967–68, 1970–72 and 1974–77. Money stock increased at a comparatively high and steady rate over the full period, with rather higher increases for 1951–52, 1959–63, 1965–67, 1970–73 and 1976–79. International reserves increased mainly in 1953–55, 1957–59, 1961, 1965, 1967, 1970–71 and 1976–80, with falls in 1952, 1963, 1968–69, 1972–73 and 1975. The interest rate, for the time covered, increased in 1970, 1973–74, 1976 and 1979–80, and fell in 1971–72, 1975 and 1977–78.

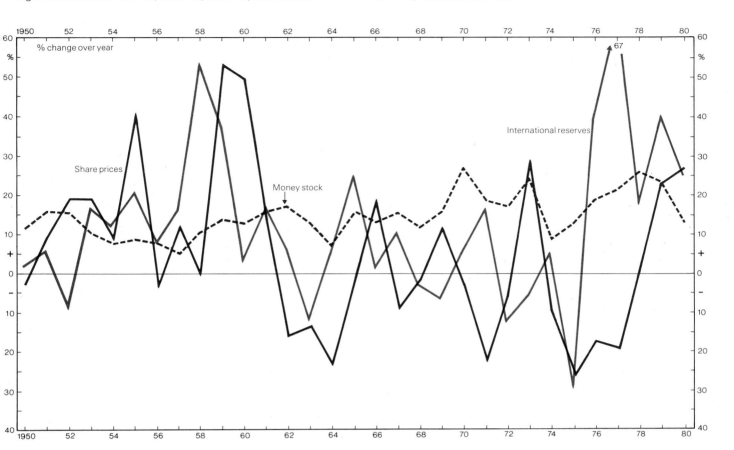

	Share prices		Money stock		International reserves		Interest rate		
	Index 1970 = 100	% change over year	Index 1970 = 100	% change over year	Index 1970 = 100	% change over year	%	Change over year[a]	
1950	22.2	−2.6	8.3	11.7	13.7	2.5	na	na	1950
1951	24.4	9.9	9.6	16.2	14.6	6.1	na	na	1951
1952	29.0	18.6	11.1	15.7	13.4	−8.1	na	na	1952
1953	34.4	18.6	12.3	10.6	15.7	17.5	na	na	1953
1954	37.8	9.9	13.3	8.3	17.8	13.4	na	na	1954
1955	53.3	41.0	14.6	9.3	21.6	21.3	na	na	1955
1956	51.8	−2.8	15.7	8.1	23.4	8.2	na	na	1956
1957	58.3	12.5	16.5	5.1	27.4	17.1	na	na	1957
1958	58.6	0.5	18.3	10.7	42.2	54.0	na	na	1958
1959	89.9	53.4	20.9	14.3	58.3	38.1	na	na	1959
1960	134.7	49.8	23.8	13.7	60.7	4.2	na	na	1960
1961	153.8	14.2	27.6	16.0	71.0	16.9	na	na	1961
1962	130.5	−15.1	32.4	17.6	76.0	7.1	na	na	1962
1963	112.8	−13.6	36.9	13.6	67.6	−11.0	na	na	1963
1964	86.6	−23.2	39.6	7.5	71.4	5.7	na	na	1964
1965	85.7	−1.0	46.2	16.4	89.7	25.5	na	na	1965
1966	101.5	18.4	52.3	13.3	91.8	2.3	na	na	1966
1967	93.4	−8.0	60.5	15.7	102.1	11.2	na	na	1967
1968	92.0	−1.5	67.7	11.9	99.8	−2.2	na	na	1968
1969	102.7	11.6	78.5	15.9	94.3	−5.5	5.00	na	1969
1970	100.0	−2.6	100.0	27.4	100.0	6.1	7.38	2.38	1970
1971	78.1	−21.9	119.0	19.0	117.4	17.4	5.76	−1.62	1971
1972	74.1	−5.1	139.5	17.3	104.7	−10.8	5.18	−0.58	1972
1973	95.7	29.1	173.4	24.3	99.7	−4.8	6.93	1.75	1973
1974	87.6	−8.5	189.7	9.4	105.9	6.3	14.57	7.64	1974
1975	65.1	−25.7	215.2	13.5	76.2	−28.1	10.64	−3.93	1975
1976	53.6	−17.6	255.8	18.9	107.0	40.4	15.68	5.04	1976
1977	43.3	−19.3	310.7	21.4	178.9	67.2	14.03	−1.65	1977
1978	43.9	1.4	393.4	26.6	213.7	19.4	11.49	−2.54	1978
1979	54.1	23.3	486.6	23.7	301.7	41.2	11.86	0.37	1979
1980	68.7	27.0	549.4	12.9	382.6	26.8	17.17	5.31	1980

[a]In percentage points

Jamaica

The main periods of expansion in gross domestic product were 1953–57, 1960–61, 1964–65, 1967–70, 1972 and 1974; there were falls or low growth in 1951–52, 1958–59, 1962–63, 1966, 1971, 1973 and 1975–80 (with falls especially in 1976 and 1980). Exports increased mainly in 1950–51, 1953–54, 1956–57, 1960–61, 1963–64, 1969–70, 1972–74 and 1977; exports fell in 1952, 1958, 1967–68, 1975–76 and 1979. Consumer prices increased mainly in 1951–52, 1973–75 and 1978–80; they rose at a comparatively stable rate for 1953–72. The interest rate increased mainly in 1952–53, 1955–58, 1961–62, 1965–66, 1972–74 and 1978–80.

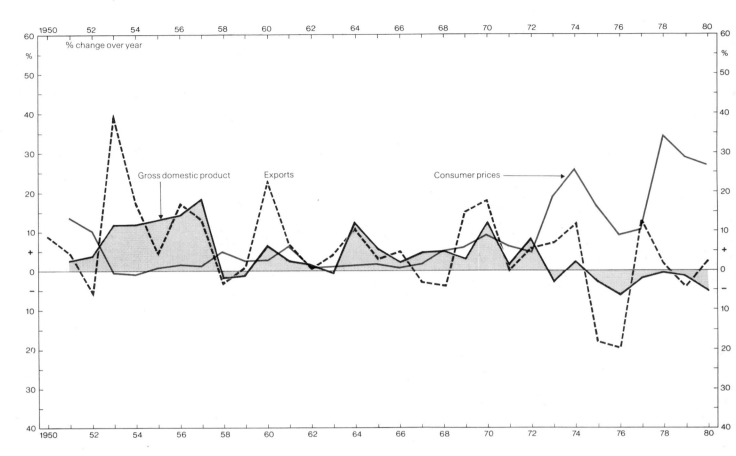

	Gross domestic product		Exports		Consumer prices		Interest rate		
	Index 1970 = 100	% change over year	Index 1970 = 100	% change over year	Index 1970 = 100	% change over year	%	Change over year[a]	
1950	30.3	na	22	9	45.1	na	1.50	0.00	1950
1951	31.0	2.3	23	4	51.3	13.7	1.50	0.00	1951
1952	32.1	3.5	22	−6	56.9	10.8	2.00	0.50	1952
1953	35.9	11.9	30	39	56.9	0.0	2.40	0.40	1953
1954	40.2	11.9	36	17	56.8	−0.2	2.00	−0.40	1954
1955	45.4	12.9	37	4	57.4	1.1	2.20	0.20	1955
1956	51.8	14.1	43	17	58.6	2.1	3.00	0.80	1956
1957	61.2	18.2	49	13	59.7	1.9	3.80	0.80	1957
1958	60.1	−1.9	47	−3	62.9	5.4	4.20	0.40	1958
1959	59.1	−1.5	48	1	64.8	3.0	3.70	−0.50	1959
1960	62.8	6.2	59	23	66.8	3.1	3.80	0.10	1960
1961	64.3	2.4	63	7	71.5	7.0	4.41	0.61	1961
1962	65.2	1.4	64	1	72.4	1.3	4.94	0.53	1962
1963	64.8	−0.6	66	4	73.6	1.7	4.01	−0.93	1963
1964	72.8	12.3	73	11	75.1	2.0	3.41	−0.60	1964
1965	76.8	5.6	75	3	77.2	2.8	4.39	0.98	1965
1966	78.6	2.3	79	5	78.7	1.9	4.65	0.26	1966
1967	82.2	4.7	77	−3	80.9	2.8	4.68	0.03	1967
1968	86.2	4.8	74	−4	85.7	5.9	4.47	−0.21	1968
1969	89.1	3.4	85	15	91.1	6.3	3.52	−0.95	1969
1970	100.0	12.2	100	18	100.0	9.8	4.03	0.51	1970
1971	101.8	1.8	100	0	106.7	6.7	3.81	−0.22	1971
1972	110.1	8.2	106	6	112.9	5.8	4.32	0.51	1972
1973	107.3	−2.6	113	7	135.4	19.9	5.54	1.22	1973
1974	110.0	2.5	126	12	171.1	26.4	7.19	1.65	1974
1975	107.2	−2.6	103	−18	200.0	16.9	6.94	−0.25	1975
1976	100.7	−6.1	82	−20	219.6	9.8	7.23	0.29	1976
1977	98.7	−1.9	93	13	244.2	11.2	7.21	−0.02	1977
1978	98.5	−0.3	95	2	329.4	34.9	8.26	1.05	1978
1979	97.1	−1.4	91	−4	425.2	29.1	9.24	0.98	1979
1980	91.8	−5.4	94	3	540.6	27.1	9.93	0.69	1980

[a]In percentage points

Japan

The main periods of expansion in gross domestic product were 1950–51, 1955–57, 1959–61, 1963–64, 1966–70, 1972–73 and 1976–79; the rate of growth slackened or fell in 1952, 1954, 1958, 1962, 1965, 1971, 1974–75 and 1980. Consumers expenditure increased at a steady rate except for lower growth in 1954, 1965, 1971, 1974 and 1980. Government expenditure changed little over 1953–57, then increased at a steady rate throughout the period, with some slackening in 1974 and 1980. Fixed investment increased mainly in 1953, 1956–57, 1959–64, 1966–70, 1972–73 and 1976–79, with a substantial fall in 1974–75 and lower growth in other years.

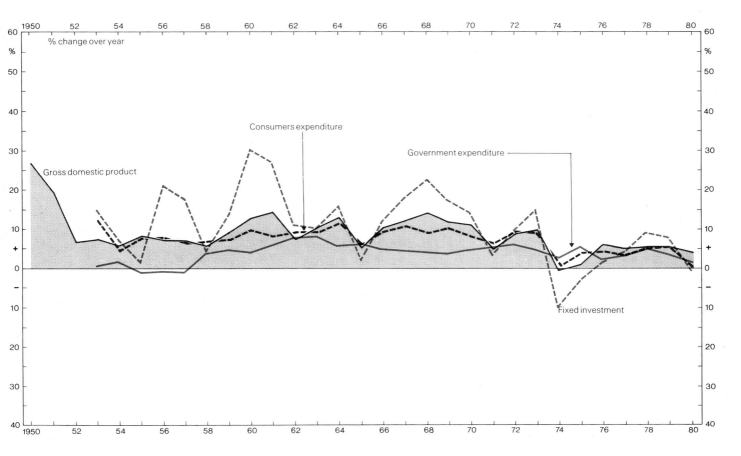

	Gross domestic product		Consumers expenditure		Government expenditure		Fixed investment		
	Index 1970 = 100	% change over year	Index 1970 = 100	% change over year	Index 1970 = 100	% change over year	Index 1970 = 100	% change over year	
1950	14.7	26.6	na	na	na	na	na	na	1950
1951	17.6	19.7	na	na	na	na	na	na	1952
1952	18.7	6.4	22.1	na	46.9	na	8.3	na	1951
1953	20.1	7.4	24.8	12.5	47.6	1.5	9.5	15.4	1953
1954	21.3	5.7	26.1	4.9	48.8	2.4	10.3	7.6	1954
1955	23.1	8.6	28.1	7.9	48.5	−0.5	10.5	2.0	1955
1956	24.8	7.5	30.3	7.8	48.3	−0.4	12.7	21.3	1956
1957	26.6	7.3	32.2	6.3	48.1	−0.6	15.1	18.4	1957
1958	28.2	5.8	34.5	7.2	50.2	4.5	15.8	4.7	1958
1959	30.8	9.1	37.2	7.8	52.9	5.2	18.0	14.4	1959
1960	34.8	13.1	41.0	10.0	55.3	4.5	23.6	30.7	1960
1961	39.9	14.6	44.4	8.4	58.6	6.1	30.1	27.8	1961
1962	42.7	7.1	48.6	9.5	63.6	8.4	33.5	11.3	1962
1963	47.1	10.5	53.3	9.6	69.1	8.7	37.0	10.4	1963
1964	53.4	13.2	59.5	11.6	73.2	6.0	43.2	16.7	1964
1965	56.1	5.1	62.9	5.6	77.9	6.3	44.6	3.2	1965
1966	62.2	10.9	68.8	9.4	82.2	5.5	50.4	13.0	1966
1967	70.0	12.4	76.2	10.8	86.4	5.1	59.8	18.7	1967
1968	79.8	14.1	83.5	9.6	90.6	4.9	73.8	23.3	1968
1969	89.5	12.2	92.2	10.4	94.8	4.6	87.1	18.1	1969
1970	100.0	11.7	100.0	8.5	100.0	5.5	100.0	14.8	1970
1971	105.1	5.1	106.6	6.6	105.9	5.9	104.2	4.2	1971
1972	114.9	9.3	117.1	9.9	113.3	7.0	115.0	10.4	1972
1973	126.4	10.0	128.3	9.5	119.4	5.3	132.6	15.3	1973
1974	125.9	−0.3	129.4	0.8	123.3	3.3	120.2	−9.4	1974
1975	127.7	1.4	134.9	4.2	131.0	6.3	117.6	−2.1	1975
1976	135.9	6.5	141.0	4.5	135.8	3.6	121.4	3.2	1976
1977	143.2	5.4	146.3	3.8	141.2	4.0	127.8	5.2	1977
1978	151.6	5.9	154.4	5.5	149.5	5.9	140.6	10.0	1978
1979	160.6	5.9	163.5	5.9	156.3	4.6	152.7	8.6	1979
1980	167.3	4.2	164.5	0.6	159.8	2.2	153.0	0.2	1980

87

Japan

Exports increased mainly in 1951, 1954–57, 1959–60, 1962–66, 1968–71, 1974, 1976–77 and 1980; there was a fall or low growth in 1952–53, 1958, 1961, 1967, 1972–73, 1975 and 1978–79. Imports increased mainly in 1951, 1953, 1956–57, 1959–61, 1963–64, 1966–70, 1972–73, 1976 and 1978–79. Unemployment increased

mainly in 1950, 1952, 1954–55, 1958–59, 1965–66, 1970–72, 1974–76 and 1978; there were falls in unemployment in 1951, 1953, 1956–57, 1960–64, 1967–69, 1973 and 1979–80. After high rates over 1951–54, consumer prices increased at a comparatively steady rate up to 1972, then at a high rate for 1973–77 and 1980.

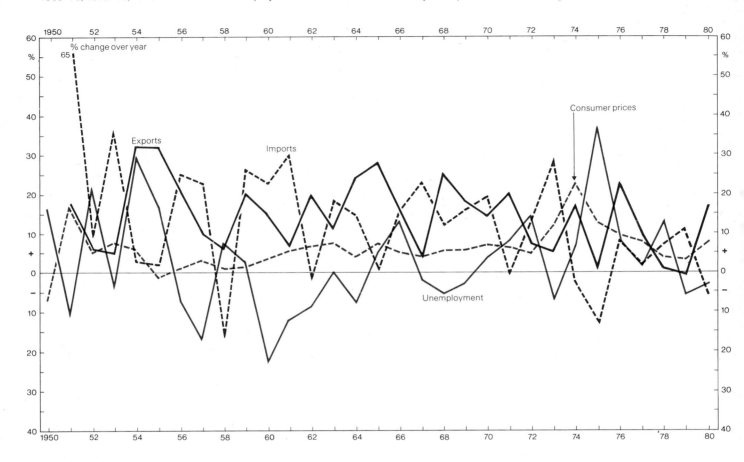

	Exports		Imports		Unemployment		Consumer prices		
	Index 1970 = 100	% change over year	Index 1970 = 100	% change over year	Number (000)	% change over year	Index 1970 = 100	% change over year	
1950	4.9	na	5.0	na	720	16	37.6	−7.1	1950
1951	5.8	18	8.2	65	639	−11	43.8	16.5	1951
1952	6.1	6	8.9	9	770	21	46.0	5.0	1952
1953	6.5	5	12.2	36	737	−4	49.5	7.6	1953
1954	8.5	32	12.5	3	950	29	52.2	5.5	1954
1955	11.2	32	12.8	2	1 113	17	51.5	−1.3	1955
1956	13.5	21	16.0	25	1 040	−7	51.9	0.8	1956
1957	14.9	10	19.7	23	864	−17	53.5	3.1	1957
1958	15.8	6	16.6	−16	923	7	54.0	0.9	1958
1959	18.9	20	20.9	26	952	3	54.8	1.5	1959
1960	21.8	15	25.7	23	733	−23	56.7	3.5	1960
1961	23.4	7	33.5	30	645	−12	59.7	5.3	1961
1962	28.0	20	33.1	−1	586	−9	63.7	6.7	1962
1963	31.2	11	39.2	18	586	0	68.7	7.8	1963
1964	38.6	24	45.1	15	542	−8	71.5	4.1	1964
1965	49.5	28	45.4	1	571	5	76.7	7.3	1965
1966	57.3	16	52.5	16	645	13	80.5	5.0	1966
1967	59.3	4	64.5	23	630	−2	83.7	4.0	1967
1968	74.0	25	72.3	12	590	−6	88.4	5.6	1968
1969	87.4	18	83.9	16	570	−3	93.3	5.5	1969
1970	100.0	14	100.0	19	590	4	100.0	7.2	1970
1971	120.2	20	99.9	0	640	8	106.3	6.3	1971
1972	128.5	7	112.9	13	730	14	111.5	4.9	1972
1973	134.9	5	144.5	28	680	−7	124.5	11.7	1973
1974	158.0	17	141.2	−2	730	7	152.7	22.7	1974
1975	159.3	1	123.3	−13	1 000	37	171.2	12.1	1975
1976	194.3	22	133.7	8	1 080	8	187.1	9.3	1976
1977	211.6	9	137.0	2	1 100	2	202.2	8.1	1977
1978	214.1	1	146.5	7	1 240	13	209.9	3.8	1978
1979	211.9	−1	162.3	11	1 170	−6	217.4	3.6	1979
1980	247.2	17	152.8	−6	1 140	−3	234.9	8.0	1980

Japan

Share prices increased mainly in 1951–53, 1955–57, 1959–61 and 1966 (recovery), 1968–73 (especially 1969 and 1972–73) and 1976–79; main falls were in 1950, 1954, 1962, 1964–65 and 1974. Money stock increased at a high and stable rate throughout the period, with a fall or low growth mainly in 1954, 1957 and 1979–80.

International reserves increased markedly in 1950–51, 1958–60, 1968–72 and 1976–78, with main falls in 1953, 1957, 1961, 1973 and 1979. The interest rate, for the time covered, increased mainly in 1961, 1964, 1967–68, 1973–74 and 1979–80, with main falls in 1958–59, 1962–63, 1965–66, 1971–72 and 1975–78.

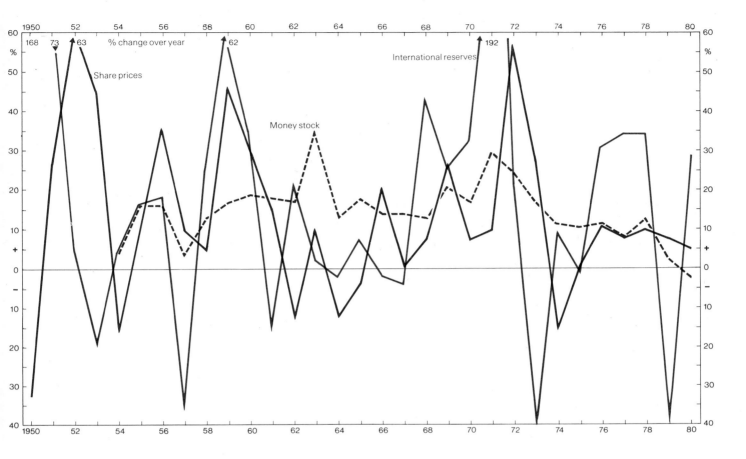

	Share prices		Money stock		International reserves		Interest rate		
	Index 1970 = 100	% change over year	Index 1970 = 100	% change over year	Index 1970 = 100	% change over year	%	Change over year[a]	
1950	7.0	−32	na	na	10.8	168	na	na	1950
1951	9.0	27	na	na	18.7	73	na	na	1951
1952	14.6	63	na	na	19.7	5	na	na	1952
1953	21.2	45	8.5	na	15.9	−19	na	na	1953
1954	17.9	−16	8.8	4	16.6	4	na	na	1954
1955	20.2	13	10.2	16	19.3	16	na	na	1955
1956	27.4	36	11.9	16	22.7	18	na	na	1956
1957	30.1	10	12.4	4	14.8	−35	11.78	na	1957
1958	31.6	5	14.0	13	18.5	25	9.69	−2.09	1958
1959	46.2	46	16.3	17	29.9	62	8.36	−1.33	1959
1960	59.5	29	19.4	19	40.3	35	8.40	0.04	1960
1961	68.6	15	23.0	18	34.4	−15	11.44	3.04	1961
1962	60.3	−12	26.8	17	41.8	21	10.31	−1.13	1962
1963	66.2	10	36.1	35	42.5	2	7.54	−2.77	1963
1964	58.5	−12	40.8	13	41.7	−2	10.03	2.49	1964
1965	56.1	−4	48.2	18	44.5	7	6.97	−3.06	1965
1966	67.2	20	54.9	14	43.8	−2	5.84	−1.13	1966
1967	67.6	1	62.6	14	41.9	−4	6.39	0.55	1967
1968	72.7	8	71.0	13	60.0	43	7.88	1.49	1968
1969	92.4	27	85.6	21	75.5	26	7.70	−0.18	1969
1970	100.0	8	100.0	17	100.0	32	8.29	0.59	1970
1971	109.9	10	129.7	30	292.3	192	6.42	−1.87	1971
1972	172.8	57	161.6	25	349.5	20	4.72	−1.70	1972
1973	221.7	28	188.7	17	209.8	−40	7.16	2.44	1973
1974	187.9	−15	210.4	12	228.1	9	12.54	5.38	1974
1975	190.6	1	233.8	11	226.2	−1	10.67	−1.87	1975
1976	212.5	11	263.0	12	295.3	31	6.98	−3.69	1976
1977	230.4	8	284.6	8	395.6	34	5.68	−1.30	1977
1978	253.9	10	322.7	13	531.3	34	4.36	−1.32	1978
1979	275.2	8	332.5	3	323.7	−39	5.86	1.50	1979
1980	289.9	5	325.7	−2	416.6	29	10.93	5.07	1980

[a] In percentage points

Jugoslavia

Over the time for which figures are available, from 1961, the main periods of expansion in gross material product were 1961–64, 1966, 1969–71, 1974 and 1977–79, with low growth for 1965 and stable growth for other years. Exports increased mainly in 1952, 1954, 1956–60, 1962–63, 1965–66, 1969, 1972–73 and 1976, with falls in 1950–51, 1953, 1955, 1975 and 1977–79. Imports increased mainly in 1951–53, 1955–58, 1960–61, 1963–64, 1966–67, 1969–71, 1973–74, 1977 and 1979, with main falls in 1950, 1954, 1962, 1972 and 1975–76. After a fall in 1952, consumer prices increased at a steady rate, but with higher price rises for 1965–66 and 1971–80.

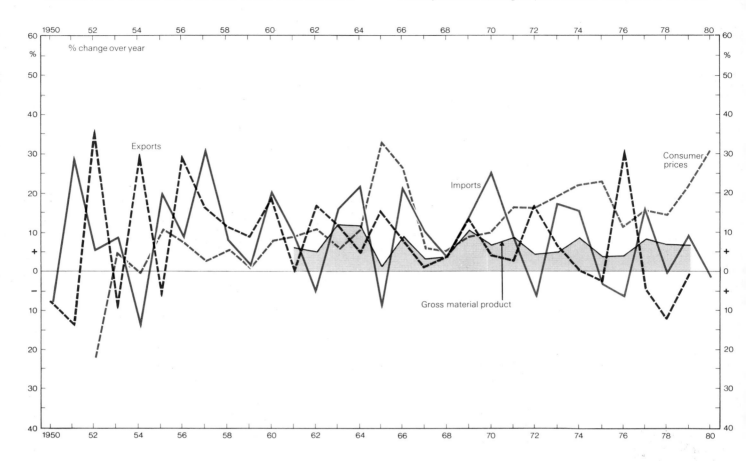

	Gross material product		Exports		Imports		Consumer prices		
	Index 1970 = 100	% change over year	Index 1970 = 100	% change over year	Index 1970 = 100	% change over year	Index 1970 = 100	% change over year	
1950	na	na	17	−8	13	−7	na	na	1950
1951	na	na	15	−13	17	29	27.1	na	1951
1952	na	na	20	35	18	6	21.0	−22	1952
1953	na	na	18	−9	19	9	22.0	5	1953
1954	na	na	23	29	17	−13	22.0	0	1954
1955	na	na	22	−6	20	20	24.4	11	1955
1956	na	na	28	29	22	9	26.3	8	1956
1957	na	na	33	17	29	31	27.1	3	1957
1958	na	na	37	12	31	8	28.7	6	1958
1959	na	na	40	9	32	2	29.0	1	1959
1960	51.8	na	47	18	38	20	31.4	8	1960
1961	55.0	6.2	47	0	42	9	34.3	9	1961
1962	57.8	5.0	55	17	40	−5	37.9	11	1962
1963	64.7	11.9	62	12	46	16	40.3	6	1963
1964	72.0	11.4	65	5	56	22	44.7	11	1964
1965	72.9	1.2	75	15	51	−9	59.4	33	1965
1966	79.4	8.8	81	8	62	22	74.9	26	1966
1967	81.7	2.9	82	1	68	10	79.7	6	1967
1968	84.9	3.9	85	4	71	4	83.8	5	1968
1969	93.6	10.2	96	13	80	13	91.3	9	1969
1970	100.0	6.9	100	4	100	25	100.0	10	1970
1971	108.3	8.3	103	3	109	9	115.7	16	1971
1972	112.8	4.2	121	17	102	−6	134.3	16	1972
1973	118.3	4.9	129	7	119	17	160.1	19	1973
1974	128.4	8.5	129	0	137	15	195.7	22	1974
1975	133.0	3.6	126	−2	133	−3	241.5	23	1975
1976	138.1	3.8	164	30	124	−7	268.6	11	1976
1977	149.1	8.0	158	−4	142	15	307.7	15	1977
1978	159.6	7.1	139	−12	141	−1	349.5	14	1978
1979	170.6	6.9	137	−1	153	8	424.2	21	1979
1980	na	na	na	na	150	−2	551.0	30	1980

Kenya

Over the time for which figures are available, from 1965, the main periods of expansion in gross domestic product were 1966–68, 1970–74 and 1976–78, with stable growth for 1979–80; low growth occurred in 1965 and 1975. Fixed investment increased mainly in 1966–67, 1970-71 and 1977–78, with falls or low growth in 1965, 1968–69, 1972–76 and 1979–80. Exports increased mainly in 1955–56, 1958–59, 1962–63, 1966, 1968–69, 1973 and 1976–77 (recovery from the fall of 1974–75); main falls were in 1957, 1967, 1974–75 and 1978–79. Imports increased mainly in 1951–52, 1954–55, 1960–61, 1965–66, 1970–71, 1974, 1977–78 and 1980.

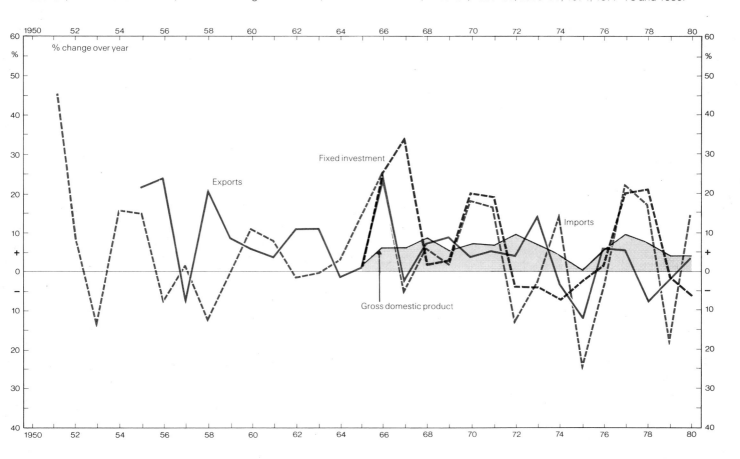

	Gross domestic product		Fixed investment		Exports		Imports		
	Index 1970 = 100	% change over year	Index 1970 = 100	% change over year	Index 1970 = 100	% change over year	Index 1970 = 100	% change over year	
1950	na	na	na	na	na	na	32	na	1950
1951	na	na	na	na	na	na	46	46	1951
1952	na	na	na	na	na	na	50	8	1952
1953	na	na	na	na	na	na	43	−13	1953
1954	na	na	na	na	27	na	50	16	1954
1955	na	na	na	na	33	22	58	15	1955
1956	na	na	na	na	41	24	53	−7	1956
1957	na	na	na	na	38	−7	54	2	1957
1958	na	na	na	na	46	21	48	−12	1958
1959	na	na	na	na	50	9	48	0	1959
1960	na	na	na	na	53	6	53	11	1960
1961	na	na	na	na	55	4	57	8	1961
1962	na	na	na	na	61	11	56	−1	1962
1963	na	na	na	na	68	11	56	0	1963
1964	70.7	na	46.9	na	67	−1	58	3	1964
1965	71.8	1.6	47.3	1	68	1	66	14	1965
1966	76.4	6.3	59.1	25	84	24	83	25	1966
1967	81.3	6.4	79.4	34	82	−2	78	−5	1967
1968	88.3	8.6	81.0	2	88	7	83	6	1968
1969	93.1	5.5	83.4	3	96	9	85	2	1969
1970	100.0	7.4	100.0	20	100	4	100	18	1970
1971	106.9	6.9	119.1	19	105	5	117	17	1971
1972	117.0	9.5	114.5	−4	109	4	102	−13	1972
1973	125.1	7.0	109.8	−4	124	14	98	−3	1973
1974	130.5	4.3	101.8	−7	120	−3	112	14	1974
1975	131.3	0.6	99.7	−2	106	−12	83	−25	1975
1976	138.5	5.5	100.6	1	112	6	80	−4	1976
1977	151.7	9.5	121.2	20	118	5	98	22	1977
1978	162.9	7.4	147.2	21	108	−8	114	17	1978
1979	169.5	4.0	145.5	−1	106	−2	93	−18	1979
1980	176.2	4.0	136.6	−6	109	3	107	14	1980

Korea, South

For the time covered, from 1954, the main periods of expansion in gross domestic product were 1954–55, 1957–59, 1961, and a long period from 1963 to 1979; there were falls in 1956 and 1980. Fixed investment increased mainly in 1954, 1957, 1962–63, 1965–69, 1973 and 1976–79, with main falls in 1955, 1958, 1964 and 1980.

Unemployment, for the time covered, increased mainly in 1960, 1962–63, 1971–72, 1974–75 and 1979–80; main reductions were in 1961, 1964–70, 1973 and 1978. Consumer prices increased markedly over 1950–55 then increased steadily from 1960, with main increases in 1963–64, 1974–75 and 1979–80.

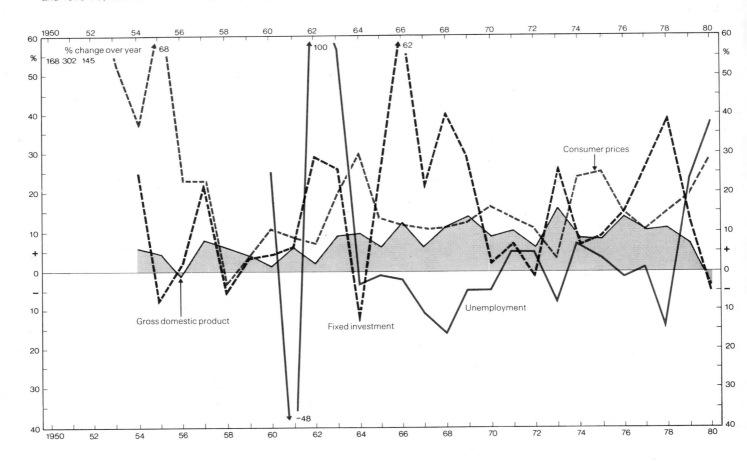

	Gross domestic product		Fixed investment		Unemployment		Consumer prices		
	Index 1970 = 100	% change over year	Index 1970 = 100	% change over year	Number (000)	% change over year	Index 1970 = 100	% change over year	
1950	na	na	na	na	na	na	0.5	167.9	1950
1951	na	na	na	na	na	na	1.9	301.9	1951
1952	na	na	na	na	na	na	4.7	144.7	1952
1953	34.3	na	10.0	na	na	na	7.1	52.6	1953
1954	36.3	5.6	12.5	25	na	na	9.8	37.0	1954
1955	37.9	4.5	11.6	−8	na	na	16.5	68.2	1955
1956	37.4	−1.3	11.8	2	na	na	20.3	23.1	1956
1957	40.3	7.6	14.4	22	na	na	25.0	23.2	1957
1958	42.5	5.5	13.6	−6	na	na	24.1	−3.7	1958
1959	44.1	3.9	14.0	3	353	na	24.8	3.1	1959
1960	44.6	1.1	14.5	4	442	25	27.4	10.2	1960
1961	47.2	5.9	15.4	6	230	−48	29.6	8.3	1961
1962	48.3	2.1	19.8	29	459	100	31.6	6.7	1962
1963	52.7	9.1	24.9	26	718	56	37.8	19.7	1963
1964	57.8	9.7	22.0	−12	695	−3	48.9	29.5	1964
1965	61.1	5.7	27.7	26	689	−1	55.6	13.6	1965
1966	68.5	12.2	44.9	62	678	−2	62.1	11.8	1966
1967	72.5	5.9	54.6	22	601	−11	69.0	11.1	1967
1968	80.8	11.3	76.6	40	505	−16	76.6	10.9	1968
1969	91.9	13.8	98.3	28	479	−5	86.2	12.5	1969
1970	100.0	8.8	100.0	2	454	−5	100.0	16.1	1970
1971	110.1	10.1	107.1	7	476	5	113.4	13.4	1971
1972	116.8	6.1	106.3	−1	499	5	126.7	11.7	1972
1973	134.7	15.3	134.5	26	461	−8	130.8	3.2	1973
1974	145.8	8.3	144.3	7	494	7	162.5	24.3	1974
1975	157.6	8.1	157.7	9	510	3	203.7	25.3	1975
1976	179.5	13.9	180.9	15	505	−1	234.8	15.3	1976
1977	197.5	10.1	229.1	27	511	1	258.7	10.1	1977
1978	219.9	11.3	319.5	39	442	−14	295.9	14.4	1978
1979	235.5	7.1	361.5	13	542	23	350.1	18.3	1979
1980	227.1	−3.6	343.9	−5	749	38	450.7	28.7	1980

Liberia

Over the time for which figures are available, from 1966, the main periods of expansion for gross domestic product were 1966–69, 1971–72, 1974, 1976 and 1978–79, with low growth or falls in 1970, 1973, 1975, 1977 and 1980. Fixed investment increased mainly in 1966–67, 1969–70, 1974–76 and 1978–79, with falls or low growth in 1968, 1971–73, 1977 and 1980. Exports increased mainly in 1964, 1966, 1968, 1970, 1972, 1976 and 1978, with main falls in 1973–75 and 1977. Consumer prices increased mainly in 1967–69, 1973–75 and 1979–80, with a negligible amount of change for 1970–71.

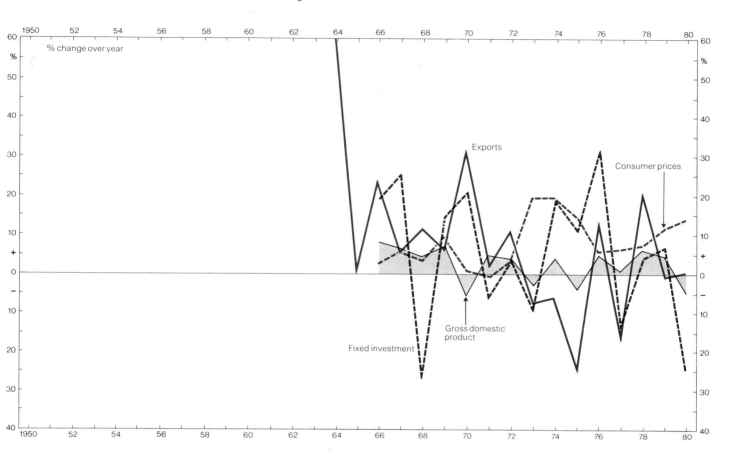

	Gross domestic product		Fixed investment		Exports		Consumer prices		
	Index 1970 = 100	% change over year	Index 1970 = 100	% change over year	Index 1970 = 100	% change over year	Index 1970 = 100	% change over year	
1950	na	na	na	na	na	na	na	na	1950
1951	na	na	na	na	na	na	na	na	1951
1952	na	na	na	na	na	na	na	na	1952
1953	na	na	na	na	na	na	na	na	1953
1954	na	na	na	na	na	na	na	na	1954
1955	na	na	na	na	na	na	na	na	1955
1956	na	na	na	na	na	na	na	na	1956
1957	na	na	na	na	na	na	na	na	1957
1958	na	na	na	na	na	na	na	na	1958
1959	na	na	na	na	na	na	na	na	1959
1960	na	na	na	na	na	na	na	na	1960
1961	na	na	na	na	na	na	na	na	1961
1962	na	na	na	na	na	na	na	na	1962
1963	na	na	na	na	30.9	na	na	na	1963
1964	na	na	na	na	49.5	59.9	na	na	1964
1965	81.5	na	67	na	49.6	0.3	80.9	na	1965
1966	87.9	7.9	79	19	61.0	22.9	82.8	2.3	1966
1967	93.9	6.8	99	25	64.4	5.5	87.3	5.4	1967
1968	98.3	4.8	72	−27	71.7	11.4	90.4	3.6	1968
1969	105.5	7.3	82	14	76.3	6.4	99.1	9.6	1969
1970	100.0	−5.2	100	21	100.0	31.0	100.0	0.9	1970
1971	104.9	4.9	94	−6	102.0	2.0	99.8	−0.2	1971
1972	108.9	3.8	98	4	112.8	10.6	103.6	3.8	1972
1973	106.2	−2.5	89	−9	104.3	−7.6	123.9	19.6	1973
1974	109.8	3.4	105	18	97.9	−6.1	147.5	19.0	1974
1975	105.5	−3.9	116	11	73.7	−24.7	168.1	14.0	1975
1976	110.6	4.8	153	31	83.0	12.5	177.5	5.6	1976
1977	111.6	0.9	131	−14	69.7	−16.0	188.6	6.2	1977
1978	118.1	5.8	137	4	84.2	20.8	202.4	7.3	1978
1979	123.7	4.8	147	7	83.6	−0.7	225.9	11.6	1979
1980	117.5	−5.0	110	−25	83.8	0.2	257.0	13.8	1980

Libya

Over the time for which figures are available, from 1961 to 1977, the main periods of expansion in gross domestic product were 1961–69 (especially 1962–65 and 1968), 1972, 1974 and 1976–77; there was low growth or a fall in 1970–71, 1973 and 1975. Exports of crude oil increased mainly over 1961–70 (exports began in 1960), then after a fall over 1971 to 1975, increased again in 1976–77 and 1979, with falls in 1978 and 1980. Consumer prices were comparatively steady throughout the period, but with a high increase for 1978, the last year for which figures are available. Money stock increased at a high rate throughout, especially for 1964–66, 1971 and 1974.

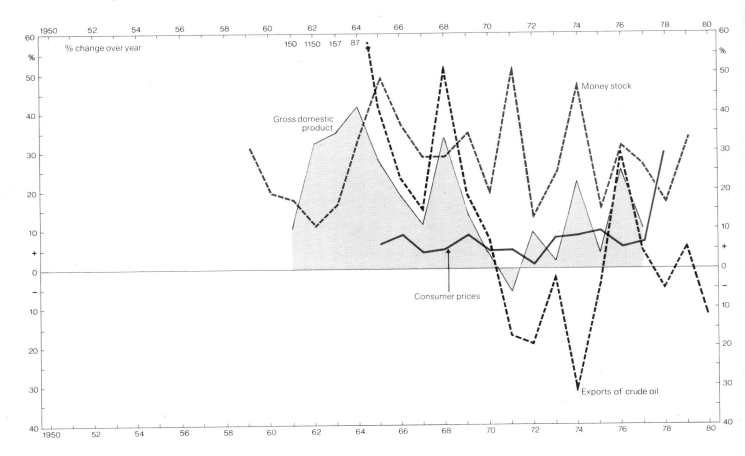

	Gross domestic product		Exports of crude oil		Consumer prices		Money stock		
	Index 1970 = 100	% change over year	Index 1970 = 100	% change over year	Index 1970 = 100	% change over year	Index 1970 = 100	% change over year	
1950	na	na	na	na	na	na	na	na	1950
1951	na	na	na	na	na	na	na	na	1951
1952	na	na	na	na	na	na	na	na	1952
1953	na	na	na	na	na	na	na	na	1953
1954	na	na	na	na	na	na	na	na	1954
1955	na	na	na	na	na	na	na	na	1955
1956	na	na	na	na	na	na	na	na	1956
1957	na	na	na	na	na	na	na	na	1957
1958	na	na	na	na	na	na	5.8	na	1958
1959	na	na	na	na	na	na	7.6	31.4	1959
1960	13.6	na	0.2	na	na	na	9.1	19.6	1960
1961	15.0	10.1	0.4	150	na	na	10.7	17.3	1961
1962	19.8	32.1	5.4	1 150	na	na	11.9	11.6	1962
1963	26.8	34.8	13.9	157	na	na	13.9	16.7	1963
1964	37.8	41.5	26.0	87	72.0	na	18.6	33.3	1964
1965	48.4	27.9	36.7	41	76.2	5.8	27.7	48.9	1965
1966	57.3	18.4	45.3	23	82.4	8.1	37.7	36.3	1966
1967	63.8	11.2	51.9	15	85.3	3.5	48.4	28.5	1967
1968	85.2	33.6	78.1	51	89.0	4.3	62.3	28.6	1968
1969	96.3	13.0	92.7	19	96.1	8.0	83.7	34.4	1969
1970	100.0	3.9	100.0	8	100.0	4.1	100.0	19.5	1970
1971	94.7	−5.3	82.9	−17	104.5	4.5	151.2	51.2	1971
1972	103.4	9.1	67.0	−19	105.6	1.1	171.3	13.3	1972
1973	105.4	2.0	65.7	−2	113.6	7.6	213.2	24.5	1973
1974	128.8	22.2	45.0	−31	122.5	7.8	312.7	46.7	1974
1975	133.9	4.0	43.2	−4	133.6	9.1	359.9	15.1	1975
1976	167.7	25.2	55.9	29	140.8	5.4	472.6	31.3	1976
1977	184.7	10.1	58.7	5	149.8	6.4	598.8	26.7	1977
1978	na	na	56.0	−5	193.7	29.3	700.0	16.9	1978
1979	na	na	59.2	6	na	na	932.1	33.1	1979
1980	na	na	52.4	−12	na	na	na	na	1980

Luxembourg

The main periods of expansion in gross domestic product were 1951–52, 1955–57, 1959–61, 1963–64, 1968–69, 1971–74 and 1978–79; there was a fall or low growth mainly in 1953, 1958, 1962, 1965–67, 1970, 1975, 1977 and 1980. Production of steel increased mainly in 1950–51, 1954–56, 1959–61, 1964, 1968–69, 1972–74 and

1978–79, with falls in 1952–53, 1958, 1962, 1966, 1970–71, 1975, 1977 and 1980. Fixed investment increased mainly in 1957, 1961–64, 1969–71 and 1973, with a low rate of increase for 1977–80 and falls in 1956, 1960, 1965–68 and 1974–76. Consumer prices increased at a stable rate, with main rises in 1951, 1973–77 and 1980.

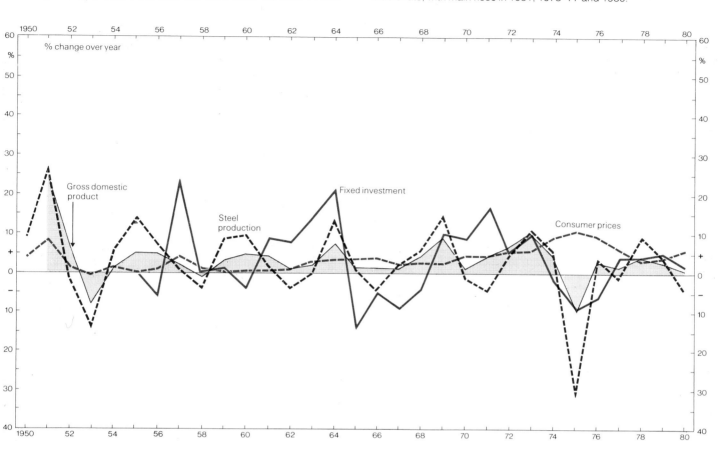

	Gross domestic product		Steel production		Fixed investment		Consumer prices		
	Index 1970 = 100	% change over year	Index 1970 = 100	% change over year	Index 1970 = 100	% change over year	Index 1970 = 100	% change over year	
1950	47.3	na	48.0	8.6	na	na	65.7	3.8	1950
1951	58.3	23.2	60.6	26.1	na	na	71.1	8.2	1951
1952	62.2	6.7	59.6	−1.6	na	na	72.2	1.6	1952
1953	57.4	−7.8	51.7	−13.3	na	na	72.0	−0.3	1953
1954	58.2	1.5	54.5	5.4	63	na	72.8	1.1	1954
1955	61.1	5.0	62.2	14.1	63	0	72.7	−0.1	1955
1956	64.2	5.0	66.7	7.2	59	−6	73.1	0.6	1956
1957	65.7	2.4	67.1	0.6	73	23	76.5	4.7	1957
1958	65.1	−0.9	64.7	−3.6	73	0	77.0	0.7	1958
1959	67.4	3.4	70.0	8.2	74	1	77.3	0.4	1959
1960	70.7	4.9	76.9	9.9	71	−4	77.6	0.4	1960
1961	73.8	4.4	78.6	2.2	78	9	78.0	0.5	1961
1962	74.7	1.2	75.6	−3.8	84	8	78.7	0.9	1962
1963	76.5	2.4	75.6	0.0	95	14	80.8	2.7	1963
1964	82.4	7.7	85.5	13.1	116	21	83.5	3.3	1964
1965	83.6	1.5	86.0	0.6	100	−13	86.2	3.2	1965
1966	84.9	1.6	82.1	−4.5	95	−5	89.1	3.4	1966
1967	86.2	1.5	83.7	1.9	87	−9	91.0	2.1	1967
1968	89.9	4.4	88.5	5.7	83	−4	93.4	2.6	1968
1969	98.4	9.4	101.3	14.5	92	10	95.6	2.4	1969
1970	100.0	1.6	100.0	−1.3	100	9	100.0	4.6	1970
1971	104.1	4.1	95.5	−4.5	117	17	104.7	4.7	1971
1972	110.2	5.9	100.1	4.8	124	6	110.1	5.2	1972
1973	121.4	10.2	111.1	11.0	136	10	116.9	6.2	1973
1974	127.0	4.7	117.0	5.3	133	−2	127.9	9.4	1974
1975	115.1	−9.4	81.0	−30.8	121	−9	141.7	10.8	1975
1976	118.4	2.9	83.6	3.2	114	−6	155.6	9.8	1976
1977	120.4	1.7	82.7	−1.1	119	4	166.1	6.7	1977
1978	125.6	4.3	90.7	9.7	125	4	171.2	3.1	1978
1979	129.0	2.7	94.0	3.6	131	5	179.0	4.6	1979
1980	129.8	0.6	90.1	−4.1	133	2	190.2	6.3	1980

Malawi

Over the time for which figures are available, from 1955, the main periods of expansion in gross domestic product were 1955–56, 1963, 1965–67, 1969, 1971–73 and 1975–79; there were falls or a low rate of growth for 1957, 1964, 1968, 1970, 1974 and 1980. Exports, for the time covered, increased mainly in 1965–67, 1971–73, 1975–77 and 1979–80, with falls or low growth in 1968–70, 1974 and 1978. Imports, for the time covered, increased mainly in 1968, 1970–72, 1975 and 1977–78, with falls in 1969, 1973, 1976 and 1980. Consumer prices increased at a comparatively steady rate, with main rises in 1970–71, 1974–75 and 1978–80.

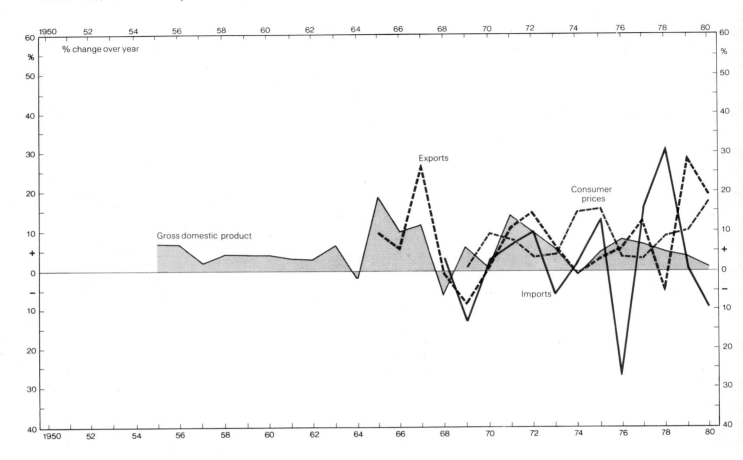

	Gross domestic product		Exports		Imports		Consumer prices		
	Index 1970 = 100	% change over year	Index 1970 = 100	% change over year	Index 1970 = 100	% change over year	Index 1970 = 100	% change over year	
1950	na	na	na	na	na	na	na	na	1950
1951	na	na	na	na	na	na	na	na	1951
1952	na	na	na	na	na	na	na	na	1952
1953	na	na	na	na	na	na	na	na	1953
1954	46	na	na	na	na	na	na	na	1954
1955	49	7	na	na	na	na	na	na	1955
1956	53	7	na	na	na	na	na	na	1956
1957	54	2	na	na	na	na	na	na	1957
1958	56	4	na	na	na	na	na	na	1958
1959	58	4	na	na	na	na	na	na	1959
1960	61	4	na	na	na	na	na	na	1960
1961	63	3	na	na	na	na	na	na	1961
1962	64	3	na	na	na	na	na	na	1962
1963	69	7	na	na	na	na	na	na	1963
1964	68	−2	72.9	na	na	na	na	na	1964
1965	80	18	80.2	10.0	na	na	na	na	1965
1966	88	10	84.7	5.6	na	na	na	na	1966
1967	98	12	107.3	26.7	106.7	na	na	na	1967
1968	93	−6	107.8	0.5	110.8	3.8	90	na	1968
1969	99	6	99.3	−7.9	96.8	−12.6	91	1	1969
1970	100	1	100.0	0.7	100.0	3.3	100	10	1970
1971	114	14	111.1	11.1	107.4	7.4	108	8	1971
1972	126	10	127.5	14.8	118.8	10.6	112	4	1972
1973	134	6	135.4	6.2	112.4	−5.4	118	5	1973
1974	133	−1	134.3	−0.8	115.2	2.5	136	15	1974
1975	141	5	138.4	3.1	130.9	13.6	157	16	1975
1976	151	8	146.6	5.9	95.7	−26.9	164	4	1976
1977	161	7	165.0	12.6	111.5	16.6	171	4	1977
1978	170	5	157.4	−4.6	146.5	31.3	185	9	1978
1979	178	4	201.5	28.1	147.9	1.0	206	11	1979
1980	179	1	240.7	19.4	135.4	−8.5	244	18	1980

Malaysia

Over the time for which figures are available, from 1961, the main periods of expansion for gross domestic product were 1961–66, 1968–69, 1971–74 and 1976–80; the growth rate slackened for 1967, 1970 and 1975. Exports increased mainly in 1954–56, 1959–61, 1963, 1965–69, 1973, 1976 and 1978–79, with falls or low growth for 1952–53, 1957–58, 1962, 1964, 1970, 1972, 1974–75, 1977 and 1980. Imports increased mainly in 1950–51, 1955–56, 1959–63, 1965, 1970, 1973–74 and 1976–80, with falls in 1952–53, 1957–58, 1966, 1971 and 1975. Consumer prices were comparatively stable throughout, but with high increases in 1950–51 and 1973–74.

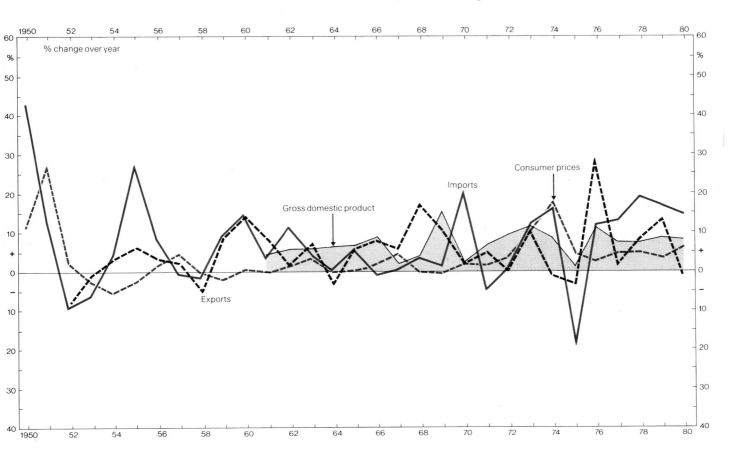

	Gross domestic product		Exports		Imports		Consumer prices		
	Index 1970 = 100	% change over year	Index 1970 = 100	% change over year	Index 1970 = 100	% change over year	Index 1970 = 100	% change over year	
1950	na	na	na	na	40	42	79.5	10.3	1950
1951	na	na	44	na	45	12	99.9	25.8	1951
1952	na	na	40	−8	41	−10	101.5	1.6	1952
1953	na	na	40	−1	38	−7	98.6	−2.9	1953
1954	na	na	41	3	39	4	92.7	−6.0	1954
1955	na	na	44	6	50	27	89.7	−3.2	1955
1956	na	na	45	3	54	8	90.5	0.9	1956
1957	na	na	46	2	53	−1	94.2	4.1	1957
1958	na	na	44	−5	52	−2	93.4	−0.8	1958
1959	na	na	47	8	56	8	91.2	−2.4	1959
1960	55.3	na	54	14	64	14	91.2	0.0	1960
1961	57.5	4.0	58	8	66	3	91.0	−0.2	1961
1962	60.9	5.9	60	2	73	11	91.1	0.1	1962
1963	64.4	5.6	64	7	77	4	94.0	3.2	1963
1964	68.5	6.4	62	−3	77	0	93.6	−0.4	1964
1965	73.3	7.0	66	6	80	5	93.5	−0.1	1965
1966	79.6	8.7	71	8	79	−1	94.4	1.0	1966
1967	81.5	2.3	75	6	80	0	98.7	4.6	1967
1968	84.9	4.2	88	17	82	3	98.5	−0.2	1968
1969	97.5	14.9	98	11	83	1	98.1	−0.4	1969
1970	100.0	2.5	100	2	100	20	100.0	1.9	1970
1971	107.1	7.1	105	5	95	−5	101.6	1.6	1971
1972	117.1	9.4	105	0	95	0	104.8	3.1	1972
1973	130.8	11.7	116	10	106	12	115.9	10.6	1973
1974	141.7	8.3	115	−1	123	16	136.0	17.3	1974
1975	142.9	0.8	112	−3	100	−19	142.2	4.6	1975
1976	158.7	11.1	143	28	112	12	145.9	2.6	1976
1977	170.7	7.6	147	2	126	13	152.9	4.8	1977
1978	183.7	7.6	158	8	150	19	160.4	4.9	1978
1979	199.4	8.6	178	13	175	17	166.2	3.6	1979
1980	215.4	8.0	177	−1	200	14	177.3	6.7	1980

Malta

Over the time from 1955, the main periods of expansion in gross domestic product were 1956, 1958, 1960, 1965–70 and 1972–79; main falls or slackening of growth occurred in 1961–63 and 1971. Exports, for the time covered, increased mainly in 1966, 1968–69, 1971–73 and 1975–77, with falls in 1967 and 1970, and low growth in 1974 and 1978–80. Imports increased mainly in 1950–51, 1955–56, 1960, 1963–64, 1966, 1968–69, 1973–74, 1976–77 and 1979–80, with falls or low growth in 1952–54, 1957–59, 1961–62, 1965, 1967, 1970–72, 1975 and 1978. Consumer prices increased slowly up to 1972; then there were main rises in 1973–75, 1977 and 1979–80.

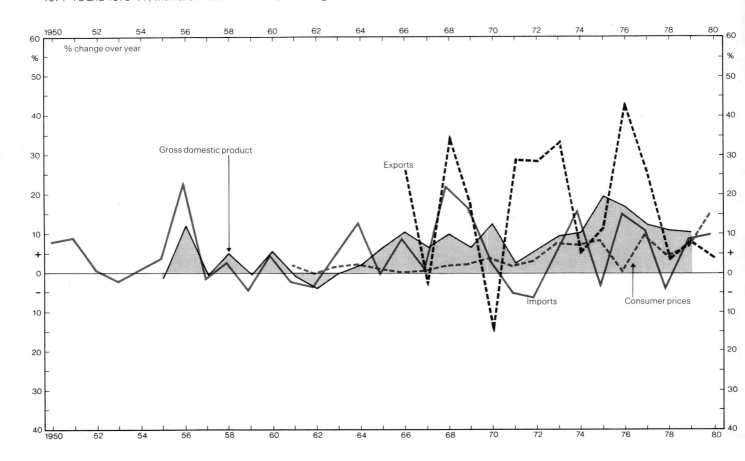

	Gross domestic product		Exports		Imports		Consumer prices		
	Index 1970 = 100	% change over year	Index 1970 = 100	% change over year	Index 1970 = 100	% change over year	Index 1970 = 100	% change over year	
1950	na	na	na	na	38	8	na	na	1950
1951	na	na	na	na	42	9	na	na	1951
1952	na	na	na	na	42	1	na	na	1952
1953	na	na	na	na	42	−2	na	na	1953
1954	50.5	na	na	na	42	1	na	na	1954
1955	50.0	−1.1	na	na	44	4	na	na	1955
1956	56.0	12.1	na	na	54	23	na	na	1956
1957	55.9	−0.2	na	na	53	−1	na	na	1957
1958	58.7	5.1	na	na	55	3	na	na	1958
1959	58.5	−0.5	na	na	53	−4	na	na	1959
1960	61.9	5.8	na	na	55	5	84.0	na	1960
1961	61.3	−0.9	na	na	54	−2	86.1	2.5	1961
1962	58.7	−4.2	na	na	52	−4	86.2	0.1	1962
1963	58.6	−0.2	na	na	54	5	87.9	2.0	1963
1964	59.8	1.9	na	na	61	13	89.8	2.2	1964
1965	64.0	7.1	61.0	na	61	0	91.2	1.6	1965
1966	70.9	10.8	76.9	26.1	67	9	91.7	0.5	1966
1967	75.8	6.9	74.9	−2.6	68	1	92.4	0.8	1967
1968	83.4	10.0	100.3	33.9	83	22	94.2	1.9	1968
1969	88.8	6.5	117.4	17.0	97	17	96.4	2.3	1969
1970	100.0	12.7	100.0	−14.8	100	3	100.0	3.7	1970
1971	102.5	2.5	128.4	28.4	95	−5	102.3	2.3	1971
1972	108.4	5.8	164.6	28.2	89	−6	105.8	3.4	1972
1973	119.0	9.8	220.1	33.7	94	5	113.9	7.7	1973
1974	131.0	10.1	231.5	5.2	109	16	122.2	7.3	1974
1975	156.6	19.5	257.7	11.3	106	−3	133.0	8.8	1975
1976	183.2	17.0	367.7	42.7	121	15	133.8	0.6	1976
1977	205.6	12.2	461.0	25.4	135	11	147.2	10.0	1977
1978	228.4	11.1	477.3	3.5	129	−4	154.0	4.6	1978
1979	252.4	10.5	515.9	8.1	141	9	165.1	7.2	1979
1980	na	na	538.3	4.3	155	10	191.1	15.8	1980

Mexico

Gross domestic product increased at a substantial rate throughout the period, with especially high rates in 1950–52 and 1954–57, and comparatively high rates in 1960, 1964, 1968, 1972–73 and 1978–80; the only fall was in 1953. Fixed investment increased mainly in 1951–52, 1954–57, 1960, 1963–64, 1966–70, 1972–75 and 1978–80;

falls or low growth occurred in 1953, 1958–59, 1961–62, 1965, 1971 and 1976–77. Consumer prices rose mainly in 1951–52, 1955, 1958 and 1973–80, with a low stable rate of increase for 1959–72. International reserves increased mainly in 1950, 1955–56, 1959, 1963–64, 1968, 1970–72, 1975, 1977 and 1979–80.

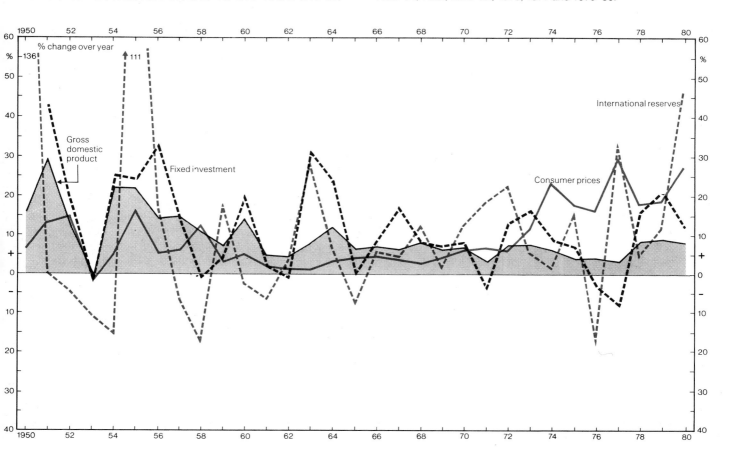

	Gross domestic product		Fixed investment		Consumer prices		International reserves		
	Index 1970 = 100	% change over year	Index 1970 = 100	% change over year	Index 1970 = 100	% change over year	Index 1970 = 100	% change over year	
1950	13.4	15.7	8	na	37.1	6.0	40	136	1950
1951	17.3	29.0	12	43	41.8	12.7	40	0	1951
1952	19.4	12.3	14	18	47.8	14.2	38	−5	1952
1953	19.3	−0.5	14	−1	47.0	−1.7	34	−11	1953
1954	23.5	21.9	17	25	49.3	4.9	28	−16	1954
1955	28.6	21.8	21	24	57.2	16.0	59	111	1955
1956	32.7	14.2	28	33	59.8	4.5	69	16	1956
1957	37.6	14.9	32	14	63.0	5.4	64	−7	1957
1958	41.7	11.1	31	−1	70.7	12.2	53	−18	1958
1959	44.7	7.2	32	4	72.6	2.7	62	17	1959
1960	50.7	13.4	39	19	76.1	4.8	59	−3	1960
1961	53.2	4.9	39	2	77.4	1.7	56	−7	1961
1962	55.7	4.7	39	−1	78.2	1.0	57	3	1962
1963	60.2	8.0	51	31	78.7	0.6	74	28	1963
1964	67.2	11.7	64	24	80.6	2.4	79	7	1964
1965	71.6	6.5	63	0	83.5	3.6	72	−8	1965
1966	76.5	6.9	69	8	87.0	4.2	76	5	1966
1967	81.4	6.3	80	17	89.6	3.0	79	4	1967
1968	88.0	8.1	86	8	91.6	2.2	88	12	1968
1969	93.5	6.3	92	7	95.1	3.8	89	1	1969
1970	100.0	6.9	100	8	100.0	5.2	100	12	1970
1971	103.4	3.4	96	−4	105.7	5.7	118	18	1971
1972	111.0	7.3	109	13	111.1	5.1	144	22	1972
1973	119.4	7.6	127	16	123.5	11.2	151	5	1973
1974	126.4	5.9	138	9	151.3	22.5	153	1	1974
1975	131.6	4.1	147	7	176.8	16.9	176	15	1975
1976	137.2	4.2	143	−3	204.7	15.8	145	−18	1976
1977	141.9	3.4	131	−8	264.3	29.1	191	32	1977
1978	153.6	8.3	152	16	310.1	17.3	199	4	1978
1979	167.7	9.2	184	21	366.7	18.2	221	11	1979
1980	181.6	8.3	206	12	463.4	26.4	322	46	1980

Morocco

The main periods of expansion in gross domestic product were 1953–54, 1958, 1960–62, 1964, 1967–68, 1970–72, 1974, 1976–77 and 1979–80; there were falls or low growth in 1955, 1957, 1959, 1963, 1965–66, 1969, 1973 and 1978. Exports increased mainly in 1950, 1953, 1955, 1958–60, 1962–64, 1968–69, 1972–73 and 1976–77, with falls in 1956–57, 1961, 1965–67, 1974–75 and 1978. Consumer prices increased mainly at a stable rate, with higher rises in 1951–52, 1956–57 and 1974–80. International reserves increased mainly in 1950, 1952–55, 1957–60, 1965, 1968–72, 1974 and 1976–78, with main falls in 1961–64, 1966–67 and 1979–80.

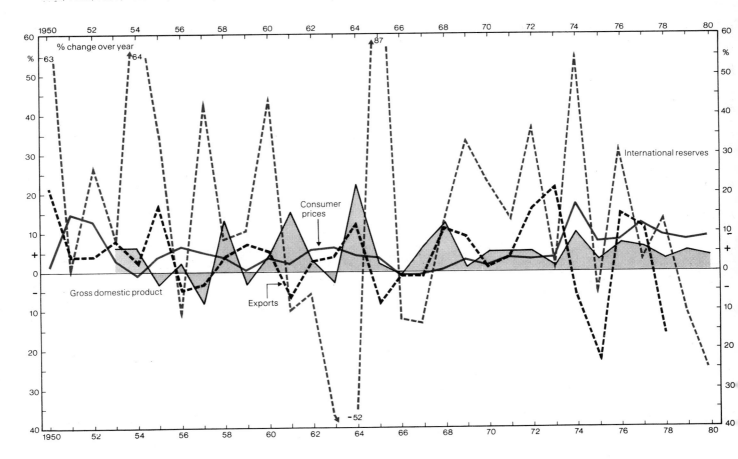

	Gross domestic product		Exports		Consumer prices		International reserves		
	Index 1970 = 100	% change over year	Index 1970 = 100	% change over year	Index 1970 = 100	% change over year	Index 1970 = 100	% change over year	
1950	na	na	55	21	49.7	0.6	22	63	1950
1951	na	na	57	4	56.9	14.4	22	0	1951
1952	48.5	na	59	4	63.9	12.4	28	26	1952
1953	51.3	6	64	8	65.5	2.5	30	8	1953
1954	54.1	6	65	2	64.8	−1.1	49	64	1954
1955	52.6	−3	76	17	67.0	3.4	67	36	1955
1956	53.7	2	72	−5	71.1	6.1	60	−11	1956
1957	49.3	−8	70	−3	74.6	4.9	86	43	1957
1958	55.6	13	73	4	77.2	3.5	93	8	1958
1959	54.0	−3	78	7	77.2	0.0	102	10	1959
1960	56.1	4	82	5	79.8	3.4	147	44	1960
1961	64.3	15	76	−7	81.2	1.8	132	−10	1961
1962	66.4	3	78	3	85.4	5.2	124	−6	1962
1963	64.3	−3	81	4	90.3	5.7	79	−37	1963
1964	78.3	22	91	12	93.9	4.0	38	−52	1964
1965	79.8	2	84	−8	97.1	3.4	71	87	1965
1966	78.7	−1	83	−1	96.2	−0.9	62	−12	1966
1967	83.8	6	82	−1	95.5	−0.7	54	−13	1967
1968	94.2	12	91	11	95.8	0.3	61	12	1968
1969	95.0	1	99	9	98.7	3.0	81	34	1969
1970	100.0	5	100	1	100.0	1.3	100	23	1970
1971	105.2	5	104	4	104.1	4.1	114	14	1971
1972	110.3	5	121	16	108.0	3.7	156	37	1972
1973	111.8	1	146	21	112.5	4.2	157	1	1973
1974	123.0	10	137	−6	132.4	17.7	243	55	1974
1975	127.1	3	105	−23	142.9	7.9	230	−5	1975
1976	136.0	7	121	15	155.0	8.5	302	31	1976
1977	144.8	6	134	11	174.6	12.6	313	4	1977
1978	149.7	3	112	−16	191.5	9.7	356	14	1978
1979	156.5	5	na	na	207.6	8.4	319	−10	1979
1980	162.8	4	na	na	227.1	9.4	241	−25	1980

Netherlands

The main periods of expansion in gross domestic product were 1950, 1953–57, 1959–60, 1964–65, 1967–70, 1973 and 1976, with a fall or low growth rate for 1951–52, 1958, 1961–63, 1966, 1975 and 1980. Consumers expenditure expanded at a generally stable rate over 1953–56 and 1959–78, with a fall or low growth rate for 1950–52,

1957–58 and 1979–80. Government expenditure, after a high increase for 1952–56 and fall for 1957–59, expanded at a low and comparatively stable rate, with a slackening in 1980. Fixed investment increased mainly in 1950, 1953–57, 1959–60, 1964–68, 1970, 1973 and 1977–78, with falls in 1951–52, 1958, 1969, 1972 and 1974–76.

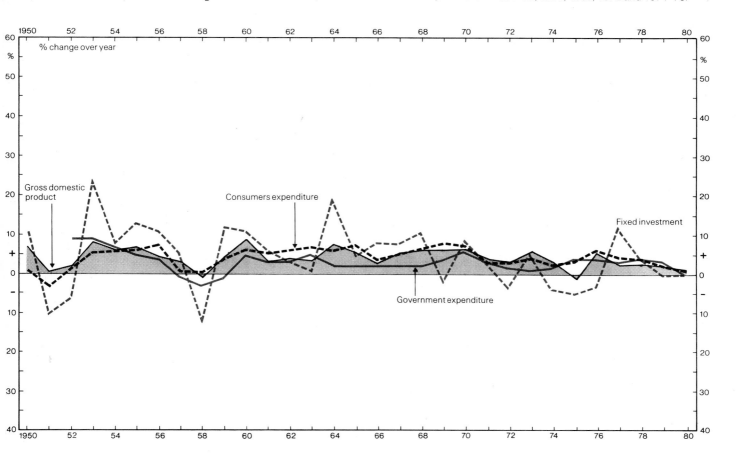

	Gross domestic product		Consumers expenditure		Government expenditure		Fixed investment		
	Index 1970 = 100	% change over year	Index 1970 = 100	% change over year	Index 1970 = 100	% change over year	Index 1970 = 100	% change over year	
1950	39.2	7.0	39.4	0.4	na	na	32.0	11	1950
1951	39.5	0.5	38.1	−3.4	52.7	na	28.7	−10	1951
1952	40.2	2.0	38.4	0.8	57.7	9	26.9	−6	1952
1953	43.5	8.2	40.4	5.2	62.7	9	33.2	23	1953
1954	46.5	6.7	42.8	6.1	67.0	7	35.8	8	1954
1955	49.7	7.0	45.6	6.4	70.6	5	40.4	13	1955
1956	51.9	4.4	49.0	7.5	73.5	4	45.0	11	1956
1957	53.5	3.0	49.1	0.3	73.1	−1	47.2	5	1957
1958	53.0	−1.0	49.3	0.3	71.0	−3	41.5	−12	1958
1959	55.4	4.7	51.5	4.4	70.0	−1	46.2	12	1959
1960	60.5	9.0	54.6	6.1	73.8	5	51.6	11	1960
1961	62.3	3.1	57.4	5.2	75.9	3	54.7	6	1961
1962	64.8	4.0	60.9	6.1	78.4	3	56.5	3	1962
1963	67.1	3.6	65.2	7.0	82.1	5	57.2	1	1963
1964	72.7	8.3	69.1	5.9	83.5	2	68.1	19	1964
1965	76.5	5.2	74.2	7.5	84.8	2	71.7	5	1965
1966	78.6	2.7	76.6	3.2	86.3	2	77.5	8	1966
1967	82.7	5.3	80.8	5.4	88.4	2	84.0	8	1967
1968	88.1	6.4	86.1	6.6	90.3	2	93.4	11	1968
1969	93.7	6.4	92.9	7.9	94.4	4	91.3	−2	1969
1970	100.0	6.7	100.0	7.7	100.0	6	100.0	9	1970
1971	104.3	4.3	103.0	3.0	103.3	3	103.4	3	1971
1972	107.8	3.4	106.3	3.2	105.2	2	100.5	−3	1972
1973	114.0	5.7	110.4	3.9	105.9	1	105.1	5	1973
1974	118.0	3.5	113.4	2.7	108.1	2	101.1	−4	1974
1975	116.8	−1.0	117.2	3.4	112.3	4	96.2	−5	1975
1976	123.0	5.3	124.0	5.7	116.8	4	93.5	−3	1976
1977	125.9	2.4	129.5	4.4	120.5	3	104.4	12	1977
1978	129.1	2.5	134.5	3.9	124.8	4	108.5	4	1978
1979	131.9	2.2	137.4	2.2	128.4	3	108.5	0	1979
1980	133.2	1.0	138.1	0.5	129.0	0	108.7	0	1980

Netherlands

Exports increased mainly in 1950–51, 1953–55, 1958–60, 1962–73 (with some slackening of growth for 1965–67 and 1972), 1976 and 1978–79; there was a fall or low growth for 1956, 1961, 1974–75, 1977 and 1980. Imports increased mainly in 1950, 1953–56, 1959–73 (with some slackening for 1962, 1965–67 and 1971–72); imports fell in 1951–52, 1958, 1974–75 and 1980. Unemployment increased mainly in 1950–52, 1957–58, 1965–67, 1971–72, 1974–75 and 1980; main reductions were in 1953–56, 1959–61, 1964 and 1968–70. Consumer prices were comparatively stable, with main increases in 1950–51, 1957, 1969, 1971–77 and 1980.

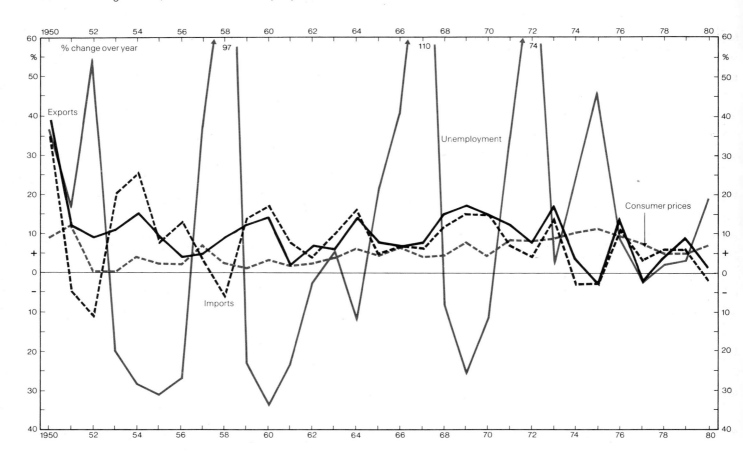

	Exports		Imports		Unemployment		Consumer prices		
	Index 1970 = 100	% change over year	Index 1970 = 100	% change over year	Number (000)	% change over year	Index 1970 = 100	% change over year	
1950	15	39	19	35	46	37	49.6	8.9	1950
1951	17	12	19	−5	54	17	55.5	12.0	1951
1952	18	9	16	−11	82	54	55.5	0.0	1952
1953	21	11	20	20	66	−20	55.5	0.0	1953
1954	24	15	25	25	48	−28	57.7	4.0	1954
1955	26	9	27	8	33	−31	58.8	1.9	1955
1956	27	4	30	13	24	−27	59.9	1.9	1956
1957	28	5	31	3	·33	37	63.8	6.5	1957
1958	30	9	29	−6	64	97	65.0	1.9	1958
1959	34	12	33	14	50	−23	65.4	0.6	1959
1960	39	14	39	17	33	−34	67.2	2.8	1960
1961	40	2	42	8	25	−24	68.2	1.5	1961
1962	42	7	44	6	24	−3	69.5	1.9	1962
1963	45	6	49	10	25	5	72.2	3.9	1963
1964	51	14	57	16	22	−12	76.2	5.5	1964
1965	55	8	60	5	27	21	79.2	3.9	1965
1966	59	7	63	7	38	40	83.8	5.8	1966
1967	64	8	67	6	79	110	86.6	3.3	1967
1968	74	15	76	12	72	−9	89.9	3.8	1968
1969	87	17	87	15	53	−26	96.5	7.3	1969
1970	100	15	100	15	47	−12	100.0	3.6	1970
1971	112	12	107	7	62	34	107.5	7.5	1971
1972	121	8	111	4	108	74	115.9	7.8	1972
1973	142	17	127	14	110	2	125.2	8.0	1973
1974	146	3	123	−3	135	23	137.3	9.7	1974
1975	142	−3	119	−3	196	45	151.3	10.2	1975
1976	160	13	132	11	212	8	164.6	8.8	1976
1977	158	−2	136	3	204	−4	175.2	6.4	1977
1978	163	4	144	6	206	1	182.3	4.1	1978
1979	178	9	152	6	210	2	190.0	4.2	1979
1980	179	1	150	−2	248	18	202.4	6.5	1980

Netherlands

Share prices increased substantially in 1953–55, 1959–61, 1967–69 and 1972–73, with falls in 1950–52, 1957, 1962, 1965–66, 1971 and 1974–80. Money stock increased mainly in 1951–55, 1958, 1968–72, 1974–75 and 1977, with falls or low growth in 1950, 1956–57, 1973 and 1978–79. International reserves increased mainly in 1950,

1952–54, 1958, 1960, 1963–64, 1967, 1970–73 and 1979–80; there were falls in 1956–57, 1962, 1968 and 1978. The interest rate increased mainly in 1955–57, 1960, 1962–66, 1969–70, 1973–74, 1976 and 1978–80, with falls in 1951–54, 1958–59, 1961, 1967–68, 1971–72, 1975 and 1977.

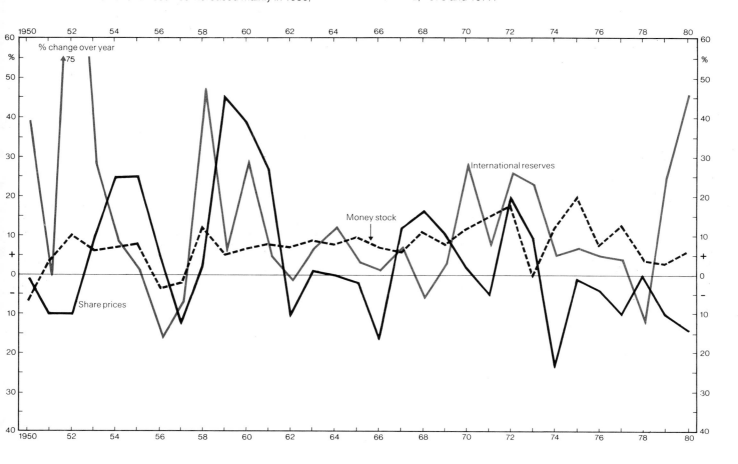

	Share prices		Money stock		International reserves		Interest rate		
	Index 1970 = 100	% change over year	Index 1970 = 100	% change over year	Index 1970 = 100	% change over year	%	Change over year[a]	
1950	27	−1	26	−7	14.7	39	1.56	0.15	1950
1951	24	−10	27	4	14.7	0	1.52	−0.04	1951
1952	22	−10	30	10	25.7	75	1.21	−0.31	1952
1953	24	10	32	6	33.3	29	0.64	−0.57	1953
1954	30	25	34	7	36.4	9	0.61	−0.02	1954
1955	37	25	37	8	36.6	1	1.07	0.46	1955
1956	39	5	36	−4	30.9	−16	2.66	1.59	1956
1957	34	−12	35	−2	28.6	−7	4.55	1.89	1957
1958	35	2	39	12	42.1	47	3.36	−1.18	1958
1959	51	45	41	5	44.5	6	2.07	−1.30	1959
1960	71	39	44	7	57.4	29	2.39	0.32	1960
1961	90	27	47	8	60.4	5	1.25	−1.14	1961
1962	81	−10	50	7	60.0	−1	2.06	0.80	1962
1963	82	1	55	9	64.8	8	2.17	0.11	1963
1964	82	0	59	8	72.4	12	3.77	1.60	1964
1965	80	−2	65	10	74.5	3	4.32	0.56	1965
1966	68	−16	70	7	75.6	1	5.30	0.97	1966
1967	76	12	74	6	80.8	7	5.11	−0.19	1967
1968	88	16	83	11	76.0	−6	4.98	−0.12	1968
1969	98	11	89	8	78.1	3	6.20	1.22	1969
1970	100	2	100	12	100.0	28	6.67	0.47	1970
1971	95	−5	115	15	107.9	8	4.85	−1.82	1971
1972	114	20	135	18	136.0	26	1.93	−2.92	1972
1973	126	10	135	0	167.4	23	6.44	4.51	1973
1974	97	−23	152	12	175.3	5	9.20	2.76	1974
1975	97	−1	182	20	187.4	7	4.17	−5.03	1975
1976	92	−4	197	8	196.2	5	7.28	3.11	1976
1977	83	−10	223	13	204.8	4	3.80	−3.48	1977
1978	83	0	232	4	179.7	−12	6.24	2.44	1978
1979	75	−10	238	3	225.3	25	9.03	2.79	1979
1980	64	−14	253	6	329.2	46	10.13	1.10	1980

[a] In percentage points

New Zealand

For the time covered, from 1955, the main periods of expansion in gross domestic product were 1955, 1957, 1959–60, 1963–66, 1969–70, 1972–74 and 1978–79; falls or low growth occurred in 1956, 1958, 1961–62, 1967–68, 1971, 1975–77 and 1980. Consumers expenditure, for the time covered, increased mainly in 1960,

1963–65, 1969–70, 1972–73 and 1978–80. Exports increased mainly in 1952, 1955–56, 1958–59, 1961–64, 1966–69, 1971–72, 1976 and 1979–80. With low numbers unemployed, changes have been extreme in percentage terms, with main increases in 1952–53, 1956–59, 1962, 1967–68, 1971–72, 1975, 1977–78 and 1980.

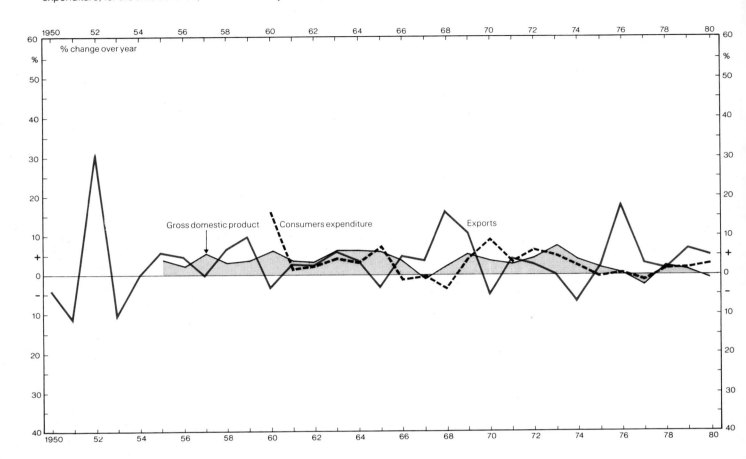

	Gross domestic product[a]		Consumers expenditure[a]		Exports		Unemployment		
	Index 1970 = 100	% change over year	Index 1970 = 100	% change over year	Index 1970 = 100	% change over year	Number (000)	% change over year	
1950	na	na	na	na	50	−4	0.04	−59	1950
1951	na	na	na	na	44	−11	0.04	0	1951
1952	na	na	na	na	58	31	0.05	24	1952
1953	na	na	na	na	52	−10	0.08	81	1953
1954	54.4	na	na	na	52	0	0.06	−32	1954
1955	56.5	3.9	na	na	55	6	0.06	−3	1955
1956	57.6	1.9	na	na	58	5	0.26	362	1956
1957	60.5	5.2	na	na	58	0	0.39	52	1957
1958	62.3	2.9	na	na	62	7	0.79	99	1958
1959	64.7	3.9	67.2	na	68	10	1.19	51	1959
1960	68.6	6.1	78.1	16.2	66	−3	0.63	−47	1960
1961	70.9	3.3	79.4	1.6	68	3	0.38	−41	1961
1962	73.1	3.1	81.2	2.4	70	3	1.04	177	1962
1963	77.6	6.1	84.5	4.0	74	6	0.85	−18	1963
1964	82.4	6.2	87.1	3.1	77	4	0.65	−24	1964
1965	87.3	6.0	93.3	7.1	75	−3	0.51	−22	1965
1966	90.6	3.8	92.0	−1.3	79	5	0.46	−10	1966
1967	89.9	−0.9	91.6	−0.5	82	4	3.85	737	1967
1968	91.8	2.2	88.1	−3.9	95	16	6.88	79	1968
1969	96.4	5.0	91.7	4.1	105	11	2.93	−57	1969
1970	100.0	3.7	100.0	9.0	100	−5	1.60	−45	1970
1971	102.5	2.5	102.8	2.8	104	4	3.11	94	1971
1972	107.1	4.4	108.9	6.0	107	3	5.68	83	1972
1973	114.7	7.2	114.2	4.9	107	0	2.32	−59	1973
1974	119.4	4.0	116.6	2.0	99	−7	0.95	−59	1974
1975	121.4	1.7	116.0	−0.5	101	2	4.17	339	1975
1976	121.6	0.1	116.1	0.1	119	18	5.36	29	1976
1977	118.2	−2.7	114.1	−1.7	123	3	7.38	38	1977
1978	121.0	2.3	116.0	1.7	125	2	22.9	210	1978
1979	122.4	1.2	117.7	1.5	134	7	25.2	10	1979
1980	121.4	−0.8	121.0	2.7	140	5	36.5	45	1980

[a]Years beginning April 1st

New Zealand

After high increases for 1950–52, consumer prices increased at a comparatively stable rate for 1953–70, then rose at a high rate for 1971–80. Share prices increased mainly in 1950–51, 1954–57, 1959–60, 1963–64, 1968–69, 1972–73, 1976 and 1979–80; main falls were in 1952, 1958, 1961–62, 1965–67, 1971, 1974–75 and 1977.

Money stock increased mainly in 1950, 1953–54, 1959–60, 1963–64, 1966, 1969–73, 1975–76 and 1978–79, with falls or low rates of increase for 1951–52, 1955–58, 1961–62, 1965, 1967–68, 1974, 1977 and 1980. The interest rate increased mainly in 1952, 1956, 1961–62, 1966–67, 1973–75 (slowly) and 1976–80 (at a high rate).

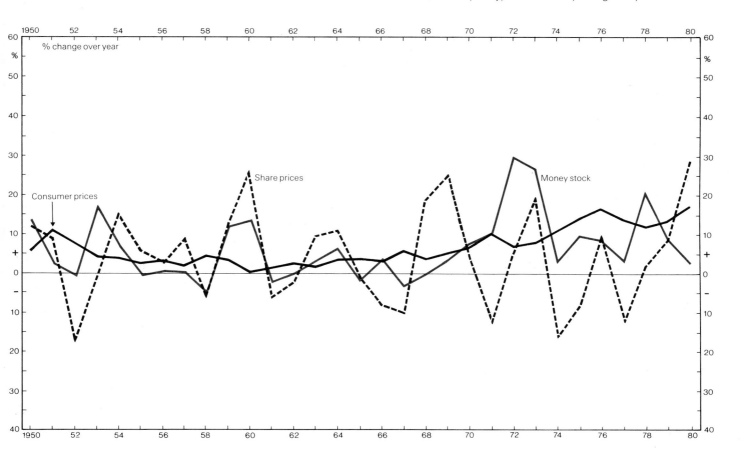

	Consumer prices		Share prices		Money stock		Interest rate[a]		
	Index 1970 = 100	% change over year	Index 1970 = 100	% change over year	Index 1970 = 100	% change over year	%	Change over year[b]	
1950	44.4	5.8	42	12	55.6	13.4	3.07	0.07	1950
1951	49.4	11.4	46	9	56.8	2.3	3.08	0.01	1951
1952	53.3	7.9	38	−17	56.5	−0.6	3.85	0.77	1952
1953	55.8	4.7	38	0	66.1	17.0	4.03	0.18	1953
1954	58.3	4.5	44	15	71.1	7.6	3.98	−0.05	1954
1955	59.8	2.6	46	6	71.0	−0.2	4.15	0.17	1955
1956	61.9	3.5	48	3	71.5	0.7	4.65	0.50	1956
1957	63.2	2.1	52	9	71.7	0.3	4.82	0.17	1957
1958	66.1	4.6	49	−6	68.0	−5.2	4.95	0.13	1958
1959	68.5	3.6	56	13	76.1	12.0	4.85	−0.10	1959
1960	69.0	0.7	70	26	86.6	13.7	4.83	−0.02	1960
1961	70.2	1.7	66	−6	84.7	−2.2	5.08	0.25	1961
1962	72.2	2.8	65	−2	84.4	−0.4	5.25	0.17	1962
1963	73.5	1.8	71	10	86.9	2.9	5.15	−0.10	1963
1964	76.0	3.4	79	11	92.5	6.5	5.06	−0.09	1964
1965	78.7	3.6	78	−1	91.1	−1.5	5.10	0.04	1965
1966	81.0	2.9	72	−8	94.0	3.2	5.28	0.18	1966
1967	85.7	5.8	65	−10	90.7	−3.6	5.51	0.23	1967
1968	89.4	4.3	77	19	90.6	−0.1	5.53	0.02	1968
1969	93.9	5.0	96	25	93.0	2.7	5.54	0.01	1969
1970	100.0	6.5	100	4	100.0	7.5	5.51	−0.03	1970
1971	110.1	10.1	88	−12	110.0	10.0	5.52	0.01	1971
1972	118.0	7.2	92	5	142.9	29.9	5.52	0.00	1972
1973	127.7	8.2	110	19	180.9	26.6	5.80	0.28	1973
1974	141.8	11.0	92	−16	186.6	3.1	6.09	0.29	1974
1975	162.6	14.7	85	−8	204.6	9.7	6.33	0.24	1975
1976	190.4	17.1	93	9	222.4	8.7	8.34	2.01	1976
1977	217.7	14.3	82	−12	229.0	3.0	9.23	0.89	1977
1978	243.7	11.9	83	2	276.2	20.6	9.97	0.74	1978
1979	276.9	13.6	91	9	298.6	8.1	12.04	2.07	1979
1980	324.5	17.2	118	29	304.6	2.0	13.29	1.25	1980

[a]Government bond yield   [b]In percentage points

105

Nicaragua

The main periods of expansion in gross domestic product were 1951–52, 1954–55, 1957, 1961–65, 1967, 1969, 1971, 1973–74 and 1976–77; there was a fall or low growth in 1956, 1958–60, 1966, 1968, 1970, 1972 and 1975, with a substantial fall in 1978–79. Fixed investment, for the time covered, rose mainly in 1962–66, 1969, 1973–74 and 1976–77, with falls or low growth in 1956–58, 1960, 1967–68, 1970–72, 1975 and 1978. Money stock increased mainly in 1951–54, 1962–65, 1972–74, 1976 and 1979–80. International reserves increased mainly in 1951–52, 1957, 1959, 1963–65, 1968, 1970–73 and 1975–76, with sharp falls in 1956, 1958, 1967 and 1978.

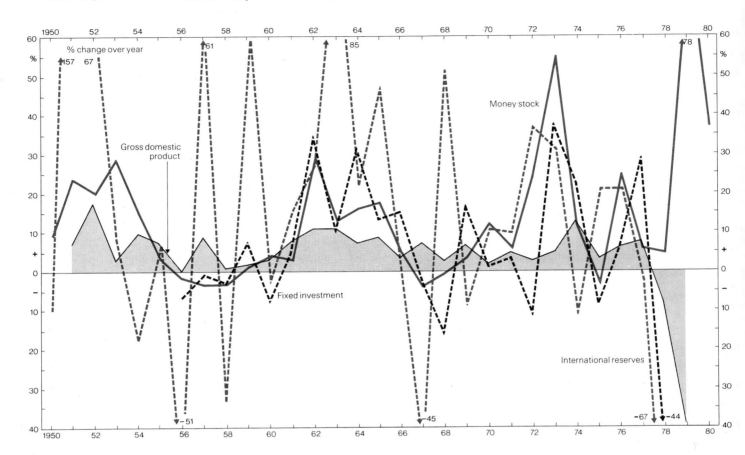

	Gross domestic product		Fixed investment		Money stock		International reserves		
	Index 1970 = 100	% change over year	Index 1970 = 100	% change over year	Index 1970 = 100	% change over year	Index 1970 = 100	% change over year	
1950	31.7	na	na	na	19	9	7	−10	1950
1951	33.8	6.7	na	na	24	23	19	157	1951
1952	39.6	16.9	na	na	29	20	31	67	1952
1953	40.5	2.4	na	na	37	28	34	8	1953
1954	44.3	9.3	na	na	42	15	28	−18	1954
1955	47.3	6.8	45	na	43	3	29	6	1955
1956	47.2	−0.1	42	−7	42	−2	14	−51	1956
1957	51.2	8.5	41	−1	41	−3	23	61	1957
1958	51.4	0.3	40	−3	40	−3	15	−33	1958
1959	52.2	1.5	43	7	40	1	24	58	1959
1960	53.6	2.7	40	−8	42	4	24	−2	1960
1961	57.7	7.6	42	5	43	3	28	15	1961
1962	63.9	10.8	56	34	56	29	35	27	1962
1963	70.9	10.9	61	10	63	13	65	85	1963
1964	75.8	7.0	80	31	73	16	79	22	1964
1965	82.6	8.9	91	13	85	17	117	47	1965
1966	85.3	3.3	104	15	90	5	118	1	1966
1967	91.3	7.0	101	−3	86	−4	65	−45	1967
1968	93.0	1.8	85	−16	86	0	99	51	1968
1969	98.7	6.2	99	16	89	4	90	−9	1969
1970	100.0	1.3	100	1	100	12	100	11	1970
1971	104.9	4.9	103	3	106	6	110	10	1971
1972	107.7	2.6	92	−11	131	24	150	37	1972
1973	113.0	5.0	126	37	203	55	197	31	1973
1974	126.9	12.3	154	22	227	12	175	−11	1974
1975	130.7	3.0	139	−9	219	−3	211	21	1975
1976	138.3	5.8	147	6	274	25	256	21	1976
1977	148.7	7.6	189	28	292	6	250	−2	1977
1978	137.0	−7.9	105	−44	306	5	81	−67	1978
1979	82.7	−39.6	na	na	544	78	na	na	1979
1980	na	na	na	na	747	37	na	na	1980

Nigeria

Over the time for which figures are available, the main periods of expansion in gross domestic product were 1954–55, 1957–60, 1962–65, 1969–74 and 1976–77; there were falls or a low growth rate in 1956, 1961, 1966–68 (Biafra civil war) and 1975. Exports increased mainly in 1952–54, 1956, 1959, 1961–62, 1964–66, 1969–74, 1976 and 1979, with falls in 1951, 1955, 1957–58, 1960, 1967–68, 1975, 1978 and 1980. Unemployment, for the time covered, increased mainly in 1958, 1960–64, 1966, 1970–74 and 1978, with reductions in 1967–69 and 1975–77. Consumer prices increased mainly in 1955–56, 1960–62, 1965–66, 1969, 1971 and 1973–80.

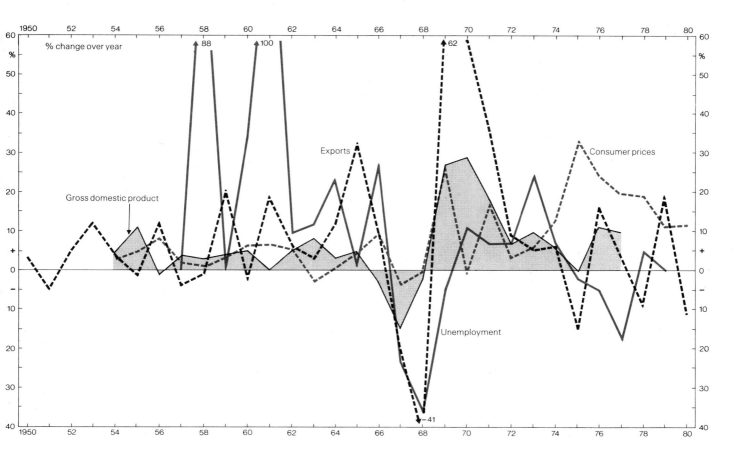

	Gross domestic product[a]		Exports		Unemployment		Consumer prices		
	Index 1970 = 100	% change over year	Index 1970 = 100	% change over year	Number (000)	% change over year	Index 1970 = 100	% change over year	
1950	na	na	26	3	na	na	na	na	1950
1951	na	na	25	−5	na	na	na	na	1951
1952	na	na	26	5	na	na	na	na	1952
1953	45.3	na	30	12	na	na	50.3	na	1953
1954	47.7	5	31	4	na	na	51.9	3.2	1954
1955	52.8	11	31	−1	na	na	54.5	5.0	1955
1956	52.3	−1	34	12	2.7	na	58.8	7.9	1956
1957	54.4	4	33	−4	2.7	0	59.9	1.9	1957
1958	56.3	3	32	−1	5.1	88	60.4	0.8	1958
1959	58.7	4	39	20	5.1	1	62.4	3.3	1959
1960	61.4	5	38	−2	6.9	34	66.4	6.4	1960
1961	61.7	0	45	19	13.7	100	70.7	6.5	1961
1962	64.6	5	48	6	15.1	10	74.4	5.2	1962
1963	70.0	8	50	3	16.8	12	72.4	−2.7	1963
1964	71.9	3	56	12	20.7	23	73.0	0.8	1964
1965	75.8	5	74	32	20.9	1	76.0	4.1	1965
1966	73.3	−3	81	9	26.6	27	83.3	9.6	1966
1967	62.3	−15	66	−19	20.1	−24	80.2	−3.7	1967
1968	61.0	−2	39	−41	12.9	−36	79.8	−0.5	1968
1969	77.4	27	63	62	12.2	−5	100.6	26.1	1969
1970	100.0	29	100	59	13.5	11	100.0	−0.6	1970
1971	118.4	18	135	35	14.4	7	116.1	16.1	1971
1972	127.0	7	147	9	15.4	7	119.3	2.8	1972
1973	139.1	10	154	5	19.1	24	126.5	6.0	1973
1974	147.4	6	164	6	20.5	7	142.2	12.4	1974
1975	147.6	0	139	−15	20.0	−2	190.1	33.7	1975
1976	163.5	11	161	16	19.0	−5	236.3	24.3	1976
1977	179.8	10	165	3	15.8	−17	281.9	19.3	1977
1978	na	na	150	−9	16.7	5	334.6	18.7	1978
1979	na	na	179	19	16.7	0	371.8	11.1	1979
1980	na	na	160	−11	na	na	414.2	11.4	1980

[a]Years beginning April 1st

Norway

Gross domestic product expanded at a comparatively steady rate throughout, with slightly higher rates of growth in 1950–51, 1953–54, 1956, 1960–67, 1969 and 1971–76, and slightly lower rates in 1955, 1957–59, 1968 and 1970. Consumers expenditure increased mainly in 1950, 1952–56, 1959–61, 1963–69 and 1971–77, with falls or low growth in 1951, 1958, 1962, 1970 and 1978–80. Fixed investment increased mainly in 1952–55, 1957–58, 1961–67, 1970–71 and 1973–77, with falls in 1951, 1959, 1968–69, 1972 and 1978–80. Exports increased mainly in 1950–51, 1954, 1956, 1959, 1963–70, 1972–73, 1976 and 1978.

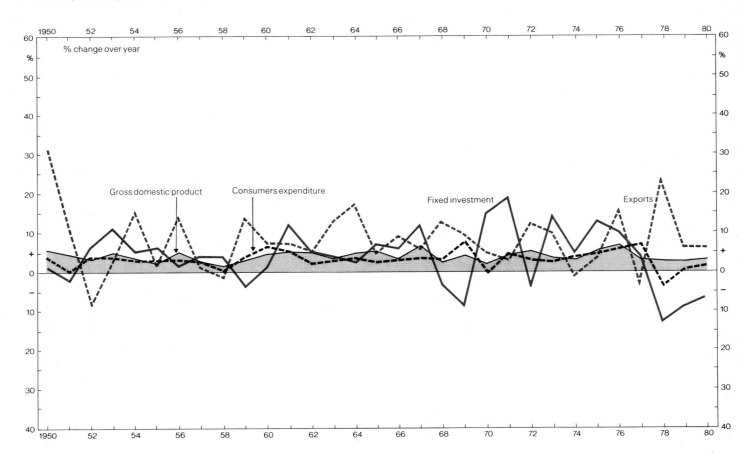

	Gross domestic product		Consumers expenditure		Fixed investment		Exports		
	Index 1970 = 100	% change over year	Index 1970 = 100	% change over year	Index 1970 = 100	% change over year	Index 1970 = 100	% change over year	
1950	46.5	5.5	52.5	4.1	45.2	1	25	31	1950
1951	48.7	4.6	52.6	0.1	44.5	−2	28	11	1951
1952	50.4	3.6	54.6	3.9	47.3	6	25	−8	1952
1953	52.9	5.0	56.8	4.1	52.7	11	26	3	1953
1954	55.0	3.8	58.6	3.0	55.3	5	30	15	1954
1955	56.1	2.1	60.4	3.1	58.4	6	31	2	1955
1956	59.0	5.1	62.3	3.1	58.8	1	35	14	1956
1957	60.4	2.3	63.7	2.3	61.1	4	35	1	1957
1958	61.2	1.3	63.8	0.3	63.6	4	35	−1	1958
1959	62.9	2.9	66.3	3.9	60.7	−4	40	14	1959
1960	65.9	4.7	70.5	6.2	61.5	1	43	7	1960
1961	69.3	5.1	74.2	5.2	69.1	12	45	7	1961
1962	72.5	4.7	75.8	2.2	72.5	5	48	5	1962
1963	75.2	3.8	78.4	3.4	75.2	4	54	13	1963
1964	79.0	5.0	81.3	3.7	77.7	3	63	17	1964
1965	83.2	5.3	83.3	2.5	83.0	7	66	5	1965
1966	86.3	3.8	86.3	3.6	87.9	6	72	9	1966
1967	91.7	6.3	89.6	3.8	98.2	12	76	6	1967
1968	93.8	2.3	92.9	3.7	95.2	−3	86	13	1968
1969	98.0	4.5	100.0	7.7	87.1	−9	95	10	1969
1970	100.0	2.0	100.0	0.0	100.0	15	100	5	1970
1971	104.6	4.6	104.6	4.6	118.8	19	103	3	1971
1972	110.0	5.2	107.7	3.0	113.9	−4	115	12	1972
1973	114.5	4.1	110.8	2.9	129.4	14	127	10	1973
1974	118.9	3.8	115.3	4.1	135.3	5	126	−1	1974
1975	125.5	5.5	121.0	4.9	152.2	13	131	4	1975
1976	134.0	6.8	128.3	6.1	167.6	10	151	15	1976
1977	138.8	3.6	137.2	6.9	173.7	4	145	−3	1977
1978	143.4	3.3	131.9	−3.8	151.3	−13	179	23	1978
1979	147.9	3.2	132.8	0.7	138.0	−9	190	6	1979
1980	153.2	3.6	134.4	1.2	128.8	−7	200	6	1980

Norway

Consumer prices, after a high rate of increase in 1951–52, were comparatively stable over 1953–69, followed by higher rises in 1970–78 and 1980. Share prices increased mainly in 1950-51, 1954–56, 1959–61, 1969–70, 1973 and 1979–80, with falls in 1952–53, 1957–58, 1962–63, 1965–67, 1972, 1974–75 and 1977–78. Changes in money stock were similar to those for consumer prices, with a high rate of increase for 1951–52, a comparatively stable rate of growth for 1953–67 and subsequent higher growth in 1968 and 1970–77. The interest rate, for the short time covered, increased in 1973–74, 1977 and 1980, with falls in 1975–76 and 1978–79.

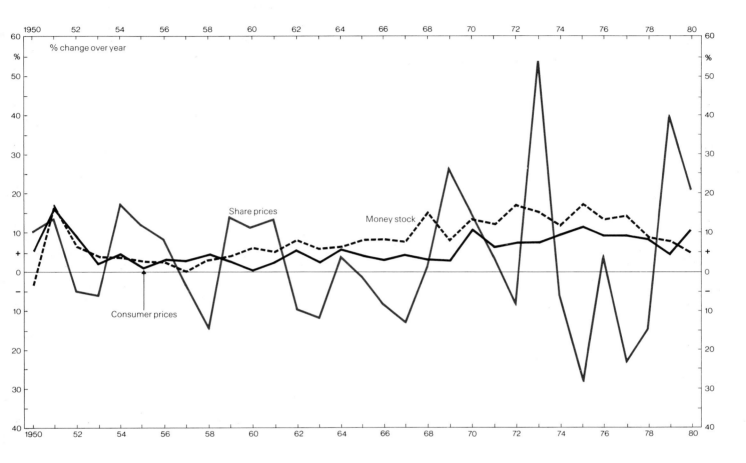

	Consumer prices		Share prices		Money stock		Interest rate		
	Index 1970 = 100	% change over year	Index 1970 = 100	% change over year	Index 1970 = 100	% change over year	%	Change over year[a]	
1950	41.4	5.3	64	10	28	−3	na	na	1950
1951	48.0	15.9	72	13	33	16	na	na	1951
1952	52.3	9.0	68	−5	35	7	na	na	1952
1953	53.3	1.9	64	−6	36	4	na	na	1953
1954	55.7	4.5	75	17	38	4	na	na	1954
1955	56.2	0.9	84	12	39	3	na	na	1955
1956	58.4	3.9	91	8	40	3	na	na	1956
1957	60.0	2.7	87	−4	40	0	na	na	1957
1958	62.8	4.7	74	−15	41	3	na	na	1958
1959	64.3	2.4	84	14	43	4	na	na	1959
1960	64.4	0.2	93	11	45	6	na	na	1960
1961	66.0	2.5	105	13	47	5	na	na	1961
1962	69.6	5.5	94	−10	51	8	na	na	1962
1963	71.4	2.6	83	−12	54	6	na	na	1963
1964	75.4	5.6	86	4	57	6	na	na	1964
1965	78.6	4.2	85	−1	62	8	na	na	1965
1966	81.3	3.4	78	−8	66	8	na	na	1966
1967	84.7	4.2	68	−13	71	7	na	na	1967
1968	87.7	3.5	69	1	82	15	na	na	1968
1969	90.4	3.1	87	26	89	8	na	na	1969
1970	100.0	10.6	100	15	100	13	na	na	1970
1971	106.2	6.2	104	4	112	12	na	na	1971
1972	113.9	7.3	95	−9	130	17	4.89	na	1972
1973	122.4	7.5	146	54	150	15	7.00	2.11	1973
1974	133.9	9.4	137	−6	168	12	8.09	1.09	1974
1975	149.5	11.7	98	−28	196	17	7.53	−0.56	1975
1976	163.3	9.2	102	4	220	13	7.43	−0.10	1976
1977	178.2	9.2	78	−23	252	14	9.84	2.41	1977
1978	192.4	8.0	67	−15	273	9	9.38	−0.46	1978
1979	201.8	4.9	93	40	294	8	8.39	−0.99	1979
1980	223.5	10.7	113	21	310	5	11.16	2.77	1980

[a] In percentage points

Pakistan

Over the time for which figures are available, from 1962, the main periods of expansion in gross domestic product were 1962–66, 1968–70, 1973–74 and 1976–80 (with rather lower growth for 1977 and 1979); there was low growth in 1967, 1971–72 and 1975. Fixed investment, for the time covered, increased mainly in 1965, 1967–68,

1970, 1974, 1976–78 and 1980, with falls in 1966, 1969, 1971–72 and 1979. Share prices, from 1961, increased mainly in 1961–63, 1968–70, 1973, 1975 and 1977–79, with falls in 1964–67, 1971–72 and 1974. The interest rate increased mainly in 1950, 1952, 1956, 1960–61, 1964–65, 1967, 1971, 1973–74 and 1977.

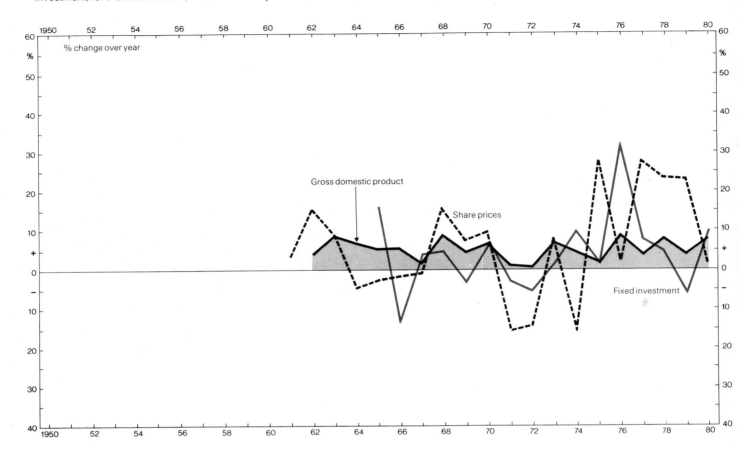

	Gross domestic product[a]		Fixed investment[a]		Share prices		Interest rate		
	Index 1970 = 100	% change over year	Index 1970 = 100	% change over year	Index 1970 = 100	% change over year	%	Change over year[b]	
1950	na	na	na	na	na	na	0.99	0.54	1950
1951	na	na	na	na	na	na	1.00	0.01	1951
1952	na	na	na	na	na	na	2.10	1.10	1952
1953	na	na	na	na	na	na	1.01	−1.09	1953
1954	na	na	na	na	na	na	1.30	0.29	1954
1955	na	na	na	na	na	na	1.45	0.15	1955
1956	na	na	na	na	na	na	2.04	0.59	1956
1957	na	na	na	na	na	na	2.06	0.02	1957
1958	na	na	na	na	na	na	1.66	−0.40	1958
1959	na	na	na	na	na	na	1.52	−0.14	1959
1960	na	na	na	na	63.5	na	3.42	1.90	1960
1961	61.5	na	na	na	65.8	3.6	3.87	0.45	1961
1962	64.1	4.1	na	na	75.9	15.3	3.38	−0.49	1962
1963	69.3	8.2	na	na	82.1	8.2	3.01	−0.37	1963
1964	74.0	6.7	92	na	78.4	−4.5	3.57	0.56	1964
1965	77.8	5.2	106	15	76.4	−2.6	5.86	2.29	1965
1966	81.9	5.2	91	−14	74.9	−2.0	4.70	−1.16	1966
1967	83.2	1.5	94	3	74.1	−1.1	6.57	1.87	1967
1968	89.9	8.1	98	4	85.3	15.1	6.24	−0.33	1968
1969	93.9	4.4	94	−4	91.5	7.3	5.40	−0.84	1969
1970	100.0	6.5	100	6	100.0	9.3	5.50	0.10	1970
1971	100.7	0.7	96	−4	84.3	−15.7	6.60	1.10	1971
1972	101.1	0.4	90	−6	71.8	−14.8	5.34	−1.26	1972
1973	108.1	6.9	91	1	77.4	7.8	6.51	1.17	1973
1974	112.6	4.2	100	9	65.5	−15.4	10.33	3.82	1974
1975	114.2	1.4	100	1	83.4	27.3	9.87	−0.46	1975
1976	123.4	8.0	132	31	84.8	1.7	9.37	−0.50	1976
1977	127.8	3.6	141	7	107.9	27.2	10.87	1.50	1977
1978	137.3	7.4	146	4	132.7	23.0	10.41	−0.46	1978
1979	142.2	3.6	136	−7	163.1	22.9	8.83	−1.58	1979
1980	152.9	7.5	148	9	164.5	0.9	8.63	−0.20	1980

[a]Years ending June 30th   [b]In percentage points

Panama

The main periods of expansion in gross domestic product were 1952–57, 1959–63, 1965–73 and 1977–80; there were falls or low growth in 1950–51, 1958, 1964 and 1974–76. Fixed investment, for the time covered, increased mainly in 1961–63, 1965–66, 1968–72, 1975–76, 1978 and 1980, with falls in 1964, 1973–74, 1977 and 1979.

Exports increased mainly in 1953–55, 1957, 1961–63, 1965–66, 1969, 1975 and 1977, with falls or a low growth rate in 1950–52, 1956, 1958, 1960, 1967, 1970, 1972–74, 1976 and 1978–80. Consumer prices were comparatively stable during the period 1952 to 1971, with main rises in 1951, 1972–75 and 1979–80.

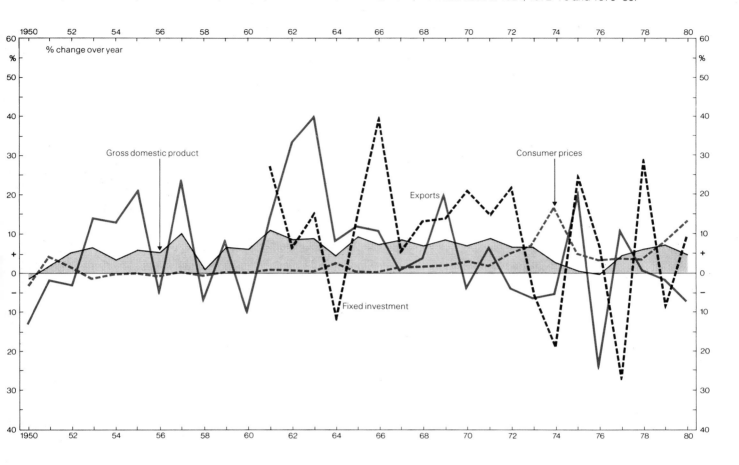

% change over year

	Gross domestic product		Fixed investment		Exports		Consumer prices		
	Index 1970 = 100	% change over year	Index 1970 = 100	% change over year	Index 1970 = 100	% change over year	Index 1970 = 100	% change over year	
1950	28.2	−1.1	na	na	19	−13	85.6	−3.2	1950
1951	28.7	1.8	na	na	18	−2	89.1	4.1	1951
1952	30.3	5.4	na	na	18	−3	90.1	1.1	1952
1953	32.1	6.1	na	na	20	14	89.0	−1.2	1953
1954	33.3	3.6	na	na	23	13	88.6	−0.4	1954
1955	35.2	5.8	na	na	28	21	88.5	−0.1	1955
1956	37.0	5.2	na	na	26	−5	88.1	−0.5	1956
1957	40.9	10.5	na	na	32	23	88.2	0.1	1957
1958	41.2	0.8	na	na	30	−7	87.9	−0.3	1958
1959	43.8	6.4	na	na	32	8	88.0	0.1	1959
1960	46.5	6.0	27.7	na	29	−10	88.1	0.1	1960
1961	51.5	10.8	35.2	27.2	33	14	88.7	0.7	1961
1962	55.8	8.3	37.6	6.9	44	33	89.3	0.7	1962
1963	60.5	8.5	43.2	14.7	62	40	89.7	0.4	1963
1964	63.2	4.4	38.3	−11.3	67	8	91.9	2.5	1964
1965	69.0	9.2	43.8	14.2	75	12	92.3	0.4	1965
1966	74.2	7.6	60.9	39.1	83	11	92.5	0.2	1966
1967	80.6	8.6	64.3	5.6	84	1	93.8	1.4	1967
1968	86.2	7.0	72.6	12.9	87	4	95.3	1.6	1968
1969	93.5	8.4	82.7	13.9	104	20	97.0	1.8	1969
1970	100.0	7.0	100.0	20.9	100	−4	100.0	3.1	1970
1971	108.7	8.7	114.8	14.8	107	7	102.0	2.0	1971
1972	115.6	6.3	139.2	21.2	103	−4	107.4	5.3	1972
1973	123.1	6.5	131.6	−5.4	97	−6	114.8	6.9	1973
1974	126.3	2.6	106.6	−19.0	92	−5	134.1	16.8	1974
1975	127.1	0.6	132.7	24.5	110	20	141.5	5.5	1975
1976	126.7	−0.3	141.3	6.5	84	−24	147.2	4.0	1976
1977	132.5	4.6	102.7	−27.3	92	11	153.8	4.5	1977
1978	141.1	6.5	131.5	28.0	94	1	160.3	4.2	1978
1979	151.1	7.1	120.3	−8.5	92	−1	173.1	7.9	1979
1980	158.5	4.9	131.1	9.0	86	−7	197.0	13.8	1980

Papua New Guinea

Over the time for which figures are available, from 1967, the main periods of expansion in gross domestic product were 1970–71, 1973 and 1977–79; there was a fall or low growth in 1975–76 and 1980. Fixed investment, for the time available, increased mainly in 1967, 1970–71, 1975 and 1977, with falls or low growth in 1968, 1972–74 and 1976. Exports of goods and services, for the time available, increased throughout 1967–75 (especially for 1972–73) and in 1977; there was a fall in 1976. Consumer prices, for the time available, increased mainly in 1974–75 and 1980, with a relatively stable rate for other years.

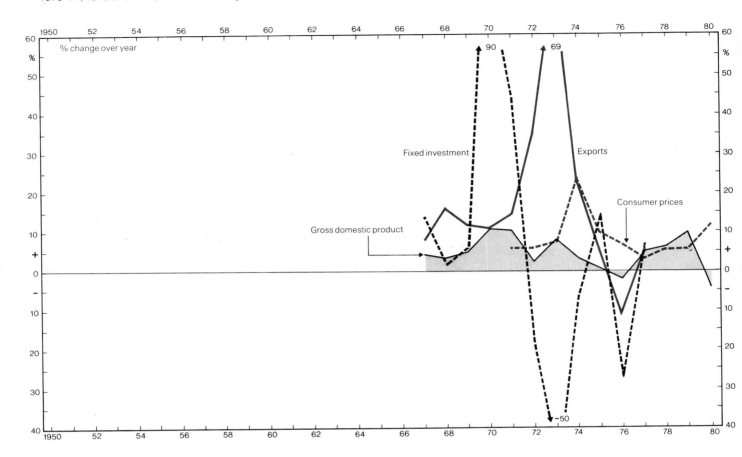

	Gross domestic product		Fixed investment[a]		Exports[a,b]		Consumer prices		
	Index 1970 = 100	% change over year	Index 1970 = 100	% change over year	Index 1970 = 100	% change over year	Index 1970 = 100	% change over year	
1950	na	na	na	na	na	na	na	na	1950
1951	na	na	na	na	na	na	na	na	1951
1952	na	na	na	na	na	na	na	na	1952
1953	na	na	na	na	na	na	na	na	1953
1954	na	na	na	na	na	na	na	na	1954
1955	na	na	na	na	na	na	na	na	1955
1956	na	na	na	na	na	na	na	na	1956
1957	na	na	na	na	na	na	na	na	1957
1958	na	na	na	na	na	na	na	na	1958
1959	na	na	na	na	na	na	na	na	1959
1960	na	na	na	na	na	na	na	na	1960
1961	na	na	na	na	na	na	na	na	1961
1962	na	na	na	na	na	na	na	na	1962
1963	na	na	na	na	na	na	na	na	1963
1964	na	na	na	na	na	na	na	na	1964
1965	na	na	na	na	na	na	na	na	1965
1966	78.9	na	42.6	na	63.8	na	na	na	1966
1967	82.6	4.6	48.6	14.2	69.2	8.4	na	na	1967
1968	85.5	3.5	49.5	1.8	80.1	15.9	na	na	1968
1969	90.0	5.3	52.5	6.2	89.9	12.1	na	na	1969
1970	100.0	11.2	100.0	90.4	100.0	11.3	100.0	na	1970
1971	110.6	10.6	144.2	44.2	114.6	14.6	105.9	5.9	1971
1972	113.3	2.5	117.8	−18.3	155.2	35.4	112.3	6.1	1972
1973	123.2	8.7	58.7	−50.2	261.7	68.6	121.8	8.4	1973
1974	127.9	3.8	55.2	−5.9	320.9	22.6	149.9	23.1	1974
1975	129.0	0.9	63.5	14.9	341.0	6.3	165.7	10.5	1975
1976	127.0	−1.6	46.3	−27.0	305.5	−10.4	178.6	7.8	1976
1977	134.0	5.5	50.3	8.4	325.3	6.5	186.4	4.4	1977
1978	142.6	6.4	na	na	na	na	197.2	5.8	1978
1979	157.6	10.5	na	na	na	na	208.6	5.8	1979
1980	151.4	−3.9	na	na	na	na	233.8	12.1	1980

[a]Years ending June 30th   [b]Including exports of services

Paraguay

The main periods of expansion in gross domestic product were 1953–58, 1961–62, 1964–65 and 1967–80; there were falls or low growth in 1951–52, 1959–60 and 1966. Fixed investment, for the time covered, increased mainly in 1957, 1960–61, 1964–67 and 1973–80, with falls in 1956, 1958–59, 1962–63, 1968 and 1970. Exports increased mainly in 1953, 1956, 1958, 1960–61, 1963–65, 1969–70, 1972–73, 1977 and 1979, with falls or low growth in 1950–52, 1954–55, 1957, 1959, 1962, 1966, 1968, 1971, 1974–76, 1978 and 1980. Consumer prices rose at very high rates for 1950–56 and at high rates for 1957–61, 1972–75 and 1978–80.

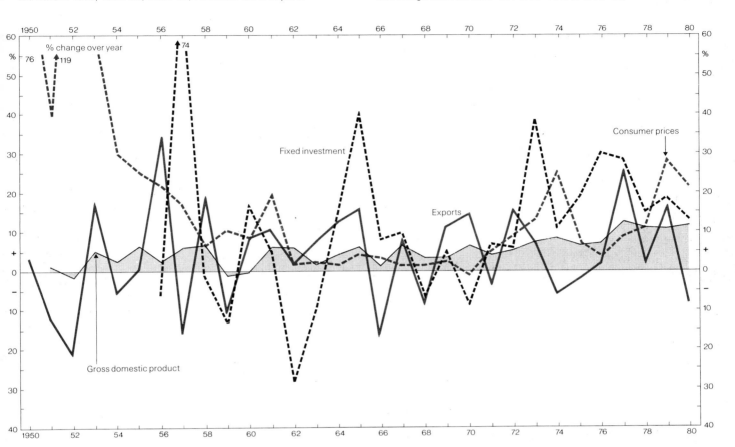

	Gross domestic product		Fixed investment		Exports		Consumer prices		
	Index 1970 = 100	% change over year	Index 1970 = 100	% change over year	Index 1970 = 100	% change over year	Index 1970 = 100	% change over year	
1950	49.4	na	na	na	69	2	5.2	76	1950
1951	49.9	1.1	na	na	59	−13	7.3	40	1951
1952	49.3	−1.1	na	na	46	−22	16.1	119	1952
1953	51.9	5.2	na	na	54	16	25.5	58	1953
1954	53.2	2.6	na	na	50	−6	33.0	29	1954
1955	56.6	6.3	52	na	50	0	40.8	24	1955
1956	57.9	2.4	49	−6	67	33	49.5	21	1956
1957	61.4	6.0	85	74	56	−16	57.4	16	1957
1958	65.5	6.6	84	−1	66	18	61.1	6	1958
1959	64.7	−1.1	73	−13	59	−11	67.2	10	1959
1960	64.5	−0.4	86	17	63	8	72.7	8	1960
1961	68.3	6.0	91	5	70	10	86.2	19	1961
1962	72.4	5.9	64	−29	71	1	87.3	1	1962
1963	73.8	2.0	58	−10	76	7	89.2	2	1963
1964	77.0	4.3	66	14	85	12	90.5	1	1964
1965	81.4	5.7	92	40	98	15	93.9	4	1965
1966	82.3	1.1	100	8	81	−17	96.7	3	1966
1967	87.5	6.3	110	10	87	7	98.0	1	1967
1968	90.7	3.7	104	−6	79	−9	98.6	1	1968
1969	94.2	3.8	109	5	88	11	100.9	2	1969
1970	100.0	6.2	100	−8	100	14	100.0	−1	1970
1971	104.4	4.4	107	7	96	−4	105.0	5	1971
1972	109.7	5.1	113	6	110	15	114.7	9	1972
1973	117.6	7.2	157	38	118	7	129.3	13	1973
1974	127.3	8.2	174	11	111	−6	161.9	25	1974
1975	135.3	6.3	208	19	109	−2	172.8	7	1975
1976	144.8	7.0	271	30	111	2	180.6	.4	1976
1977	163.4	12.8	348	28	138	25	197.3	9	1977
1978	181.1	10.8	399	15	142	2	218.4	11	1978
1979	200.5	10.7	473	19	165	16	279.9	28	1979
1980	223.4	11.4	533	13	152	−8	342.8	22	1980

Peru

The main periods of expansion in gross domestic product were 1955–57, 1960–67, 1969–76 and 1979–80; there was a fall or low growth in 1954, 1958, 1968 and 1977–78. Fixed investment increased mainly in 1956, 1960–62, 1965–66, 1970–71 and 1973–75, with falls or low growth in 1954–55, 1958–59, 1963–64, 1967–68, 1972 and

1976–78. Consumer prices increased at a comparatively stable and high rate over 1950–73, with especially high rates for 1950, 1959, 1964–65 and 1968; there were very high rates for 1974–80. Share prices increased mainly in 1951–54, 1956–57, 1971, 1977–78 and 1980, with main falls in 1958–59, 1961–63, 1969, 1973–75 and 1979.

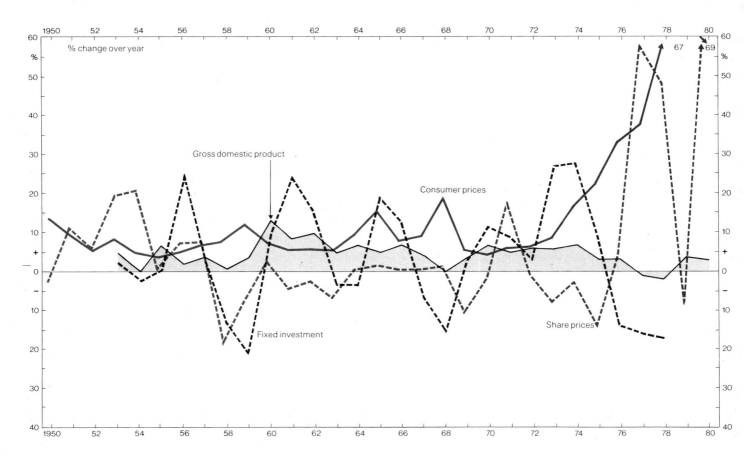

	Gross domestic product		Fixed investment		Consumer prices		Share prices		
	Index 1970 = 100	% change over year	Index 1970 = 100	% change over year	Index 1970 = 100	% change over year	Index 1970 = 100	% change over year	
1950	na	na	na	na	19.5	14.0	74	−2	1950
1951	na	na	na	na	21.5	10.2	83	12	1951
1952	40	na	62	na	22.8	6.2	89	7	1952
1953	42	5	64	2	24.9	9.2	107	20	1953
1954	42	0	62	−2	26.2	5.2	130	21	1954
1955	45	7	63	0	27.4	4.6	131	1	1955
1956	46	2	78	25	28.9	5.5	142	8	1956
1957	48	4	81	3	31.1	7.6	153	8	1957
1958	49	1	70	−13	33.6	8.0	125	−18	1958
1959	51	4	55	−21	37.8	12.5	116	−7	1959
1960	57	13	61	10	41.1	8.7	119	3	1960
1961	62	9	76	24	43.6	6.1	114	−4	1961
1962	69	10	87	16	46.5	6.7	112	−2	1962
1963	72	5	84	−3	49.2	5.8	105	−6	1963
1964	77	7	82	−3	54.1	10.0	106	1	1964
1965	81	5	98	19	62.9	16.3	108	2	1965
1966	86	7	110	13	68.5	8.9	109	1	1966
1967	89	4	102	−7	75.3	9.9	110	1	1967
1968	89	0	87	−15	89.6	19.0	112	2	1968
1969	93	4	89	3	95.2	6.2	101	−10	1969
1970	100	7	100	12	100.0	5.0	100	−1	1970
1971	105	5	109	9	106.8	6.8	118	18	1971
1972	111	6	112	3	114.4	7.1	118	0	1972
1973	118	6	142	27	125.3	9.5	110	−7	1973
1974	126	7	182	28	146.5	16.9	108	−2	1974
1975	130	3	196	8	181.1	23.6	93	−14	1975
1976	134	3	168	−14	241.8	33.5	98	5	1976
1977	133	−1	142	−16	333.8	38.1	154	58	1977
1978	130	−2	117	−17	526.8	57.8	230	49	1978
1979	135	4	na	na	878.2	66.7	213	−7	1979
1980	140	3	na	na	1 398.1	59.2	361	69	1980

Philippines

Gross national product increased at a steady rate of between about 5% and 10% per year over 1950 to 1980, with rather lower growth only for 1958, 1960, 1964 and 1970. Fixed investment increased mainly in 1953–57, 1960–61, 1963–64, 1967, 1971, 1974–76 and 1978–80, with falls or low growth in 1958–59, 1962, 1968–70, 1972–73 and

1977. Consumer prices rose mainly in 1950–51, 1960, 1962–64, 1966–67 and 1970–80 (with especially high rises in 1970–74 and 1979–80). Share prices increased mainly in 1956, 1958–59, 1963, 1967–68, 1973–74 and 1978, with falls in 1953, 1955, 1960–61, 1964–65, 1969–72, 1975, 1977 and 1979–80.

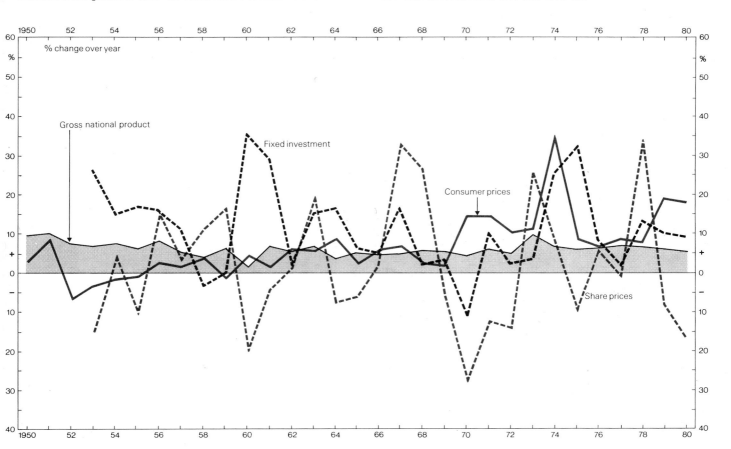

	Gross national product		Fixed investment		Consumer prices		Share prices		
	Index 1970 = 100	% change over year	Index 1970 = 100	% change over year	Index 1970 = 100	% change over year	Index 1970 = 100	% change over year	
1950	32.7	9.7	na	na	55.7	3.1	na	na	1950
1951	36.0	10.1	na	na	60.4	8.6	na	na	1951
1952	38.6	7.5	17	na	56.5	−6.5	89.4	na	1952
1953	41.4	7.0	21	26	54.6	−3.4	75.8	−15.2	1953
1954	44.5	7.7	24	15	53.8	−1.5	79.0	4.2	1954
1955	47.4	6.4	28	17	53.3	−0.9	70.9	−10.3	1955
1956	51.1	7.9	33	16	54.7	2.6	81.5	15.0	1956
1957	53.8	5.3	36	11	55.6	1.6	84.1	3.2	1957
1958	56.0	4.0	35	−3	57.6	3.6	93.4	11.1	1958
1959	59.5	6.3	35	0	57.0	−1.0	108.4	16.1	1959
1960	60.3	1.4	47	35	59.4	4.2	86.9	−19.8	1960
1961	64.4	6.9	61	29	60.3	1.5	83.0	−4.5	1961
1962	68.0	5.5	62	2	63.8	5.8	83.8	1.0	1962
1963	72.7	6.9	72	15	67.4	5.6	100.0	19.3	1963
1964	75.2	3.4	83	16	72.9	8.2	92.3	−7.7	1964
1965	79.0	5.0	88	6	74.8	2.6	86.7	−6.1	1965
1966	82.4	4.4	93	5	78.8	5.3	88.0	1.5	1966
1967	86.4	4.8	107	16	83.8	6.3	116.6	32.5	1967
1968	91.0	5.4	109	2	85.7	2.3	146.8	25.9	1968
1969	95.9	5.3	112	3	87.4	2.0	138.2	−5.9	1969
1970	100.0	4.3	100	−11	100.0	14.4	100.0	−27.6	1970
1971	105.8	5.8	110	10	114.6	14.6	87.2	−12.8	1971
1972	111.0	4.9	112	2	126.3	10.2	74.4	−14.7	1972
1973	121.7	9.6	115	3	140.2	11.0	93.2	25.3	1973
1974	129.4	6.3	144	25	188.4	34.4	100.0	7.3	1974
1975	137.0	5.9	190	32	203.4	8.0	90.4	−9.6	1975
1976	145.3	6.1	206	8	216.0	6.2	95.1	5.2	1976
1977	155.5	7.0	210	2	233.1	7.9	94.4	−0.8	1977
1978	166.0	6.8	237	13	250.8	7.6	126.4	33.9	1978
1979	176.1	6.1	260	10	298.0	18.8	115.7	−8.4	1979
1980	185.7	5.4	284	9	351.1	17.8	96.1	−17.0	1980

Portugal

The main periods of expansion in gross domestic product were 1951, 1954–57, 1959–65, 1967–68, 1970–73, 1976–77 and 1979–80; there was a fall or low growth in 1952–53, 1958, 1969, 1974–75 and 1978. Consumers expenditure increased mainly in 1954–56, 1959–61, 1963–65, 1968, 1971, 1973–74 and 1980, with falls or low growth in 1957–58, 1962, 1967, 1972, 1975 and 1977–79. Fixed investment increased mainly in 1957–61, 1963, 1965–67, 1969–73 and 1977–78, with a fall or low growth in 1962, 1968, 1974–76 and 1979. Imports increased mainly in 1953–58, 1960–61, 1963–66, 1968–74, 1976–77 and 1979–80, with falls in 1950, 1962 and 1975.

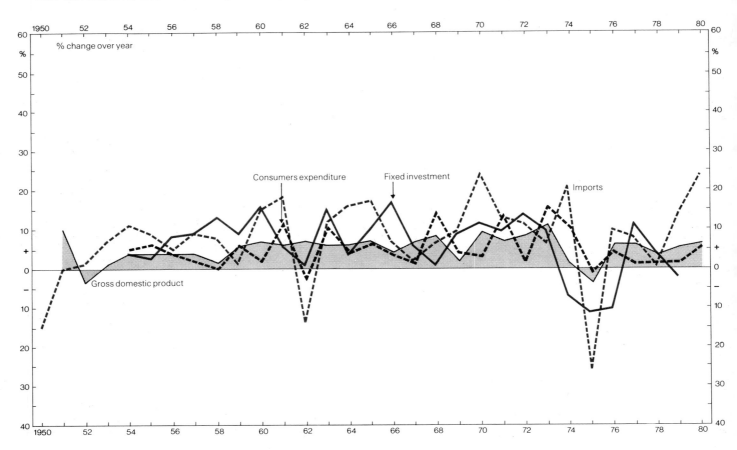

	Gross domestic product		Consumers expenditure		Fixed investment		Imports		
	Index 1970 = 100	% change over year	Index 1970 = 100	% change over year	Index 1970 = 100	% change over year	Index 1970 = 100	% change over year	
1950	38	na	na	na	na	na	22	−15	1950
1951	41	10	na	na	na	na	22	0	1951
1952	40	−3	na	na	na	na	22	1	1952
1953	41	1	46	na	26	na	24	7	1953
1954	42	4	49	5	27	4	26	11	1954
1955	44	4	51	6	28	3	29	9	1955
1956	46	4	54	4	30	8	30	5	1956
1957	48	4	55	2	32	9	33	9	1957
1958	49	2	55	0	37	13	35	8	1958
1959	52	6	58	6	40	9	36	1	1959
1960	55	7	60	2	46	16	41	15	1960
1961	58	6	66	11	49	6	48	18	1961
1962	62	7	64	−3	50	1	41	−14	1962
1963	66	6	71	10	57	15	46	12	1963
1964	70	6	74	4	59	4	54	16	1964
1965	75	7	78	6	66	10	63	17	1965
1966	77	4	81	3	77	17	67	7	1966
1967	82	7	82	1	82	6	68	2	1967
1968	89	8	93	14	82	1	73	7	1968
1969	91	2	97	4	90	9	80	10	1969
1970	100	9	100	3	100	12	100	24	1970
1971	107	7	113	13	110	10	113	13	1971
1972	115	8	114	1	125	14	127	12	1972
1973	128	11	131	15	137	10	136	7	1973
1974	130	1	144	10	127	−7	164	21	1974
1975	124	−4	143	−1	113	−11	122	−26	1975
1976	132	6	149	4	101	−10	135	10	1976
1977	139	6	150	1	114	12	145	8	1977
1978	143	3	151	1	118	4	146	1	1978
1979	150	5	153	1	116	−2	166	14	1979
1980	158	6	160	5	na	na	207	24	1980

Portugal

Consumer prices were comparatively stable up to 1965, then rose at a gradually increasing rate up to 1973; from 1974 to 1980 they rose at a high rate. Money stock increased mainly in 1951, 1954–60, 1962–65, 1967–70, 1972–73, 1975 and 1978–79; there was comparatively stable growth for 1952–60 and 1965–71. International reserves increased mainly in 1950–51, 1953–54, 1959, 1962–68, 1971–73 and 1979, with falls in 1957, 1961, 1974–76 and 1980. The interest rate (government bond yield) increased mainly in 1950, 1959, 1961–63, 1967, 1971–72 and 1977–79; also between 1973 and 1976 (1974 and 1975 figures being not available).

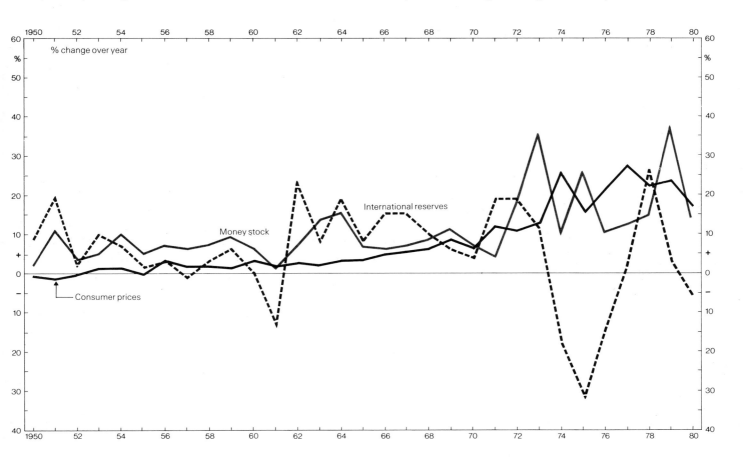

	Consumer prices		Money stock		International reserves		Interest rate[a]			
	Index 1970 = 100	% change over year	Index 1970 = 100	% change over year	Index 1970 = 100	% change over year	%	Change over year[b]		
1950	58.2	−0.7	23.5	2	26	9	3.92	0.16	1950
1951	57.4	−1.4	26.1	11	30	19	3.79	−0.13	1951
1952	57.2	−0.4	26.8	3	31	2	3.48	−0.31	1952
1953	57.8	1.0	28.2	5	34	10	3.38	−0.10	1953
1954	58.4	1.0	30.9	10	37	7	3.27	−0.11	1954
1955	58.3	−0.2	32.4	5	37	2	3.18	−0.09	1955
1956	60.2	3.3	34.6	7	39	3	3.03	−0.15	1956
1957	61.1	1.5	36.6	6	38	−1	3.05	0.02	1957
1958	62.0	1.5	39.3	7	40	3	3.03	−0.02	1958
1959	62.7	1.1	42.8	9	42	6	3.45	0.42	1959
1960	64.6	3.0	45.5	6	42	0	3.46	0.01	1960
1961	65.6	1.5	46.0	1	37	−13	3.82	0.36	1961
1962	67.3	2.6	49.3	7	45	23	3.96	0.14	1962
1963	68.7	2.1	55.8	13	49	8	4.18	0.22	1963
1964	71.0	3.3	64.1	15	58	19	3.94	−0.24	1964
1965	73.5	3.5	68.4	7	62	8	3.88	−0.06	1965
1966	77.2	5.0	72.8	6	72	15	3.96	0.08	1966
1967	81.4	5.4	77.5	7	82	15	5.00	1.04	1967
1968	86.4	6.1	84.1	8	91	10	5.11	0.11	1968
1969	94.0	8.8	93.5	11	96	6	5.15	0.04	1969
1970	100.0	6.4	100.0	7	100	4	5.28	0.13	1970
1971	111.9	11.9	104.4	4	119	19	5.70	0.42	1971
1972	123.9	10.7	121.7	17	142	19	6.01	0.31	1972
1973	139.9	12.9	164.9	35	156	11	5.50	−0.51	1973
1974	175.1	25.2	181.7	10	128	−18	na	na	1974
1975	201.8	15.2	226.3	25	87	−32	na	na	1975
1976	244.4	21.1	248.4	10	74	−15	9.74	na	1976
1977	311.0	27.3	277.4	12	76	2	10.80	1.06	1977
1978	380.8	22.5	316.6	14	96	26	16.17	5.37	1978
1979	471.6	23.8	431.2	36	98	3	16.68	0.51	1979
1980	549.7	16.6	489.3	13	93	−6	16.68	0.00	1980

[a]Government bond yield   [b]In percentage points

117

Saudi Arabia

Over the time for which figures are available, from 1968, the main periods of expansion in gross domestic product were 1968, 1970–74, 1976–77 and 1979–80; there was low growth in 1975 and comparatively low growth in 1969 and 1978. Exports of crude oil increased mainly in 1950–52, 1954, 1956, 1958–75 (with high but lower growth in 1963–64 and 1967–69), 1976 and 1979; exports fell in 1955, 1957, 1975 and 1978. Consumer prices, for the time covered, were comparatively stable, except for high rises in 1973–77. Money stock, for the time covered, increased mainly in 1962–63, 1966–68, and 1971–79 (with especially high rises for 1972–77).

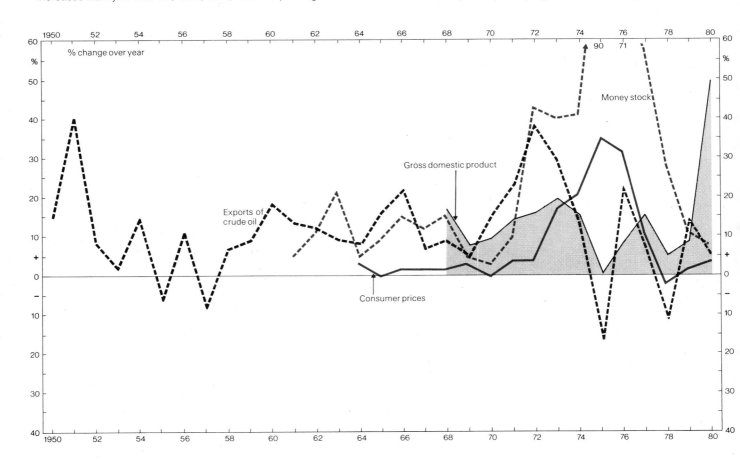

	Gross domestic product[a]		Exports of crude oil		Consumer prices		Money stock		
	Index 1970 = 100	% change over year	Index 1970 = 100	% change over year	Index 1970 = 100	% change over year	Index 1970 = 100	% change over year	
1950	na	na	14	15	na	na	na	na	1950
1951	na	na	20	40	na	na	na	na	1951
1952	na	na	22	8	na	na	na	na	1952
1953	na	na	22	2	na	na	na	na	1953
1954	na	na	25	14	na	na	na	na	1954
1955	na	na	24	−6	na	na	na	na	1955
1956	na	na	27	11	na	na	na	na	1956
1957	na	na	25	−8	na	na	na	na	1957
1958	na	na	26	7	na	na	na	na	1958
1959	na	na	29	9	na	na	na	na	1959
1960	na	na	34	18	na	na	38.3	na	1960
1961	na	na	38	13	na	na	40.4	5	1961
1962	na	na	43	12	na	na	45.0	11	1962
1963	na	na	46	9	89	na	54.6	21	1963
1964	na	na	50	8	91	3	57.1	5	1964
1965	na	na	58	16	92	0	62.5	9	1965
1966	na	na	71	22	93	2	71.7	15	1966
1967	73.0	na	76	7	95	2	80.0	12	1967
1968	84.9	16.3	83	9	96	2	91.7	15	1968
1969	91.4	7.7	87	5	100	3	96.7	5	1969
1970	100.0	9.4	100	15	100	0	100.0	3	1970
1971	114.4	14.4	123	23	104	4	110.4	10	1971
1972	132.0	15.4	169	38	109	4	157.5	43	1972
1973	158.0	19.7	218	29	127	17	220.4	40	1973
1974	181.8	15.1	246	13	154	21	311.7	41	1974
1975	182.3	0.3	205	−17	208	35	590.8	90	1975
1976	198.1	8.6	250	22	273	32	1011.2	71	1976
1977	228.0	15.1	267	7	304	11	1600.4	58	1977
1978	240.8	5.6	239	−11	299	−2	2050.4	28	1978
1979	262.3	8.9	274	14	305	2	2279.2	11	1979
1980	391.8[b]	49.4[b]	287	5	316	4	2456.7	8	1980

[a]Years ending June 30th   [b]Estimate

118

Singapore

Over the time for which figures are available, from 1961, the main periods of expansion for gross domestic product were 1961–63, 1965–66, 1968–74 and 1976–80; there were falls in 1964 and 1967, and a slackening of growth in 1975. Fixed investment, for the time covered, increased mainly in 1969–74 and 1978–79, with a fall in 1975 and low growth for 1976–77. Consumer prices, for the time covered, were comparatively stable for 1961–72 and 1975–76, with high rises in 1973–74 and rises again for 1977–80. International reserves increased mainly in 1955, 1958–59, 1962–63 and 1967–80, with falls in 1951–52, 1954, 1956–57, 1960 and 1966.

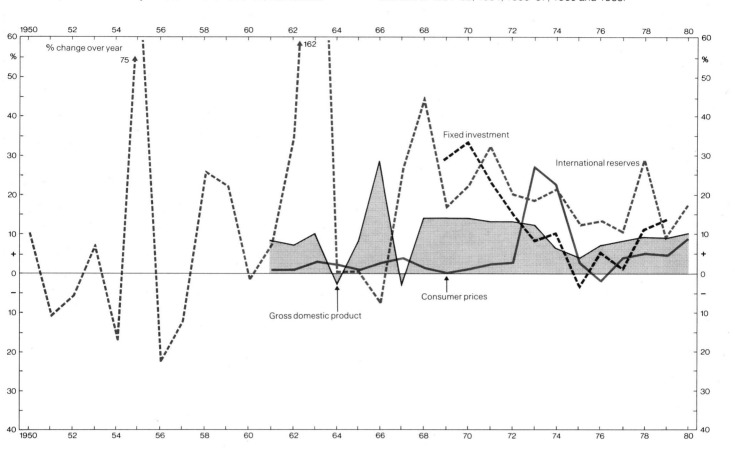

	Gross domestic product		Fixed investment		Consumer prices		International reserves		
	Index 1970 = 100	% change over year	Index 1970 = 100	% change over year	Index 1970 = 100	% change over year	Index 1970 = 100	% change over year	
1950	na	na	na	na	na	na	9	10	1950
1951	na	na	na	na	na	na	8	−11	1951
1952	na	na	na	na	na	na	7	−6	1952
1953	na	na	na	na	na	na	8	7	1953
1954	na	na	na	na	na	na	6	−17	1954
1955	na	na	na	na	na	na	11	75	1955
1956	na	na	na	na	na	na	9	−23	1956
1957	na	na	na	na	na	na	8	−13	1957
1958	na	na	na	na	na	na	9	25	1958
1959	na	na	na	na	na	na	12	22	1959
1960	41	na	na	na	89.8	na	11	−2	1960
1961	45	8	na	na	90.1	0.4	12	7	1961
1962	48	7	na	na	90.4	0.4	16	34	1962
1963	53	10	na	na	92.6	2.4	43	162	1963
1964	51	−3	na	na	93.9	1.4	43	0	1964
1965	55	8	na	na	94.2	0.4	42	0	1965
1966	70	28	na	na	96.0	1.9	39	−8	1966
1967	68	−3	na	na	99.2	3.3	49	26	1967
1968	77	14	58	na	99.8	0.7	70	44	1968
1969	88	14	75	29	99.7	−0.2	82	16	1969
1970	100	14	100	33	100.0	0.3	100	22	1970
1971	113	13	123	23	101.8	1.8	132	32	1971
1972	128	13	141	15	104.0	2.1	159	20	1972
1973	142	12	153	8	131.4	26.3	187	18	1973
1974	151	6	168	10	160.7	22.4	227	21	1974
1975	158	4	162	−4	165.0	2.7	254	12	1975
1976	169	7	170	5	161.7	−2.0	286	13	1976
1977	183	8	172	1	167.0	3.3	314	10	1977
1978	198	9	191	11	174.9	4.7	402	28	1978
1979	217	9	215	13	182.0	4.1	436	9	1979
1980	239	10	na	na	197.5	8.5	509	17	1980

South Africa

The main periods of expansion in gross domestic product were 1950–57, 1959–71, 1973–74 and 1978–80; growth over the period 1950 to 1974 was comparatively stable, with low growth in 1958, 1972 and 1975–77. Consumers expenditure also increased at a comparatively stable rate for 1950–74, with low growth in 1950, 1959 and 1961; there followed low growth or a fall in 1976–78, with further expansion in 1979–80. Fixed investment rose mainly in 1951–52, 1957–58, 1963–65, 1969–71, 1974–75 and 1980, with falls in 1950, 1954–56, 1959, 1962 and 1976–78. Exports rose mainly in 1950–51, 1953–57, 1959–62, 1966–68, 1972 and 1976–79.

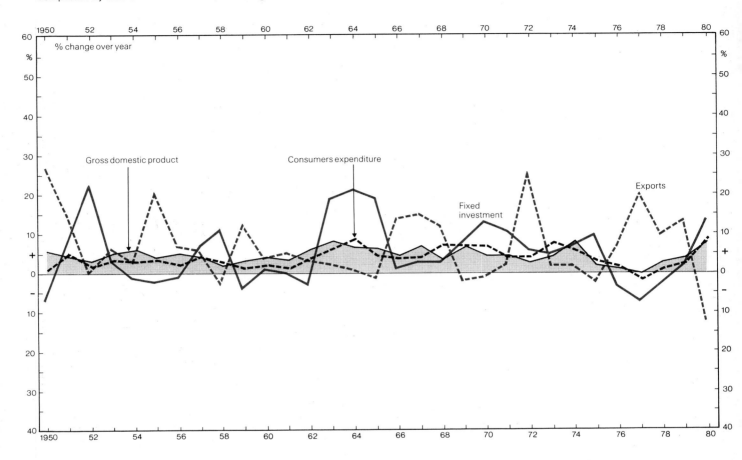

	Gross domestic product		Consumers expenditure		Fixed investment		Exports		
	Index 1970 = 100	% change over year	Index 1970 = 100	% change over year	Index 1970 = 100	% change over year	Index 1970 = 100	% change over year	
1950	37.1	5.8	41.8	1.2	30	−7	33	27	1950
1951	38.9	4.9	43.9	5.0	33	8	38	15	1951
1952	40.3	3.5	44.7	2.0	40	22	38	0	1952
1953	42.3	5.1	46.6	4.2	42	3	40	6	1953
1954	44.8	5.8	48.3	3.6	41	−1	41	3	1954
1955	46.8	4.5	50.4	4.3	41	−2	49	20	1955
1956	49.2	5.1	51.6	2.3	40	−1	52	7	1956
1957	51.5	4.7	54.0	4.7	43	7	55	6	1957
1958	52.5	1.9	55.8	3.2	47	11	54	−3	1958
1959	54.3	3.5	56.7	1.6	45	−4	60	12	1959
1960	56.7	4.4	58.1	2.5	46	1	63	4	1960
1961	58.6	3.4	58.9	1.4	46	0	66	5	1961
1962	62.2	6.1	61.3	4.1	45	−3	68	3	1962
1963	67.2	8.1	65.1	6.3	53	19	70	2	1963
1964	71.7	6.7	71.1	9.1	64	21	71	1	1964
1965	76.5	6.6	74.6	4.9	76	19	70	−1	1965
1966	80.1	4.7	77.8	4.4	77	1	80	14	1966
1967	86.0	7.3	81.4	4.6	80	3	92	15	1967
1968	89.4	4.0	87.4	7.3	82	3	103	12	1968
1969	95.4	6.8	93.4	6.9	89	8	101	−2	1969
1970	100.0	4.8	100.0	7.1	100	13	100	−1	1970
1971	104.9	4.9	104.7	4.7	111	11	102	2	1971
1972	107.8	2.7	109.0	4.1	117	6	127	25	1972
1973	112.7	4.6	117.7	7.9	123	5	129	2	1973
1974	122.0	8.3	124.7	6.0	131	7	132	2	1974
1975	124.7	2.2	129.1	3.5	144	10	130	−2	1975
1976	126.6	1.5	131.4	1.7	140	−3	139	7	1976
1977	126.6	0.0	129.8	−1.2	130	−7	166	20	1977
1978	130.2	2.9	131.2	1.1	126	−3	183	10	1978
1979	135.5	4.1	134.6	2.5	128	2	209	14	1979
1980	146.1	7.8	146.5	8.9	146	14	183	−12	1980

South Africa

Consumer prices increased at a comparatively stable rate for 1953 to 1970; there were higher rates of increase for 1951–52 and 1973–80. Share prices increased mainly in 1951, 1955, 1962–64, 1967–69, 1972–73 and 1978–80; main falls were in 1952–53, 1956, 1960, 1965–66, 1970–71, 1974 and 1977. Money stock increased mainly in 1950, 1953–54, 1959, 1962–64, 1966–69, 1971–75 and 1978–80, with falls or low rates of increase in 1951–52, 1955–58, 1960–61, 1965, 1970 and 1976–77. The interest rate increased mainly in 1952–53, 1955, 1961, 1964–65, 1967, 1971 and 1974–77; main falls were in 1962–63, 1969–70, 1973 and 1979–80.

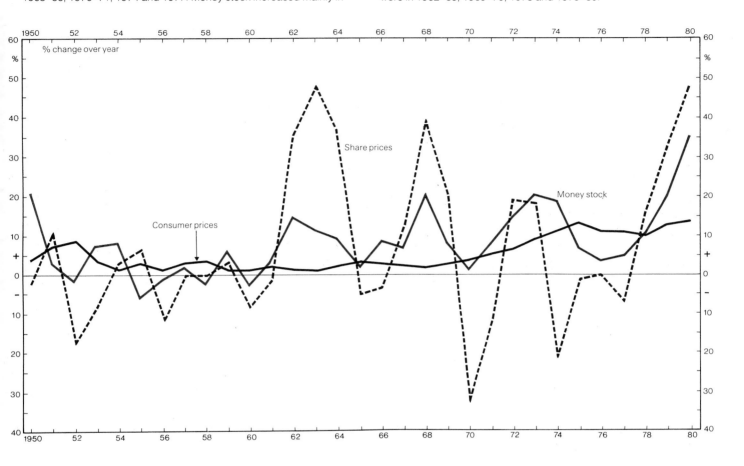

	Consumer prices		Share prices		Money stock		Interest rate		
	Index 1970 = 100	% change over year	Index 1970 = 100	% change over year	Index 1970 = 100	% change over year	%	Change over year[a]	
1950	53.7	3.9	38	−2	40.6	20.2	1.00	0.00	1950
1951	57.6	7.3	42	11	41.5	2.2	1.00	0.00	1951
1952	62.7	8.9	35	−17	40.7	−1.9	1.50	0.50	1952
1953	64.9	3.5	32	−8	43.5	7.0	1.88	0.38	1953
1954	66.1	1.8	33	3	47.0	7.9	1.94	0.06	1954
1955	68.2	3.2	36	7	44.0	−6.4	3.00	1.06	1955
1956	69.4	1.8	32	−11	43.4	−1.3	3.25	0.25	1956
1957	71.5	3.0	32	0	44.0	1.4	3.25	0.00	1957
1958	74.0	3.5	32	0	42.8	−2.7	3.60	0.35	1958
1959	75.0	1.4	33	3	45.3	5.7	3.45	−0.15	1959
1960	76.1	1.5	30	−8	43.9	−2.9	3.60	0.15	1960
1961	77.7	2.1	30	−1	45.3	3.1	4.25	0.65	1961
1962	78.7	1.3	41	36	51.9	14.7	2.78	−1.47	1962
1963	79.7	1.3	60	48	58.0	11.7	1.99	−0.79	1963
1964	81.8	2.6	83	37	63.4	9.3	2.90	0.91	1964
1965	85.0	3.9	79	−5	64.7	2.0	4.04	1.14	1965
1966	88.1	3.6	77	−3	70.7	9.3	4.20	0.16	1966
1967	91.1	3.4	87	13	75.6	6.9	4.87	0.67	1967
1968	93.0	2.1	121	39	90.8	20.2	4.90	0.03	1968
1969	96.0	3.2	146	21	98.4	8.4	4.61	−0.29	1969
1970	100.0	4.2	100	−32	100.0	1.6	4.39	−0.22	1970
1971	105.6	5.6	89	−11	108.3	8.3	5.38	0.99	1971
1972	112.5	6.5	106	19	124.4	14.9	5.30	−0.08	1972
1973	123.2	9.5	125	18	149.8	20.4	3.18	−2.12	1973
1974	137.5	11.6	99	−21	177.6	18.6	5.43	2.25	1974
1975	156.0	13.5	98	−1	189.8	6.9	6.12	0.69	1975
1976	173.5	11.2	98	0	196.5	3.5	7.44	1.32	1976
1977	192.8	11.2	91	−7	205.8	4.8	7.87	0.43	1977
1978	212.5	10.2	106	16	227.3	10.4	7.81	−0.06	1978
1979	240.4	13.1	141	33	274.5	20.7	5.26	−2.55	1979
1980	273.5	13.8	209	48	371.9	35.5	4.65	−0.61	1980

[a]In percentage points

Spain

For the time covered, from 1955, the main periods of expansion in gross domestic product were 1955–58, 1961–66, 1968–69, 1972–74 and 1976–78; there was a fall or low growth in 1959–60, 1975 and 1979–80. Consumers expenditure increased mainly in 1955–58, 1961–63, 1965–69, 1972–74 and 1976; there was a comparatively stable rate of growth throughout, with a major fall in 1960 and low growth for 1977–79. Fixed investment increased mainly in 1955–58, 1960–66, 1968–69 and 1972–74, with falls in 1959, 1971 and 1975–79. Exports increased mainly in 1950–51, 1953, 1959–60, 1964, 1966–73, 1976 and 1978–79.

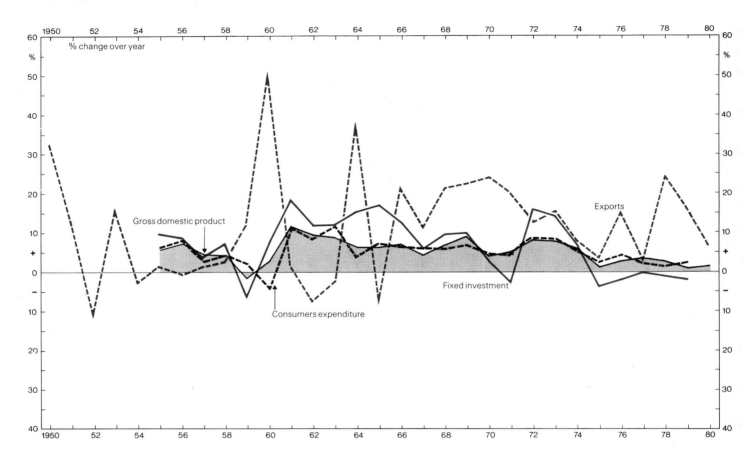

	Gross domestic product		Consumers expenditure		Fixed investment		Exports		
	Index 1970 = 100	% change over year	Index 1970 = 100	% change over year	Index 1970 = 100	% change over year	Index 1970 = 100	% change over year	
1950	na	na	na	na	na	na	18	32	1950
1951	na	na	na	na	na	na	20	13	1951
1952	na	na	na	na	na	na	18	−11	1952
1953	na	na	na	na	na	na	20	15	1953
1954	39.9	na	42.1	na	26.2	na	20	−3	1954
1955	42.0	5.2	44.4	5.4	28.7	9.6	20	1	1955
1956	45.0	7.2	47.7	7.4	31.1	8.1	20	−1	1956
1957	46.9	4.3	49.2	3.2	32.4	4.2	20	1	1957
1958	49.1	4.5	51.4	4.4	34.4	6.2	21	3	1958
1959	48.1	−1.9	52.2	1.7	32.1	−6.6	23	12	1959
1960	49.3	2.4	49.9	−4.5	34.5	7.3	35	50	1960
1961	55.1	11.8	55.3	11.0	40.6	17.9	35	1	1961
1962	60.2	9.3	60.2	8.8	45.3	11.4	33	−7	1962
1963	65.5	8.8	67.0	11.3	50.4	11.4	32	−3	1963
1964	69.6	6.2	69.9	4.3	58.0	15.0	43	37	1964
1965	74.0	6.3	74.8	7.0	67.7	16.6	40	−7	1965
1966	79.2	7.1	79.9	6.9	76.3	12.7	49	21	1966
1967	82.6	4.3	84.7	6.0	80.8	6.0	55	11	1967
1968	88.2	6.8	89.7	6.0	88.5	9.4	66	21	1968
1969	96.1	8.9	96.0	7.0	97.1	9.8	81	22	1969
1970	100.0	4.1	100.0	4.2	100.0	3.0	100	24	1970
1971	105.0	5.0	104.9	4.9	97.1	−2.9	120	20	1971
1972	113.5	8.1	113.7	8.3	112.5	15.8	136	13	1972
1973	122.4	7.9	122.8	8.0	128.6	14.3	157	15	1973
1974	129.4	5.7	129.2	5.2	137.1	6.6	168	7	1974
1975	130.8	1.1	132.3	2.4	131.8	−3.9	174	3	1975
1976	134.8	3.0	138.4	4.7	129.2	−2.0	199	15	1976
1977	139.2	3.3	141.9	2.5	128.9	−0.2	206	3	1977
1978	143.0	2.7	144.1	1.5	127.5	−1.1	256	24	1978
1979	144.2	0.8	147.1	2.1	124.9	−2.0	297	16	1979
1980	145.9	1.2	na	na	na	na	314	6	1980

Spain

Unemployment increased mainly in 1950, 1954, 1960–61, 1964–65, 1967–68, 1971 and 1975–80; main reductions were in 1951–52, 1955–59, 1962, 1966, 1969–70 and 1973. Consumer prices increased mainly in 1950–51, 1956–59, 1962–67 and 1971–80, with low rises or a fall in 1952–54, 1960–61 and 1969. Share prices increased mainly in 1954–56, 1961–63, 1968–70 and 1972–73, with falls in 1953, 1958–60, 1964 and 1975–80. Money stock increased at high rates throughout, with especially large rates of increase for 1951–52, 1954–58, 1961–69, 1971–78 and 1980, and lower rates for 1953, 1959–60, 1970 and 1979.

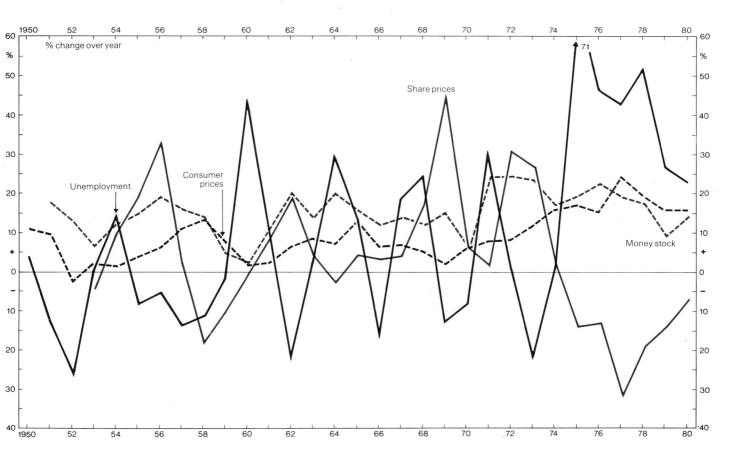

	Unemployment		Consumer prices		Share prices		Money stock		
	Number (000)	% change over year	Index 1970 = 100	% change over year	Index 1970 = 100	% change over year	Index 1970 = 100	% change over year	
1950	166.2	3.8	33.0	10.7	na	na	8.9	na	1950
1951	144.2	−13.2	36.2	9.6	na	na	10.5	18	1951
1952	106.5	−26.1	35.5	−2.0	29.5	na	11.8	13	1952
1953	107.2	0.6	36.1	1.7	28.1	−4.7	12.7	7	1953
1954	122.6	14.4	36.5	1.1	30.9	10.0	14.1	12	1954
1955	112.1	−8.6	38.0	4.1	36.9	19.4	16.3	15	1955
1956	105.9	−5.5	40.2	5.8	49.3	33.6	19.4	19	1956
1957	91.1	−14.0	44.5	10.7	50.4	2.2	22.5	16	1957
1958	81.0	−11.1	50.5	13.5	41.6	−17.5	25.7	14	1958
1959	79.9	−1.4	54.2	7.3	37.4	−10.1	27.1	5	1959
1960	114.4	43.2	54.9	1.3	37.3	−0.3	27.6	2	1960
1961	124.6	8.9	55.9	1.8	40.2	7.8	30.6	11	1961
1962	97.8	−21.5	59.3	6.1	48.0	19.4	36.6	20	1962
1963	100.2	2.5	64.5	8.8	50.2	4.6	41.9	14	1963
1964	129.6	29.3	69.0	7.0	49.0	−2.4	50.1	20	1964
1965	147.1	13.5	78.1	13.2	51.2	4.5	57.7	15	1965
1966	123.2	−16.2	82.9	6.1	53.0	3.5	64.6	12	1966
1967	146.3	18.7	88.2	6.4	55.2	4.2	73.4	14	1967
1968	182.0	24.4	92.6	5.0	64.9	17.6	82.4	12	1968
1969	158.9	−12.7	94.6	2.2	93.9	44.7	94.3	15	1969
1970	145.6	−8.4	100.0	5.7	100.0	6.5	100.0	6	1970
1971	190.3	30.7	108.2	8.2	101.4	1.4	123.8	24	1971
1972	190.9	0.3	117.2	8.3	132.7	30.9	153.7	24	1972
1973	149.6	−21.6	130.6	11.4	167.9	26.5	189.8	23	1973
1974	150.3	0.5	151.1	15.7	170.1	1.3	222.6	17	1974
1975	256.6	70.7	176.7	16.9	146.1	−14.1	264.2	19	1975
1976	376.4	46.7	203.4	15.1	126.2	−13.6	321.9	22	1976
1977	539.6	43.4	253.2	24.5	86.6	−31.4	381.7	19	1977
1978	818.5	51.7	303.4	19.8	70.0	−19.2	447.6	17	1978
1979	1 037.2	26.7	350.7	15.6	60.2	−14.0	485.9	9	1979
1980	1 277.3	23.1	405.5	15.6	56.1	−6.8	551.5	14	1980

Sri Lanka

The main periods of expansion in gross domestic product were 1951–52, 1954–55, 1957–60, 1964, 1966–70, 1972–74 and 1976–80; there was a fall for 1953, 1956, 1963, 1971 and 1975. Fixed investment increased mainly in 1951–52, 1954–55, 1962–64, 1966–69, 1972, 1975–76 and 1978–80, with falls or low growth in 1953, 1956–57, 1959–61, 1965, 1970–71 and 1977. Exports increased mainly in 1950, 1953–55, 1960–62, 1964–65 and 1975, with falls in 1956–57, 1959, 1963, 1966, 1969, 1971–72, 1974, 1976–77 and 1980. Consumer prices were comparatively stable, except for main rises in 1968–70, 1972–75 and 1978–80.

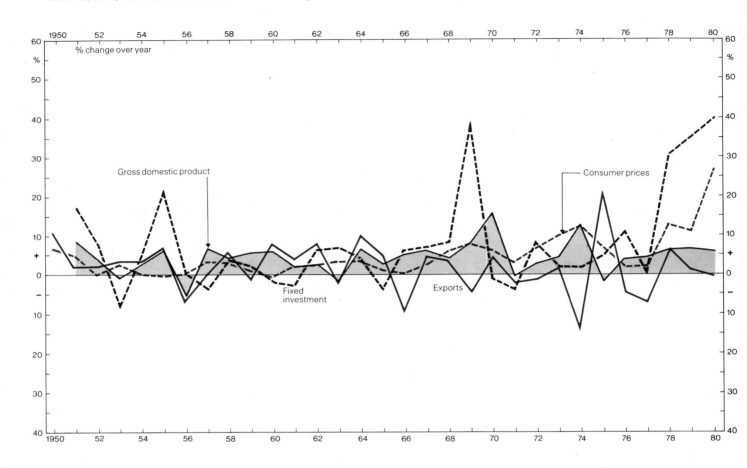

	Gross domestic product		Fixed investment		Exports		Consumer prices		
	Index 1970 = 100	% change over year	Index 1970 = 100	% change over year	Index 1970 = 100	% change over year	Index 1970 = 100	% change over year	
1950	43.4	na	37	na	74	10	70.1	5.4	1950
1951	47.1	8.4	43	17	75	1	73.0	4.1	1951
1952	48.8	3.7	46	7	76	1	72.4	−0.8	1952
1953	48.3	−1.0	42	−8	78	3	73.5	1.5	1953
1954	49.7	3.0	44	5	80	3	73.2	−0.4	1954
1955	52.8	6.2	54	21	85	6	72.7	−0.7	1955
1956	49.9	−5.5	54	0	79	−7	72.5	−0.3	1956
1957	53.1	6.5	52	−4	78	−1	74.4	2.6	1957
1958	55.6	4.7	54	4	82	5	76.0	2.2	1958
1959	58.5	5.2	55	2	80	−2	76.1	0.1	1959
1960	61.8	5.5	54	−2	86	7	74.9	−1.6	1960
1961	62.8	1.7	52	−3	89	3	75.8	1.2	1961
1962	64.3	2.4	55	6	95	7	76.9	1.5	1962
1963	63.1	−2.0	59	7	92	−3	78.7	2.3	1963
1964	67.0	6.2	61	4	100	9	81.2	3.2	1964
1965	68.6	2.4	59	−4	104	4	81.4	0.2	1965
1966	72.1	5.1	63	6	94	−10	81.3	−0.1	1966
1967	76.5	6.1	67	7	98	4	83.1	2.2	1967
1968	79.8	4.4	73	8	101	3	87.9	5.8	1968
1969	86.3	8.2	101	38	96	−5	94.4	7.4	1969
1970	100.0	15.8	100	−1	100	4	100.0	5.9	1970
1971	99.9	−0.1	96	−4	97	−3	102.7	2.7	1971
1972	103.0	3.0	104	8	95	−2	109.2	6.3	1972
1973	107.8	4.7	105	2	96	1	119.7	9.6	1973
1974	121.8	13.1	107	2	83	−14	134.4	12.3	1974
1975	120.3	−1.2	113	5	100	20	143.3	6.6	1975
1976	125.9	4.7	125	11	95	−5	145.0	1.2	1976
1977	131.9	4.8	125	0	88	−7	146.9	1.3	1977
1978	140.2	6.2	164	31	93	6	164.7	12.1	1978
1979	149.0	6.3	221	35	94	1	182.3	10.7	1979
1980	157.7	5.8	308	40	93	−1	230.0	26.2	1980

Surinam

For the time for which figures are available for gross domestic product in quantity terms, there has been a high growth for 1974 and 1976–78 and a fall or low growth in 1975 and 1979. Exports (of bauxite only before 1965) increased mainly in 1951–52, 1956, 1959–60, 1963–67, 1969, 1971–72 and 1976–78, with a fall or low growth in 1950, 1955, 1957–58, 1961–62, 1970, 1973–75 and 1979–80. Consumer prices, for the time covered, increased mainly in 1957, 1967, 1969 and 1973–80, with a comparatively stable period for 1958–66. International reserves, for the time covered, increased mainly in 1959, 1963–66, 1969–76 and 1978–80.

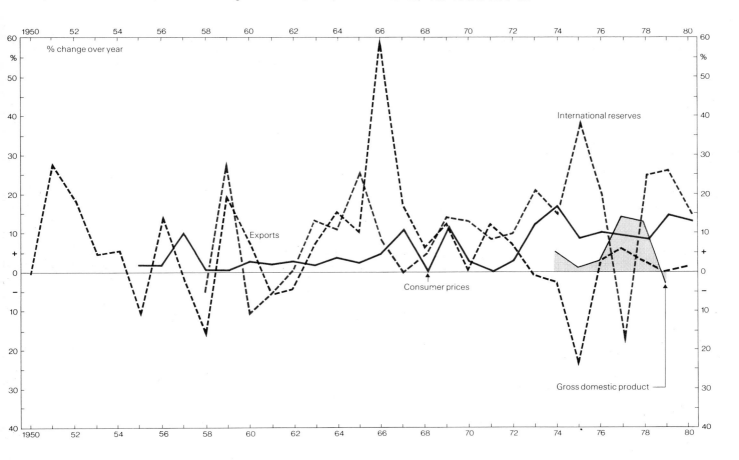

	Gross domestic product		Exports[a]		Consumer prices		International reserves		
	Index[b] 1975 = 100	% change over year	Index 1970 = 100	% change over year	Index 1970 = 100	% change over year	Index 1970 = 100	% change over year	
1950	na	na	22	−1	na	na	na	na	1950
1951	na	na	28	27	na	na	na	na	1951
1952	na	na	33	18	na	na	na	na	1952
1953	na	na	34	4	na	na	na	na	1953
1954	na	na	36	5	58.5	na	na	na	1954
1955	na	na	32	−11	59.1	1.0	na	na	1955
1956	na	na	36	14	59.7	1.0	na	na	1956
1957	na	na	35	−3	65.5	9.7	44	na	1957
1958	na	na	30	−16	65.5	0.0	42	−6	1958
1959	na	na	35	19	65.5	0.0	53	27	1959
1960	na	na	38	7	67.1	2.5	47	−11	1960
1961	na	na	36	−6	68.3	1.8	44	−6	1961
1962	na	na	34	−5	70.1	2.6	44	0	1962
1963	na	na	36	7	71.3	1.7	50	13	1963
1964	na	na	42	15	73.9	3.7	56	11	1964
1965	na	na	46	10	75.7	2.4	69	25	1965
1966	na	na	72	58	79.1	4.5	75	8	1966
1967	na	na	84	17	87.7	10.9	75	0	1967
1968	na	na	89	6	87.7	0.0	78	4	1968
1969	na	na	100	12	97.5	11.1	89	14	1969
1970	na	na	100	0	100.0	2.6	100	13	1970
1971	na	na	112	12	100.3	0.3	108	8	1971
1972	na	na	120	7	103.6	3.2	119	10	1972
1973	94	na	118	−1	116.9	12.9	144	21	1973
1974	99	5	115	−3	136.6	16.9	167	15	1974
1975	100	1	88	−24	148.1	8.5	231	38	1975
1976	103	3	90	3	163.1	10.1	278	20	1976
1977	118	14	96	6	179.0	9.7	231	−17	1977
1978	133	13	99	3	194.7	8.8	289	25	1978
1979	129	−3	98	0	223.7	14.9	364	26	1979
1980	na	na	100	1	255.3	14.1	417	15	1980

[a]Exports of bauxite only before 1965   [b]Index with 1975 = 100 (1970 not being available)

125

Sweden

The main periods of expansion in gross domestic product were 1951, 1953–56, 1959–65, 1967–70, 1973–75 and 1979–80; there was a fall or low growth rate in 1952, 1957–58, 1966, 1971–72 and 1976–78. Consumers expenditure increased mainly in 1952–56, 1958–59, 1961–65, 1968–69, 1972–76 and 1979, with falls in 1951, 1971

and 1977–78. Fixed investment increased mainly in 1953–54, 1958–59, 1961–67, 1969–70, 1972–73, 1975–76 and 1979–80, with falls or low growth in 1955, 1968, 1971, 1974 and 1977–78. Exports increased mainly in 1950, 1953–54, 1956–57, 1959–66, 1968–70, 1973 and 1978–79, with falls in 1952, 1975 and 1980.

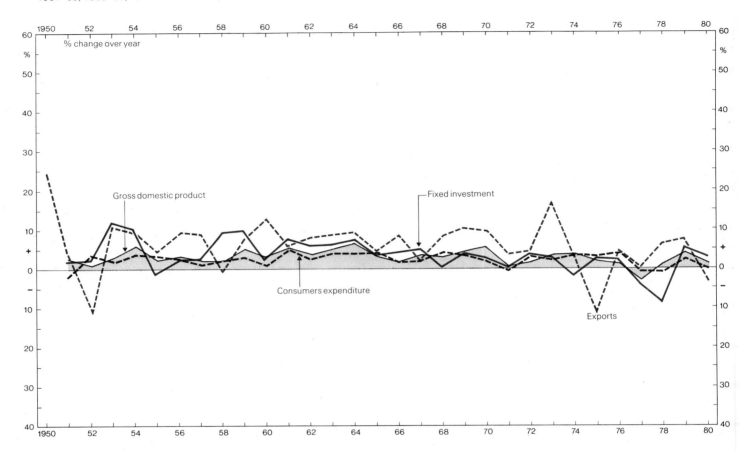

	Gross domestic product		Consumers expenditure		Fixed investment		Exports		
	Index 1970 = 100	% change over year	Index 1970 = 100	% change over year	Index 1970 = 100	% change over year	Index 1970 = 100	% change over year	
1950	45.8	na	54.6	na	35.2	na	27	25	1950
1951	47.1	3.0	54.0	−1.1	36.1	2.4	28	4	1951
1952	47.9	1.7	56.0	3 7	37.2	3.2	25	−11	1952
1953	49.5	3.2	57.4	2.6	41.8	12.2	28	11	1953
1954	52.4	6.0	59.8	4.1	46.3	10.9	31	10	1954
1955	54.0	3.0	61.6	3.1	46.0	−0.8	32	5	1955
1956	55.8	3.3	63.4	2.9	47.3	2.9	35	10	1956
1957	57.1	2.4	64.4	1.5	48.5	2.5	38	9	1957
1958	58.5	2.4	65.9	2.4	53.3	9.9	38	0	1958
1959	61.5	5.2	68.3	3.6	58.6	10.0	41	8	1959
1960	63.9	3.8	69.4	1.6	60.7	3.6	47	13	1960
1961	67.5	5.7	73.1	5.3	65.6	8.0	50	6	1961
1962	70.4	4.3	75.5	3.3	69.7	6.2	53	8	1962
1963	74.1	5.2	78.8	4.4	74.4	6.8	58	9	1963
1964	79.2	6.9	82.3	4.3	80.2	7.8	64	10	1964
1965	82.5	4.1	85.8	4.3	83.6	4.2	67	5	1965
1966	84.3	2.2	87.7	2.2	87.4	4.5	73	9	1966
1967	87.3	3.6	90.1	2.8	92.2	5.5	75	3	1967
1968	90.5	3.7	94.0	4.3	92.8	0.7	82	9	1968
1969	94.8	4.8	97.9	4.1	96.8	4.2	91	11	1969
1970	100.0	5.5	100.0	2.1	100.0	3.3	100	10	1970
1971	101.0	1.0	99.9	−0.1	101.0	1.0	104	4	1971
1972	103.1	2.1	103.5	3.6	104.9	3.9	109	5	1972
1973	107.0	3.8	106.3	2.6	108.3	3.2	127	17	1973
1974	111.4	4.1	110.5	4.0	106.8	−1.3	132	4	1974
1975	114.2	2.5	114.1	3.3	110.2	3.2	117	−11	1975
1976	116.0	1.6	118.8	4.2	113.2	2.7	123	5	1976
1977	113.2	−2.4	117.8	−0.8	108.6	−4.1	124	1	1977
1978	114.8	1.4	116.9	−0.8	99.5	−8.4	132	7	1978
1979	119.4	4.0	119.9	2.6	104.8	5.3	143	8	1979
1980	121.6	1.8	119.9	0.0	108.1	3.1	138	−3	1980

Sweden

Consumer prices rose at a comparatively steady rate over 1953–69, after a high rate of increase for 1951–52; then followed comparatively high rates of increase, especially for 1974–78 and 1980. Share prices increased mainly in 1950–51, 1954–55, 1959–60, 1963–65, 1968–69, 1971–76 and 1980, with falls in 1952, 1956, 1962, 1966–67, 1970 and 1977. Money stock increased mainly in 1950–51, 1956, 1959, 1961–67, 1970–75 and 1977–79, with a fall or low increase in 1954–55, 1958, 1960, 1968–69 and 1976. The interest rate (government bond yield) increased mainly in 1955, 1957, 1960, 1964–66, 1968–70 and 1974–80, with main falls in 1962 and 1967.

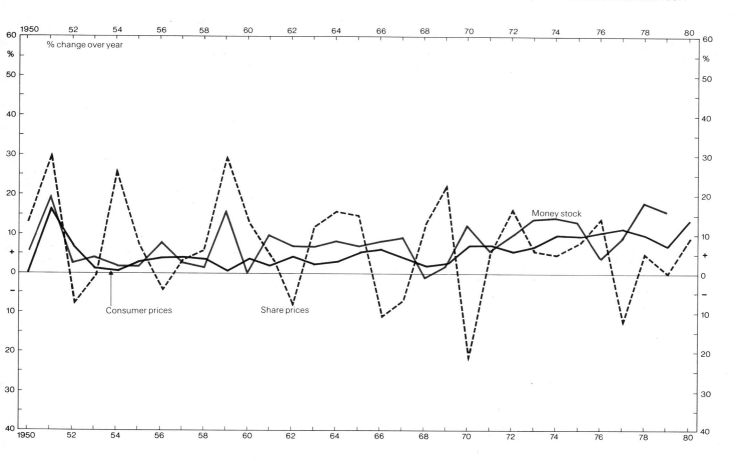

	Consumer prices		Share prices		Money stock		Interest rate[a]		
	Index 1970 = 100	% change over year	Index 1970 = 100	% change over year	Index 1970 = 100	% change over year	%	Change over year[b]	
1950	42.7	0.7	30	14	29.3	6	3.11	0.09	1950
1951	49.6	16.2	38	30	35.0	19	3.23	0.12	1951
1952	53.4	7.7	36	−7	36.2	3	3.28	0.05	1952
1953	54.1	1.4	36	0	37.8	4	3.27	−0.01	1953
1954	54.5	0.8	45	26	38.4	2	3.24	−0.03	1954
1955	56.3	3.2	49	8	39.2	2	3.70	0.46	1955
1956	58.8	4.4	47	−4	42.3	8	3.75	0.05	1956
1957	61.4	4.5	49	4	43.8	3	4.33	0.58	1957
1958	64.1	4.3	52	6	44.5	2	4.33	0.00	1958
1959	64.7	0.9	67	30	51.7	16	4.28	−0.05	1959
1960	67.3	4.1	76	13	51.7	0	5.19	0.91	1960
1961	68.8	2.2	80	5	56.6	10	5.33	0.14	1961
1962	72.0	4.7	74	−8	60.9	7	4.99	−0.34	1962
1963	74.0	2.9	83	12	65.0	7	4.93	−0.06	1963
1964	76.5	3.4	96	16	70.2	8	5.64	0.71	1964
1965	80.5	5.2	110	15	74.7	7	6.18	0.54	1965
1966	85.6	6.4	98	−11	80.4	8	6.57	0.39	1966
1967	89.3	4.3	91	−7	87.8	9	6.06	−0.51	1967
1968	91.1	2.0	103	13	87.0	−1	6.31	0.25	1968
1969	93.4	2.6	127	23	89.1	2	6.98	0.67	1969
1970	100.0	7.1	100	−21	100.0	12	7.39	0.41	1970
1971	107.5	7.5	106	6	106.2	6	7.23	−0.16	1971
1972	113.9	6.0	123	16	117.0	10	7.29	0.06	1972
1973	121.6	6.7	130	6	132.8	14	7.39	0.10	1973
1974	133.6	9.9	136	5	151.3	14	7.79	0.40	1974
1975	146.6	9.8	147	8	170.6	13	8.79	1.00	1975
1976	161.7	10.3	168	14	178.0	4	9.28	0.49	1976
1977	180.2	11.4	147	−12	194.9	9	9.74	0.46	1977
1978	198.1	9.9	154	5	230.8	18	10.09	0.35	1978
1979	212.5	7.3	154	0	268.4	16	10.47	0.38	1979
1980	241.5	13.7	168	9	na	na	11.74	1.27	1980

[a]Government bond yield   [b]In percentage points

127

Switzerland

The main periods of expansion in gross domestic product were 1950–51, 1953–57, 1959–64, 1968–73, 1977 and 1979–80; there were falls or a low growth rate in 1952, 1958, 1966, 1974–76 and 1978. Consumers expenditure increased mainly in 1950, 1953–56, 1959–72, 1977–78 and 1980; there were falls or a low growth rate in 1951–52, 1958, 1974–76 and 1979. Fixed investment increased mainly in 1951, 1953–57, 1959–64, 1969–72 and 1978–80, with a fall or low growth rate in 1952, 1958, 1965–68 and 1974–77. Exports increased mainly in 1950–51, 1953–57, 1959–60, 1962–66, 1968–70, 1972–73 and 1976–77, with falls in 1952, 1958 and 1975.

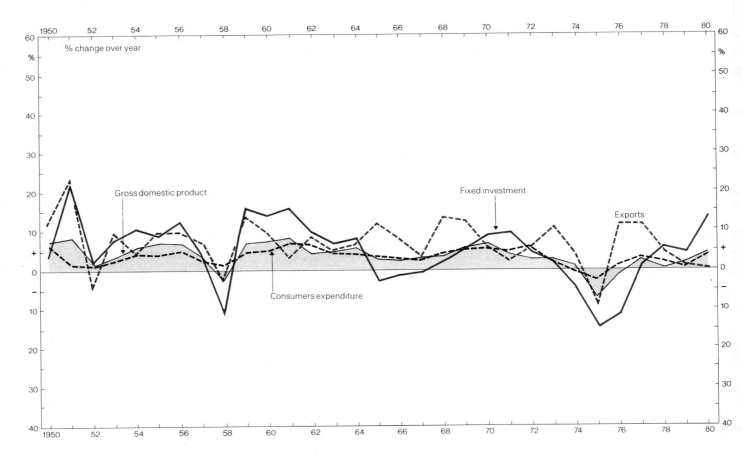

% change over year

Gross domestic product

Consumers expenditure

Fixed investment

Exports

	Gross domestic product		Consumers expenditure		Fixed investment		Exports		
	Index 1970 = 100	% change over year	Index 1970 = 100	% change over year	Index 1970 = 100	% change over year	Index 1970 = 100	% change over year	
1950	40.2	7.3	46.3	5.9	25.6	4	21	12	1950
1951	43.4	8.1	46.8	1.1	31.2	22	25	23	1951
1952	43.8	0.8	47.2	1.0	31.9	2	24	−4	1952
1953	45.3	3.5	48.5	2.7	34.6	8	27	10	1953
1954	47.9	5.6	50.5	4.1	38.3	11	28	5	1954
1955	51.1	6.8	52.5	4.0	41.8	9	31	10	1955
1956	54.5	6.6	55.1	4.9	47.0	13	34	10	1956
1957	56.6	4.0	56.6	2.6	49.3	5	37	7	1957
1958	55.4	−2.1	57.5	1.7	44.6	−10	36	−2	1958
1959	58.9	6.3	60.3	4.8	51.7	16	41	14	1959
1960	63.1	7.0	63.3	5.0	58.6	14	45	10	1960
1961	68.2	8.1	67.6	6.8	67.8	16	47	4	1961
1962	71.4	4.8	72.0	6.4	74.8	10	51	9	1962
1963	74.9	4.9	75.4	4.8	80.2	7	54	6	1963
1964	78.9	5.3	79.0	4.7	86.8	8	58	7	1964
1965	81.4	3.2	81.7	3.5	84.7	−2	65	12	1965
1966	83.4	2.5	84.2	3.0	84.0	−1	70	8	1966
1967	85.9	3.1	86.6	2.9	84.1	0	73	4	1967
1968	89.0	3.6	90.0	3.9	86.7	3	83	14	1968
1969	94.0	5.6	94.9	5.5	91.8	6	94	13	1969
1970	100.0	6.4	100.0	5.4	100.0	9	100	6	1970
1971	104.1	4.1	104.8	4.8	109.9	10	103	3	1971
1972	107.4	3.2	110.5	5.4	115.3	5	109	6	1972
1973	110.7	3.1	113.5	2.8	118.7	3	121	11	1973
1974	112.3	1.5	113.0	−0.5	113.6	−4	126	4	1974
1975	104.1	−7.3	109.7	−2.9	98.2	−14	116	−8	1975
1976	102.7	−1.4	110.8	1.0	87.9	−11	130	12	1976
1977	105.2	2.4	114.2	3.0	89.3	2	145	12	1977
1978	105.5	0.3	116.7	2.2	94.8	6	152	5	1978
1979	107.8	2.2	117.9	1.0	99.7	5	155	2	1979
1980	112.6	4.4	122.5	3.9	113.3	14	158	1	1980

Switzerland

Consumer prices were comparatively stable throughout the period, but with rather higher rises in 1951–52, 1962–67, 1970–75 and 1979–80. Share prices increased mainly in 1950–51, 1954–56, 1959–61, 1968–69, 1972, 1976–77 and 1979, with falls in 1953, 1957–58, 1962–66, 1970, 1973–75, 1978 and 1980. Money stock increased mainly in 1956, 1958, 1960–64, 1967–71, 1976 and 1978, with falls or low rates of increase in 1965–66, 1973–74, 1977 and 1979–80. The interest rate (government bond yield) increased mainly in 1951, 1955–57, 1964, 1966–67, 1969–70, 1973–74 and 1980; main falls were in 1950, 1953, 1958, 1971–72 and 1975–78.

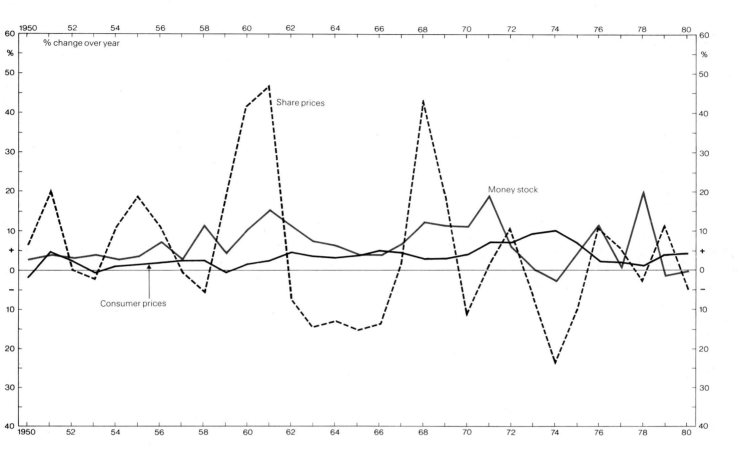

	Consumer prices		Share prices		Money stock		Interest rate[a]		
	Index 1970 = 100	% change over year	Index 1970 = 100	% change over year	Index 1970 = 100	% change over year	%	Change over year[b]	
1950	62.6	−1.6	33.5	6.7	25.5	3.0	2.67	−0.27	1950
1951	65.5	4.6	40.2	20.0	26.6	4.3	2.95	0.28	1951
1952	67.2	2.7	40.2	0.0	27.5	3.3	2.84	−0.11	1952
1953	66.7	−0.7	39.4	−2.0	28.7	4.3	2.55	−0.29	1953
1954	67.2	0.7	43.7	10.9	29.5	2.8	2.62	0.07	1954
1955	67.9	1.0	51.7	18.3	30.5	3.3	2.97	0.35	1955
1956	68.9	1.5	57.3	10.8	32.6	7.2	3.11	0.14	1956
1957	70.2	1.9	57.0	−0.5	33.5	2.7	3.64	0.53	1957
1958	71.5	1.9	53.6	−6.0	37.2	11.1	3.19	−0.45	1958
1959	71.0	−0.7	64.0	19.4	39.0	4.8	3.08	−0.11	1959
1960	72.0	1.4	90.4	41.2	43.0	10.3	3.09	0.01	1960
1961	73.4	1.9	132.2	46.2	49.6	15.3	2.96	−0.13	1961
1962	76.6	4.4	121.9	−7.8	55.2	11.3	3.13	0.17	1962
1963	79.2	3.4	104.0	−14.7	59.2	7.3	3.25	0.12	1963
1964	81.6	3.0	89.9	−13.6	63.1	6.5	3.97	0.72	1964
1965	84.5	3.6	75.8	−15.7	65.5	3.8	3.95	−0.02	1965
1966	88.5	4.7	65.1	−14.1	68.0	3.8	4.16	0.21	1966
1967	92.0	4.0	66.2	1.7	72.5	6.7	4.61	0.45	1967
1968	94.1	2.3	94.7	43.1	81.2	11.9	4.37	−0.24	1968
1969	96.5	2.6	113.1	19.4	90.1	11.0	4.90	0.53	1969
1970	100.0	3.6	100.0	−11.6	100.0	11.0	5.82	0.92	1970
1971	106.6	6.6	100.6	0.6	118.4	18.4	5.27	−0.55	1971
1972	113.7	6.7	111.0	10.3	125.1	5.7	4.97	−0.30	1972
1973	123.6	8.7	102.9	−7.3	125.1	0.0	5.60	0.63	1973
1974	135.7	9.8	77.9	−24.3	120.9	−3.3	7.15	1.55	1974
1975	144.8	6.7	69.9	−10.3	126.3	4.4	6.44	−0.71	1975
1976	147.3	1.7	77.2	10.4	139.7	10.6	4.99	−1.45	1976
1977	149.6	1.6	81.2	5.2	140.6	0.6	4.05	−0.94	1977
1978	150.7	0.8	78.1	−3.7	168.3	19.7	3.33	−0.72	1978
1979	156.1	3.6	86.5	10.7	166.2	−1.2	3.45	0.12	1979
1980	162.5	4.1	82.0	−5.3	165.4	−0.5	4.77	1.32	1980

[a]Government bond yield   [b]In percentage points

Syria

Over the time for which figures are available, from 1958, the main periods of expansion in gross domestic product were 1961–62, 1964–65, 1967, 1969, 1971–72, 1974–76 and 1978–80; there were falls or low growth in 1958–60, 1963, 1966, 1968, 1970, 1973 and 1977. Fixed investment, for the time covered, increased mainly in 1961–62, 1966, 1968–69, 1971–72, 1974–75, 1977 and 1980, with falls in 1963, 1965, 1970, 1973 and 1976. Exports, for the time covered, increased mainly in 1960, 1962–63, 1969, 1972, 1975 and 1978–79. Consumer prices increased mainly in 1951–52, 1956, 1959–60, 1964, 1973–77 and 1980.

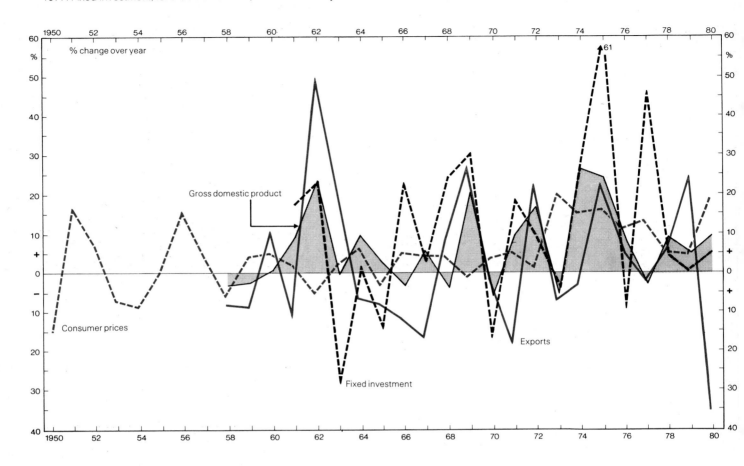

	Gross domestic product		Fixed investment		Exports		Consumer prices		
	Index 1970 = 100	% change over year	Index 1970 = 100	% change over year	Index 1970 = 100	% change over year	Index 1970 = 100	% change over year	
1950	na	na	na	na	na	na	65	−15	1950
1951	na	na	na	na	na	na	76	16	1951
1952	na	na	na	na	na	na	81	7	1952
1953	na	na	na	na	na	na	75	−7	1953
1954	na	na	na	na	na	na	68	−9	1954
1955	na	na	na	na	na	na	68	0	1955
1956	na	na	na	na	na	na	78	15	1956
1957	63.0	na	na	na	83	na	81	4	1957
1958	60.9	−3.3	na	na	76	−8	76	−6	1958
1959	59.6	−2.1	na	na	69	−9	79	4	1959
1960	59.8	0.3	64	na	76	10	83	5	1960
1961	65.0	8.7	75	17	67	−12	85	2	1961
1962	80.4	23.7	92	23	99	48	81	−5	1962
1963	80.3	−0.1	67	−28	119	20	83	2	1963
1964	87.8	9.3	67	1	111	−7	88	6	1964
1965	89.8	2.3	58	−14	102	−8	85	−3	1965
1966	87.2	−2.9	71	22	90	−12	89	5	1966
1967	91.9	5.3	73	3	75	−17	93	4	1967
1968	88.6	−3.6	91	24	81	8	97	4	1968
1969	106.3	20.0	118	30	102	26	96	−1	1969
1970	100.0	−5.9	100	−15	100	−2	100	4	1970
1971	109.5	9.5	118	18	82	−18	105	5	1971
1972	127.7	16.6	128	9	100	22	106	1	1972
1973	120.9	−5.3	123	−4	93	−7	127	20	1973
1974	153.0	26.6	159	29	90	−3	146	15	1974
1975	189.6	23.9	254	61	110	22	170	16	1975
1976	205.0	8.1	232	−9	116	5	189	11	1976
1977	199.9	−2.5	336	45	113	−2	213	13	1977
1978	217.3	8.7	350	4	120	6	223	5	1978
1979	228.9	5.3	352	1	149	24	233	5	1979
1980	251.1	9.7	374	6	95	−36	277	19	1980

Taiwan

There was a generally high rate of growth for gross domestic product throughout the period 1952 to 1973, with especially high rates for 1963–65 and 1970–73; there was then a low growth rate in 1974, followed by expansion in 1976–80, with some slackening of growth in 1979–80. Fixed investment increased mainly in 1952–53, 1956, 1958–60, 1963, 1965–68, 1970–75 and 1978–80, with falls or low growth in 1955, 1957, 1961–62, 1964 and 1976–77. Exports increased mainly in 1953, 1955, 1957–58, 1962–73 and 1976–80, with falls in 1953, 1956, 1959–60 and 1974. Consumer prices rose mainly in 1951–53, 1955–57, 1959–61, 1973–74 and 1979–80.

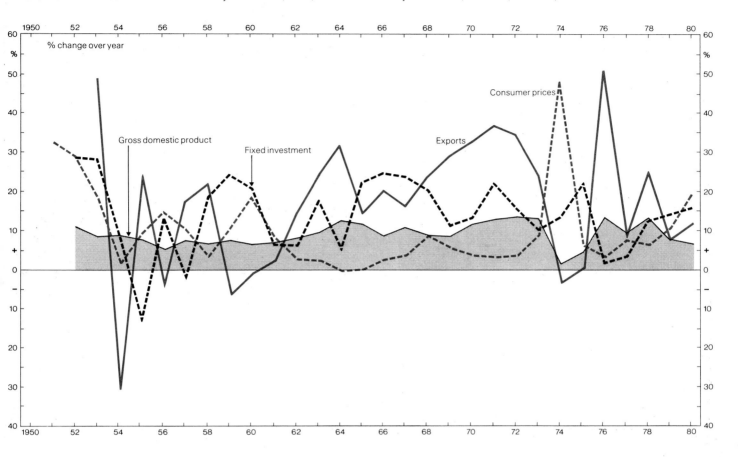

	Gross domestic product		Fixed investment		Exports		Consumer prices		
	Index 1970 = 100	% change over year	Index 1970 = 100	% change over year	Index 1970 = 100	% change over year	Index 1970 = 100	% change over year	
1950	na	na	na	na	na	na	18.5	na	1950
1951	20.5	na	8.3	na	na	na	24.6	32.7	1951
1952	22.8	10.9	10.7	28.6	10	na	31.7	29.0	1952
1953	24.7	8.3	13.7	28.0	15	49	37.5	18.3	1953
1954	26.8	8.7	14.8	8.1	10	−31	38.1	1.6	1954
1955	28.9	7.7	12.7	−13.7	13	24	41.8	9.8	1955
1956	30.4	5.3	14.5	13.4	12	−4	48.0	14.8	1956
1957	32.6	7.4	14.2	−1.9	14	17	53.0	10.5	1957
1958	34.8	6.7	16.8	18.8	17	22	54.8	3.3	1958
1959	37.5	7.6	20.9	24.0	16	−6	60.6	10.6	1959
1960	39.9	6.3	25.2	20.6	16	−1	71.8	18.5	1960
1961	42.6	6.9	26.8	6.5	16	2	77.4	7.8	1961
1962	46.0	7.9	28.5	6.1	19	14	79.3	2.4	1962
1963	50.3	9.4	33.4	17.3	23	24	81.0	2.2	1963
1964	56.4	12.2	35.2	5.5	30	31	80.8	−0.2	1964
1965	62.7	11.2	43.0	22.0	35	14	80.8	−0.1	1965
1966	68.3	8.9	53.4	24.3	42	20	82.4	2.0	1966
1967	75.6	10.7	66.0	23.6	48	16	85.2	3.4	1967
1968	82.5	9.1	79.4	20.3	59	23	91.9	7.9	1968
1969	89.8	8.9	88.3	11.2	76	28	96.6	5.1	1969
1970	100.0	11.3	100.0	13.3	100	32	100.0	3.6	1970
1971	112.8	12.8	121.7	21.7	136	36	102.8	2.8	1971
1972	127.7	13.2	140.6	15.6	182	34	105.9	3.0	1972
1973	144.1	12.9	154.9	10.2	224	23	114.6	8.2	1973
1974	145.8	1.1	175.4	13.2	215	−4	169.0	47.5	1974
1975	152.8	4.8	213.7	21.8	215	0	177.8	5.2	1975
1976	173.6	13.7	216.3	1.2	323	50	182.2	2.5	1976
1977	190.6	9.8	224.8	3.9	348	8	195.0	7.0	1977
1978	216.1	13.4	253.2	12.6	432	24	206.3	5.8	1978
1979	232.9	7.8	288.9	14.1	461	7	226.4	9.8	1979
1980	248.8	6.8	333.6	15.5	510	11	269.5	19.0	1980

Tanzania

Over the time for which figures are available, from 1966, the main periods of expansion in gross domestic product were 1966–68, 1970–72 and 1975–79; there was comparatively low growth for 1969, 1973–74 and 1980. Exports of coffee increased mainly in 1950–52, 1954, 1956, 1958–59, 1964, 1966, 1972–73, 1975–76, 1978 and 1980, with main falls in 1953, 1957, 1965, 1967, 1970–71, 1974, 1977 and 1979. Consumer prices, for the time covered, increased mainly in 1966–69, 1973–75 and 1977–80, with especially high rates in 1974–75 and 1980. Money stock, for the time covered, increased mainly in 1968–69, 1971–77 and 1979–80.

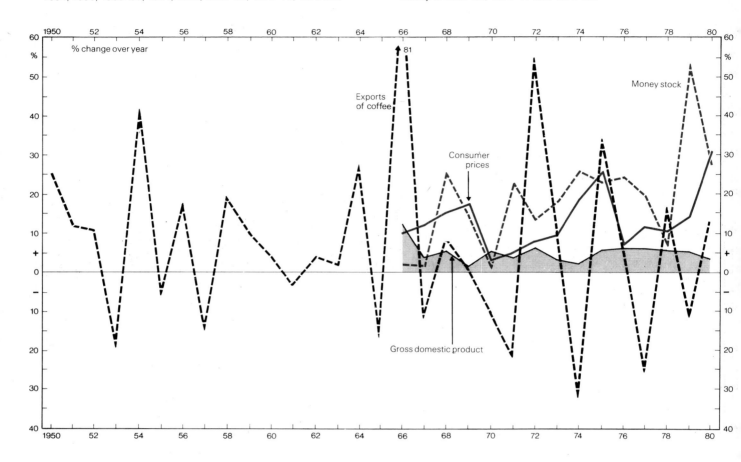

	Gross domestic product		Exports of coffee		Consumer prices		Money stock		
	Index 1970 = 100	% change over year	Index 1970 = 100	% change over year	Index 1970 = 100	% change over year	Index 1970 = 100	% change over year	
1950	na	na	31	25	na	na	na	na	1950
1951	na	na	34	12	na	na	na	na	1951
1952	na	na	38	11	na	na	na	na	1952
1953	na	na	31	−18	na	na	na	na	1953
1954	na	na	44	42	na	na	na	na	1954
1955	na	na	42	−5	na	na	na	na	1955
1956	na	na	49	17	na	na	na	na	1956
1957	na	na	42	−14	na	na	na	na	1957
1958	na	na	50	19	na	na	na	na	1958
1959	na	na	55	10	na	na	na	na	1959
1960	na	na	57	4	na	na	na	na	1960
1961	na	na	56	−2	na	na	na	na	1961
1962	na	na	58	4	na	na	na	na	1962
1963	na	na	59	2	na	na	na	na	1963
1964	na	na	75	27	na	na	na	na	1964
1965	75.2	na	63	−16	58	na	65.6	na	1965
1966	84.8	12.8	114	81	64	10	66.9	2.1	1966
1967	88.2	4.0	101	−11	72	12	68.4	2.1	1967
1968	92.8	5.2	110	9	83	15	85.9	25.6	1968
1969	94.5	1.8	111	1	97	17	98.6	14.8	1969
1970	100.0	5.8	100	−10	100	3	100.0	1.4	1970
1971	104.2	4.2	79	−21	105	5	122.6	22.6	1971
1972	111.2	6.7	122	54	113	8	138.6	13.0	1972
1973	114.6	3.1	134	10	124	10	163.7	18.1	1973
1974	117.4	2.5	92	−31	148	19	205.9	25.8	1974
1975	124.4	5.9	122	33	188	26	255.2	23.9	1975
1976	132.4	6.4	129	6	201	7	317.6	24.5	1976
1977	141.0	6.6	98	−25	224	12	380.2	19.7	1977
1978	149.2	5.8	113	16	249	11	406.6	7.0	1978
1979	157.3	5.5	101	−11	283	14	621.7	52.9	1979
1980	163.0	3.6	115	13	369	30	794.9	27.9	1980

Thailand

The main periods of expansion in gross domestic product were 1952–53, 1955–56 and 1959–80, with rather higher growth in 1960, 1962–63, 1965–69, 1973 and 1978; there were falls in 1954 and 1957. Fixed investment increased mainly in 1952–53, 1956–57, 1959–60, 1962–64, 1966–69, 1973–74 and 1977–79, with falls or comparatively low growth in 1954–55, 1958, 1961, 1965, 1970–72, 1975–76 and 1980. Exports increased in 1955, 1957, 1959–61, 1964–66, 1970–72 and 1976–79, with falls or low growth in 1951–54, 1956, 1958, 1962–63, 1967–68, 1973–75 and 1980. Consumer prices increased mainly in 1951–53, 1955–58, 1973–74 and 1977–80.

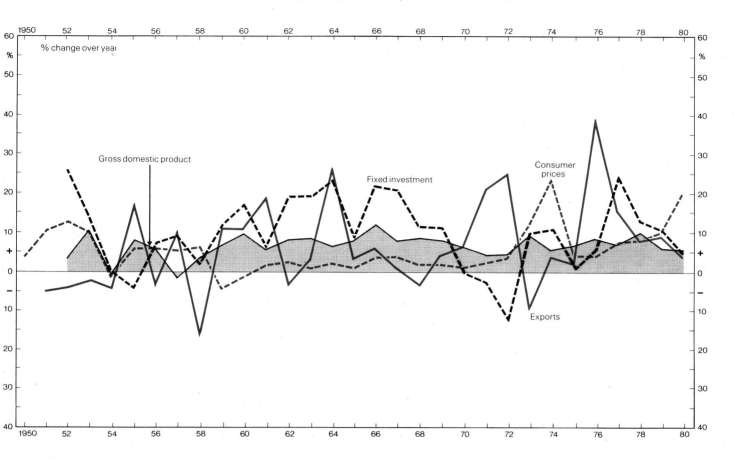

	Gross domestic product		Fixed investment		Exports		Consumer prices		
	Index 1970 = 100	% change over year	Index 1970 = 100	% change over year	Index 1970 = 100	% change over year	Index 1970 = 100	% change over year	
1950	na	na	na	na	51.2	na	51.0	3.5	1950
1951	30.0	na	13	na	48.7	−5	56.2	10.2	1951
1952	31.1	3.4	16	26	46.6	−4	63.1	12.3	1952
1953	34.3	10.5	19	14	45.8	−2	69.4	10.0	1953
1954	34.1	−0.5	19	0	43.9	−4	68.8	−0.9	1954
1955	36.9	8.0	18	−4	51.5	17	72.8	5.8	1955
1956	39.1	6.0	19	7	49.9	−3	77.2	6.0	1956
1957	38.5	−1.6	21	9	54.7	10	81.2	5.2	1957
1958	39.8	3.4	20	−2	45.7	−16	86.2	6.2	1958
1959	42.5	6.9	23	12	50.6	11	82.7	−4.1	1959
1960	46.7	9.9	27	17	56.0	11	81.8	−1.1	1960
1961	49.2	5.3	29	6	66.8	19	82.9	1.3	1961
1962	53.2	8.1	34	19	64.7	−3	84.9	2.4	1962
1963	57.7	8.4	40	19	66.9	3	85.7	0.9	1963
1964	61.5	6.6	49	23	84.6	26	87.4	2.0	1964
1965	66.3	7.9	54	9	87.5	3	88.1	0.8	1965
1966	74.4	12.2	66	22	92.6	6	91.5	3.9	1966
1967	80.2	7.8	79	21	93.7	1	95.1	3.9	1967
1968	87.0	8.5	89	12	90.8	−3	97.1	2.1	1968
1969	93.9	7.9	100	12	94.4	4	99.1	2.1	1969
1970	100.0	6.5	100	0	100.0	6	100.0	0.9	1970
1971	104.7	4.7	98	−2	121.2	21	102.0	2.0	1971
1972	109.7	4.8	87	−12	151.8	25	106.0	3.9	1972
1973	120.1	9.4	95	10	138.6	−9	118.4	11.7	1973
1974	126.6	5.4	105	11	144.8	4	146.0	23.3	1974
1975	135.7	7.1	106	1	148.2	2	152.0	4.1	1975
1976	147.5	8.7	112	6	205.8	39	158.4	4.2	1976
1977	158.1	7.2	139	24	235.8	15	170.4	7.6	1977
1978	174.0	10.1	157	13	254.6	8	183.8	7.9	1978
1979	184.6	6.1	174	11	277.6	9	202.0	9.9	1979
1980	195.2	5.8	183	5	289.1	4	241.8	19.7	1980

Trinidad and Tobago

The main periods of expansion in gross domestic product, for the time covered, were 1953–57, 1959–61, 1963–64, 1967–68, 1970–72 and 1975–78; there was comparatively low growth in 1958, 1962, 1965–66, 1969 and 1973–74. Exports, for the time covered, increased mainly in 1967–69 and 1976, with falls in 1971, 1973–75 and 1977–80. Imports, for the time covered, increased mainly in 1968–71, 1974, 1976 and 1979–80, with falls or low increases for 1967, 1972–73, 1975 and 1977. Consumer prices rose at a comparatively stable rate for 1953 to 1971 (with a higher rate for 1968), then rose at a high rate for 1972–80.

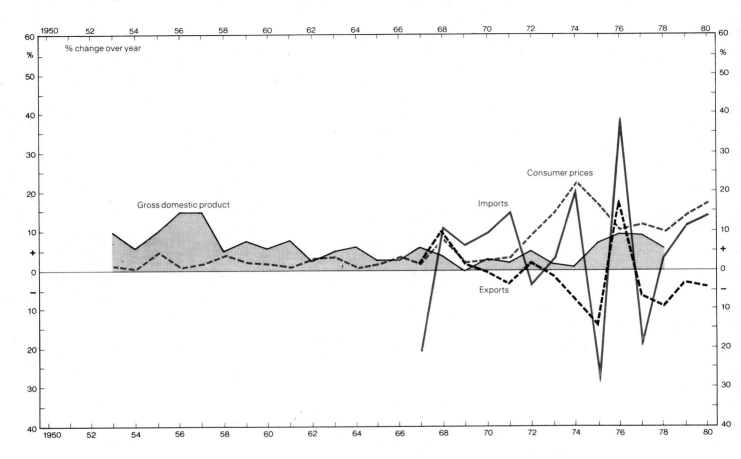

	Gross domestic product		Exports		Imports		Consumer prices		
	Index 1970 = 100	% change over year	Index 1970 = 100	% change over year	Index 1970 = 100	% change over year	Index 1970 = 100	% change over year	
1950	na	na	na	na	na	na	na	na	1950
1951	na	na	na	na	na	na	na	na	1951
1952	33	na	na	na	na	na	61.4	na	1952
1953	36	10	na	na	na	na	62.4	1.6	1953
1954	38	6	na	na	na	na	62.8	0.6	1954
1955	42	10	na	na	na	na	65.9	4.9	1955
1956	49	15	na	na	na	na	66.6	1.1	1956
1957	56	15	na	na	na	na	68.0	2.1	1957
1958	59	5	na	na	na	na	71.0	4.4	1958
1959	64	8	na	na	na	na	72.8	2.5	1959
1960	68	6	na	na	na	na	74.3	2.1	1960
1961	73	8	na	na	na	na	75.4	1.5	1961
1962	75	3	na	na	na	na	77.6	2.9	1962
1963	79	5	na	na	na	na	80.6	3.9	1963
1964	84	6	na	na	na	na	81.3	0.9	1964
1965	86	3	na	na	na	na	82.7	1.7	1965
1966	89	3	87	na	96	na	86.1	4.1	1966
1967	94	6	89	2	77	−20	87.9	2.1	1967
1968	97	4	98	10	85	11	95.2	8.3	1968
1969	97	0	100	2	91	7	97.5	2.4	1969
1970	100	3	100	0	100	10	100.0	2.6	1970
1971	102	2	97	−3	115	15	103.5	3.5	1971
1972	107	5	99	2	112	−3	113.1	9.3	1972
1973	109	2	98	−1	114	3	129.8	14.8	1973
1974	110	1	91	−7	138	20	158.5	22.1	1974
1975	118	7	79	−14	101	−27	185.4	17.0	1975
1976	129	9	92	17	139	38	204.9	10.5	1976
1977	141	9	86	−6	114	−18	229.2	11.9	1977
1978	149	6	78	−9	119	4	252.5	10.2	1978
1979	na	na	76	−3	133	12	289.6	14.7	1979
1980	na	na	73	−4	151	14	340.4	17.5	1980

Tunisia

Over the time for which figures are available, from 1961, the main periods of expansion in gross domestic product were 1961, 1963–66, 1968–72, 1974–76 and 1978–80; there was a fall or low growth in 1962, 1967 and 1973. Fixed investment, for the time covered, increased mainly in 1961–65, 1968–69, 1971–72 and 1974–79, with falls or low growth in 1966–67, 1970, 1973 and 1980. Exports increased mainly in 1950, 1954, 1957–59, 1963–64, 1966, 1968, 1971–72 and 1978–79, with falls in 1951, 1955–56, 1960–61, 1965, 1973, 1975 and 1977. Consumer prices increased mainly in 1951–52, 1956–58, 1965, 1971, 1975 and 1979–80.

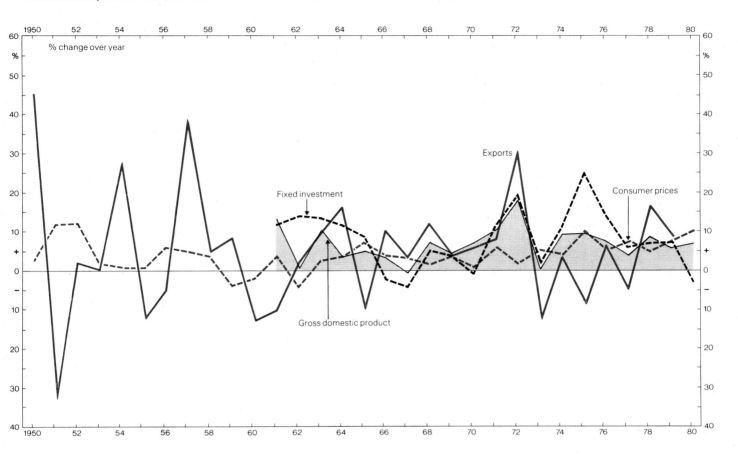

	Gross domestic product		Fixed investment		Exports		Consumer prices		
	Index 1970 = 100	% change over year	Index 1970 = 100	% change over year	Index 1970 = 100	% change over year	Index 1970 = 100	% change over year	
1950	na	na	na	na	67	45	52	3	1950
1951	na	na	na	na	46	−32	59	12	1951
1952	na	na	na	na	46	2	66	12	1952
1953	na	na	na	na	46	0	68	2	1953
1954	na	na	na	na	59	28	68	1	1954
1955	na	na	na	na	52	−12	69	1	1955
1956	na	na	na	na	49	−5	73	6	1956
1957	na	na	na	na	68	38	77	5	1957
1958	na	na	na	na	71	5	80	4	1958
1959	na	na	na	na	77	8	77	−4	1959
1960	58.6	na	56	na	67	−13	76	−2	1960
1961	66.2	13.1	62	12	61	−10	79	4	1961
1962	66.7	0.7	71	14	62	2	76	−4	1962
1963	73.8	10.7	81	13	68	10	78	3	1963
1964	76.7	3.9	91	12	79	16	81	4	1964
1965	80.5	5.0	99	9	71	−10	87	7	1965
1966	83.0	3.1	96	−2	78	10	90	4	1966
1967	82.9	−0.1	92	−4	80	3	93	3	1967
1968	88.9	7.2	97	5	90	12	95	2	1968
1969	93.0	4.6	101	4	94	4	99	4	1969
1970	100.0	7.5	100	−1	100	6	100	1	1970
1971	110.9	10.9	112	12	108	8	106	6	1971
1972	130.7	17.8	133	19	140	30	108	2	1972
1973	131.3	0.4	134	1	123	−12	113	5	1973
1974	143.9	9.6	148	11	127	3	118	4	1974
1975	157.9	9.8	186	25	117	−8	129	10	1975
1976	170.4	7.9	212	14	124	6	136	5	1976
1977	177.5	4.1	225	6	118	−5	145	7	1977
1978	193.2	8.9	240	7	137	16	153	5	1978
1979	204.5	5.8	256	7	150	9	164	8	1979
1980	218.4	6.8	247	−3	na	na	181	10	1980

Turkey

The main periods of expansion in gross domestic product were 1950–53, 1955–59, 1962–64, 1966–72 and 1974–77; there was a fall or low rate of growth for 1954, 1960–61, 1965 and 1979–80. Consumers expenditure similarly increased mainly in 1950–53, 1955–59, 1962–63, 1966–69, 1971–72, 1974–76 and 1979–80, with a fall or low growth in 1954, 1960–61, 1964–65, 1970, 1973 and 1977–78. Government expenditure increased mainly in 1953–55, 1958–61, 1963–64, 1966–69, 1971–73 and 1975–77. Fixed investment rose mainly in 1950–53, 1959–63, 1966–70, 1972–73 and 1975–77, with main falls in 1954, 1956, 1971 and 1978–79.

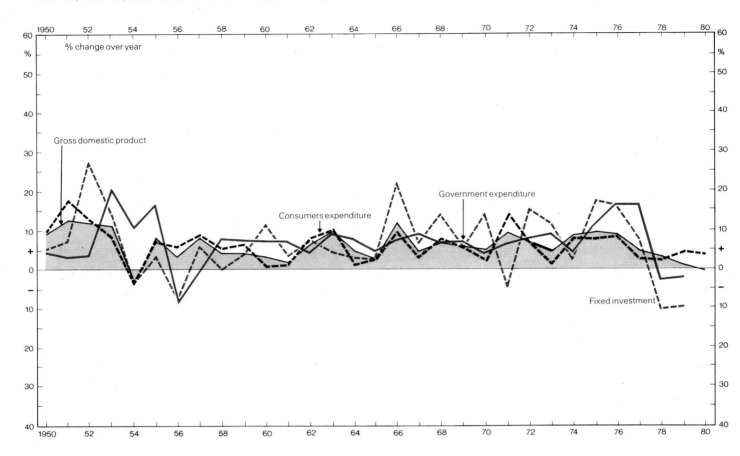

	Gross domestic product		Consumers expenditure		Government expenditure		Fixed investment		
	Index 1970 = 100	% change over year	Index 1970 = 100	% change over year	Index 1970 = 100	% change over year	Index 1970 = 100	% change over year	
1950	31.1	9.4	32.6	9.7	28.3	4.6	26.9	5.0	1950
1951	35.1	12.8	38.3	17.5	29.4	3.7	28.7	6.8	1951
1952	39.3	12.0	43.2	12.8	30.6	4.0	36.5	26.9	1952
1953	43.7	11.2	46.8	8.3	36.7	20.0	41.5	13.7	1953
1954	42.5	−2.9	45.0	−3.9	40.5	10.4	39.8	−4.0	1954
1955	45.9	8.1	48.4	7.6	47.1	16.4	41.2	3.4	1955
1956	47.4	3.3	51.1	5.5	43.0	−8.8	38.0	−7.8	1956
1957	51.2	7.9	55.3	8.3	42.9	−0.1	39.9	5.2	1957
1958	53.5	4.6	58.1	5.1	46.2	7.7	39.9	−0.1	1958
1959	56.0	4.6	61.8	6.3	49.6	7.3	41.5	4.1	1959
1960	57.6	2.9	62.1	0.6	53.2	7.2	46.1	11.0	1960
1961	58.6	1.7	62.7	1.0	57.1	7.3	47.7	3.4	1961
1962	62.1	6.1	67.6	7.8	59.4	4.2	50.9	6.7	1962
1963	68.0	9.4	74.3	9.9	64.5	8.5	53.2	4.7	1963
1964	70.8	4.1	75.1	1.0	69.4	7.6	54.8	2.9	1964
1965	72.7	2.6	77.0	2.6	72.7	4.8	56.2	2.5	1965
1966	81.2	11.7	84.0	9.1	78.1	7.4	68.6	22.2	1966
1967	84.8	4.5	86.6	3.1	84.9	8.7	73.0	6.4	1967
1968	90.5	6.7	92.9	7.3	90.6	6.8	82.8	13.4	1968
1969	95.3	5.3	97.8	5.3	96.5	6.5	88.1	6.4	1969
1970	100.0	4.9	100.0	2.2	100.0	3.6	100.0	13.5	1970
1971	109.1	9.1	113.5	13.5	106.1	6.1	95.0	−5.0	1971
1972	116.2	6.6	120.8	6.4	113.8	7.3	109.1	14.8	1972
1973	121.4	4.4	122.2	1.1	123.6	8.6	121.3	11.2	1973
1974	131.7	8.5	131.5	7.6	129.3	4.7	123.9	2.1	1974
1975	143.4	8.9	141.4	7.5	144.1	11.4	144.8	16.8	1975
1976	155.5	8.5	152.4	7.8	167.3	16.1	167.4	15.6	1976
1977	162.4	4.4	156.2	2.5	193.7	15.8	179.7	7.4	1977
1978	167.3	3.0	159.7	2.2	187.2	−3.3	160.1	−10.9	1978
1979	168.3	0.6	166.2	4.1	181.8	−2.9	143.9	−10.1	1979
1980	167.1	−0.7	171.8	3.4	na	na	na	na	1980

Turkey

Exports (of goods and services) increased mainly in 1951–53, 1955–59, 1962–64, 1966–67, 1969–73, 1975–76 and 1978; there was a fall or comparatively low growth for 1954, 1960–61, 1965, 1968, 1974, 1977 and 1979–80. Imports (of goods and services) increased mainly in 1951–52, 1955, 1959, 1961–63, 1966, 1968, 1970–73, 1975–76 and 1980 with falls in 1956–57, 1964–65, 1967 and 1977–79. Consumer prices increased mainly in 1954–60, 1963, 1966–67 and 1970–77, followed by very high rises for 1978–80. Money stock increased at a high rate throughout, with especially high increases in 1951–57, 1964–66 and 1971–78.

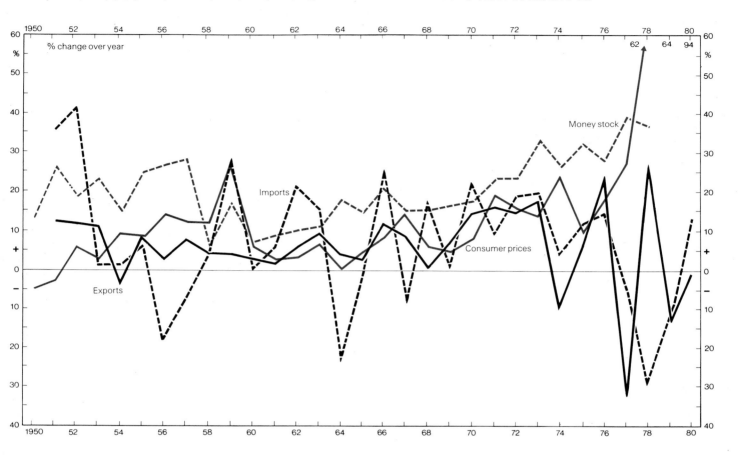

	Exports[a]		Imports[b]		Consumer prices		Money stock		
	Index 1970 = 100	% change over year	Index 1970 = 100	% change over year	Index 1970 = 100	% change over year	Index 1970 = 100	% change over year	
1950	28.9	na	23.2	na	22.9	−4.9	4.5	13	1950
1951	32.6	12.8	31.4	35.6	22.4	−2.1	5.6	27	1951
1952	36.5	11.9	44.4	41.5	23.8	6.3	6.7	19	1952
1953	40.6	11.2	45.1	1.5	24.6	3.4	8.3	23	1953
1954	39.5	−2.9	45.9	1.7	26.9	9.3	9.5	15	1954
1955	42.7	8.1	48.7	6.2	29.3	8.9	11.9	25	1955
1956	44.0	3.2	40.3	−17.2	33.4	14.0	15.1	27	1956
1957	47.5	7.9	37.7	−6.7	37.5	12.3	19.4	28	1957
1958	49.7	4.6	39.4	4.6	42.1	12.3	20.7	7	1958
1959	52.0	4.6	50.7	28.6	53.2	26.4	24.2	17	1959
1960	53.5	2.9	50.9	0.4	56.6	6.4	25.9	7	1960
1961	54.4	1.7	54.2	6.5	58.1	2.7	27.9	8	1961
1962	57.7	6.1	65.7	21.3	60.3	3.8	30.6	10	1962
1963	63.2	9.4	76.0	15.6	64.3	6.6	34.0	11	1963
1964	65.8	4.1	59.7	−21.5	64.4	0.2	40.2	18	1964
1965	67.5	2.6	59.4	−0.5	67.4	4.7	46.3	15	1965
1966	75.4	11.7	74.2	24.9	73.0	8.3	55.8	21	1966
1967	81.8	8.4	68.4	−7.8	83.3	14.1	64.0	15	1967
1968	81.9	0.1	80.4	17.6	88.4	6.1	73.8	15	1968
1969	87.5	6.9	82.0	1.9	92.7	4.9	85.3	16	1969
1970	100.0	14.3	100.0	22.0	100.0	7.9	100.0	17	1970
1971	115.5	15.5	109.7	9.7	119.0	19.0	123.5	23	1971
1972	132.3	14.6	130.6	19.0	137.3	15.4	151.4	23	1972
1973	155.4	17.5	156.5	19.8	156.6	14.1	200.8	33	1973
1974	140.6	−9.5	163.4	4.4	194.0	23.9	255.3	27	1974
1975	150.1	6.8	183.3	12.2	213.0	9.8	336.2	32	1975
1976	185.6	23.6	209.0	14.0	250.3	17.5	430.4	28	1976
1977	126.4	−31.9	202.4	−3.2	315.2	26.0	598.3	39	1977
1978	160.9	27.2	143.6	−29.1	510.3	61.9	819.8	37	1978
1979	138.8	−13.7	129.9	−9.5	834.5	63.5	na	na	1979
1980	137.6	−0.8	147.0	13.1	1621.1	94.3	na	na	1980

[a]Including exports of services   [b]Including imports of services

Uganda

Over the time for which figures are available, from 1968, the main periods of expansion in gross domestic product were 1968–71 and 1976–77, with falls or low growth for 1972–75 and 1978. Exports of coffee increased mainly in 1950–51, 1955, 1957, 1959–60, 1962–63, 1965–66, 1969–70, 1972 and 1979, with falls in 1952–54, 1956, 1958, 1961, 1964, 1967–68, 1971, 1973–78 and 1980. Consumer prices, for the time covered, increased mainly in 1961, 1964–65, 1969–71 and 1973–78 (especially 1973–74 and 1976–78). Money stock, for the time covered, increased mainly in 1966–68, 1970, 1972–74 and 1976–80.

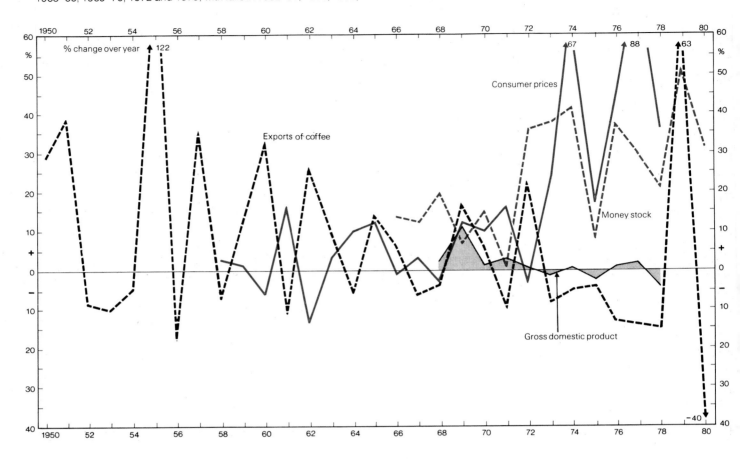

	Gross domestic product		Exports of coffee		Consumer prices		Money stock		
	Index 1970 = 100	% change over year	Index 1970 = 100	% change over year	Index 1970 = 100	% change over year	Index 1970 = 100	% change over year	
1950	na	na	16	29	na	na	na	na	1950
1951	na	na	23	39	na	na	na	na	1951
1952	na	na	21	−8	na	na	na	na	1952
1953	na	na	19	−10	na	na	na	na	1953
1954	na	na	18	−5	na	na	na	na	1954
1955	na	na	40	122	na	na	na	na	1955
1956	na	na	33	−18	na	na	na	na	1956
1957	na	na	45	36	66.4	na	na	na	1957
1958	na	na	42	−7	67.8	2	na	na	1958
1959	na	na	47	12	68.5	1	na	na	1959
1960	na	na	62	32	64.4	−6	na	na	1960
1961	na	na	55	−11	74.7	16	na	na	1961
1962	na	na	70	27	64.4	−14	na	na	1962
1963	na	na	77	10	66.4	3	na	na	1963
1964	na	na	73	−5	73.3	10	na	na	1964
1965	na	na	83	14	82.2	12	53.8	na	1965
1966	na	na	88	6	81.5	−1	60.5	13	1966
1967	86.5	na	83	−6	84.2	3	68.0	12	1967
1968	88.7	2.6	80	−4	81.5	−3	81.3	20	1968
1969	98.5	11.0	94	17	91.1	12	87.0	7	1969
1970	100.0	1.6	100	6	100.0	10	100.0	15	1970
1971	103.0	3.0	91	−9	115.8	16	101.3	1	1971
1972	103.6	0.6	112	23	112.3	−3	138.0	36	1972
1973	102.6	−1.0	103	−8	139.7	24	189.8	38	1973
1974	103.1	0.5	98	−5	233.2	67	269.0	42	1974
1975	101.0	−2.0	94	−4	273.1	17	290.8	8	1975
1976	101.8	0.7	82	−13	400.4	47	399.2	37	1976
1977	103.4	1.6	71	−14	754.6	88	518.1	30	1977
1978	99.2	−4.0	60	−15	1 029.9	36	626.4	21	1978
1979	na	na	98	63	na	na	953.7	52	1979
1980	na	na	58	−40	na	na	1 253.1	31	1980

United Kingdom

The main periods of expansion in gross domestic product were 1950–51, 1953–57, 1959–61, 1963–68, 1970–73 and 1976–79; there was a fall or low rate of growth in 1952, 1958, 1962, 1969, 1974–75 and 1980. Consumers expenditure increased mainly in 1950, 1953–55, 1959–60, 1963–68, 1970–73 and 1978–79, with falls in 1951–52, 1974–75 and 1977. Government expenditure increased mainly in 1951–53, 1961–62, 1965–67, 1971–73, 1975 and 1978–80. Fixed investment increased mainly in 1950, 1953–57, 1959–61, 1964–65, 1967–68, 1970–71, 1973 and 1978, with falls or low growth in 1951–52, 1958, 1962–63, 1969, 1972, 1974–77 and 1979–80.

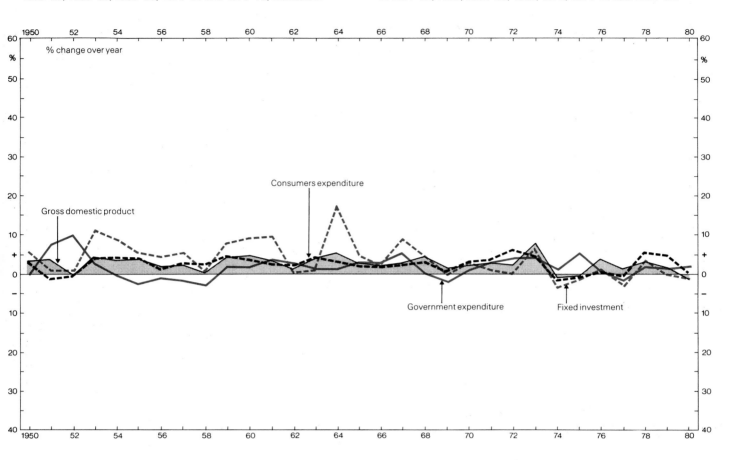

	Gross domestic product		Consumers expenditure		Government expenditure		Fixed investment		
	Index 1970 = 100	% change over year	Index 1970 = 100	% change over year	Index 1970 = 100	% change over year	Index 1970 = 100	% change over year	
1950	57.4	3.1	62.1	2.8	70.7	−0.2	36.1	5.7	1950
1951	59.5	3.6	61.3	−1.4	75.9	7.4	36.4	0.7	1951
1952	59.4	−0.2	61.0	−0.5	83.4	9.9	36.6	0.7	1952
1953	62.1	4.6	63.7	4.5	85.6	2.6	40.6	11.0	1953
1954	64.5	3.8	66.3	4.1	85.2	−0.4	44.2	8.7	1954
1955	67.0	3.8	69.0	4.1	83.0	−2.6	46.8	5.9	1955
1956	68.1	1.7	69.7	1.0	82.1	−1.0	49.0	4.7	1956
1957	69.4	1.9	71.1	2.1	80.7	−1.7	51.7	5.5	1957
1958	69.5	0.1	72.8	2.4	78.6	−2.7	52.1	0.8	1958
1959	72.2	4.0	76.0	4.3	80.0	1.8	56.1	7.7	1959
1960	75.6	4.7	78.9	3.9	81.5	1.9	61.2	9.0	1960
1961	78.1	3.3	80.7	2.3	84.4	3.6	67.2	9.8	1961
1962	78.8	0.9	82.4	2.1	87.0	3.1	67.3	0.2	1962
1963	82.0	4.1	86.0	4.3	88.4	1.6	68.2	1.3	1963
1964	86.3	5.3	88.7	3.1	89.8	1.6	79.6	16.8	1964
1965	88.4	2.4	90.2	1.7	92.2	2.7	83.5	4.8	1965
1966	90.2	2.1	92.0	2.0	94.7	2.7	85.5	2.5	1966
1967	92.6	2.6	94.1	2.3	100.1	5.7	92.8	8.5	1967
1968	96.4	4.2	96.9	3.0	100.4	0.4	97.0	4.6	1968
1969	97.8	1.4	97.4	0.5	98.6	−1.9	97.4	0.4	1969
1970	100.0	2.2	100.0	2.7	100.0	1.5	100.0	2.7	1970
1971	102.7	2.7	103.3	3.3	103.0	3.0	101.5	1.5	1971
1972	105.1	2.3	109.4	5.9	107.2	4.1	101.9	0.4	1972
1973	112.9	7.5	114.7	4.8	112.3	4.7	108.9	6.9	1973
1974	111.8	−1.0	112.6	−1.8	114.0	1.5	105.7	−3.0	1974
1975	111.2	−0.5	112.0	−0.6	120.6	5.8	104.9	−0.7	1975
1976	115.3	3.6	112.1	0.1	121.5	0.8	106.1	1.1	1976
1977	116.7	1.3	111.7	−0.4	120.1	−1.1	103.6	−2.4	1977
1978	120.6	3.3	118.0	5.6	122.7	2.1	107.1	3.3	1978
1979	122.3	1.4	123.5	4.7	124.8	1.7	107.4	0.3	1979
1980	120.6	−1.4	123.6	0.1	127.6	2.3	106.7	−0.7	1980

The amount invested in new stocks was increased mainly in 1951, 1955, 1959–60, 1963–64, 1973, 1976–77 and 1979; stocks were reduced mainly in 1950, 1952, 1958, 1961–62, 1965–67, 1970–72, 1974–75, 1978 and 1980. Exports increased mainly in 1950, 1953–56, 1959–61, 1963–66, 1968–69, 1973–74 and 1976–77, with falls in 1951–52, 1958, 1967 and 1975. Imports increased mainly in 1951, 1955, 1959–60, 1962–64, 1967–68, 1970–73 and 1978–79, with falls in 1952, 1956, 1961, 1975 and 1980. Unemployment rose mainly in 1952, 1957–58, 1962–63, 1967, 1971–72, 1975–76 and 1980, with main falls in 1951, 1954–55, 1960–61, 1964–65 and 1973.

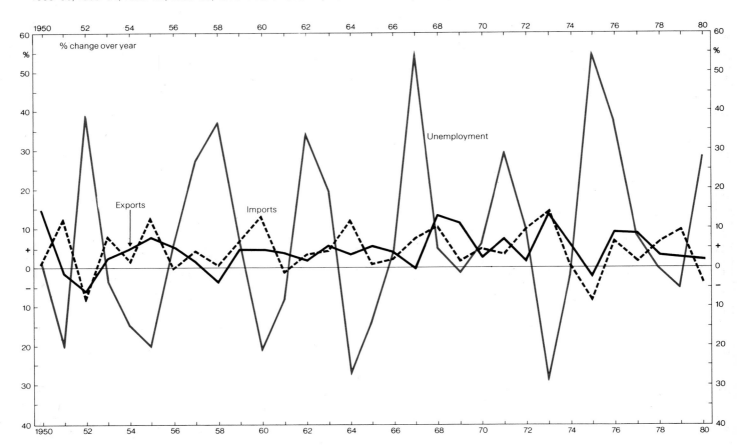

	Stock investment		Exports		Imports		Unemployment		
	£ mn[a]	Change over year[b]	Index 1970 = 100	% change over year	Index 1970 = 100	% change over year	Number (000)	% change over year	
1950	−525	−696	53.3	14.5	41.4	0.6	327	1	1950
1951	1 175	1 700	52.5	−1.5	46.4	12.0	260	−20	1951
1952	126	−1 049	49.2	−6.2	42.5	−8.3	361	39	1952
1953	257	131	50.3	2.1	45.8	7.6	349	−3	1953
1954	122	−135	52.6	4.7	46.4	1.4	297	−15	1954
1955	704	582	56.5	7.4	52.0	12.1	239	−20	1955
1956	548	−156	59.5	5.3	51.7	−0.5	254	6	1956
1957	562	14	60.3	1.3	54.0	4.3	322	27	1957
1958	249	−313	57.8	−4.1	54.1	0.2	442	37	1958
1959	468	219	60.4	4.5	58.0	7.1	468	6	1959
1960	1 460	992	63.1	4.5	65.4	12.9	368	−21	1960
1961	703	−757	65.1	3.1	64.7	−1.1	339	−8	1961
1962	23	−680	66.1	1.6	66.5	2.9	454	34	1962
1963	438	415	69.8	5.5	69.3	4.1	539	19	1963
1964	1 738	1 300	71.8	3.0	77.2	11.5	394	−27	1964
1965	1 120	−618	75.6	5.2	77.6	0.5	338	−14	1965
1966	697	−423	78.3	3.6	79.1	1.9	353	4	1966
1967	548	−149	78.0	−0.4	85.0	7.5	547	55	1967
1968	977	429	88.0	12.8	93.9	10.5	574	5	1968
1969	1 019	42	97.6	10.9	95.4	1.6	566	−1	1969
1970	802	−217	100.0	2.5	100.0	4.8	602	6	1970
1971	278	−524	106.9	6.9	103.7	3.7	776	29	1971
1972	−19	−297	108.2	1.2	113.9	9.9	855	10	1972
1973	2 483	2 502	122.3	13.0	129.6	13.8	611	−29	1973
1974	1 386	−1 097	128.7	5.2	130.1	0.4	600	−2	1974
1975	−1 483	−2 869	125.8	−2.2	118.9	−8.6	929	55	1975
1976	624	2 107	136.6	8.6	126.6	6.5	1 273	37	1976
1977	1 387	763	148.1	8.4	128.9	1.8	1 378	8	1977
1978	833	−554	152.2	2.8	137.5	6.6	1 376	0	1978
1979	1 504	671	155.7	2.3	150.7	9.6	1 307	−5	1979
1980	−1 978	−3 482	158.5	1.8	144.2	−4.3	1 668	28	1980

[a]At 1975 price levels   [b]Actual amount of change

United Kingdom

The main periods of expansion for industrial production were 1950–51, 1953–55, 1959–60, 1963–65, 1968–69, 1972–73 and 1976–79; there were falls or low growth in 1952, 1956–58, 1961–62, 1966–67, 1970–71, 1974–75 and 1980. Production of coal increased mainly in 1951–52, 1973, 1975 and 1980, with falling production for most other years. Electricity production increased mainly in 1950–51, 1953–56, 1958–65, 1968–70, 1973 and 1977–79, with falls in 1974 and 1980. Steel production increased mainly in 1950, 1952–57, 1959–60, 1963–65, 1968–70, 1972–73, 1976 and 1979, with main falls in 1951, 1958, 1961–62, 1966, 1971, 1974–75, 1977 and 1980.

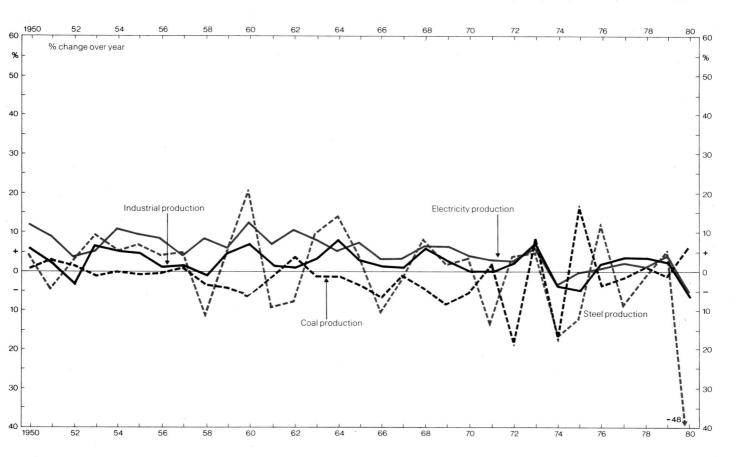

	Industrial production		Coal production		Electricity production[a]		Steel production		
	Index 1970 = 100	% change over year	Index 1970 = 100	% change over year	Index 1970 = 100	% change over year	Index 1970 = 100	% change over year	
1950	57.1	6.1	149.8	0.5	24.8	11.8	59.6	4.8	1950
1951	58.4	2.3	154.3	3.1	27.1	9.0	57.2	−4.0	1951
1952	56.6	−3.1	156.8	1.6	28.1	3.9	58.9	3.0	1952
1953	60.2	6.4	155.2	−1.0	29.6	5.4	64.4	9.3	1953
1954	63.3	5.1	155.2	0.0	32.9	11.0	67.7	5.2	1954
1955	66.4	4.9	154.1	−0.7	36.1	9.7	72.4	6.9	1955
1956	66.9	0.8	153.7	−0.3	39.1	8.6	75.5	4.4	1956
1957	68.1	1.8	154.9	0.8	40.8	4.3	79.3	5.0	1957
1958	67.5	−0.9	149.4	−3.5	44.1	8.1	70.2	−11.5	1958
1959	70.9	5.0	142.9	−4.4	47.0	6.5	73.8	5.2	1959
1960	75.8	6.9	134.5	−5.9	53.0	12.9	88.9	20.4	1960
1961	76.7	1.2	132.6	−1.4	56.9	7.3	80.7	−9.1	1961
1962	77.4	0.9	137.7	3.9	63.1	10.9	74.9	−7.2	1962
1963	79.7	3.0	136.3	−1.1	68.5	8.6	82.3	9.9	1963
1964	86.5	8.5	134.6	−1.2	72.3	5.5	94.2	14.4	1964
1965	89.1	3.0	130.3	−3.2	77.8	7.7	98.7	4.7	1965
1966	90.6	1.7	121.6	−6.6	80.7	3.7	88.8	−10.0	1966
1967	91.7	1.2	120.7	−0.7	83.8	3.8	87.3	−1.7	1967
1968	97.1	5.9	115.5	−4.3	89.6	6.9	94.5	8.2	1968
1969	99.7	2.7	105.8	−8.4	95.7	6.8	96.5	2.2	1969
1970	100.0	0.3	100.0	−5.5	100.0	4.5	100.0	3.6	1970
1971	100.1	0.1	101.6	1.6	103.3	3.3	86.9	−13.1	1971
1972	102.3	2.2	82.8	−18.5	106.4	3.0	91.0	4.7	1972
1973	109.8	7.4	89.7	8.4	113.4	6.6	95.7	5.1	1973
1974	105.5	−3.9	75.1	−16.3	109.7	−3.2	80.3	−16.1	1974
1975	100.4	−4.9	87.5	16.5	110.1	0.3	71.2	−11.4	1975
1976	102.4	2.0	84.2	−3.8	111.7	1.5	80.1	12.6	1976
1977	106.3	3.8	83.0	−1.3	114.8	2.8	73.4	−8.4	1977
1978	110.2	3.7	84.0	1.2	116.9	1.8	73.1	−0.5	1978
1979	113.1	2.6	83.2	−1.0	122.4	4.7	77.2	5.7	1979
1980	105.7	−6.5	88.4	6.3	116.7	−4.7	40.6	−47.5	1980

[a]Public supply only

141

Production of cement rose mainly in 1950–52, 1954–56, 1959–61, 1964, 1967–68, 1971–73 and 1978–79, with falls or low growth in 1953, 1957–58, 1962–63, 1965–66, 1969–70, 1974–77 and 1980. Sulphuric acid production increased mainly in 1950, 1953–57, 1959–60, 1963–65, 1973 and 1976–77, with falls in 1951–52, 1958, 1961, 1966, 1969, 1972, 1974–75 and 1980. Passenger car production rose mainly in 1950, 1953–55, 1957–60, 1962–64, 1968 and 1971–72, falling in 1951–52, 1956, 1961, 1965–67, 1969–70, 1973–75 and 1977–80. Ships built increased mainly in 1954, 1956, 1965, 1970, 1974–76 and 1978, with falls in most other years.

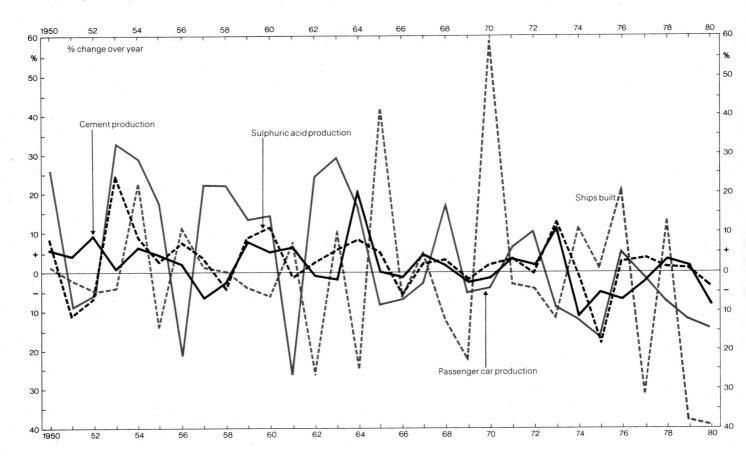

	Cement production		Sulphuric acid production		Passenger car production		Ships built		
	Index 1970 = 100	% change over year	Index 1970 = 100	% change over year	Index 1970 = 100	% change over year	Index 1970 = 100	% change over year	
1950	57.7	5.8	54.6	8.6	31.8	26	106.5	1	1950
1951	60.3	4.5	48.7	−10.9	29.0	−9	104.0	−2	1951
1952	65.9	9.3	45.6	−6.3	27.3	−6	98.4	−5	1952
1953	66.4	0.7	56.8	24.6	36.3	33	94.7	−4	1953
1954	70.8	6.6	61.9	8.9	46.9	29	115.6	22	1954
1955	74.1	4.6	63.6	2.7	54.7	17	99.3	−14	1955
1956	75.5	2.0	68.2	7.3	43.2	−21	110.4	11	1956
1957	70.8	−6.3	70.8	3.8	52.5	22	111.6	1	1957
1958	69.1	−2.5	67.9	−4.1	64.1	22	112.0	0	1958
1959	74.5	7.9	73.6	8.4	72.6	13	107.0	−4	1959
1960	78.7	5.5	81.9	11.2	82.4	14	100.5	−6	1960
1961	83.8	6.5	80.7	−1.5	61.2	−26	107.2	7	1961
1962	83.0	−0.9	82.8	2.6	76.2	24	78.8	−26	1962
1963	81.9	−1.4	87.3	5.5	98.0	29	86.9	10	1963
1964	98.8	20.7	95.0	8.8	113.8	16	65.4	−25	1964
1965	98.9	0.0	100.2	5.4	105.0	−8	92.8	42	1965
1966	97.8	−1.1	94.5	−5.7	97.7	−7	87.1	−6	1966
1967	102.6	4.9	96.5	2.1	94.6	−3	91.9	5	1967
1968	104.5	1.8	99.5	3.1	110.7	17	80.6	−12	1968
1969	101.7	−2.7	98.1	−1.4	104.7	−5	62.8	−22	1969
1970	100.0	−1.7	100.0	2.0	100.0	−4	100.0	59	1970
1971	103.1	3.1	103.2	3.2	106.2	6	97.1	−3	1971
1972	105.1	2.0	102.9	−0.3	117.1	10	93.1	−4	1972
1973	116.4	10.7	115.9	12.7	106.5	−9	82.4	−12	1973
1974	103.6	−11.0	115.0	−0.8	93.5	−12	91.7	11	1974
1975	98.4	−5.0	94.5	−17.9	77.2	−17	92.8	1	1975
1976	91.9	−6.6	97.6	3.3	81.3	5	112.6	21	1976
1977	90.0	−2.0	101.6	4.1	80.2	−1	77.6	−31	1977
1978	92.7	3.0	103.0	1.4	74.5	−7	87.5	13	1978
1979	94.0	1.4	104.4	1.3	65.3	−12	54.5	−38	1979
1980	86.2	−8.3	100.9	−3.4	56.3	−14	33.2	−39	1980

United Kingdom

Wholesale prices, for the time covered, increased mainly in 1955–57, 1961–62, 1964–66, 1970–71, 1974–77 and 1979–80. Consumer prices rose mainly in 1951–52, 1955–58, 1961–62, 1964–66, 1968–71, 1974–77 and 1979–80, with comparatively low rises for other years. Wages rose mainly in 1951–52, 1955–57, 1961–66,

1968, 1970–76 and 1978–80; for the years from 1970, the change in wages was about one year ahead of the change in consumer prices. Shipping freight rates fluctuated markedly, with main rises in 1951, 1954–56, 1959–61, 1963–65, 1970, 1973–74 and 1978–80, and falls in 1952–53, 1957–58, 1962, 1966, 1971, 1975 and 1977.

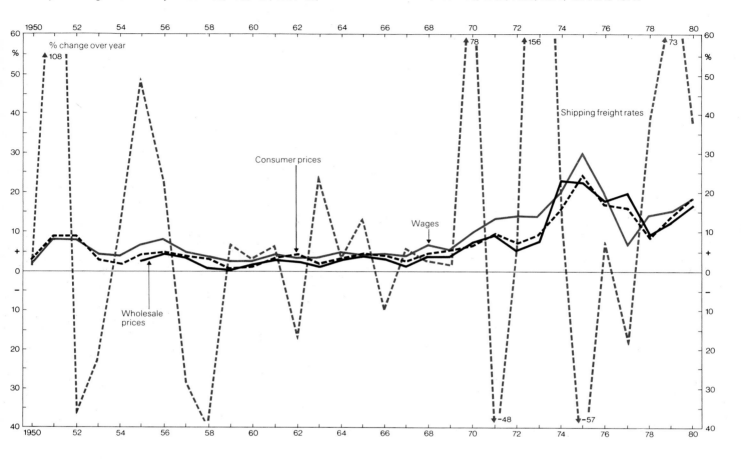

	Wholesale prices		Consumer prices		Wages[a]		Shipping freight rates		
	Index 1970 = 100	% change over year	Index 1970 = 100	% change over year	Index 1970 = 100	% change over year	Index 1970 = 100	% change over year	
1950	na	na	45.2	3.2	36.0	1.8	45.3	1.5	1950
1951	na	na	49.3	9.1	39.1	8.5	94.3	108.1	1951
1952	na	na	53.8	9.1	42.4	8.4	60.4	−35.9	1952
1953	na	na	55.4	3.0	44.3	4.5	46.7	−22.7	1953
1954	65.1	na	56.5	2.0	46.2	4.3	51.8	10.9	1954
1955	66.7	2.5	59.0	4.4	49.4	6.9	76.9	48.6	1955
1956	69.6	4.3	61.9	4.9	53.3	8.0	94.3	22.5	1956
1957	71.8	3.2	64.2	3.7	56.0	5.0	67.6	−28.3	1957
1958	72.3	0.7	66.2	3.1	58.0	3.6	40.3	−40.4	1958
1959	72.5	0.3	66.5	0.5	59.5	2.6	43.1	7.0	1959
1960	73.5	1.4	67.2	1.1	61.0	2.6	44.6	3.4	1960
1961	75.5	2.7	69.5	3.4	63.6	4.2	47.5	6.4	1961
1962	77.2	2.3	72.5	4.3	65.9	3.6	39.6	−16.7	1962
1963	78.0	1.0	73.9	1.9	68.3	3.7	48.9	23.6	1963
1964	80.3	2.9	76.3	3.2	71.6	4.8	50.4	3.0	1964
1965	83.3	3.7	80.0	4.8	74.6	4.3	56.8	12.8	1965
1966	85.6	2.8	83.1	3.9	78.0	4.6	51.0	−10.1	1966
1967	86.5	1.1	85.2	2.5	81.1	3.9	54.0	5.7	1967
1968	89.9	3.9	89.2	4.7	86.4	6.6	55.4	2.6	1968
1969	93.4	3.9	94.0	5.4	91.0	5.3	56.1	1.3	1969
1970	100.0	7.1	100.0	6.4	100.0	9.9	100.0	78.2	1970
1971	109.1	9.1	109.4	9.4	112.9	12.9	51.8	−48.2	1971
1972	114.8	5.3	117.2	7.1	128.6	13.8	54.7	5.6	1972
1973	123.3	7.4	128.0	9.2	146.2	13.7	140.2	156.4	1973
1974	151.2	22.6	148.4	16.0	175.1	19.8	157.5	12.3	1974
1975	184.8	22.2	184.4	24.2	226.8	29.5	67.6	−57.1	1975
1976	216.8	17.3	214.9	16.5	270.6	19.3	71.9	6.4	1976
1977	259.7	19.8	249.0	15.8	288.5	6.6	58.3	−19.0	1977
1978	283.4	9.1	269.6	8.3	329.1	14.1	80.5	38.2	1978
1979	317.9	12.2	305.8	13.4	378.3	15.0	139.6	73.3	1979
1980	369.7	16.3	360.8	18.0	446.4	18.0	191.3	37.1	1980

[a]Basic wage rates

United Kingdom

Share prices rose mainly in 1950–51, 1953–55, 1959–60, 1963–64, 1967–68, 1971–72 and 1975–78, with falls in 1952, 1956, 1958, 1962, 1965–66, 1969–70, 1973–74 and 1979–80. Money stock increased mainly in 1953–54, 1958–59, 1962–65, 1967–68, 1970–72 and 1974–79. International reserves rose mainly in 1950, 1953–54, 1958,

1960, 1965, 1970–71, 1977 and 1979–80, with falls in 1951–52, 1955–57, 1959, 1961–64, 1967–68, 1972, 1975–76 and 1978. The interest rate increased mainly in 1952, 1955–56, 1960–61, 1964–66, 1968–69, 1973–74, 1976 and 1978–80, with main falls in 1954, 1959, 1962–63, 1967, 1970–71, 1975 and 1977.

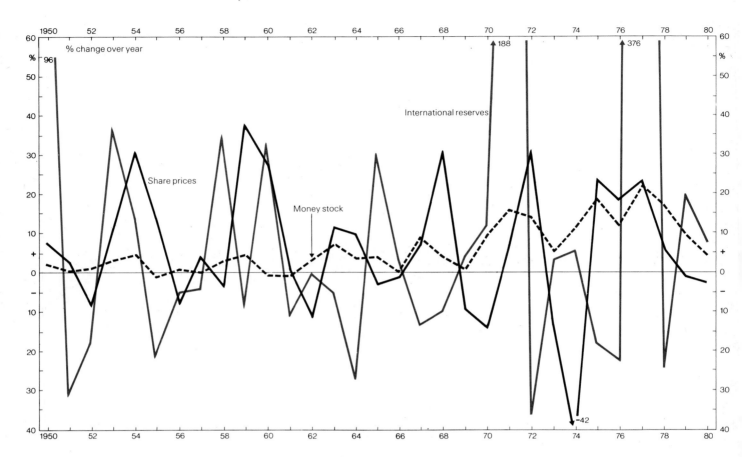

	Share prices		Money stock		International reserves		Interest rate		
	Index 1970 = 100	% change over year	Index 1970 = 100	% change over year	Index 1970 = 100	% change over year	%	Change over year[a]	
1950	34.9	7.4	59.5	1.8	127.0	96.4	0.516	−0.005	1950
1951	35.9	2.7	59.6	0.1	87.6	−31.0	0.577	0.061	1951
1952	32.8	−8.7	60.0	0.7	72.2	−17.6	2.196	1.619	1952
1953	36.3	11.0	61.8	3.0	98.5	36.5	2.304	0.108	1953
1954	47.4	30.5	64.6	4.5	111.9	13.6	1.794	−0.510	1954
1955	54.0	13.9	63.8	−1.2	88.3	−21.0	3.753	1.959	1955
1956	50.0	−7.4	64.2	0.6	83.9	−5.0	4.945	1.192	1956
1957	52.2	4.3	64.2	−0.1	80.4	−4.2	4.814	−0.131	1957
1958	50.4	−3.4	65.9	2.7	108.5	34.9	4.563	−0.251	1958
1959	69.3	37.5	69.0	4.7	99.0	−8.7	3.375	−1.188	1959
1960	88.3	27.3	68.5	−0.7	131.6	32.8	4.887	1.512	1960
1961	88.6	0.4	68.1	−0.7	117.4	−10.8	5.141	0.254	1961
1962	79.1	−10.7	70.5	3.6	117.0	−0.3	4.171	−0.970	1962
1963	87.8	11.0	75.4	6.9	111.4	−4.8	3.667	−0.504	1963
1964	96.1	9.5	77.8	3.2	81.9	−26.5	4.594	0.927	1964
1965	93.4	−2.8	80.8	3.9	106.3	29.8	5.909	1.315	1965
1966	91.9	−1.6	80.7	−0.1	109.6	3.2	6.122	0.213	1966
1967	98.3	7.0	87.6	8.5	95.3	−13.0	5.810	−0.312	1967
1968	128.3	30.5	91.2	4.1	85.7	−10.1	7.031	1.221	1968
1969	116.3	−9.4	91.5	0.3	89.4	4.3	7.627	0.596	1969
1970	100.0	−14.0	100.0	9.3	100.0	11.9	6.999	−0.628	1970
1971	107.0	7.0	115.1	15.1	287.8	187.8	5.554	−1.445	1971
1972	139.6	30.5	131.4	14.2	184.0	−36.1	5.541	−0.013	1972
1973	120.7	−13.5	138.1	5.1	189.9	3.2	9.306	3.765	1973
1974	69.6	−42.3	153.0	10.8	200.5	5.6	11.357	2.051	1974
1975	86.1	23.8	181.5	18.6	164.9	−17.7	10.187	−1.170	1975
1976	101.9	18.3	202.0	11.3	128.8	−21.9	11.157	0.970	1976
1977	125.3	22.9	245.6	21.5	613.2	376.1	7.630	−3.527	1977
1978	132.8	6.0	285.8	16.4	463.4	−24.4	8.535	0.905	1978
1979	131.7	−0.8	311.8	9.1	552.7	19.3	12.988	4.453	1979
1980	128.7	−2.3	324.1	3.9	596.1	7.8	15.127	2.139	1980

[a]In percentage points

144

United States

The main periods of expansion in gross domestic product were 1950–53, 1955–57, 1959, 1962–66, 1968–69, 1971–73 and 1976–79, with falls in 1954, 1958, 1970, 1974–75 and 1980 and low growth in 1960–61 and 1967. Consumers expenditure rose mainly in 1950, 1952–53, 1955, 1959, 1962–66, 1968–69, 1971–73 and 1976–78, with low growth or a fall for other years. Government expenditure increased mainly in 1951–53, 1957–58, 1961–62 and 1965–68, with falls in 1954–55 and 1969–71. Fixed investment increased mainly in 1950, 1953, 1955, 1959,1962–66, 1968–69, 1971–73 and 1976–79, with falls in1951–52, 1957–58, 1961, 1967, 1970,1974–75 and 1980.

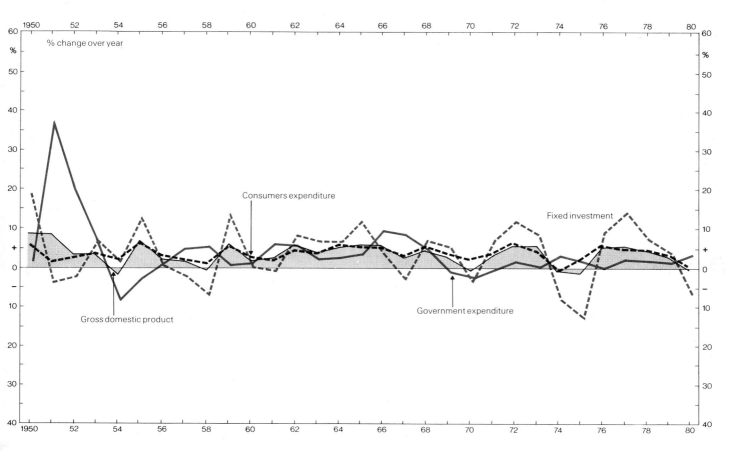

	Gross domestic product		Consumers expenditure		Government expenditure[a]		Fixed investment[b]		
	Index 1970 = 100	% change over year	Index 1970 = 100	% change over year	Index 1970 = 100	% change over year	Index 1970 = 100	% change over year	
1950	49.4	8.7	50.2	5.6	39.1	1.3	53.6	18.9	1950
1951	53.4	8.2	50.8	1.3	53.2	36.3	51.8	−3.4	1951
1952	55.4	3.7	52.1	2.5	63.6	19.5	50.8	−1.9	1952
1953	57.5	3.8	54.1	3.8	67.7	6.4	54.1	6.5	1953
1954	56.8	−1.2	55.1	1.8	62.1	−8.3	55.1	1.8	1954
1955	60.6	6.7	58.6	6.5	60.7	−2.4	62.1	12.7	1955
1956	61.9	2.1	60.3	2.9	61.1	0.8	62.5	0.7	1956
1957	62.9	1.8	61.6	2.1	64.2	5.0	61.7	−1.3	1957
1958	62.8	−0.3	62.2	1.0	67.6	5.3	57.7	−6.5	1958
1959	66.5	6.0	65.5	5.4	67.9	0.5	65.2	13.0	1959
1960	67.9	2.1	67.3	2.6	68.8	1.3	65.4	0.3	1960
1961	69.7	2.6	68.7	2.1	72.8	5.8	65.2	−0.3	1961
1962	73.7	5.7	71.7	4.5	76.9	5.6	70.9	8.7	1962
1963	76.6	4.0	74.5	3.8	78.7	2.3	75.9	7.1	1963
1964	80.6	5.2	78.6	5.5	80.7	2.5	81.3	7.1	1964
1965	85.5	6.0	82.9	5.6	83.6	3.6	90.5	11.3	1965
1966	90.7	6.1	87.1	5.1	91.5	9.5	94.4	4,4	1966
1967	93.2	2.7	89.7	2.9	99.0	8.2	92.2	−2.4	1967
1968	97.4	4.6	94.4	5.3	103.6	4.7	98.6	6.9	1968
1969	100.2	2.8	97.9	3.7	102.5	−1.1	103.6	5.1	1969
1970	100.0	−0.2	100.0	2.2	100.0	−2.4	100.0	−3.5	1970
1971	103.3	3.3	103.7	3.7	99.6	−0.4	107.1	7.1	1971
1972	109.0	5.6	109.7	5.8	100.8	1.2	119.4	11.5	1972
1973	115.1	5.5	114.3	4.3	101.0	0.2	129.5	8.4	1973
1974	114.2	−0.7	113.6	−0.6	104.0	3.0	118.8	−8.2	1974
1975	113.2	−0.9	116.1	2.2	106.2	2.1	104.3	−12.2	1975
1976	119.2	5.3	122.6	5.6	106.3	0.0	114.1	9.4	1976
1977	125.7	5.4	128.5	4.9	108.4	2.1	130.0	13.9	1977
1978	131.5	4.6	134.6	4.7	110.6	2.0	139.4	7.3	1978
1979	135.1	2.8	138.5	2.9	112.2	1.4	143.7	3.1	1979
1980	134.8	−0.2	139.1	0.5	115.5	2.9	133.5	−7.1	1980

[a]Including government investment   [b]Excluding government investment

United States

The amount invested in new stocks was increased mainly in 1950–51, 1955, 1959, 1962, 1965–66, 1969, 1971–73 and 1976–77; stocks were reduced in 1952–54, 1956–58, 1960–61, 1963–64, 1967–68, 1970, 1974–75 and 1979–80. Exports increased mainly in 1951, 1954–57, 1960, 1962–64, 1966–70, 1972–74 and 1978–80, with falls in 1950, 1952–53, 1958, 1971 and 1975. Imports increased mainly in 1950, 1952–53, 1955–56, 1959, 1962, 1964–66, 1968, 1971–73 and 1976–78. Unemployment rose mainly in 1954, 1958, 1961, 1970–71, 1974–75 and 1980, with reductions in 1950–53, 1955–56, 1959, 1962, 1964–66, 1968, 1972–73 and 1976–79.

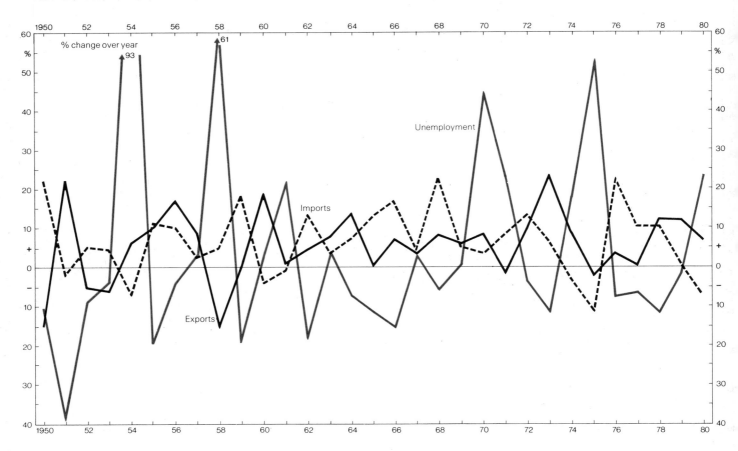

	Stock investment		Exports		Imports		Unemployment		
	$ bn[a]	Change over year[b]	Index 1970 = 100	% change over year	Index 1970 = 100	% change over year	Number (000)	% change over year	
1950	10.6	15.0	34.6	−15.2	29.2	22.0	3 288	−10	1950
1951	13.7	3.1	42.3	22.1	28.7	−1.5	2 055	−38	1951
1952	4.3	−9.4	40.2	−5.0	30.1	5.0	1 883	−8	1952
1953	1.5	−2.8	37.8	−6.0	31.6	4.7	1 834	−3	1953
1954	−2.2	−3.7	40.1	6.2	29.5	−6.7	3 532	93	1954
1955	7.7	9.9	44.1	10.1	32.8	11.2	2 852	−19	1955
1956	5.8	−1.9	51.7	17.0	36.1	10.1	2 750	−4	1956
1957	1.5	−4.3	56.3	8.9	37.0	2.5	2 859	4	1957
1958	−1.8	−3.3	47.7	−15.2	38.8	4.9	4 602	61	1958
1959	7.0	8.8	47.7	0.0	45.8	18.0	3 740	−19	1959
1960	3.5	−3.5	56.7	18.8	43.9	−4.1	3 852	3	1960
1961	3.0	−0.5	57.1	0.9	43.4	−1.0	4 714	22	1961
1962	7.8	4.8	59.6	4.4	49.4	13.7	3 911	−17	1962
1963	7.5	−0.3	64.0	7.3	51.2	3.7	4 070	4	1963
1964	7.1	−0.4	72.8	13.7	54.8	7.2	3 786	−7	1964
1965	11.8	4.7	73.0	0.3	62.1	13.2	3 366	−11	1965
1966	16.8	5.0	78.0	6.7	72.1	16.2	2 875	−15	1966
1967	12.2	−4.6	80.7	3.5	75.1	4.2	2 975	3	1967
1968	9.0	−3.2	87.3	8.2	91.9	22.3	2 817	−5	1968
1969	11.1	2.1	92.6	6.0	96.7	5.2	2 832	1	1969
1970	3.8	−7.3	100.0	8.0	100.0	3.4	4 093	45	1970
1971	8.1	4.3	98.8	−1.2	108.6	8.6	5 016	23	1971
1972	10.2	2.1	108.4	9.7	123.1	13.4	4 882	−3	1972
1973	17.2	7.0	133.7	23.3	130.7	6.2	4 365	−11	1973
1974	11.6	−5.6	145.7	9.0	126.3	−3.4	5 156	18	1974
1975	−6.7	−18.3	142.6	−2.1	112.2	−11.1	7 929	54	1975
1976	7.8	14.5	147.5	3.4	136.8	21.9	7 406	−7	1976
1977	12.3	4.5	147.8	0.2	150.9	10.3	6 991	−6	1977
1978	14.0	1.7	165.4	11.9	166.2	10.2	6 202	−11	1978
1979	10.2	−3.8	183.9	11.2	166.6	0.2	6 137	−1	1979
1980	−2.9	−13.1	196.3	6.7	154.8	−7.1	7 637	24	1980

[a]At 1972 price levels   [b]Actual amount of change

United States

The main periods of expansion for industrial production were 1950–53, 1955–56, 1959, 1962–66, 1968–69, 1972–73 and 1976–79, with falls or low growth in 1954, 1957–58, 1960–61, 1967, 1970–71, 1974–75 and 1980. Production of coal increased mainly in 1950, 1955–56, 1962–67, 1969–70, 1972, 1975–76 and 1979–80.

Electricity production increased at a high rate throughout, with comparatively low rates of growth for 1958, 1970, 1974–75 and 1979–80. Steel production increased mainly in 1950–51, 1953, 1955, 1959–60, 1963–65, 1968–69, 1972–73, 1976 and 1978; there were main falls in 1952, 1954, 1958, 1967, 1970–71, 1974–75 and 1980.

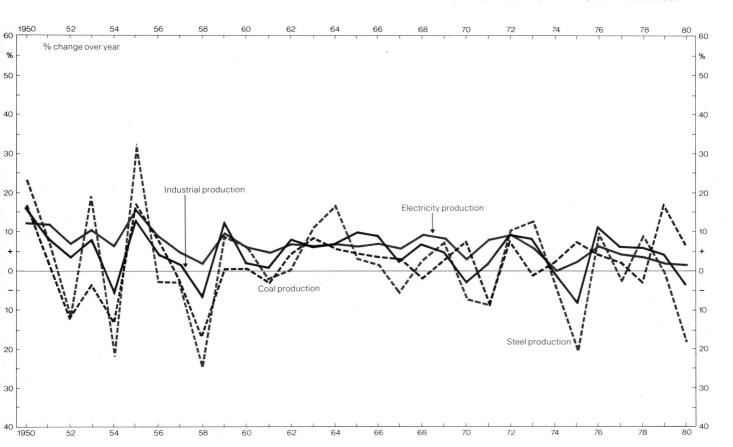

	Industrial production		Coal production		Electricity production[a]		Steel production		
	Index 1970 = 100	% change over year	Index 1970 = 100	% change over year	Index 1970 = 100	% change over year	Index 1970 = 100	% change over year	
1950	41.7	15.7	91.5	16.6	22.1	13.1	73.6	24.2	1950
1951	45.2	8.5	94.1	2.8	24.8	12.6	80.0	8.6	1951
1952	46.9	3.9	82.8	−12.0	26.8	7.7	70.8	−11.4	1952
1953	50.8	8.3	79.7	−3.8	29.7	10.9	84.9	19.8	1953
1954	48.1	−5.3	68.7	−13.8	31.6	6.6	67.2	−20.9	1954
1955	54.3	12.7	80.1	16.6	36.7	16.0	89.0	32.5	1955
1956	56.7	4.4	86.5	7.9	40.3	9.8	87.6	−1.6	1956
1957	57.4	1.3	84.6	−2.2	42.3	5.1	85.7	−2.2	1957
1958	53.7	−6.5	70.4	−16.7	43.2	2.2	64.8	−24.4	1958
1959	60.1	11.9	70.6	0.2	47.6	10.1	71.1	9.6	1959
1960	61.4	2.2	70.9	0.4	50.5	6.1	75.5	6.2	1960
1961	61.9	0.8	68.6	−3.2	53.1	5.1	74.5	−1.3	1961
1962	67.0	8.2	71.7	4.4	57.1	7.6	74.8	0.3	1962
1963	71.0	6.0	77.9	8.7	61.3	7.3	83.1	11.1	1963
1964	75.8	6.8	82.3	5.7	66.0	7.6	96.6	16.3	1964
1965	83.3	9.9	86.0	4.5	70.7	7.2	100.0	3.5	1965
1966	90.7	8.9	89.3	3.8	76.7	8.4	102.0	2.0	1966
1967	92.8	2.2	92.2	3.3	81.4	6.1	96.7	−5.1	1967
1968	98.6	6.3	90.9	−1.4	89.1	9.5	100.0	3.3	1968
1969	103.1	4.5	93.2	2.6	96.7	8.5	107.4	7.5	1969
1970	100.0	−3.0	100.0	7.3	100.0	3.5	100.0	−6.9	1970
1971	101.7	1.7	91.6	−8.4	108.0	8.0	91.6	−8.4	1971
1972	111.0	9.2	98.3	7.4	117.4	8.7	101.3	10.6	1972
1973	120.4	8.4	97.7	−0.7	124.5	6.1	114.7	13.2	1973
1974	119.9	−0.4	99.6	1.9	125.1	0.5	110.8	−3.4	1974
1975	109.3	−8.9	106.9	7.3	128.6	2.7	88.7	−20.0	1975
1976	121.1	10.8	111.8	4.6	136.6	6.3	97.3	9.7	1976
1977	128.2	5.9	113.8	1.8	142.4	4.2	95.3	−2.0	1977
1978	135.5	5.7	109.6	−3.7	147.9	3.9	104.2	9.3	1978
1979	141.5	4.4	127.5	16.4	150.6	1.9	103.7	−0.5	1979
1980	136.4	−3.6	135.4	6.2	153.2	1.7	85.0	−18.0	1980

[a]Utilities only (excludes production by industrial establishments)

Production of cement rose mainly in 1950–56, 1958–59, 1961–64, 1968–69, 1971–73 and 1976–78, with falls in 1957, 1960, 1967, 1970, 1974–75 and 1980. Sulphuric acid production increased mainly in 1950–51, 1953–55, 1959, 1962–66, 1972–74 and 1976–80, with falls in 1952, 1957–58, 1961, 1968, 1971 and 1975. Passenger car

production rose mainly in 1950, 1953, 1955, 1959–60, 1962–63, 1965, 1968, 1971–73 and 1976–77, falling in 1951–52, 1954, 1956, 1958, 1961, 1966–67, 1969–70, 1974–75 and 1978–80. Ships built rose mainly in 1952–53, 1957–59, 1968–69, 1973, 1976–77 and 1979, with main falls in 1950–51, 1955, 1960–61, 1964–66, 1975 and 1980.

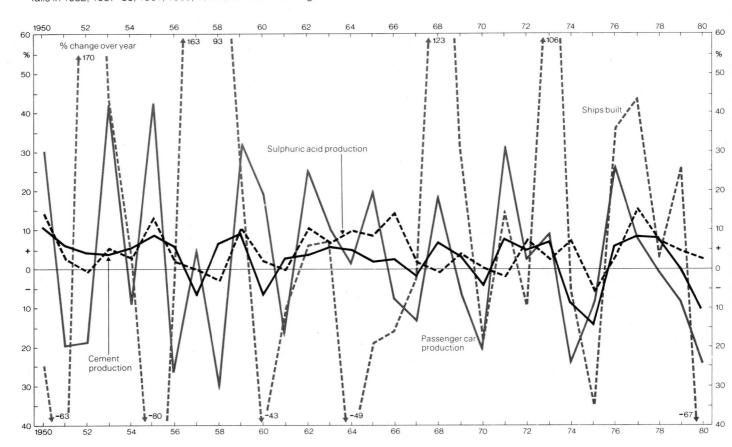

	Cement production[a]		Sulphuric acid production		Passenger car production[b]		Ships built		
	Index 1970 = 100	% change over year	Index 1970 = 100	% change over year	Index 1970 = 100	% change over year	Index 1970 = 100	% change over year	
1950	58.3	10.5	44.1	14.0	101.8	30.2	118	−25	1950
1951	61.8	5.9	45.3	2.6	81.5	−19.9	43	−63	1951
1952	64.3	4.1	45.1	−0.5	66.0	−19.1	117	170	1952
1953	66.8	3.9	47.4	5.2	93.4	41.6	167	43	1953
1954	70.2	5.1	48.7	2.7	84.9	−9.1	171	3	1954
1955	75.9	8.1	55.1	13.1	121.0	42.5	35	−80	1955
1956	79.8	5.2	55.9	1.5	88.8	−26.6	33	−5	1956
1957	74.7	−6.4	55.7	−0.2	93.4	5.1	87	163	1957
1958	79.3	6.1	54.0	−3.1	65.0	−30.4	167	93	1958
1959	86.6	9.1	59.6	10.4	85.4	31.3	209	25	1959
1960	80.7	−6.8	60.6	1.6	102.0	19.4	120	−43	1960
1961	82.6	2.5	60.5	−0.2	84.7	−17.0	108	−10	1961
1962	85.7	3.7	66.7	10.4	105.9	25.1	115	6	1962
1963	90.2	5.3	70.9	6.3	116.7	10.2	122	7	1963
1964	94.5	4.8	77.6	9.5	118.4	1.5	62	−49	1964
1965	95.8	1.4	84.2	8.4	142.1	20.0	51	−19	1965
1966	97.5	1.8	96.1	14.2	131.3	−7.6	43	−16	1966
1967	95.8	−1.8	97.6	1.5	113.6	−13.5	42	−2	1967
1968	101.8	6.3	96.7	−0.9	134.8	18.6	93	123	1968
1969	105.0	3.1	100.0	3.5	125.6	−6.8	122	31	1969
1970	100.0	−4.7	100.0	0.0	100.0	−20.4	100	−18	1970
1971	107.6	7.6	98.3	−1.7	131.1	31.1	115	15	1971
1972	112.8	4.8	105.6	7.4	134.8	2.8	104	−9	1972
1973	120.5	6.8	108.2	2.5	147.5	9.4	215	106	1973
1974	110.5	−8.3	115.8	7.0	112.0	−24.1	204	−5	1974
1975	94.1	−14.8	109.6	−5.3	102.5	−8.4	132	−35	1975
1976	99.2	5.4	113.5	3.5	129.8	26.6	180	36	1976
1977	107.3	8.1	130.4	14.9	140.5	8.3	258	44	1977
1978	115.6	7.8	139.9	7.3	140.0	−0.4	267	3	1978
1979	115.6	0.0	146.3	4.6	128.6	−8.1	336	26	1979
1980	103.6	−10.4	149.9	2.5	97.8	−24.0	110	−67	1980

[a]Shipments of Portland cement   [b]Factory sales

United States

After a high increase in 1951, wholesale prices moved at a comparatively stable level from 1952 to 1972, then rose mainly in 1973–75 and 1977–80. Consumer prices followed a similar pattern with, however, rather higher rises for 1968–71; main rises were in 1951, 1973–75 and 1977–80. Wages rose more steadily throughout the period, with main rises in 1950–53, 1955–57, 1959 and 1968–80. Corporate profits, in value terms, increased mainly in 1950–51, 1955, 1959, 1962–66, 1968, 1971–73 and 1975–79; there were falls in profits for 1952, 1954, 1956–58, 1960, 1967, 1969–70, 1974 and 1980.

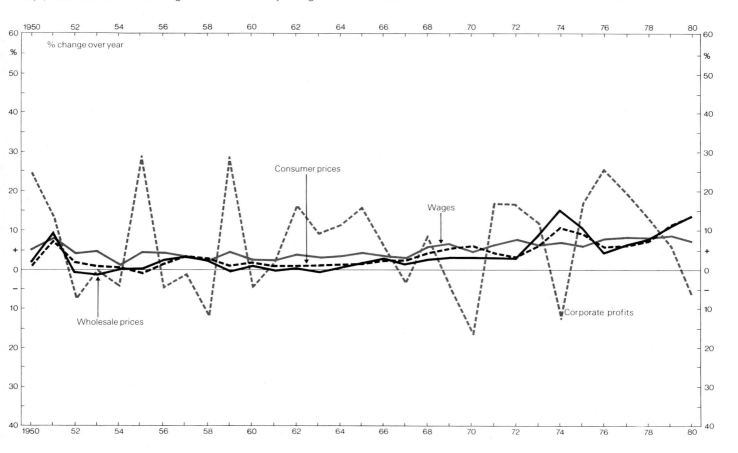

	Wholesale prices		Consumer prices		Wages[a]		Corporate profits[b]		
	Index 1970 = 100	% change over year	Index 1970 = 100	% change over year	Index 1970 = 100	% change over year	Index 1970 = 100	% change over year	
1950	71.6	1.8	62.0	1.0	44.3	5.8	47.5	25.1	1950
1951	78.4	9.5	66.9	7.9	48.3	8.9	54.2	14.2	1951
1952	78.0	−0.6	68.4	2.2	50.6	4.8	50.6	−6.7	1952
1953	77.2	−1.0	68.9	0.8	53.2	5.1	50.8	0.6	1953
1954	77.3	0.2	69.2	0.5	53.8	1.2	49.3	−3.0	1954
1955	77.5	0.2	69.0	−0.4	56.5	5.0	63.7	29.3	1955
1956	79.7	2.8	70.0	1.5	59.0	4.5	61.2	−4.0	1956
1957	82.6	3.6	72.5	3.6	61.2	3.7	60.6	−0.9	1957
1958	84.5	2.3	74.5	2.7	62.7	2.4	53.9	−11.1	1958
1959	84.3	−0.2	75.1	0.8	65.7	4.9	69.5	28.8	1959
1960	85.0	0.8	76.3	1.6	67.3	2.4	66.7	−4.0	1960
1961	85.0	0.0	77.0	1.0	68.9	2.4	68.1	2.1	1961
1962	85.2	0.3	77.9	1.1	71.7	4.0	79.3	16.5	1962
1963	85.0	−0.3	78.8	1.2	73.8	3.0	87.0	9.7	1963
1964	85.3	0.4	79.9	1.3	76.2	3.2	96.9	11.4	1964
1965	86.8	1.7	81.3	1.7	79.7	4.5	112.0	15.6	1965
1966	89.6	3.2	83.6	2.9	82.5	3.5	119.2	6.4	1966
1967	90.7	1.2	86.0	2.9	85.0	3.1	115.4	−3.2	1967
1968	93.2	2.8	89.6	4.2	89.9	5.8	124.8	8.1	1968
1969	96.6	3.7	94.4	5.4	95.6	6.4	119.2	−4.5	1969
1970	100.0	3.5	100.0	5.9	100.0	4.6	100.0	−16.1	1970
1971	103.1	3.1	104.3	4.3	106.2	6.2	116.5	16.5	1971
1972	106.3	3.1	107.7	3.3	114.2	7.5	135.3	16.1	1972
1973	116.0	9.1	114.4	6.2	121.3	6.2	151.7	12.1	1973
1974	133.7	15.3	127.0	11.0	129.1	6.4	132.9	−12.4	1974
1975	148.1	10.8	138.6	9.1	136.5	5.7	154.8	16.4	1975
1976	154.7	4.4	146.6	5.8	146.4	7.3	193.4	25.0	1976
1977	164.7	6.5	156.1	6.5	157.7	7.7	230.7	19.3	1977
1978	177.6	7.8	168.0	7.7	170.0	7.8	259.8	12.6	1978
1979	197.4	11.1	186.9	11.3	183.5	8.0	275.6	6.1	1979
1980	223.9	13.5	212.2	13.5	196.2	6.9	255.9	−7.2	1980

[a]Weekly earnings (private non-agricultural) [b]At current prices (value terms)

United States

Share prices rose mainly in 1950–52, 1954–56, 1958–59, 1961, 1963–65, 1967–68, 1971–72, 1975–76 and 1979–80, with falls in 1957, 1960, 1962, 1966, 1969–70, 1973–74 and 1977–78. Money stock increased at a comparatively stable rate throughout, with main rises in 1951–52, 1963–65, 1967–68, 1970–73 and 1976–80.

International reserves increased mainly in 1952, 1956–57, 1968–69, 1974–77 and 1980, with falls in 1950, 1953–55, 1958–67, 1970–73 and 1978. The interest rate increased mainly in 1950–53, 1955–57, 1959, 1962–66, 1968–69, 1973–74 and 1978–80, with reductions in 1954, 1958, 1960–61, 1967, 1970–72 and 1975–76.

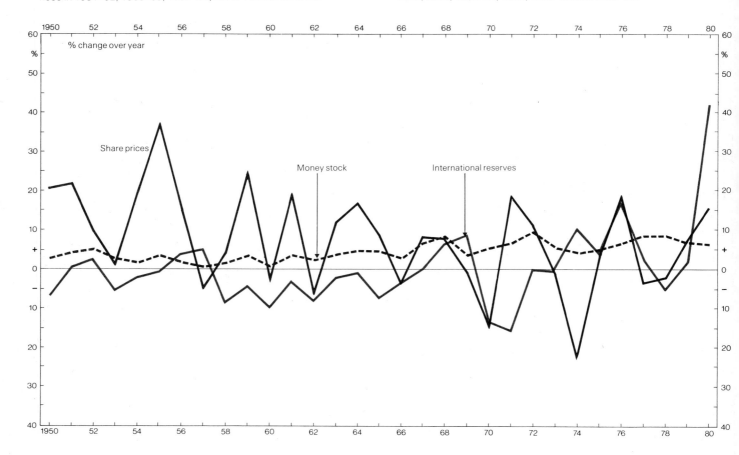

	Share prices		Money stock		International reserves		Interest rate		
	Index 1970 = 100	% change over year	Index 1970 = 100	% change over year	Index 1970 = 100	% change over year	%	Change over year[a]	
1950	22.1	20.8	51.9	2.7	167.5	−6.8	1.218	0.116	1950
1951	26.8	21.4	54.2	4.5	167.7	0.1	1.552	0.334	1951
1952	29.4	9.7	56.9	5.0	170.6	1.7	1.766	0.214	1952
1953	29.7	0.9	58.3	2.5	161.9	−5.1	1.931	0.165	1953
1954	35.7	20.1	59.2	1.5	158.6	−2.0	0.953	−0.978	1954
1955	48.7	36.4	61.1	3.2	157.4	−0.8	1.753	0.800	1955
1956	56.0	15.1	61.8	1.2	163.4	3.8	2.658	0.905	1956
1957	53.3	−4.8	62.2	0.5	171.4	4.9	3.267	0.609	1957
1958	55.6	4.2	62.9	1.2	155.6	−9.2	1.839	−1.428	1958
1959	68.9	24.1	65.1	3.6	148.4	−4.6	3.405	1.566	1959
1960	67.1	−2.7	65.6	0.7	133.6	−10.0	2.928	−0.477	1960
1961	79.6	18.7	67.7	3.2	129.4	−3.1	2.378	−0.550	1961
1962	75.0	−5.9	68.9	1.8	118.9	−8.2	2.778	0.400	1962
1963	84.0	12.0	71.4	3.7	116.3	−2.2	3.157	0.379	1963
1964	97.8	16.5	74.7	4.6	115.1	−1.0	3.549	0.392	1964
1965	105.9	8.4	78.2	4.7	106.6	−7.3	3.954	0.405	1965
1966	102.5	−3.3	80.2	2.5	102.7	−3.7	4.881	0.927	1966
1967	110.5	7.8	85.4	6.6	102.4	−0.3	4.321	−0.560	1967
1968	118.6	7.4	92.0	7.7	108.4	5.9	5.339	1.018	1968
1969	117.6	−0.9	95.0	3.2	117.1	8.0	6.677	1.338	1969
1970	100.0	−14.9	100.0	5.3	100.0	−14.6	6.458	−0.219	1970
1971	118.1	18.1	106.5	6.5	83.9	−16.1	4.348	−2.110	1971
1972	131.2	11.1	116.4	9.3	83.6	−0.3	4.071	−0.277	1972
1973	129.1	−1.6	122.9	5.5	82.3	−1.6	7.041	2.970	1973
1974	99.6	−22.9	128.2	4.4	90.5	10.0	7.886	0.845	1974
1975	103.5	4.0	134.6	5.0	93.6	3.4	5.838	−2.048	1975
1976	122.6	18.4	143.5	6.6	108.8	16.2	4.989	−0.849	1976
1977	118.0	−3.7	155.2	8.1	110.2	1.3	5.265	0.276	1977
1978	115.4	−2.2	168.0	8.3	103.8	−5.8	7.221	1.956	1978
1979	123.8	7.3	180.1	7.2	104.7	0.9	10.041	2.820	1979
1980	142.7	15.3	191.7	6.4	148.3	41.6	11.506	1.465	1980

[a]In percentage points

Uruguay

For the time covered, the main periods of expansion in gross domestic product were 1956–57, 1960–61, 1963–66, 1968–70, 1974–76 and 1978–80, with falls or low growth in 1958–59, 1962, 1967, 1971–73 and 1977. Fixed investment, for the time covered, increased mainly in 1959–61, 1967, 1969–71 and 1974–77, with falls in 1956, 1958, 1963–66, 1968, 1972–73 and 1978. Consumer prices rose at a high rate throughout, with especially high rises in 1951–52, 1959–60, 1964–68 and 1972–80. International reserves increased mainly in 1950, 1952–53, 1969, 1972–73, 1976–77 and 1979–80, with main falls in 1951, 1954–57, 1963–67, 1970–71, 1974–75 and 1978.

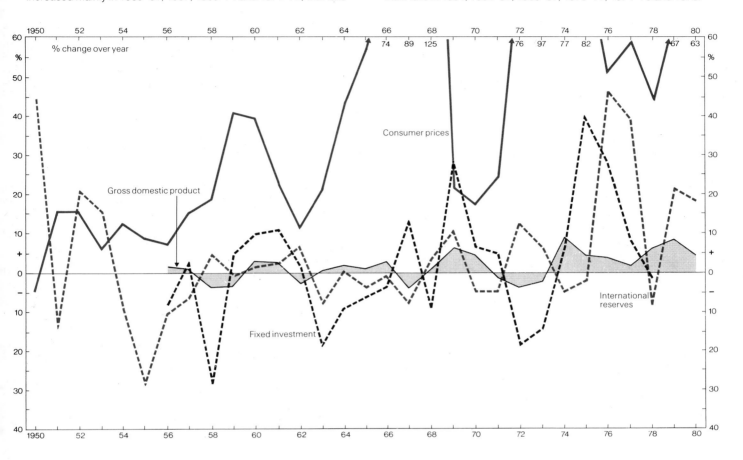

	Gross domestic product		Fixed investment		Consumer prices		International reserves		
	Index 1970 = 100	% change over year	Index 1970 = 100	% change over year	Index 1970 = 100	% change over year	Index 1970 = 100	% change over year	
1950	na	na	na	na	0.6	−5	165	44	1950
1951	na	na	na	na	0.6	15	142	−14	1951
1952	na	na	na	na	0.7	15	170	20	1952
1953	na	na	na	na	0.8	6	195	15	1953
1954	na	na	na	na	0.9	12	177	−10	1954
1955	85.7	na	114	na	0.9	8	125	−29	1955
1956	87.2	1.8	105	−8	1.0	7	111	−11	1956
1957	88.3	1.2	108	3	1.2	15	103	−7	1957
1958	85.2	−3.5	78	−28	1.4	18	107	4	1958
1959	82.7	−3.0	82	5	1.9	40	106	−1	1959
1960	85.7	3.7	90	10	2.6	39	107	1	1960
1961	88.3	3.0	100	11	3.2	22	109	2	1961
1962	86.2	−2.3	103	2	3.6	11	116	6	1962
1963	86.7	0.6	84	−18	4.3	21	106	−8	1963
1964	88.3	1.8	77	−9	6.1	43	106	0	1964
1965	89.3	1.2	72	−6	9.6	57	102	−4	1965
1966	92.4	3.4	70	−3	16.7	74	101	−1	1966
1967	88.8	−3.9	79	13	31.6	89	93	−8	1967
1968	89.8	1.1	73	−8	71.1	125	95	3	1968
1969	95.4	6.3	94	28	85.7	21	105	10	1969
1970	100.0	4.8	100	7	100.0	17	100	−5	1970
1971	99.0	−1.0	105	5	123.6	24	95	−5	1971
1972	95.4	−3.6	85	−18	218.1	76	107	12	1972
1973	93.4	−2.1	73	−14	429.7	97	114	6	1973
1974	102.0	9.3	78	6	761.4	77	108	−5	1974
1975	106.6	4.5	109	40	1382.8	82	106	−2	1975
1976	111.2	4.3	139	28	2083.8	51	155	46	1976
1977	113.3	1.8	150	8	3295.1	58	216	39	1977
1978	120.4	6.3	149	−1	4763.6	45	199	−8	1978
1979	130.6	8.5	na	na	7946.8	67	241	21	1979
1980	136.7	4.7	na	na	12992.5	63	285	18	1980

Venezuela

The main periods of expansion in gross domestic product were 1951–57, 1959–65, 1967–70 and 1973–78, with a fall or low growth for 1958, 1966, 1971–72 and 1979–80. Fixed investment increased mainly in 1951–52, 1954, 1956–57, 1959, 1964–65, 1968–69, 1971–73 and 1975–77, with falls or low growth in 1953, 1955, 1958,

1960–61, 1966–67, 1970, 1974 and 1978–80. Consumer prices rose mainly in 1951, 1958–60 and 1974–80, with periods of low rises or falls from 1952 to 1957 and 1961 to 1973. Share prices increased mainly in 1951–53, 1957, 1964–65, 1968–69 and 1972–77, with main falls in 1950, 1958–61, 1966–67 and 1978–80.

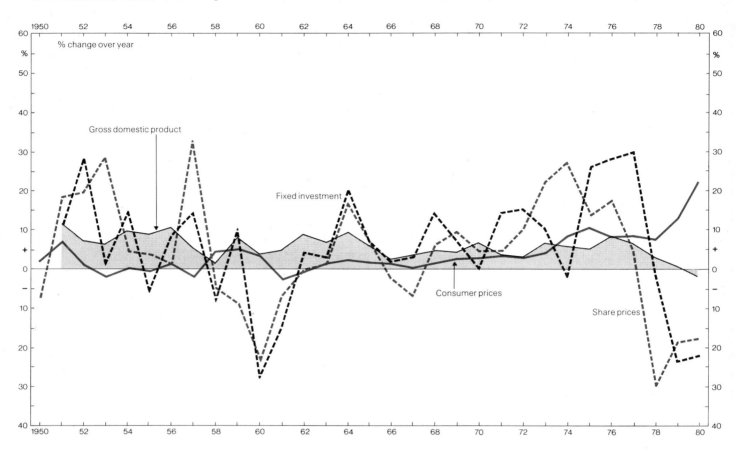

	Gross domestic product		Fixed investment		Consumer prices		Share prices		
	Index 1970 = 100	% change over year	Index 1970 = 100	% change over year	Index 1970 = 100	% change over year	Index 1970 = 100	% change over year	
1950	27.9	na	47	na	75.7	2.0	44.6	−7.1	1950
1951	31.2	11.7	52	11	81.1	7.1	52.8	18.6	1951
1952	33.5	7.3	67	28	82.0	1.1	63.3	19.8	1952
1953	35.6	6.2	68	1	80.9	−1.3	81.2	28.3	1953
1954	39.0	9.7	78	14	81.0	0.1	85.2	4.9	1954
1955	42.4	8.9	73	−6	80.7	−0.4	88.6	4.0	1955
1956	46.9	10.6	80	8	81.4	0.9	89.4	0.9	1956
1957	49.4	5.3	91	14	79.7	−2.1	118.6	32.7	1957
1958	50.0	1.3	83	−8	83.6	4.9	112.9	−4.8	1958
1959	54.1	8.1	92	10	87.8	5.0	102.4	−9.3	1959
1960	56.2	4.0	66	−28	90.8	3.4	78.5	−23.3	1960
1961	59.0	4.9	56	−15	88.4	−2.6	73.0	−7.0	1961
1962	64.4	9.1	59	4	88.0	−0.5	72.7	−0.4	1962
1963	68.9	7.0	60	3	89.0	1.1	73.5	1.1	1963
1964	75.5	9.6	72	20	90.9	2.1	85.4	16.2	1964
1965	80.1	6.0	78	7	92.4	1.7	91.0	6.6	1965
1966	82.1	2.5	79	2	94.0	1.7	89.0	−2.2	1966
1967	85.2	3.8	82	3	94.1	0.1	82.8	−7.0	1967
1968	89.4	4.9	94	14	95.2	1.2	87.5	5.7	1968
1969	93.4	4.5	100	7	97.5	2.4	95.6	9.3	1969
1970	100.0	7.1	100	0	100.0	2.6	100.0	4.6	1970
1971	103.3	3.3	114	14	103.2	3.2	104.7	4.7	1971
1972	106.5	3.0	131	15	106.2	2.9	115.1	9.9	1972
1973	113.6	6.7	144	10	110.6	4.1	140.2	21.8	1973
1974	120.2	5.8	141	−2	119.7	8.2	177.3	26.5	1974
1975	126.5	5.2	177	26	132.0	10.3	201.2	13.5	1975
1976	137.1	8.4	226	28	142.2	7.7	235.0	16.8	1976
1977	146.5	6.8	293	30	153.1	7.7	245.3	4.4	1977
1978	151.1	3.2	291	−1	164.1	7.2	171.0	−30.3	1978
1979	152.4	0.9	222	−24	184.3	12.3	138.4	−19.1	1979
1980	150.6	−1.2	174	−22	224.0	21.6	112.7	−18.6	1980

Zaire

Over the time for which figures are available, the main periods of expansion in gross domestic product were 1966, 1968–71 and 1973–74; there were falls or low growth in 1967, 1972 and 1975–80. Fixed investment, for the time covered, increased mainly in 1967, 1969–72, 1974, 1977 and 1980 (recovery), with falls in 1973, 1975–76 and 1978–79. Consumer prices, for the time covered, increased markedly in 1964, 1967–68 and 1974–80, with comparatively low rises for 1969–71. International reserves increased mainly in 1950, 1952–53, 1963–64, 1967–69, 1972–73, 1977 and 1979, with main falls in 1957, 1959–62, 1965, 1971 and 1974–75.

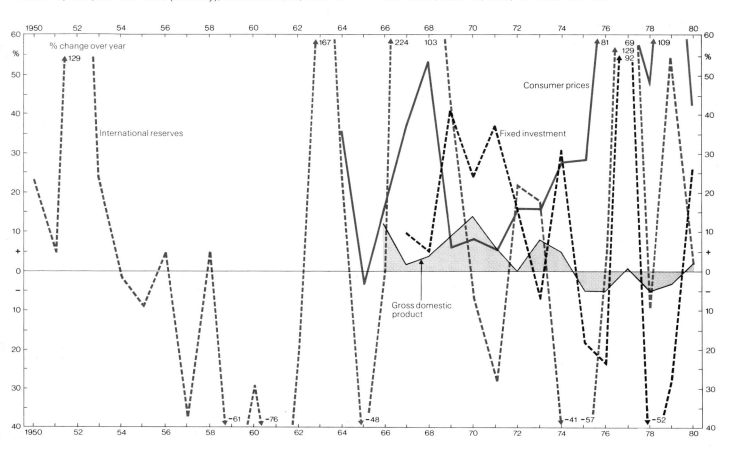

	Gross domestic product		Fixed investment		Consumer prices		International reserves		
	Index 1970 = 100	% change over year	Index 1970 = 100	% change over year	Index 1970 = 100	% change over year	Index 1970 = 100	% change over year	
1950	na	na	na	na	na	na	63	24	1950
1951	na	na	na	na	na	na	67	6	1951
1952	na	na	na	na	na	na	153	129	1952
1953	na	na	na	na	na	na	190	24	1953
1954	na	na	na	na	na	na	187	−1	1954
1955	na	na	na	na	na	na	172	−8	1955
1956	na	na	na	na	na	na	181	5	1956
1957	na	na	na	na	na	na	113	−37	1957
1958	na	na	na	na	na	na	119	5	1958
1959	na	na	na	na	na	na	47	−61	1959
1960	na	na	na	na	na	na	33	−29	1960
1961	na	na	na	na	na	na	8	−76	1961
1962	na	na	na	na	na	na	6	−20	1962
1963	na	na	na	na	27.2	na	17	167	1963
1964	na	na	na	na	36.9	35.7	22	25	1964
1965	67	na	na	na	35.9	−2.7	11	−48	1965
1966	75	12	49	na	41.6	15.9	11	0	1966
1967	77	2	54	10	56.9	36.8	37	224	1967
1968	80	4	57	5	87.2	53.3	74	103	1968
1969	88	9	81	41	92.6	6.2	107	44	1969
1970	100	14	100	24	100.0	8.0	100	−7	1970
1971	106	6	137	37	105.8	5.8	72	−28	1971
1972	106	0	159	16	122.5	15.8	88	22	1972
1973	115	8	148	−7	141.7	15.7	104	18	1973
1974	120	5	193	31	180.5	27.4	62	−41	1974
1975	114	−5	159	−18	232.0	28.5	27	−57	1975
1976	108	−5	121	−24	419.2	80.7	28	4	1976
1977	109	1	233	92	708.5	69.0	64	129	1977
1978	104	−5	111	−52	1051.9	48.5	58	−10	1978
1979	100	−3	79	−28	2194.5	108.6	89	55	1979
1980	103	2	100	26	3118.1	42.1	91	2	1980

Zambia

Over the time for which figures are available, the main periods of expansion in gross domestic product were 1955, 1959–60, 1964–65, 1967–70, 1972, 1974 and 1976; there were falls or low growth for 1956–58, 1961–63, 1966, 1971, 1973, 1975 and 1977–80. Fixed investment, for the time covered, increased mainly in 1955–57, 1964–68, 1970, 1972, 1975 and 1980 (recovery), with main falls in 1958–60, 1962–63, 1971, 1973 and 1976–79. Exports, for the time covered, rose mainly in 1967, 1969, 1972, 1976 and 1979, with main falls in 1966, 1970–71 and 1977–78. Consumer prices rose mainly in 1965–68 and 1974–80.

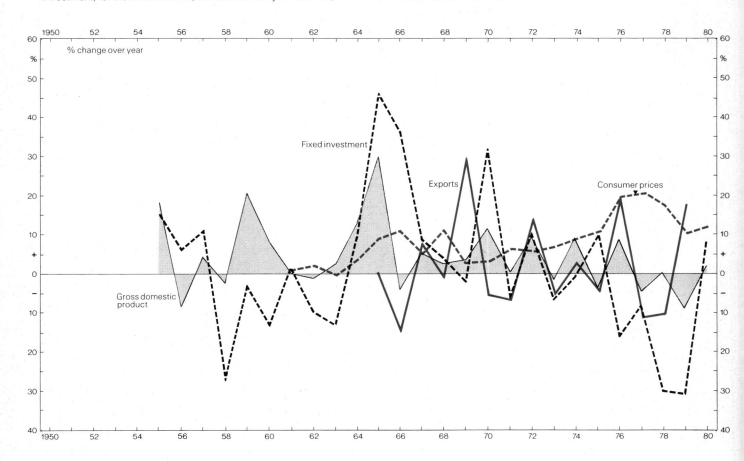

	Gross domestic product		Fixed investment		Exports		Consumer prices		
	Index 1970 = 100	% change over year	Index 1970 = 100	% change over year	Index 1970 = 100	% change over year	Index 1970 = 100	% change over year	
1950	na	na	na	na	na	na	na	na	1950
1951	na	na	na	na	na	na	na	na	1951
1952	na	na	na	na	na	na	na	na	1952
1953	na	na	na	na	na	na	na	na	1953
1954	39.6	na	48	na	na	na	na	na	1954
1955	46.8	18.3	55	15	na	na	na	na	1955
1956	42.7	−8.7	58	6	na	na	na	na	1956
1957	44.6	4.4	65	11	na	na	na	na	1957
1958	43.5	−2.6	48	−27	na	na	na	na	1958
1959	52.4	20.6	46	−3	na	na	na	na	1959
1960	56.6	8.1	40	−13	na	na	65.9	na	1960
1961	56.6	0.0	41	1	na	na	66.0	0.2	1961
1962	56.0	−1.1	37	−10	na	na	66.9	1.4	1962
1963	57.3	2.3	32	−13	na	na	66.6	−0.4	1963
1964	64.6	12.9	35	9	92	na	68.6	3.0	1964
1965	83.7	29.5	50	46	93	0	74.2	8.2	1965
1966	80.2	−4.1	69	36	78	−15	81.8	10.2	1966
1967	84.3	5.1	75	9	83	7	85.9	5.0	1967
1968	86.5	2.5	78	4	82	−1	95.1	10.7	1968
1969	89.3	3.2	76	−2	106	29	97.5	2.5	1969
1970	100.0	12.0	100	32	100	−6	100.0	2.6	1970
1971	100.1	0.1	94	−6	93	−7	106.0	6.0	1971
1972	109.2	9.2	103	10	104	13	111.7	5.4	1972
1973	107.3	−1.8	96	−7	98	−6	118.8	6.4	1973
1974	117.8	9.7	95	−1	100	2	128.8	8.4	1974
1975	113.3	−3.8	104	10	95	−5	141.7	10.0	1975
1976	122.8	8.4	87	−16	112	18	168.3	18.8	1976
1977	117.3	−4.5	80	−8	99	−12	201.6	19.8	1977
1978	118.0	0.5	56	−30	88	−11	234.7	16.4	1978
1979	107.4	−8.9	39	−31	103	17	257.5	9.7	1979
1980	109.8	2.2	42	8	na	na	287.5	11.7	1980

Aluminium

The main periods of expansion in world production were 1950–56, 1959–60, 1962–74 (a long period of comparatively stable growth) and 1976–79; there was a fall in production or a low growth rate for 1957–58, 1961, 1975 and 1980. The aluminium price increased mainly over 1950–57, 1964–65, 1969–70, 1974–75 and 1977–80; overall there was a comparatively stable period for the price from 1958 to 1971, with a significant fall in 1972, and a period of high increases from 1974 to 1980 (although with only a small increase for 1976).

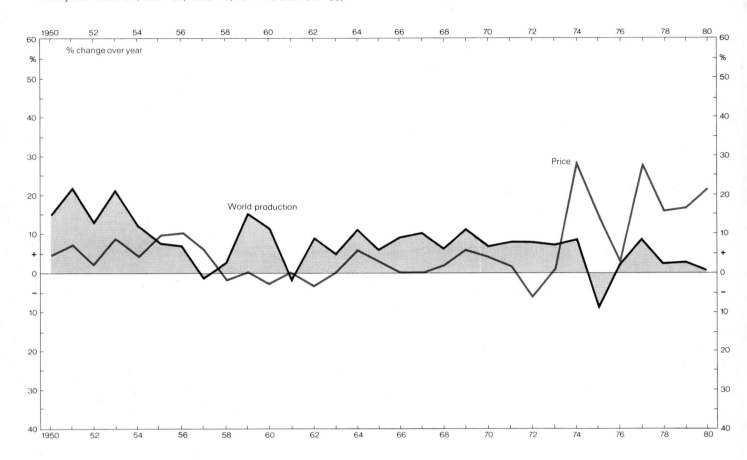

	World production[a]			Price[b]			
	Tonnes (000)	Index 1970 = 100	% change over year	$ per tonne	Index 1970 = 100	% change over year	
1950	1659	17.3	14.9	350	57	4	1950
1951	2027	21.2	22.1	375	61	7	1951
1952	2293	23.9	13.1	383	62	2	1952
1953	2774	29.0	21.0	414	67	8	1953
1954	3116	32.5	12.3	430	70	4	1954
1955	3357	35.1	7.7	468	76	9	1955
1956	3610	37.7	7.5	514	84	10	1956
1957	3547	37.0	−1.8	543	88	6	1957
1958	3635	38.0	2.5	531	86	−2	1958
1959	4180	43.7	15.0	531	86	0	1959
1960	4674	48.8	11.8	514	84	−3	1960
1961	4585	47.9	−1.9	514	84	0	1961
1962	5016	52.4	9.4	498	81	−3	1962
1963	5265	55.0	5.0	498	81	0	1963
1964	5854	61.1	11.2	527	86	6	1964
1965	6213	64.9	6.1	540	88	3	1965
1966	6781	70.8	9.1	540	88	0	1966
1967	7479	78.1	10.3	540	88	0	1967
1968	7975	83.3	6.6	553	90	2	1968
1969	8934	93.3	12.0	589	96	6	1969
1970	9575	100.0	7.2	615	100	4	1970
1971	10337	108.0	8.0	626	102	2	1971
1972	11161	116.6	8.0	591	96	−6	1972
1973	12034	125.7	7.8	600	97	1	1973
1974	13090	136.7	8.8	765	124	28	1974
1975	12016	125.5	−8.2	869	141	14	1975
1976	12329	128.8	2.6	891	145	3	1976
1977	13389	139.8	8.6	1144	186	28	1977
1978	13758	143.7	2.8	1325	215	16	1978
1979	14181	148.1	3.1	1550	252	17	1979
1980	14221	148.5	0.3	1885	306	22	1980

[a]Primary; excluding China   [b]Canadian aluminium (UK price); linked to US primary ingots price before 1960.

Bananas

The main periods of expansion in world production were 1953, 1955, 1957, 1959–60, 1963–65, 1969–71, 1976–77 and 1980; there were falls in production or comparatively low growth in 1950–52, 1954, 1956, 1958, 1961–62, 1968, 1972 and 1975. The banana price increased mainly in 1950, 1954, 1957, 1963, 1969–70, 1972, 1974–75 and 1979–80; prices were comparatively stable over 1950–57, then fell from 1958 to 1962, for 1965–66, 1968 and 1971.

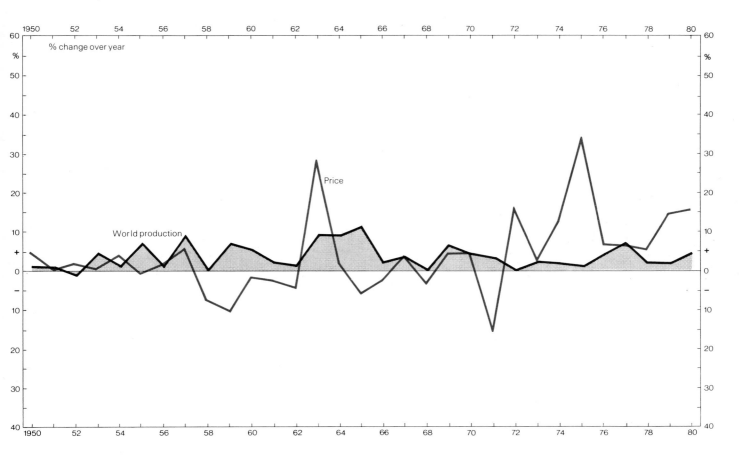

	World production			Price[a]			
	Tonnes (000)	Index 1970 = 100	% change over year	$ per tonne	Index 1970 = 100	% change over year	
1950	13869	46	1	161	97	4	1950
1951	14013	46	1	161	97	0	1951
1952	13854	46	−1	163	98	1	1952
1953	14346	47	4	163	98	0	1953
1954	14452	48	1	168	101	3	1954
1955	15467	51	7	165	99	−1	1955
1956	15591	51	1	168	101	1	1956
1957	17051	56	9	176	106	5	1957
1958	17049	56	0	163	98	−8	1958
1959	18259	60	7	146	88	−11	1959
1960	19093	63	5	143	86	−2	1960
1961	19509	64	2	139	84	−3	1961
1962	19781	65	1	132	80	−5	1962
1963	21623	71	9	168	101	27	1963
1964	23634	78	9	170	102	1	1964
1965	26239	87	11	159	95	−6	1965
1966	26681	88	2	154	93	−3	1966
1967	27490	91	3	159	95	3	1967
1968	27609	91	0	153	92	−4	1968
1969	29227	96	6	160	96	4	1969
1970	30319	100	4	166	100	4	1970
1971	31175	103	3	140	84	−16	1971
1972	31147	103	0	162	97	15	1972
1973	31776	105	2	165	99	2	1973
1974	32374	107	2	184	111	12	1974
1975	32805	108	1	245	147	33	1975
1976	34165	113	4	259	156	6	1976
1977	36509	120	7	273	164	6	1977
1978	37135	122	2	287	172	5	1978
1979	38011	125	2	326	196	14	1979
1980	39417	130	4	375	226	15	1980

[a]US wholesale price (Latin American bananas)

Beef

The main periods of expansion in world production were 1953–56, 1960–63, 1966–69 and 1974–76; there were falls or slackening in growth during 1951, 1957–59, 1964 and 1978–80, with a comparatively stable period for production during 1969–73. The price of beef increased and fell for alternate years from 1950 to 1955, with a sharp fall in 1956; thereafter there were main increases in 1958–59, 1964–65, 1968, 1970–74, 1976–77 and 1979–80, with main falls in 1961–62, 1966–67, 1969 and 1975.

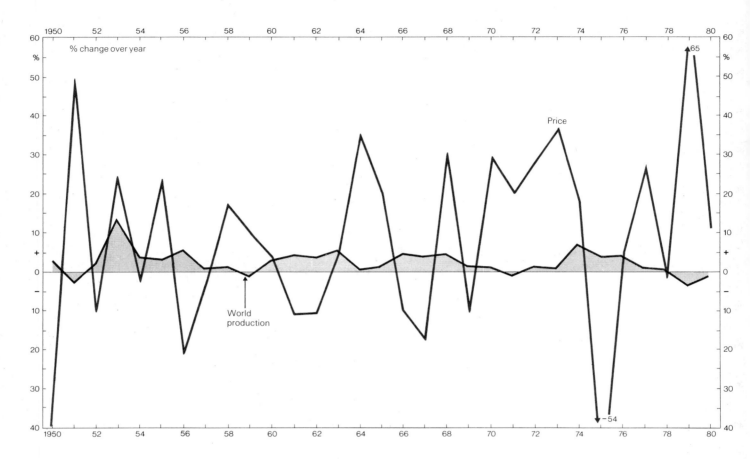

	World production[a]			Price[b]			
	Tonnes (000)	Index 1970 = 100	% change over year	$ per tonne	Index 1970 = 100	% change over year	
1950	21 852	54.4	3.1	208	28.5	−39.7	1950
1951	21 317	53.1	−2.5	312	42.7	49.7	1951
1952	21 774	54.2	2.1	282	38.6	−9.5	1952
1953	24 650	61.4	13.2	351	48.1	24.5	1953
1954	25 576	63.7	3.8	345	47.2	−1.8	1954
1955	26 494	66.0	3.6	427	58.4	23.7	1955
1956	28 017	69.8	5.7	338	46.2	−20.9	1956
1957	28 263	70.4	0.9	329	45.0	−2.7	1957
1958	28 572	71.2	1.1	387	53.0	17.7	1958
1959	28 263	70.4	−1.1	427	58.5	10.4	1959
1960	29 088	72.4	2.9	447	61.2	4.6	1960
1961	30 326	75.5	4.3	400	54.8	−10.5	1961
1962	31 460	78.3	3.7	360	49.2	−10.1	1962
1963	33 082	82.4	5.2	381	52.1	5.9	1963
1964	33 225	82.7	0.4	516	70.6	35.5	1964
1965	33 838	84.3	1.8	625	85.6	21.2	1965
1966	35 499	88.4	4.9	568	77.7	−9.2	1966
1967	37 076	92.3	4.4	473	64.8	−16.7	1967
1968	38 876	96.8	4.9	618	84.6	30.6	1968
1969	39 658	98.8	2.0	562	77.0	−9.0	1969
1970	40 158	100.0	1.3	731	100.0	29.9	1970
1971	39 795	99.1	−0.9	885	121.2	21.2	1971
1972	40 223	100.2	1.1	1 143	156.4	29.1	1972
1973	40 582	101.1	0.9	1 569	214.7	37.3	1973
1974	43 548	108.4	7.3	1 851	253.4	18.0	1974
1975	45 432	113.1	4.3	857	117.3	−53.7	1975
1976	47 500	118.3	4.6	910	124.6	6.2	1976
1977	47 993	119.5	1.0	1 165	159.5	28.1	1977
1978	48 162	119.9	0.4	1 158	158.5	−0.6	1978
1979	46 804	116.6	−2.8	1 916	262.3	65.4	1979
1980	46 313	115.3	−1.0	2 148	293.9	12.1	1980

[a]Including veal   [b]Argentina frozen beef (unit value)

Butter

The main periods of expansion in world production were 1953–54, 1956–58, 1961–62, 1964–65, 1967–68, 1972–73 and 1975–77; main falls in production occurred in 1951–52, 1963, 1966, 1969–70, 1974 and 1980, with a slackening in the rate of growth in 1959–60 and 1978–79. Main increases in the butter price were in 1951, 1957, 1959–60, 1962–64, 1971–72, 1975 and 1977–78; main falls were in 1950, 1954, 1958, 1961, 1966–68, 1973 and 1976.

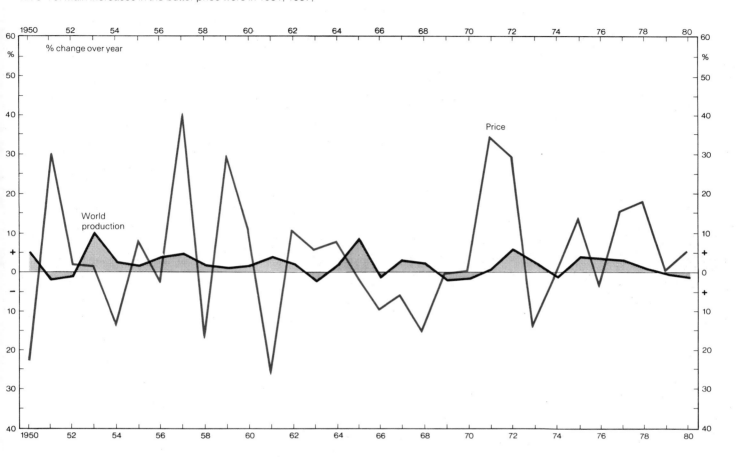

	World production[a]			Price[b]			
	Tonnes (000)	Index 1970 = 100	% change over year	$ per tonne	Index 1970 = 100	% change over year	
1950	3 884	67.7	5.0	406	64.3	−22.4	1950
1951	3 819	66.5	−1.7	531	84.1	30.8	1951
1952	3 780	65.9	−1.0	546	86.5	2.8	1952
1953	4 158	72.5	10.0	557	88.3	2.1	1953
1954	4 263	74.3	2.5	485	76.9	−12.9	1954
1955	4 337	75.6	1.7	526	83.5	8.5	1955
1956	4 507	78.5	3.9	517	81.9	−1.8	1956
1957	4 721	82.3	4.8	730	115.8	41.3	1957
1958	4 823	84.0	2.1	610	96.8	−16.4	1958
1959	4 871	84.9	1.0	795	126.1	30.3	1959
1960	4 937	86.0	1.4	880	139.5	10.6	1960
1961	5 130	89.4	3.9	658	104.3	−25.3	1961
1962	5 240	91.3	2.1	733	116.2	11.5	1962
1963	5 125	89.3	−2.2	781	123.9	6.6	1963
1964	5 229	91.1	2.0	849	134.7	8.7	1964
1965	5 682	99.0	8.7	842	133.6	−0.8	1965
1966	5 619	97.9	−1.1	769	121.8	−8.8	1966
1967	5 804	101.1	3.3	730	115.8	−5.0	1967
1968	5 934	103.4	2.2	623	98.7	−14.7	1968
1969	5 810	101.2	−2.1	624	98.9	0.2	1969
1970	5 738	100.0	−1.2	631	100.0	1.1	1970
1971	5 755	100.3	0.3	856	135.8	35.8	1971
1972	6 084	106.0	5.7	1 116	176.9	30.3	1972
1973	6 230	108.6	2.4	974	154.5	−12.7	1973
1974	6 176	107.6	−0.9	972	154.2	−0.2	1974
1975	6 437	112.2	4.2	1 112	176.2	14.3	1975
1976	6 670	116.2	3.6	1 088	172.4	−2.2	1976
1977	6 868	119.7	3.0	1 266	200.7	16.4	1977
1978	6 928	120.7	0.9	1 501	238.0	18.6	1978
1979	6 909	120.4	−0.3	1 529	242.4	1.9	1979
1980	6 831	119.0	−1.1	1 627	258.0	6.4	1980

[a]Including ghee   [b]New Zealand (unit value)

Coal

The main periods of expansion in world production were 1950–51, 1955–60, 1962–66, 1968–70 and 1973–80 (including comparatively large increases in 1975, 1977 and 1979); falls in production occurred in 1952–54, 1961 and 1967, with comparatively stable levels for 1971–72. The coal price increased mainly in 1950–51, 1956–57, 1963–64, 1967–75 (including the very large increase in 1974–75 associated with the crude oil price rise) and 1980; main falls were in 1954–55, 1959–60, 1965–66 and 1978.

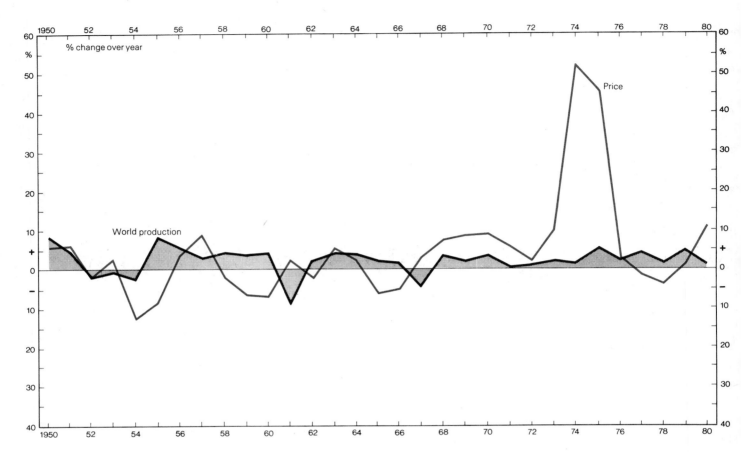

	World production[a]			Price[b]			
	Tonnes (million)	Index 1970 = 100	% change over year	$ per tonne	Index 1970 = 100	% change over year	
1950	1 466	68.7	8.3	15	84.2	6.2	1950
1951	1 536	72.0	4.7	16	90.0	6.9	1951
1952	1 508	70.7	−1.8	16	88.6	−1.6	1952
1953	1 502	70.4	−0.4	17	91.5	3.3	1953
1954	1 465	68.7	−2.5	15	80.6	−11.9	1954
1955	1 582	74.1	8.0	14	74.4	−7.7	1955
1956	1 671	78.3	5.6	14	77.5	4.2	1956
1957	1 718	80.5	2.8	16	85.1	9.8	1957
1958	1 801	84.4	4.8	15	84.1	−1.2	1958
1959	1 875	87.9	4.1	14	79.0	−6.0	1959
1960	1 965	92.1	4.8	14	74.0	−6.3	1960
1961	1 783	83.6	−9.2	14	76.1	2.8	1961
1962	1 826	85.6	2.4	14	75.2	−1.2	1962
1963	1 894	88.8	3.7	15	79.5	5.8	1963
1964	1 960	91.8	3.5	15	81.9	3.0	1964
1965	2 005	94.0	2.3	14	77.7	−5.1	1965
1966	2 042	95.7	1.8	14	74.0	−4.8	1966
1967	1 946	91.2	−4.7	14	76.8	3.8	1967
1968	2 014	94.4	3.5	15	83.1	8.2	1968
1969	2 055	96.3	2.0	17	91.0	9.4	1969
1970	2 134	100.0	3.8	18	100.0	9.9	1970
1971	2 139	100.2	0.2	20	106.6	6.6	1971
1972	2 156	101.0	0.8	20	109.6	2.8	1972
1973	2 204	103.3	2.2	22	120.8	10.2	1973
1974	2 241	105.0	1.7	34	184.8	53.0	1974
1975	2 358	110.5	5.2	49	270.2	46.3	1975
1976	2 418	113.3	2.5	51	279.8	3.5	1976
1977	2 523	118.2	4.3	51	277.9	−0.7	1977
1978	2 569	120.4	1.8	49	269.3	−3.1	1978
1979	2 696	126.3	4.9	50	274.9	2.1	1979
1980	2 741	128.5	1.7	56	307.2	11.7	1980

[a]Excludes lignite and brown coal   [b]Pennsylvania mines (wholesale price)

Cocoa

The main periods of expansion in world production were 1952, 1955–56, 1958–60, 1963–64, 1966–67, 1969–71, 1974 and 1977–79; there were falls in production for 1951, 1953, 1957, 1961, 1965, 1968, 1972–73 and 1975–76. The cocoa price increased mainly in 1950–51, 1954, 1957–58, 1963, 1966–69, 1972–74 and 1976–77; main falls occurred in 1952–53, 1955–56, 1959–61, 1970–71, 1975 and 1978–80.

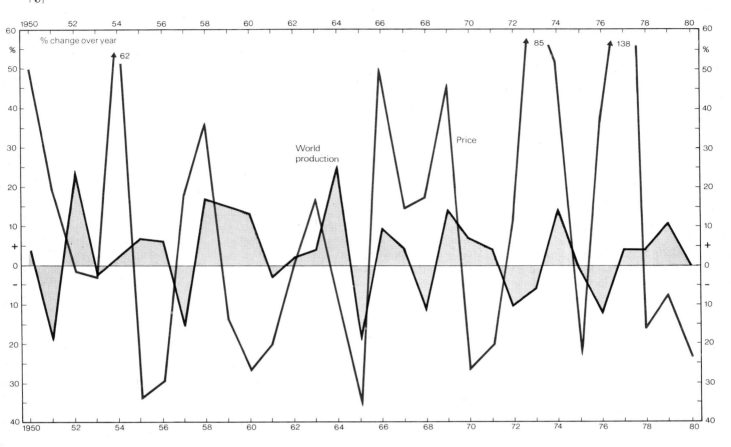

	World production[a]			Price[b]			
	Tonnes (000)	Index 1970 = 100	% change over year	$ per tonne	Index 1970 = 100	% change over year	
1950	826	53	4	596	91.9	50.3	1950
1951	666	43	−19	722	111.3	21.2	1951
1952	816	53	23	713	109.9	−1.3	1952
1953	800	52	−2	692	106.7	−2.9	1953
1954	815	53	2	1 121	172.8	62.0	1954
1955	869	56	7	746	115.0	−33.5	1955
1956	921	60	6	534	82.4	−28.4	1956
1957	788	51	−15	635	98.0	18.9	1957
1958	924	60	17	864	133.3	36.1	1958
1959	1 061	69	15	747	115.2	−13.6	1959
1960	1 203	78	13	551	85.0	−26.2	1960
1961	1 169	76	−3	441	68.0	−20.0	1961
1962	1 196	77	2	438	67.5	−0.7	1962
1963	1 239	80	4	510	78.6	16.5	1963
1964	1 544	100	25	466	71.9	−8.6	1964
1965	1 249	81	−19	301	46.4	−35.4	1965
1966	1 364	88	9	451	69.5	49.7	1966
1967	1 418	92	4	517	79.8	14.8	1967
1968	1 266	82	−11	608	93.7	17.5	1968
1969	1 441	93	14	882	136.0	45.1	1969
1970	1 545	100	7	649	100.0	−26.5	1970
1971	1 614	104	4	518	79.9	−20.1	1971
1972	1 459	94	−10	578	89.2	11.7	1972
1973	1 366	88	−6	1 069	164.9	84.9	1973
1974	1 553	101	14	1 617	249.3	51.2	1974
1975	1 542	100	−1	1 248	192.4	−22.8	1975
1976	1 363	88	−12	1 698	261.8	36.1	1976
1977	1 422	92	4	4 046	623.8	138.3	1977
1978	1 483	96	4	3 385	521.9	−16.3	1978
1979	1 651	107	11	3 103	478.3	−8.3	1979
1980	1 650	107	0	2 360	363.9	−23.9	1980

[a]Cocoa beans   [b]Brazil (unit value)

Coffee

The main periods of expansion in world production were 1951–52, 1955, 1957–59, 1961, 1965, 1967, 1969, 1971, 1974 and 1977–79; there were falls in production or comparatively low growth for 1950, 1953–54, 1956, 1960, 1962–64, 1966, 1968, 1970, 1972–73, 1975–76 and 1980. The coffee price increased mainly in 1950–51, 1953–54, 1964, 1969–70, 1972–73, 1975–77 and 1979–80; there were main falls in 1955, 1958–59, 1962, 1965–67, 1971 and 1978.

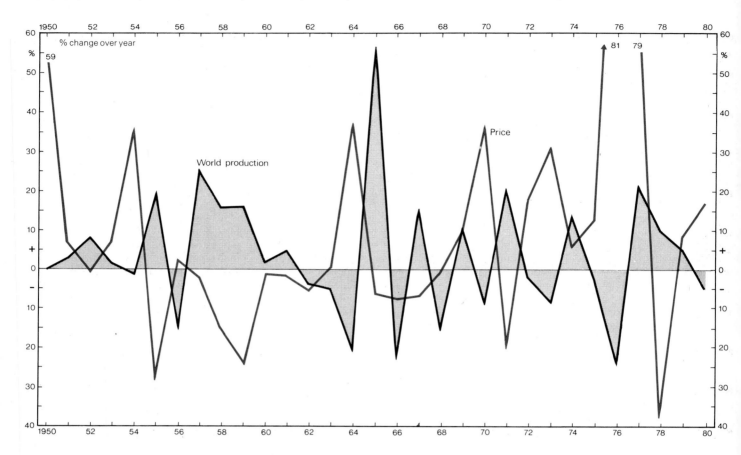

	World production[a]			Price[b]			
	Tonnes (000)	Index 1970 = 100	% change over year	$ per tonne	Index 1970 = 100	% change over year	
1950	2 197	56	0	1 114	90.5	59.1	1950
1951	2 264	58	3	1 195	97.1	7.3	1951
1952	2 441	63	8	1 191	96.8	−0.3	1952
1953	2 470	63	1	1 277	103.8	7.2	1953
1954	2 453	63	−1	1 735	141.1	35.9	1954
1955	2 919	75	19	1 259	102.3	−27.5	1955
1956	2 488	64	−15	1 281	104.1	1.8	1956
1957	3 117	80	25	1 254	102.0	−2.1	1957
1958	3 604	93	16	1 067	86.8	−14.9	1958
1959	4 190	108	16	815	66.3	−23.6	1959
1960	4 280	110	2	807	65.6	−1.1	1960
1961	4 487	115	5	793	64.5	−1.7	1961
1962	4 328	111	−4	749	60.9	−5.6	1962
1963	4 128	106	−5	752	61.1	0.4	1963
1964	3 287	84	−20	1 029	83.6	36.8	1964
1965	5 165	133	57	965	78.4	−6.2	1965
1966	3 968	102	−23	894	72.7	−7.3	1966
1967	4 544	117	15	832	67.6	−7.0	1967
1968	3 882	100	−15	824	67.0	−1.0	1968
1969	4 277	110	10	902	73.3	9.5	1969
1970	3 893	100	−9	1 230	100.0	36.4	1970
1971	4 676	120	20	986	80.1	−19.9	1971
1972	4 591	118	−2	1 159	94.2	17.6	1972
1973	4 217	108	−8	1 526	124.0	31.6	1973
1974	4 784	123	13	1 617	131.4	6.0	1974
1975	4 652	119	−3	1 821	148.0	12.6	1975
1976	3 555	91	−24	3 295	267.9	81.0	1976
1977	4 316	111	21	5 890	478.8	78.7	1977
1978	4 738	122	10	3 644	296.2	−38.1	1978
1979	4 995	128	5	3 935	319.8	8.0	1979
1980	4 756	122	−5	4 603	374.2	17.0	1980

[a]Green coffee   [b]Brazilian coffee (New York wholesale price)

Copper

The main periods of expansion in world production were 1950–51, 1955–56, 1959–62, 1964–66, 1968–70, 1972–73 and 1976; slackening or falls in growth occurred in 1952–54, 1957–58, 1963, 1967, 1971, 1975 and 1977–80. The copper price increased mainly in 1951–52, 1955, 1959, 1964–66, 1968–69, 1973–74, 1976 (minor recovery) and 1979–80; main falls in price were in 1953, 1956–58, 1961, 1967, 1971, 1975 and 1977.

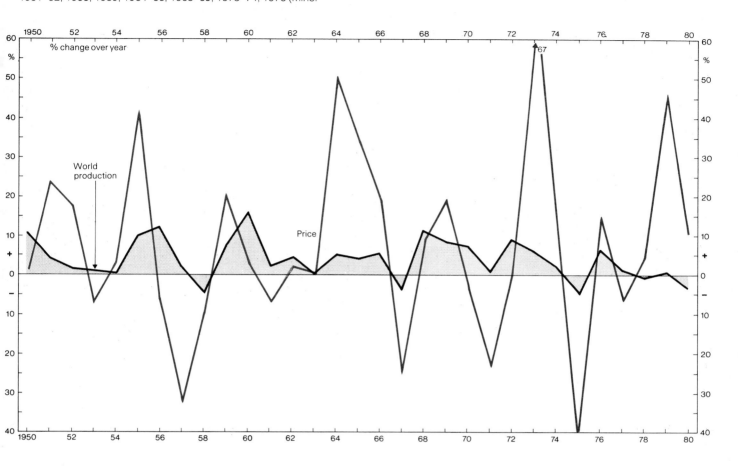

	World production[a]			Price[b]			
	Tonnes (000)	Index 1970 = 100	% change over year	$ per tonne	Index 1970 = 100	% change over year	
1950	2 604	39.8	10.7	493	34.8	1.1	1950
1951	2 719	41.6	4.4	607	42.9	23.3	1951
1952	2 765	42.3	1.7	715	50.5	17.7	1952
1953	2 799	42.8	1.2	664	46.9	−7.1	1953
1954	2 811	43.0	0.4	685	48.4	3.2	1954
1955	3 098	47.4	10.2	968	68.5	41.4	1955
1956	3 463	53.0	11.8	907	64.1	−6.4	1956
1957	3 540	54.2	2.2	605	42.8	−33.3	1957
1958	3 385	51.8	−4.4	544	38.4	−10.1	1958
1959	3 662	56.0	8.2	655	46.3	20.5	1959
1960	4 248	65.0	16.0	678	47.9	3.4	1960
1961	4 359	66.7	2.6	633	44.7	−6.6	1961
1962	4 555	69.7	4.5	645	45.6	1.9	1962
1963	4 575	70.0	0.4	646	45.6	0.1	1963
1964	4 807	73.5	5.1	967	68.4	49.9	1964
1965	5 010	76.6	4.2	1 290	91.2	33.3	1965
1966	5 277	80.7	5.3	1 530	108.1	18.6	1966
1967	5 056	77.4	−4.2	1 136	80.3	−25.7	1967
1968	5 624	86.0	11.2	1 240	87.6	9.1	1968
1969	6 099	93.3	8.5	1 466	103.6	18.3	1969
1970	6 537	100.0	7.2	1 415	100.0	−3.5	1970
1971	6 602	101.0	1.0	1 081	76.4	−23.6	1971
1972	7 201	110.2	9.1	1 069	75.5	−1.2	1972
1973	7 644	116.9	6.2	1 782	125.9	66.7	1973
1974	7 823	119.7	2.3	2 052	145.0	15.2	1974
1975	7 432	113.7	−5.0	1 231	87.0	−40.0	1975
1976	7 925	121.2	6.6	1 403	99.1	13.9	1976
1977	8 020	122.7	1.2	1 310	92.6	−6.6	1977
1978	7 978	122.0	−0.5	1 361	96.2	4.0	1978
1979	8 034	122.9	0.7	1 982	140.1	45.6	1979
1980	7 800	119.3	−2.9	2 187	154.6	10.3	1980

[a]Metal content of ores and concentrates; excluding China   [b]United Kingdom (wholesale price)

Copra

The main periods of expansion in world production were 1950–51, 1954–56, 1960, 1963, 1966, 1968, 1970–72, 1975–76 and 1980; there were falls in production for 1952–53, 1958–59, 1962, 1964–65, 1967, 1969, 1973–74 and 1977–79. The copra price increased mainly in 1950, 1953, 1958–59, 1962–65, 1968, 1970, 1973–74, 1977 and 1979; main falls in price were in 1952, 1954–56, 1960–61, 1966, 1969, 1971–72, 1975–76 and 1980.

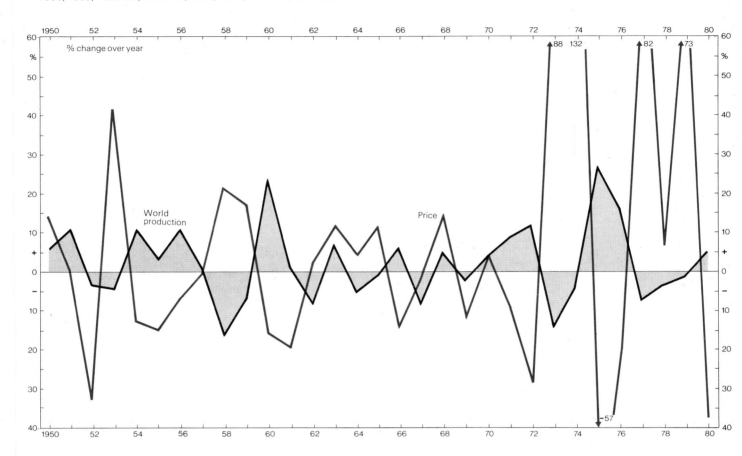

	World production			Price[a]			
	Tonnes (000)	Index 1970 = 100	% change over year	$ per tonne	Index 1970 = 100	% change over year	
1950	2 729	82	6	195.07	108.4	15.1	1950
1951	3 035	91	11	197.59	109.8	1.3	1951
1952	2 932	88	−3	135.17	75.1	−31.6	1952
1953	2 821	85	−4	192.72	107.1	42.6	1953
1954	3 136	94	11	170.44	94.7	−11.6	1954
1955	3 235	97	3	147.47	82.0	−13.5	1955
1956	3 587	108	11	138.78	77.1	−5.9	1956
1957	3 609	108	1	139.92	77.8	0.8	1957
1958	3 021	91	−16	171.30	95.2	22.4	1958
1959	2 821	85	−7	202.72	112.7	18.3	1959
1960	3 457	104	23	172.35	95.8	−15.0	1960
1961	3 487	105	1	140.56	78.1	−18.4	1961
1962	3 201	96	−8	144.93	80.6	3.1	1962
1963	3 432	103	7	162.93	90.6	12.4	1963
1964	3 270	98	−5	171.53	95.3	5.3	1964
1965	3 228	97	−1	192.42	107.0	12.2	1965
1966	3 425	103	6	167.12	92.9	−13.1	1966
1967	3 138	94	−8	166.98	92.8	−0.1	1967
1968	3 284	98	5	192.17	106.8	15.1	1968
1969	3 221	97	−2	171.58	95.4	−10.7	1969
1970	3 335	100	4	179.91	100.0	4.9	1970
1971	3 642	109	9	164.68	91.5	−8.5	1971
1972	4 079	122	12	119.36	66.3	−27.5	1972
1973	3 500	105	−14	224.79	124.9	88.3	1973
1974	3 347	100	−4	522.15	290.2	132.3	1974
1975	4 236	127	27	226.41	125.8	−56.6	1975
1976	4 901	147	16	181.99	101.2	−19.6	1976
1977	4 537	136	−7	331.64	184.3	82.2	1977
1978	4 392	132	−3	356.00	197.9	7.3	1978
1979	4 340	130	−1	615.27	342.0	72.8	1979
1980	4 552	136	5	390.45	217.0	−36.5	1980

[a]Philippines (unit value)

Cotton

The main periods of expansion in world production were 1951–52, 1955, 1958–59, 1962–65, 1968, 1971–72, 1977 and 1979; there were falls in production for 1950, 1954, 1956–57, 1960–61, 1966–67, 1975–76, 1978 and 1980. The cotton price increased mainly in 1950, 1954, 1961–62, 1968, 1971–73, 1976 and 1979–80; there were falls in price for 1951–53, 1955, 1959–60, 1964–67, 1969–70, 1975 and 1977–78.

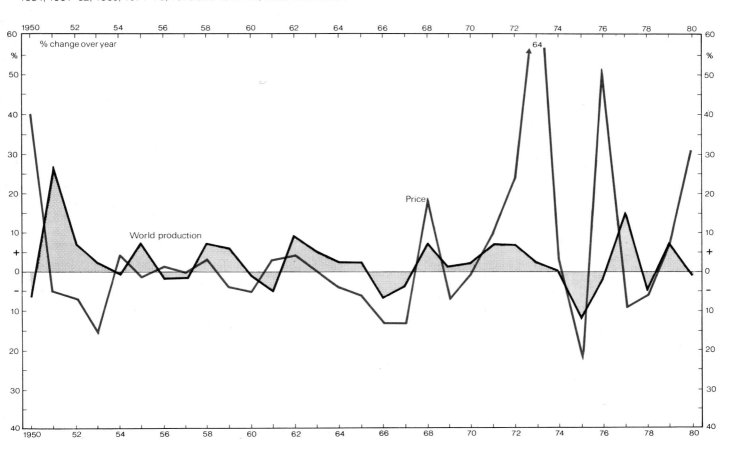

	World production[a]			Price[b]			
	Tonnes (000)	Index 1970 = 100	% change over year	$ per tonne	Index 1970 = 100	% change over year	
1950	6861	58	−7	970	175	40	1950
1951	8629	73	26	917	166	−5	1951
1952	9202	78	7	853	154	−7	1952
1953	9378	79	2	723	131	−15	1953
1954	9316	79	−1	750	135	4	1954
1955	9935	84	7	741	134	−1	1955
1956	9693	82	−2	747	135	1	1956
1957	9533	80	−2	745	135	0	1957
1958	10222	86	7	765	138	3	1958
1959	10829	91	6	732	132	−4	1959
1960	10707	90	−1	692	125	−5	1960
1961	10220	86	−5	710	128	3	1961
1962	11145	94	9	741	134	4	1962
1963	11697	99	5	741	134	0	1963
1964	11917	100	2	711	128	−4	1964
1965	12192	103	2	670	121	−6	1965
1966	11183	94	−8	582	105	−13	1966
1967	10769	91	−4	507	92	−13	1967
1968	11520	97	7	600	108	18	1968
1969	11625	98	1	560	101	−7	1969
1970	11863	100	2	553	100	−1	1970
1971	12724	107	7	611	110	10	1971
1972	13674	115	7	756	137	24	1972
1973	13883	117	2	1237	224	64	1973
1974	13943	118	0	1276	231	3	1974
1975	12269	103	−12	994	180	−22	1975
1976	12066	102	−2	1499	271	51	1976
1977	13857	117	15	1358	245	−9	1977
1978	13230	112	−5	1270	229	−6	1978
1979	14292	120	8	1369	247	8	1979
1980	14202	120	−1	1792	324	31	1980

[a]Cotton (lint)   [b]United States (wholesale price)

Crude oil

The rate of increase in world production was comparatively stable over 1950–73, but with higher increases in growth in 1950–51, 1955, 1970 and 1973; there was recovery in 1976 from the fall in production in 1975, and a fall in 1980. Prices also were comparatively stable over the period 1950–70, although with falls in 1950, 1957–64 and 1968–69. There were high increases in price during 1971–73 preceding the very large increase in 1974, and substantial increases again in 1979–80.

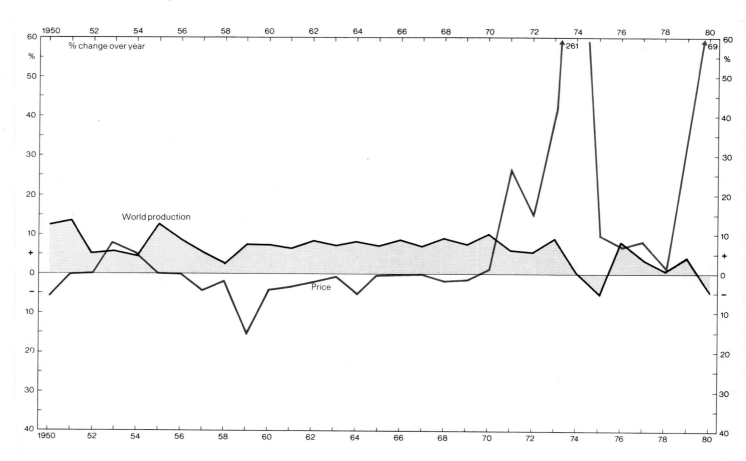

	World production[a]			Price[b]			
	Tonnes (million)	Index 1970 = 100	% change over year	$ per tonne	Index 1970 = 100	% change over year	
1950	521	22.9	12.5	12.7	131.5	−6	1950
1951	590	25.9	13.2	12.7	131.5	0	1951
1952	621	27.3	5.2	12.7	131.5	0	1952
1953	657	28.9	5.9	13.6	141.5	8	1953
1954	688	30.3	4.7	14.3	148.5	5	1954
1955	776	34.1	12.7	14.3	148.5	0	1955
1956	843	37.1	8.7	14.3	148.5	0	1956
1957	889	39.1	5.5	13.8	143.1	−4	1957
1958	911	40.0	2.4	13.5	140.8	−2	1958
1959	981	43.1	7.7	11.5	120.0	−15	1959
1960	1054	46.3	7.5	11.1	115.4	−4	1960
1961	1123	49.4	6.5	10.7	111.5	−3	1961
1962	1217	53.5	8.4	10.5	109.2	−2	1962
1963	1306	57.4	7.3	10.4	107.7	−1	1963
1964	1410	62.0	7.9	9.8	102.3	−5	1964
1965	1510	66.4	7.1	9.8	102.3	0	1965
1966	1639	72.0	8.5	9.8	102.3	0	1966
1967	1759	77.3	7.3	9.8	102.3	0	1967
1968	1920	84.4	9.2	9.6	100.0	−2	1968
1969	2066	90.8	7.6	9.5	98.5	−2	1969
1970	2275	100.0	10.1	9.6	100.0	2	1970
1971	2413	106.1	6.1	12.2	126.9	27	1971
1972	2548	112.0	5.6	14.1	146.2	15	1972
1973	2780	122.2	9.1	20.0	207.7	42	1973
1974	2789	122.6	0.3	72.2	750.8	261	1974
1975	2646	116.3	−5.1	79.3	824.6	10	1975
1976	2872	126.2	8.5	85.2	885.4	7	1976
1977	2975	130.8	3.6	91.8	953.8	8	1977
1978	3007	132.2	1.1	94.0	976.9	2	1978
1979	3123	137.3	3.9	125.6	1305.4	34	1979
1980	2976	130.8	−4.7	212.2	2205.4	69	1980

[a]Oil well production; excluding shale oil, coal distillation, etc   [b]Saudi Arabia (Ras Tanura), converted from $ per barrel

Gold

The main periods of expansion in world production were 1950, 1952, 1954–65 (a long period of steady growth), 1968–70, 1976 and 1978; there were falls in production or low growth for 1951, 1953, 1966–67, 1971–75, 1977 and 1979–80. The United States price of gold was fixed at $35 per fine ounce throughout the 1950s and 1960s; gold convertibility of the dollar was suspended on August 15, 1971, and was followed by main rises in the gold price for 1971–74 and 1977–80. There were falls in the gold price for 1970 (UK price) and 1976, with little change in price for 1975. The 1968–69 rise in the UK price followed the 1967 devaluation of the pound (16.7%).

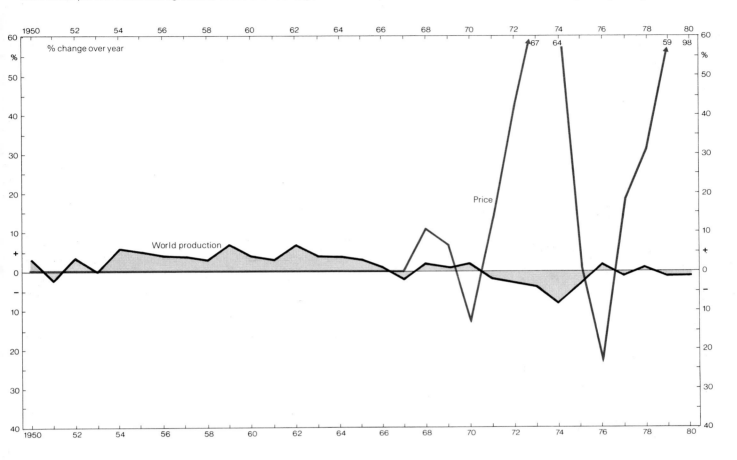

	World production[a]			Price[b]			
	Tonnes (000)	Index 1970 = 100	% change over year	$ per ounce (troy)	Index 1970 = 100	% change over year	
1950	0.84	56	3	35.0	97.4	0.0	1950
1951	0.82	55	−2	35.0	97.4	0.0	1951
1952	0.84	57	3	35.0	97.4	0.0	1952
1953	0.84	57	0	35.0	97.4	0.0	1953
1954	0.89	60	6	35.0	97.4	0.0	1954
1955	0.93	63	5	35.0	97.4	0.0	1955
1956	0.97	65	4	35.0	97.4	0.0	1956
1957	1.01	68	4	35.0	97.4	0.0	1957
1958	1.04	70	3	35.0	97.4	0.0	1958
1959	1.11	75	7	35.0	97.4	0.0	1959
1960	1.16	79	4	35.0	97.4	0.0	1960
1961	1.20	81	3	35.0	97.4	0.0	1961
1962	1.28	87	7	35.0	97.4	0.0	1962
1963	1.34	90	4	35.0	97.4	0.0	1963
1964	1.40	94	4	35.0	97.4	0.0	1964
1965	1.44	97	3	35.0	97.4	0.0	1965
1966	1.45	98	1	35.0	97.4	0.0	1966
1967	1.41	96	−2	35.0	97.4	0.0	1967
1968	1.44	97	2	38.6	107.5	10.4	1968
1969	1.45	98	1	41.1	114.3	6.4	1969
1970	1.48	100	2	35.9	100.0	−12.5	1970
1971	1.45	98	−2	40.8	113.6	13.6	1971
1972	1.40	95	−3	58.2	161.8	42.5	1972
1973	1.35	91	−4	97.3	270.8	67.3	1973
1974	1.23	83	−8	159.2	443.1	63.6	1974
1975	1.19	80	−3	161.0	448.1	1.1	1975
1976	1.21	82	2	124.8	347.3	−22.5	1976
1977	1.20	81	−1	147.7	411.0	18.3	1977
1978	1.22	82	1	193.2	537.7	30.8	1978
1979	1.20	81	−1	306.7	853.3	58.7	1979
1980	1.19	80	−1	607.9	1 691.3	98.2	1980

[a]Metal content of gold-bearing ores; includes estimates for Soviet Union production   [b]United Kingdom (wholesale price)

Groundnuts (peanuts)

The main periods of expansion in world production were 1950–51, 1953–58, 1960–64, 1967, 1969–71, 1973, 1975 and 1978; there were falls in production or comparatively low growth for 1952, 1959, 1965–66, 1968, 1972, 1976–77 and 1979–80. The groundnuts price increased mainly in 1951, 1956, 1959–60, 1964–65, 1969–71, 1973–74 and 1977–78; there were falls in 1952, 1954–55, 1957–58, 1961–62, 1966–68, 1975–76 and 1979–80.

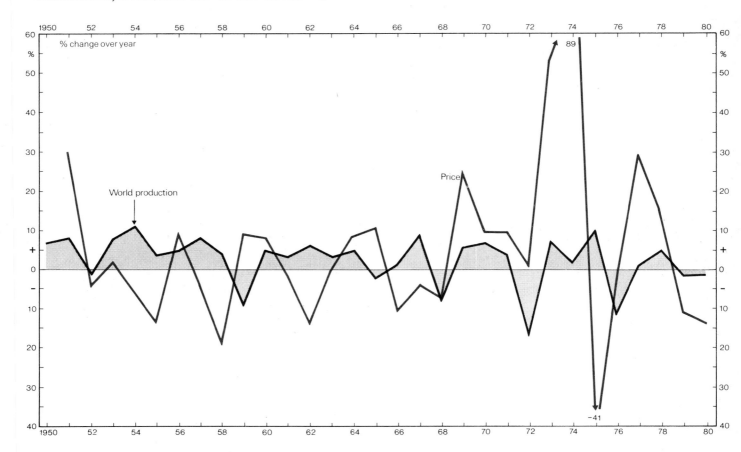

	World production[a]			Price[b]			
	Tonnes (000)	Index 1970 = 100	% change over year	$ per tonne	Index 1970 = 100	% change over year	
1950	9655	51	7	178.38	78	na	1950
1951	10440	55	8	233.75	102	31	1951
1952	10307	54	−1	225.64	99	−3	1952
1953	11097	58	8	229.07	100	2	1953
1954	12321	65	11	217.59	95	−5	1954
1955	12756	67	4	190.09	83	−13	1955
1956	13432	71	5	209.44	92	10	1956
1957	14521	76	8	203.50	89	−3	1957
1958	15138	80	4	166.35	73	−18	1958
1959	13733	72	−9	182.17	80	10	1959
1960	14441	76	5	197.99	87	9	1960
1961	14838	78	3	195.69	86	−1	1961
1962	15712	83	6	170.77	75	−13	1962
1963	16158	85	3	171.44	75	0	1963
1964	16968	89	5	186.65	82	9	1964
1965	16570	87	−2	206.56	91	11	1965
1966	16684	88	1	186.65	82	−10	1966
1967	18149	96	9	179.29	79	−4	1967
1968	16694	88	−8	166.06	73	−7	1968
1969	17665	93	6	206.78	91	25	1969
1970	18987	100	7	228.17	100	10	1970
1971	19759	104	4	250.92	110	10	1971
1972	16490	87	−17	253.95	111	1	1972
1973	17583	93	7	391.31	171	54	1973
1974	17883	94	2	739.07	324	89	1974
1975	19743	104	10	432.97	190	−41	1975
1976	17476	92	−11	422.99	185	−2	1976
1977	17716	93	1	546.86	240	29	1977
1978	18660	98	5	630.92	277	15	1978
1979	18488	97	−1	562.75	247	−11	1979
1980	18286	96	−1	485.57	213	−14	1980

[a]Groundnuts in shell   [b]Nigerian groundnuts (London wholesale price)

Iron ore

The main periods of expansion in world production were 1950–51, 1953, 1955–57, 1959–60, 1962–66, 1968–71 and 1973–74; there were main falls in production for 1954, 1958, 1961 and 1977, with other falls or low growth in 1952, 1967, 1972, 1975–76 and 1978–80. The price of iron ore increased mainly in 1950–52, 1955–57, 1961, 1970, 1973–75 and 1979–80; there were falls in price for 1953–54, 1958–59, 1962–63, 1966–69, 1971–72 and 1976–78.

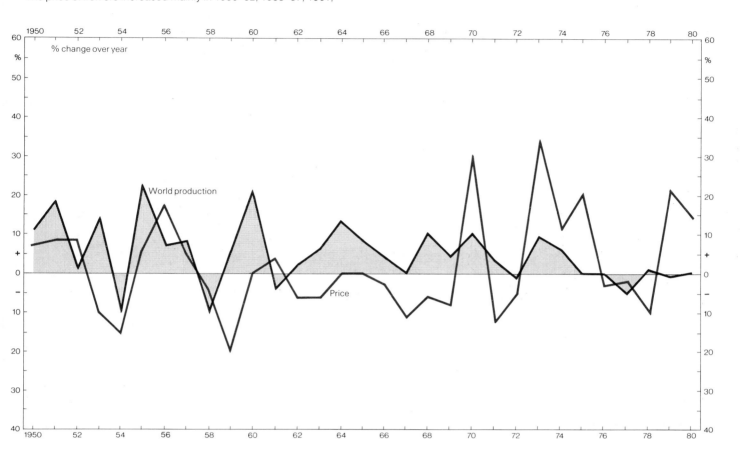

	World production[a]			Price[b]			
	Tonnes (million)	Index 1970 = 100	% change over year	$ per tonne	Index 1970 = 100	% change over year	
1950	234	30	11	19.14	125.7	7	1950
1951	276	36	18	20.63	135.5	8	1951
1952	279	36	1	22.30	146.5	8	1952
1953	317	41	14	20.05	131.7	−10	1953
1954	285	37	−10	17.10	112.4	−15	1954
1955	347	45	22	18.20	119.6	6	1955
1956	373	49	7	21.36	140.3	17	1956
1957	403	53	8	22.45	147.5	5	1957
1958	363	47	−10	21.48	141.1	−4	1958
1959	385	50	6	17.08	112.2	−20	1959
1960	465	61	21	17.08	112.2	0	1960
1961	445	58	−4	17.79	116.9	4	1961
1962	456	59	2	16.75	110.1	−6	1962
1963	481	63	6	15.69	103.1	−6	1963
1964	544	71	13	15.69	103.1	0	1964
1965	590	77	8	15.69	103.1	0	1965
1966	613	80	4	15.25	100.2	−3	1966
1967	611	80	0	13.50	88.7	−11	1967
1968	673	88	10	12.63	83.0	−6	1968
1969	700	91	4	11.68	76.7	−8	1969
1970	767	100	10	15.22	100.0	30	1970
1971	787	103	3	13.46	88.4	−12	1971
1972	778	101	−1	12.79	84.0	−5	1972
1973	846	110	9	17.13	112.5	34	1973
1974	895	117	6	19.00	124.8	11	1974
1975	894	117	0	22.81	149.9	20	1975
1976	895	117	0	22.10	145.2	−3	1976
1977	853	111	−5	21.59	141.9	−2	1977
1978	865	113	1	19.39	127.4	−10	1978
1979	855	111	−1	23.44	154.0	21	1979
1980	856	112	0	26.70	175.4	14	1980

[a]Gross weight   [b]Brazil (US wholesale price)

Jute

The main periods of expansion in world production were 1950–52, 1954–55, 1958, 1961, 1963, 1965–66, 1969, 1972–73 and 1975–78; there were falls in production or a low growth rate for 1953, 1956–57, 1959–60, 1962, 1964, 1967–68, 1970–71, 1974 and 1979–80. The price of jute increased mainly in 1951, 1954, 1957, 1960–61, 1964–66, 1974 and 1977–78; there were falls in price for 1950, 1952–53, 1955, 1959, 1962–63, 1967–68, 1970, 1973, 1976 and 1979–80.

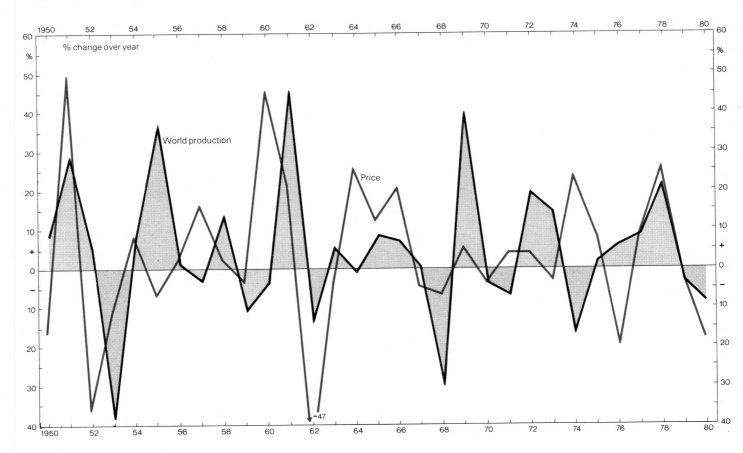

	World production[a]			Price[b]			
	Tonnes (000)	Index 1970 = 100	% change over year	$ per tonne	Index 1970 = 100	% change over year	
1950	1883	62	8	202	75	−16	1950
1951	2413	79	28	301	112	49	1951
1952	2544	84	5	192	71	−36	1952
1953	1587	52	−38	172	64	−11	1953
1954	1717	56	8	185	68	8	1954
1955	2332	77	36	171	63	−7	1955
1956	2357	77	1	174	64	2	1956
1957	2284	75	−3	201	74	16	1957
1958	2576	85	13	205	76	2	1958
1959	2293	75	−11	197	73	−4	1959
1960	2198	72	−4	286	106	45	1960
1961	3196	105	45	345	128	21	1961
1962	2756	91	−14	184	68	−47	1962
1963	2887	95	5	179	66	−3	1963
1964	2844	93	−1	224	83	25	1964
1965	3085	101	8	251	93	12	1965
1966	3303	109	7	302	112	20	1966
1967	3289	108	0	288	107	−5	1967
1968	2292	75	−30	267	99	−7	1968
1969	3177	104	39	281	104	5	1969
1970	3043	100	−4	270	100	−4	1970
1971	2842	93	−7	282	104	4	1971
1972	3377	111	19	294	109	4	1972
1973	3859	127	14	284	105	−3	1973
1974	3194	105	−17	348	129	23	1974
1975	3251	107	2	371	137	7	1975
1976	3460	114	6	295	109	−20	1976
1977	3730	123	8	319	118	8	1977
1978	4507	148	21	398	147	25	1978
1979	4381	144	−3	385	143	−3	1979
1980	3987	131	−9	314	116	−18	1980

[a]Including jute-like fibres   [b]Bangladesh (wholesale price); estimated before 1957

Lamb

The main periods of expansion in world production were 1952–56, 1958–62, 1967–68, 1970–71, 1975–76, 1978 and 1980; there were falls in production or low growth for 1950–51, 1957, 1963–66, 1969, 1972–74, 1977 and 1979. The price of lamb rose mainly in 1951–55, 1957, 1960, 1963–65, 1969, 1972–74 and 1977–80; the price fell in 1950, 1956, 1958–59, 1961, 1966–68, 1971 and 1975.

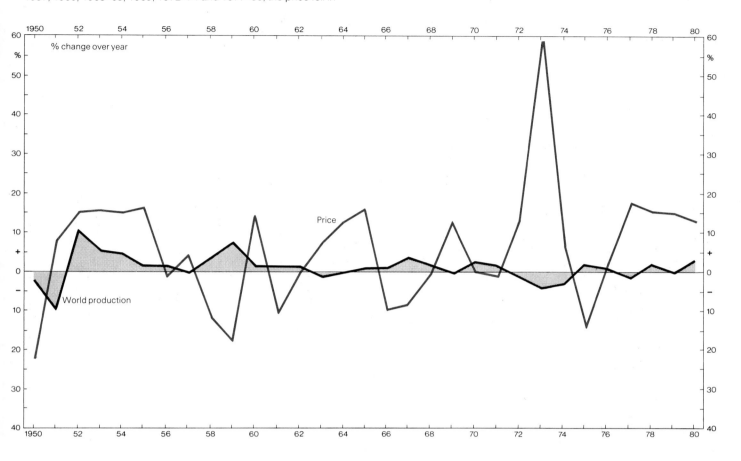

	World production[a]			Price[b]			
	Tonnes (000)	Index 1970 = 100	% change over year	$ per tonne	Index 1970 = 100	% change over year	
1950	4975	66	−2	275	51.3	−22.1	1950
1951	4520	60	−9	298	55.5	8.3	1951
1952	5019	67	11	343	63.9	15.1	1952
1953	5313	71	6	396	73.8	15.5	1953
1954	5582	74	5	455	84.9	15.0	1954
1955	5720	76	2	528	98.4	15.9	1955
1956	5837	78	2	522	97.2	−1.1	1956
1957	5837	78	0	544	101.5	4.4	1957
1958	6070	81	4	480	89.6	−11.7	1958
1959	6537	87	8	397	74.1	−17.3	1959
1960	6654	88	2	453	84.5	14.0	1960
1961	6771	90	2	406	75.7	−10.4	1961
1962	6893	92	2	406	75.8	0.1	1962
1963	6854	91	−1	437	81.4	7.4	1963
1964	6829	91	0	491	91.5	12.4	1964
1965	6923	92	1	569	106.0	15.9	1965
1966	6965	92	1	513	95.7	−9.7	1966
1967	7214	96	4	473	88.2	−7.9	1967
1968	7361	98	2	471	87.9	−0.4	1968
1969	7335	97	0	536	99.9	13.7	1969
1970	7530	100	3	536	100.0	0.1	1970
1971	7645	102	2	533	99.3	−0.7	1971
1972	7592	101	−1	602	112.2	12.9	1972
1973	7324	97	−4	960	179.0	59.5	1973
1974	7132	95	−3	1021	190.3	6.3	1974
1975	7307	97	2	877	163.5	−14.1	1975
1976	7389	98	1	902	168.1	2.8	1976
1977	7352	98	−1	1062	197.9	17.8	1977
1978	7524	100	2	1226	228.6	15.5	1978
1979	7517	100	0	1410	262.8	15.0	1979
1980	7726	103	3	1593	297.1	13.0	1980

[a]Including mutton   [b]New Zealand (unit value)

Lead

The main periods of expansion in world production were 1950, 1952–57, 1960–62, 1965–66, 1968–70, 1972 and 1977–79; there was a slight fall or low growth in 1958–59, 1963–64, 1967, 1971, 1973–76 and 1980. The price of lead rose mainly in 1951, 1954–56, 1963–65, 1969–70, 1972–74 and 1977–79; there were falls in the price for 1950,   1952–53, 1957–58, 1960–62, 1966–68, 1971, 1975 and 1980.

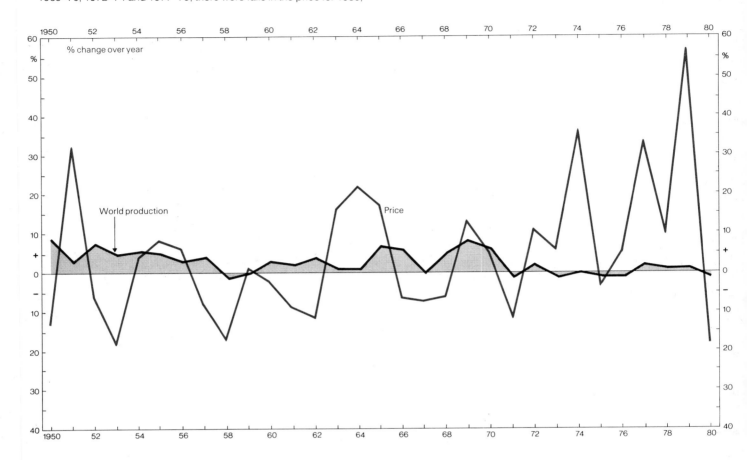

	World production[a]			Price[b]			
	Tonnes (000)	Index 1970 = 100	% change over year	$ per tonne	Index 1970 = 100	% change over year	
1950	1 667	49	9	293	85	−13	1950
1951	1 713	50	3	386	111	32	1951
1952	1 853	54	8	363	105	−6	1952
1953	1 947	57	5	297	86	−18	1953
1954	2 056	60	6	310	90	4	1954
1955	2 153	63	5	334	96	8	1955
1956	2 221	65	3	353	102	6	1956
1957	2 310	67	4	323	93	−8	1957
1958	2 283	67	−1	267	77	−17	1958
1959	2 276	66	0	269	78	1	1959
1960	2 349	69	3	263	76	−2	1960
1961	2 396	70	2	240	69	−9	1961
1962	2 502	73	4	212	61	−11	1962
1963	2 518	74	1	246	71	16	1963
1964	2 541	74	1	300	87	22	1964
1965	2 710	79	7	353	102	17	1965
1966	2 868	84	6	333	96	−6	1966
1967	2 870	84	0	309	89	−7	1967
1968	3 000	88	5	291	84	−6	1968
1969	3 240	95	8	329	95	13	1969
1970	3 424	100	6	346	100	5	1970
1971	3 396	99	−1	306	89	−11	1971
1972	3 456	101	2	340	98	11	1972
1973	3 408	100	−1	362	105	6	1973
1974	3 415	100	0	492	142	36	1974
1975	3 395	99	−1	476	138	−3	1975
1976	3 375	99	−1	507	147	6	1976
1977	3 436	100	2	677	196	33	1977
1978	3 470	101	1	745	215	10	1978
1979	3 519	103	1	1 168	338	57	1979
1980	3 482	102	−1	959	277	−18	1980

[a]Metal content of ores and concentrates   [b]United States (wholesale price)

Maize (corn)

The main periods of expansion in world production were 1951–53, 1955–56, 1958–60, 1962–63, 1965–67, 1969, 1971, 1973, 1975 and 1977–79; there were falls in production or comparatively low growth for 1950, 1954, 1957, 1961, 1964, 1968, 1970, 1972, 1974, 1976 and 1980. The maize price rose mainly in 1950–51, 1963, 1966, 1969–70, 1973–74 and 1978–80; there were falls in the price for 1952–57, 1960–61, 1967–68, 1972 and 1975–77.

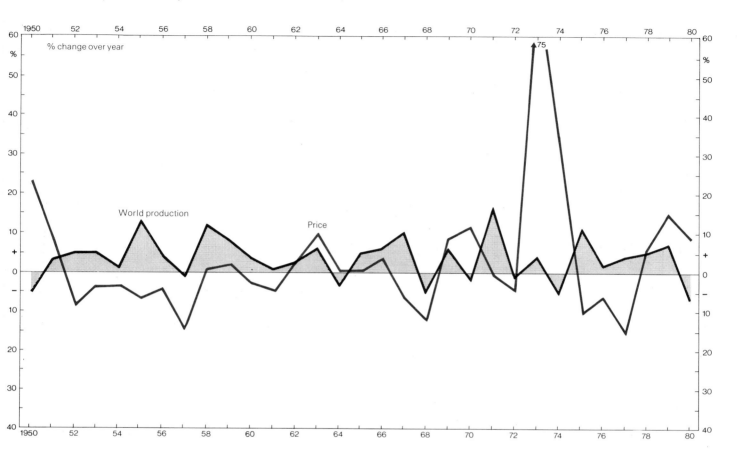

	World production			Price[a]			
	Tonnes (million)	Index 1970 = 100	% change over year	$ per tonne	Index 1970 = 100	% change over year	
1950	131.0	47.6	−5	67.8	116	23	1950
1951	134.7	48.9	3	74.0	127	9	1951
1952	141.4	51.3	5	67.8	116	−8	1952
1953	147.7	53.7	5	66.0	113	−3	1953
1954	148.6	54.0	1	63.8	109	−3	1954
1955	167.5	60.8	13	59.8	103	−6	1955
1956	173.5	63.0	4	57.1	98	−4	1956
1957	172.4	62.6	−1	49.2	84	−14	1957
1958	193.6	70.3	12	49.6	85	1	1958
1959	209.2	76.0	8	50.8	87	2	1959
1960	215.7	78.3	3	49.6	85	−2	1960
1961	216.9	78.8	1	47.6	82	−4	1961
1962	221.6	80.5	2	48.8	84	2	1962
1963	233.8	84.9	6	53.9	93	10	1963
1964	226.8	82.4	−3	54.7	94	1	1964
1965	238.7	86.7	5	55.5	95	1	1965
1966	254.0	92.2	6	57.9	99	4	1966
1967	280.0	101.7	10	54.3	93	−6	1967
1968	265.3	96.3	−5	47.6	82	−12	1968
1969	280.9	102.0	6	52.0	89	9	1969
1970	275.4	100.0	−2	58.3	100	12	1970
1971	318.6	115.7	16	58.3	100	0	1971
1972	315.7	114.6	−1	55.9	96	−4	1972
1973	328.7	119.4	4	97.6	168	75	1973
1974	313.0	113.7	−5	132.3	227	35	1974
1975	345.9	125.6	11	119.3	205	−10	1975
1976	354.4	128.7	2	112.2	193	−6	1976
1977	369.9	134.4	4	95.3	164	−15	1977
1978	390.1	141.7	5	100.8	173	6	1978
1979	418.6	152.0	7	115.7	199	15	1979
1980	390.9	142.0	−7	125.6	216	9	1980

[a]United States (wholesale price); converted from dollars per bushel price

Manganese

The main periods of expansion in world production were 1950–53; 1955–57, 1959–60, 1962–65, 1968–71, 1973–74, 1976 and 1979; there were falls in production for 1954, 1958, 1961, 1967 and 1977–78, with low growth for 1972 and 1975. The price of manganese increased mainly in 1951, 1954, 1956–57, 1965, 1970–71, 1973–75 and 1980; there were falls in price for 1952–53, 1955, 1958–60, 1962–64, 1967–69 and 1978–79.

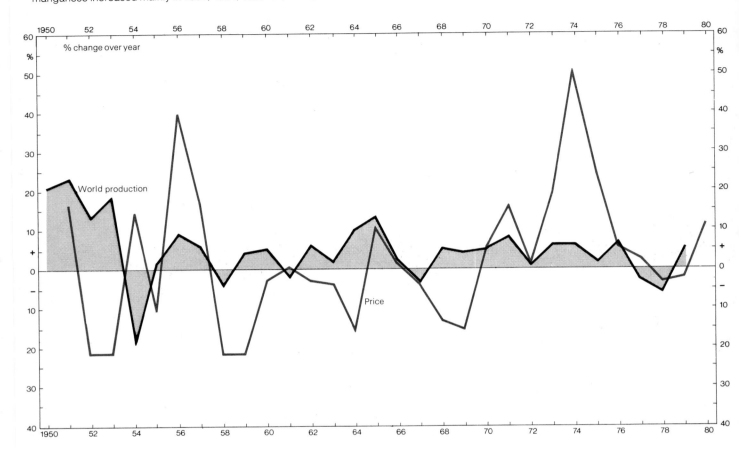

	World production[a]			Price[b]			
	Tonnes (million)	Index 1970 = 100	% change over year	$ per tonne	Index 1970 = 100	% change over year	
1950	3.06	41	21	127	233	na	1950
1951	3.77	50	23	148	271	16	1951
1952	4.27	57	13	115	211	−22	1952
1953	5.04	67	18	90	164	−22	1953
1954	4.09	54	−19	102	188	14	1954
1955	4.19	56	2	91	167	−11	1955
1956	4.55	60	9	127	233	39	1956
1957	4.82	64	6	148	271	16	1957
1958	4.64	62	−4	115	211	−22	1958
1959	4.82	64	4	90	164	−22	1959
1960	5.08	67	5	87	160	−3	1960
1961	4.98	66	−2	87	160	0	1961
1962	5.28	70	6	85	155	−3	1962
1963	5.37	71	2	81	149	−4	1963
1964	5.89	78	10	68	125	−16	1964
1965	6.65	88	13	75	138	10	1965
1966	6.81	90	2	76	139	1	1966
1967	6.57	87	−3	73	133	−4	1967
1968	6.91	92	5	62	114	−14	1968
1969	7.20	96	4	52	96	−16	1969
1970	7.53	100	5	54	100	5	1970
1971	8.15	108	8	63	115	15	1971
1972	8.22	109	1	63	117	1	1972
1973	8.73	116	6	75	138	18	1973
1974	9.24	123	6	112	206	50	1974
1975	9.45	125	2	138	253	23	1975
1976	10.11	134	7	145	266	5	1976
1977	9.83	130	−3	148	272	2	1977
1978	9.20	122	−6	142	261	−4	1978
1979	9.67	128	5	138	253	−3	1979
1980	na	na	na	153	281	11	1980

[a]Metal content of ores and concentrates   [b]India (US wholesale price)

Newsprint

The main periods of expansion in world production were 1950–51, 1954–56, 1959–60, 1963–66, 1968–70, 1972–74, 1976 and 1978–80; there were falls in production for 1958, 1971 and 1975, with low growth in 1962, 1967 and 1977. The price of newsprint increased mainly in 1951–52, 1956–57, 1974–75 and 1979–80, with a comparatively steady rate of increase for 1966–73 and 1976–78; there were falls in price for 1955, 1958, 1960–63 and 1965.

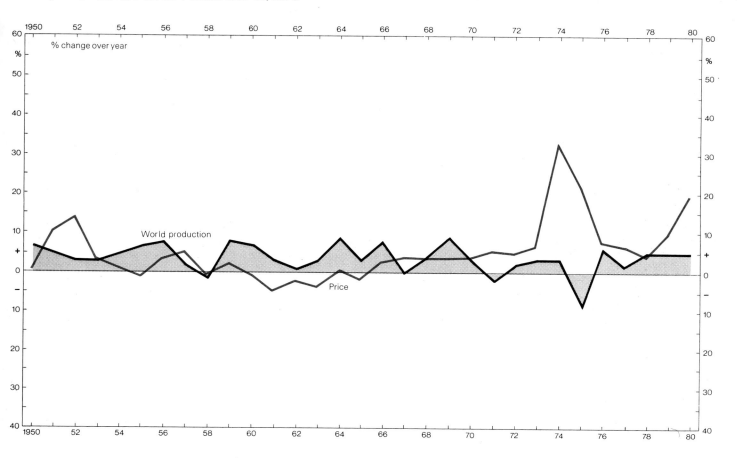

	World production			Price[a]			
	Tonnes (000)	Index 1970 = 100	% change over year	$ per tonne	Index 1970 = 100	% change over year	
1950	9013	41.6	7	99.6	68.9	0.4	1950
1951	9443	43.5	5	109.8	76.1	10.3	1951
1952	9706	44.8	3	125.1	86.6	13.9	1952
1953	10010	46.2	3	129.1	89.4	3.2	1953
1954	10556	48.7	5	130.4	90.3	1.0	1954
1955	11332	52.3	7	129.2	89.5	−0.9	1955
1956	12190	56.2	8	133.0	92.1	3.0	1956
1957	12478	57.5	2	139.4	96.5	4.8	1957
1958	12260	56.5	−2	137.9	95.5	−1.0	1958
1959	13206	60.9	8	140.4	97.2	1.8	1959
1960	14131	65.2	7	139.2	96.4	−0.9	1960
1961	14507	66.9	3	132.5	91.7	−4.8	1961
1962	14723	67.9	1	129.2	89.5	−2.5	1962
1963	15160	69.9	3	124.7	86.4	−3.4	1963
1964	16464	75.9	9	124.9	86.5	0.1	1964
1965	17003	78.4	3	123.3	85.4	−1.3	1965
1966	18354	84.6	8	126.2	87.4	2.3	1966
1967	18441	85.0	0	130.5	90.4	3.4	1967
1968	19268	88.9	4	135.0	93.5	3.4	1968
1969	21004	96.9	9	139.4	96.5	3.3	1969
1970	21685	100.0	3	144.4	100.0	3.6	1970
1971	21286	98.2	−2	151.8	105.1	5.1	1971
1972	21810	100.6	2	159.1	110.2	4.8	1972
1973	22434	103.5	3	169.0	117.0	6.2	1973
1974	23176	106.9	3	223.6	154.8	32.3	1974
1975	21060	97.1	−9	270.5	187.3	21.0	1975
1976	22392	103.3	6	290.3	201.0	7.3	1976
1977	22900	105.6	2	308.2	213.4	6.2	1977
1978	24100	111.1	5	321.6	222.7	4.3	1978
1979	25300	116.7	5	353.6	244.8	10.0	1979
1980	26547	122.4	5	422.1	292.3	19.4	1980

[a]Canada (unit value)

Nickel

The main periods of expansion in world production were 1951–57, 1959–61, 1964–65, 1967–68, 1970, 1973–74, 1976 and 1979–80; there were falls in production for 1958, 1962–63, 1966, 1969, 1972 and 1978, with low growth in 1950, 1971, 1975 and 1977. The price of nickel increased mainly in 1950–53, 1955, 1957, 1961–62, 1967–70, 1973–76 and 1979–80; there were falls or low increases in 1954, 1956, 1958–60, 1963–66, 1971 and 1978.

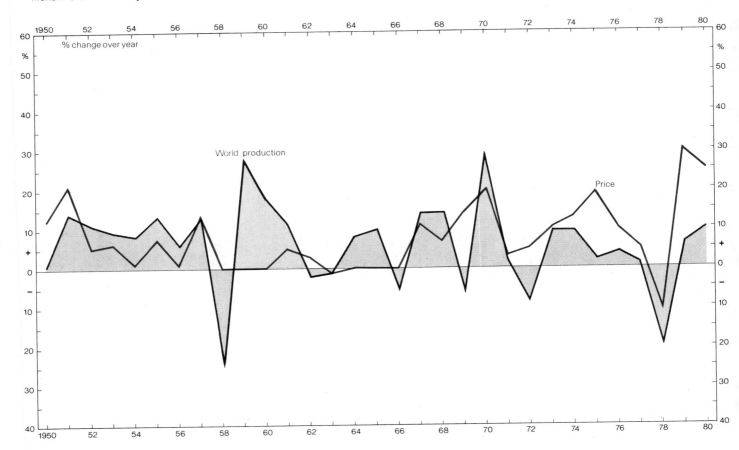

	World production[a]			Price[b]			
	Tonnes (000)	Index 1970 = 100	% change over year	$ per tonne	Index 1970 = 100	% change over year	
1950	148	22	1	988	35	12	1950
1951	168	25	14	1 190	42	21	1951
1952	187	28	11	1 246	44	5	1952
1953	204	31	9	1 321	46	6	1953
1954	221	33	8	1 334	47	1	1954
1955	249	38	13	1 422	50	7	1955
1956	265	40	6	1 437	51	1	1956
1957	299	45	13	1 631	57	13	1957
1958	227	34	−24	1 631	57	0	1958
1959	290	44	28	1 631	57	0	1959
1960	342	52	18	1 631	57	0	1960
1961	378	57	11	1 711	60	5	1961
1962	371	56	−2	1 761	62	3	1962
1963	366	55	−1	1 742	61	−1	1963
1964	397	60	8	1 742	61	0	1964
1965	437	66	10	1 735	61	0	1965
1966	416	63	−5	1 742	61	0	1966
1967	476	72	14	1 932	68	11	1967
1968	545	82	14	2 074	73	7	1968
1969	514	78	−6	2 363	83	14	1969
1970	663	100	29	2 846	100	20	1970
1971	679	102	2	2 932	103	3	1971
1972	626	94	−8	3 079	108	5	1972
1973	681	103	9	3 373	119	10	1973
1974	745	112	9	3 825	134	13	1974
1975	757	114	2	4 538	159	19	1975
1976	788	119	4	4 973	175	10	1976
1977	799	121	1	5 203	183	5	1977
1978	643	97	−20	4 609	162	−11	1978
1979	680	103	6	5 986	210	30	1979
1980	750	113	10	7 468	262	25	1980

[a]Metal content of ores and concentrates   [b]Canada (wholesale price)

Palm oil

The main periods of expansion in world production were 1950, 1952–54, 1956, 1958–60, 1963–64, 1966, 1968–72, 1974–77 and 1979–80. There was substantial growth throughout the period from 1968 to 1980, with comparatively low, but still high, growth for 1973 and 1978; before 1968 there were falls in production for 1951, 1955, 1957, 1961, 1965 and 1967. The price of palm oil rose mainly in 1951–52, 1955–56, 1959, 1964–65, 1970, 1973–74, 1977 and 1979; there were falls in 1950, 1953, 1958, 1960, 1962–63, 1966–69, 1972, 1975–76 and 1980.

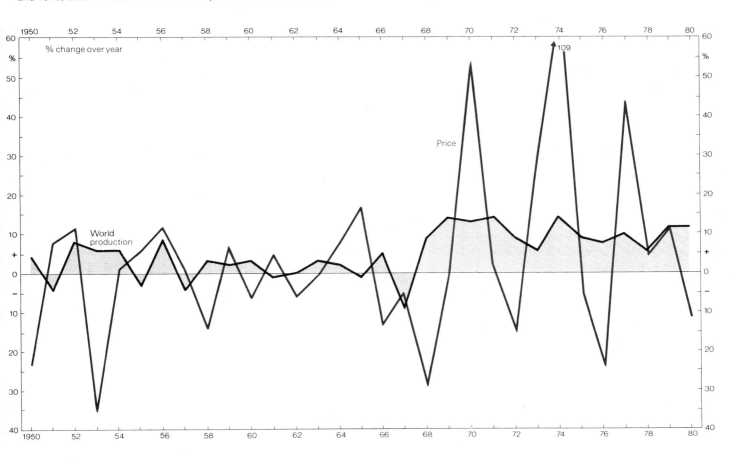

	World production			Price[a]			
	Tonnes (000)	Index 1970 = 100	% change over year	$ per tonne	Index 1970 = 100	% change over year	
1950	1 126	57	4	259.2	120.7	−23.8	1950
1951	1 078	55	−4	278.6	129.7	7.5	1951
1952	1 169	59	8	310.0	144.3	11.3	1952
1953	1 241	63	6	199.5	92.9	−35.7	1953
1954	1 314	67	6	201.0	93.6	0.7	1954
1955	1 272	64	−3	211.6	98.5	5.3	1955
1956	1 368	69	8	236.2	110.0	11.7	1956
1957	1 318	67	−4	237.8	110.7	0.7	1957
1958	1 357	69	3	202.4	94.2	−14.9	1958
1959	1 379	70	2	216.0	100.5	6.7	1959
1960	1 419	72	3	202.8	94.4	−6.1	1960
1961	1 411	71	−1	211.0	98.2	4.0	1961
1962	1 416	72	0	198.0	92.2	−6.2	1962
1963	1 457	74	3	195.8	91.1	−1.1	1963
1964	1 480	75	2	210.1	97.8	7.3	1964
1965	1 469	74	−1	244.5	113.8	16.4	1965
1966	1 546	78	5	212.3	98.9	−13.2	1966
1967	1 410	71	−9	200.6	93.4	−5.5	1967
1968	1 532	78	9	142.2	66.2	−29.1	1968
1969	1 739	88	14	140.1	65.2	−1.5	1969
1970	1 974	100	13	214.8	100.0	53.3	1970
1971	2 245	114	14	217.3	101.2	1.2	1971
1972	2 437	123	9	184.5	85.9	−15.1	1972
1973	2 591	131	6	239.3	111.4	29.7	1973
1974	2 949	149	14	500.4	233.0	109.1	1974
1975	3 218	163	9	471.8	219.6	−5.7	1975
1976	3 476	176	8	356.8	166.1	−24.4	1976
1977	3 821	194	10	510.6	237.7	43.1	1977
1978	4 049	205	6	532.0	247.7	4.2	1978
1979	4 550	231	12	593.9	276.4	11.6	1979
1980	5 080	257	12	528.8	246.2	−11.0	1980

[a]Malaysia (unit value)

Phosphate rock

The main periods of expansion in world production were 1950–51, 1953–54, 1956, 1958–66, 1968, 1970–74 and 1977–80; there were falls in production or low growth for 1952, 1955, 1957, 1967, 1969 and 1975–76. The price of phosphate rock rose mainly in 1964–65, 1973–75 and 1979–80; there was a long period of steady or falling prices for 1951–63, then falling prices in 1966–70 and 1976–78.

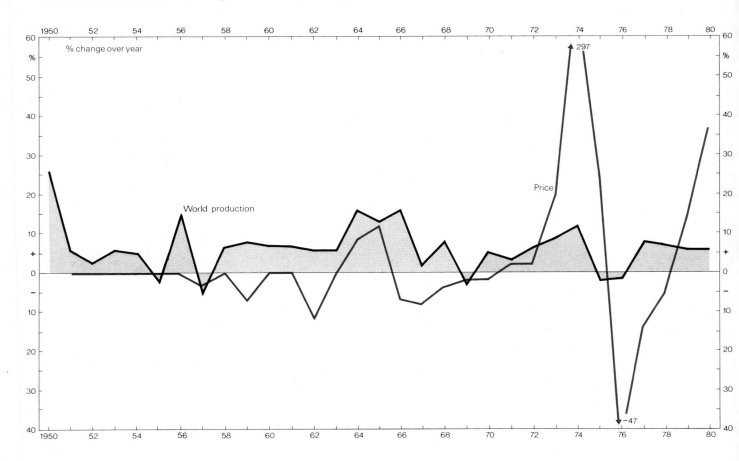

	World production			Price[a]			
	Tonnes (million)	Index 1970 = 100	% change over year	$ per tonne	Index 1970 = 100	% change over year	
1950	24.5	30	26	14.5	132	na	1950
1951	26.0	32	6	14.5	132	0	1951
1952	26.8	33	3	14.5	132	0	1952
1953	28.3	35	6	14.5	132	0	1953
1954	29.7	36	5	14.5	132	0	1954
1955	29.1	36	−2	14.5	132	0	1955
1956	33.6	41	15	14.5	132	0	1956
1957	32.0	39	−5	14.0	127	−3	1957
1958	34.3	42	7	14.0	127	0	1958
1959	37.1	46	8	13.0	118	−7	1959
1960	39.8	49	7	13.0	118	0	1960
1961	42.6	52	7	13.0	118	0	1961
1962	45.0	55	6	11.5	105	−12	1962
1963	47.9	59	6	11.5	105	0	1963
1964	55.4	68	16	12.5	114	9	1964
1965	62.6	77	13	14.0	127	12	1965
1966	72.7	89	16	13.0	118	−7	1966
1967	74.2	91	2	12.0	109	−8	1967
1968	80.0	98	8	11.5	105	−4	1968
1969	77.9	96	−3	11.2	102	−2	1969
1970	81.5	100	5	11.0	100	−2	1970
1971	85.0	104	4	11.2	102	2	1971
1972	90.8	111	7	11.5	105	2	1972
1973	99.2	122	9	13.7	125	20	1973
1974	110.6	136	12	54.5	496	297	1974
1975	108.5	133	−2	67.2	611	23	1975
1976	107.6	132	−1	35.8	326	−47	1976
1977	115.8	142	8	30.7	279	−14	1977
1978	123.7	152	7	29.0	264	−5	1978
1979	130.9	161	6	33.0	300	14	1979
1980	138.8	170	6	45.0	409	36	1980

[a]Morocco (wholesale price)

Rice

.The main periods of expansion in world production were 1950–53, 1955–56, 1958, 1960–61, 1963–64, 1967–70, 1973, 1975, 1977–78 and 1980; there were falls in production or comparatively low growth in 1954, 1957, 1959, 1962, 1965–66, 1971–72, 1974, 1976 and 1979. The price of rice increased mainly in 1951–53, 1958, 1961–62, 1966–67, 1972–74, 1977–78 and 1980; main falls in price were in 1950, 1954–56, 1959–60, 1963–65, 1968–71, 1975–76 and 1979.

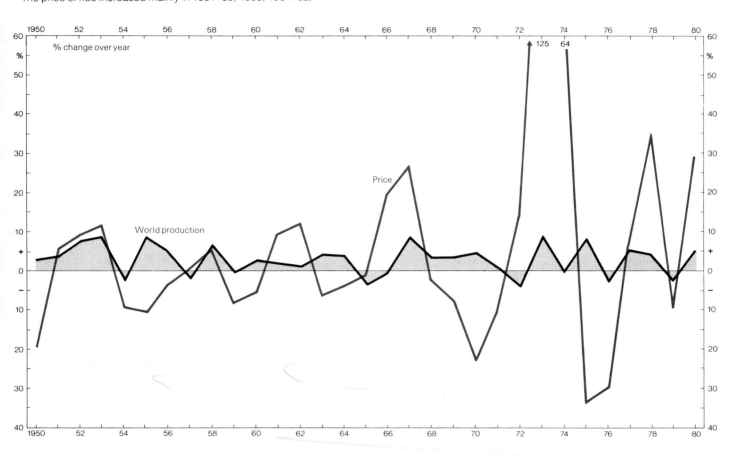

	World production[a]			Price[b]			
	Tonnes (million)	Index 1970 = 100	% change over year	$ per tonne	Index 1970 = 100	% change over year	
1950	169.6	53.7	2.6	136.70	94.9	−19.4	1950
1951	175.6	55.7	3.5	144.40	100.3	5.6	1951
1952	188.4	59.7	7.3	156.30	108.5	8.2	1952
1953	204.5	64.8	8.5	174.70	121.3	11.8	1953
1954	199.9	63.4	−2.2	157.90	109.7	−9.6	1954
1955	216.8	68.7	8.4	141.50	98.3	−10.4	1955
1956	227.7	72.2	5.0	136.90	95.1	−3.3	1956
1957	223.8	70.9	−1.7	137.18	95.3	0.2	1957
1958	239.0	75.7	6.8	144.80	100.6	5.6	1958
1959	238.2	75.5	−0.3	132.17	91.8	−8.7	1959
1960	244.3	77.4	2.5	124.70	86.6	−5.7	1960
1961	248.8	78.9	1.8	136.51	94.8	9.5	1961
1962	251.0	79.6	0.9	152.78	106.1	11.9	1962
1963	261.5	82.9	4.2	143.35	99.5	−6.2	1963
1964	271.3	86.0	3.7	137.73	95.6	−3.9	1964
1965	262.3	83.1	−3.3	136.34	94.7	−1.0	1965
1966	260.6	82.6	−0.6	163.24	113.4	19.7	1966
1967	282.6	89.6	8.4	205.98	143.0	26.2	1967
1968	292.5	92.7	3.5	201.64	140.0	−2.1	1968
1969	301.8	95.6	3.2	186.88	129.8	−7.3	1969
1970	315.5	100.0	4.6	144.00	100.0	−22.9	1970
1971	317.5	100.6	0.6	128.96	89.6	−10.4	1971
1972	305.6	96.9	−3.8	147.12	102.2	14.1	1972
1973	332.2	105.3	8.7	330.42	229.5	124.6	1973
1974	332.1	105.3	0.0	542.02	376.4	64.0	1974
1975	358.2	113.5	7.9	363.06	252.1	−33.0	1975
1976	350.1	111.0	−2.3	254.59	176.8	−29.9	1976
1977	369.0	117.0	5.4	272.20	189.0	6.9	1977
1978	385.1	122.1	4.4	367.51	255.2	35.0	1978
1979	375.9	119.1	−2.4	334.19	232.1	−9.1	1979
1980	396.1	125.6	5.4	433.70	301.2	29.8	1980

[a]Paddy rice   [b]Thailand (wholesale price)

Rubber

The main periods of expansion in world production were 1950, 1954–55, 1958–59, 1961, 1964–65, 1967–70, 1973, 1976 and 1978–79; there were falls in production or low growth rates for 1951–53, 1956–57, 1960, 1962–63, 1966, 1971–72, 1974–75, 1977 and 1980. The rubber price increased mainly in 1950–51, 1955, 1959–60, 1969, 1973–74, 1976 and 1978–80; there were falls in price for 1952–53, 1956–58, 1961–64, 1966–68, 1970–71 and 1975.

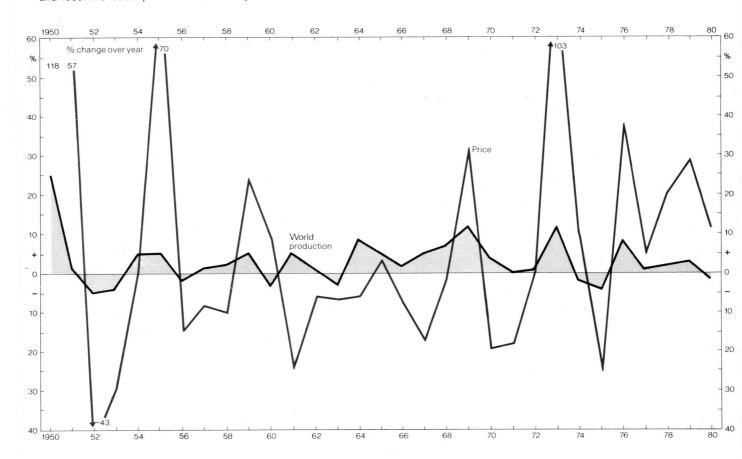

	World production[a]			Price[b]			
	Tonnes (million)	Index 1970 = 100	% change over year	$ per tonne	Index 1970 = 100	% change over year	
1950	1.89	61	25	779	192	118	1950
1951	1.92	62	1	1 221	301	57	1951
1952	1.82	59	−5	692	170	−43	1952
1953	1.75	57	−4	486	120	−30	1953
1954	1.83	59	5	485	119	0	1954
1955	1.92	62	5	822	202	70	1955
1956	1.89	61	−2	697	172	−15	1956
1957	1.91	62	1	639	157	−8	1957
1958	1.94	63	2	578	142	−10	1958
1959	2.04	66	5	716	176	24	1959
1960	1.98	64	−3	782	193	9	1960
1961	2.09	68	5	597	147	−24	1961
1962	2.12	69	1	564	139	−6	1962
1963	2.07	67	−3	522	128	−7	1963
1964	2.24	72	8	491	121	−6	1964
1965	2.34	76	5	505	124	3	1965
1966	2.38	77	2	472	116	−7	1966
1967	2.51	81	5	390	96	−17	1967
1968	2.68	87	7	383	94	−2	1968
1969	2.99	97	12	503	124	31	1969
1970	3.09	100	4	406	100	−19	1970
1971	3.08	100	0	333	82	−18	1971
1972	3.11	101	1	333	82	0	1972
1973	3.50	113	12	676	166	103	1973
1974	3.44	111	−2	745	183	10	1974
1975	3.31	107	−4	569	140	−24	1975
1976	3.56	115	8	783	193	38	1976
1977	3.59	116	1	824	203	5	1977
1978	3.68	119	2	993	244	20	1978
1979	3.78	122	3	1 277	314	29	1979
1980	3.74	121	−1	1 435	353	12	1980

[a]Natural rubber only [b]Malaysia (Singapore wholesale price)

Silver

The main periods of expansion in world production were 1950, 1952–53, 1955–58, 1960, 1962–63, 1965–66, 1968–70, 1972–73 and 1976–78; there were falls in production or low growth rates for 1951, 1954, 1959, 1961, 1964, 1967, 1971, 1974–75 and 1979–80. The price of silver rose mainly in 1950–51, 1955, 1962–63, 1967–68, 1973–74 and 1978–80; there were falls in the price for 1952, 1958, 1969–71 and 1975–76, and comparatively stable periods for 1953–54, 1956–57, 1960–61 and 1964–66.

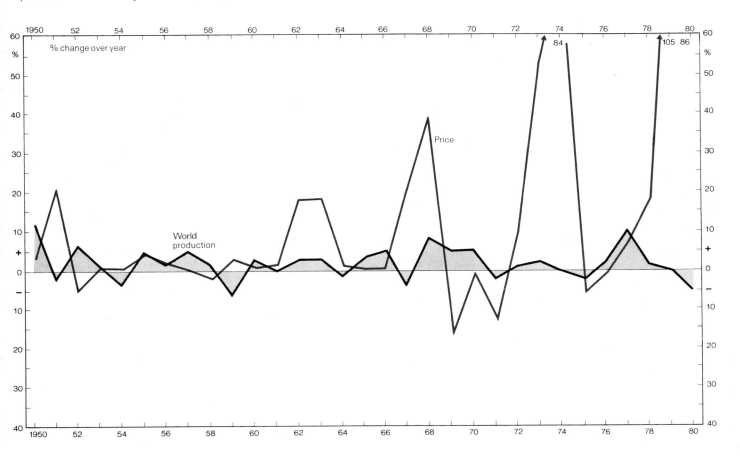

	World production[a]			Price[b]			
	Tonnes (000)	Index 1970 = 100	% change over year	$ per ounce (troy)	Index 1970 = 100	% change over year	
1950	6.57	68	12	0.74	41.9	3.2	1950
1951	6.45	67	−2	0.89	50.5	20.5	1951
1952	6.92	72	7	0.85	47.9	−5.0	1952
1953	7.04	73	2	0.85	48.1	0.4	1953
1954	6.80	70	−3	0.85	48.2	0.1	1954
1955	7.15	74	5	0.89	50.3	4.5	1955
1956	7.27	75	2	0.91	51.3	1.9	1956
1957	7.61	79	5	0.91	51.3	0.0	1957
1958	7.73	80	2	0.89	50.3	−2.0	1958
1959	7.26	75	−6	0.91	51.5	2.5	1959
1960	7.48	77	3	0.91	51.6	0.2	1960
1961	7.48	77	0	0.92	52.2	1.1	1961
1962	7.70	80	3	1.08	61.3	17.4	1962
1963	7.92	82	3	1.28	72.2	17.9	1963
1964	7.84	81	−1	1.29	73.0	1.1	1964
1965	8.07	83	3	1.29	73.0	0.0	1965
1966	8.49	88	5	1.29	73.0	0.0	1966
1967	8.16	84	−4	1.55	87.5	19.9	1967
1968	8.79	91	8	2.14	121.1	38.4	1968
1969	9.24	96	5	1.79	101.1	−16.5	1969
1970	9.67	100	5	1.77	100.0	−1.1	1970
1971	9.43	98	−2	1.55	87.3	−12.7	1971
1972	9.54	99	1	1.68	95.1	9.0	1972
1973	9.75	101	2	2.56	144.4	51.8	1973
1974	9.75	101	0	4.71	265.8	84.1	1974
1975	9.52	98	−2	4.42	249.5	−6.1	1975
1976	9.73	101	2	4.35	245.8	−1.5	1976
1977	10.66	110	10	4.62	261.0	6.2	1977
1978	10.85	112	2	5.40	305.0	16.8	1978
1979	10.84	112	0	11.09	626.2	105.3	1979
1980	10.30	106	−5	20.58	1 161.9	85.6	1980

[a]Metal content of ores and concentrates   [b]United States (wholesale price)

Soyabeans

The main periods of expansion in world production were 1950–52, 1954–56, 1958, 1961, 1965–68, 1972–73, 1975, 1977 and 1979; there were falls in production for 1953, 1959–60, 1962, 1974, 1976 and 1980. The period from 1965 to 1973 was one of comparatively steady expansion. The price of soyabeans increased mainly in 1950–51, 1961, 1963, 1965–66, 1970–73 (with an especially large rise in 1973), 1976–77 and 1979; there were falls in price for 1954–60, 1962, 1967–69, 1974–75 and 1978.

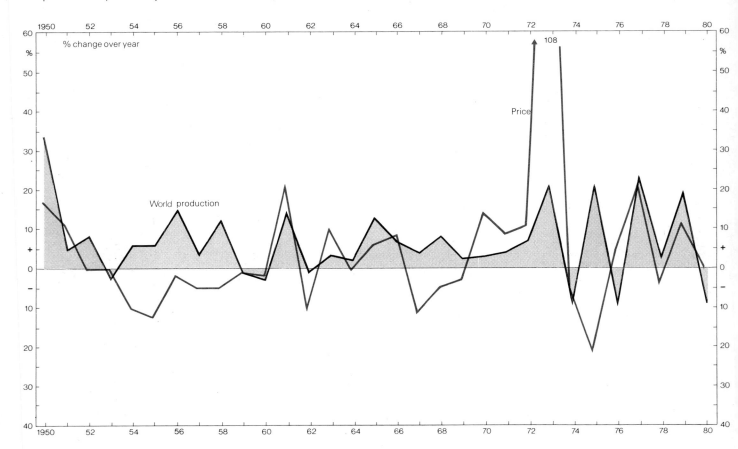

	World production			Price[a]			
	Tonnes (000)	Index 1970 = 100	% change over year	$ per tonne	Index 1970 = 100	% change over year	
1950	16534	37	34	122	104	17	1950
1951	17349	39	5	135	115	11	1951
1952	18686	41	8	135	115	0	1952
1953	18301	41	−2	135	115	0	1953
1954	19368	43	6	122	104	−10	1954
1955	20445	45	6	107	92	−12	1955
1956	23483	52	15	105	90	−2	1956
1957	24498	54	4	100	85	−5	1957
1958	27385	61	12	95	81	−5	1958
1959	27154	60	−1	94	80	−1	1959
1960	26442	59	−3	92	79	−2	1960
1961	30185	67	14	111	95	21	1961
1962	29897	66	−1	100	85	−10	1962
1963	30693	68	3	110	94	10	1963
1964	31357	70	2	110	94	0	1964
1965	35382	79	13	117	100	6	1965
1966	37874	84	7	126	108	8	1966
1967	39479	88	4	112	96	−11	1967
1968	42642	95	8	106	91	−5	1968
1969	43815	97	3	103	88	−3	1969
1970	45057	100	3	117	100	14	1970
1971	46940	104	4	126	108	8	1971
1972	50313	112	7	140	120	11	1972
1973	60671	135	21	291	249	108	1973
1974	55180	122	−9	277	237	−5	1974
1975	66501	148	21	220	188	−21	1975
1976	60719	135	−9	231	197	5	1976
1977	74807	166	23	279	238	21	1977
1978	76723	170	3	268	229	−4	1978
1979	91449	203	19	297	254	11	1979
1980	83481	185	−9	297	254	0	1980

[a]Netherlands (wholesale price); linked to US price before 1957

Sugar

The main periods of expansion in world production were 1950–52, 1954, 1956–61, 1964–65, 1967, 1969–70, 1972–73 and 1975–77; there were falls in production or comparatively low growth for 1953, 1955, 1962–63, 1966, 1968, 1971, 1974 and 1978–80. The sugar price increased mainly in 1951, 1957, 1960, 1962–63, 1966, 1972–75 and 1980; there were main falls in 1952–54, 1958–59, 1961, 1965 and 1976–77.

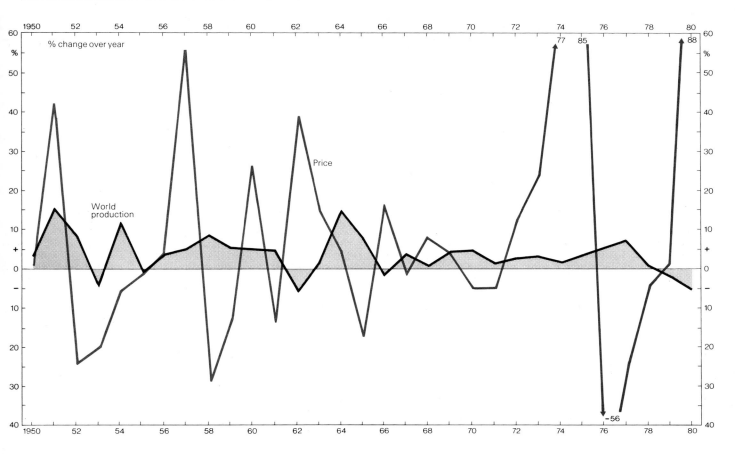

	World production[a]			Price[b]			
	Tonnes (000)	Index 1970 = 100	% change over year	$ per tonne	Index 1970 = 100	% change over year	
1950	29646	41.6	3.4	88	65	1	1950
1951	34280	48.1	15.6	126	93	43	1951
1952	37030	52.0	8.0	95	70	−24	1952
1953	35496	49.8	−4.1	76	56	−20	1953
1954	39672	55.7	11.8	72	53	−5	1954
1955	39258	55.1	−1.0	72	53	−1	1955
1956	40725	57.2	3.7	74	55	4	1956
1957	42765	60.0	5.0	116	86	56	1957
1958	46250	64.9	8.2	84	62	−28	1958
1959	48651	68.3	5.2	74	54	−12	1959
1960	51105	71.7	5.0	94	69	27	1960
1961	53505	75.1	4.7	80	59	−14	1961
1962	50440	70.8	−5.7	112	82	39	1962
1963	51381	72.1	1.9	128	94	15	1963
1964	58836	82.6	14.5	133	98	4	1964
1965	63396	89.0	7.8	111	82	−17	1965
1966	62585	87.9	−1.3	128	95	16	1966
1967	64872	91.1	3.7	127	93	−1	1967
1968	65302	91.7	0.7	137	101	8	1968
1969	68004	95.5	4.1	143	105	4	1969
1970	71229	100.0	4.7	136	100	−5	1970
1971	72266	101.5	1.5	129	95	−5	1971
1972	73922	103.8	2.3	145	107	13	1972
1973	76038	106.8	2.9	180	133	24	1973
1974	77138	108.3	1.4	319	235	77	1974
1975	79601	111.8	3.2	590	435	85	1975
1976	83754	117.6	5.2	262	193	−56	1976
1977	89811	126.1	7.2	199	147	−24	1977
1978	90289	126.8	0.5	190	140	−4	1978
1979	88788	124.7	−1.7	192	142	1	1979
1980	84177	118.2	−5.2	362	267	88	1980

[a]Centrifugal sugar (raw value)   [b]Dominican Republic (unit value)

Tea

The main periods of expansion in world production were 1950–51, 1954–55, 1957–58, 1961, 1964, 1966, 1968–70, 1972–73, 1975–78 and 1980; there was a fall in production only for 1952, with low growth in 1953, 1956, 1960, 1962–63, 1967, 1971, 1974 and 1979. The tea price rose mainly in 1953–54, 1957, 1962–63, 1965, 1970–72, 1974–77 (especially for 1977) and 1980; there were falls in the price for 1950–52, 1956, 1958–59, 1961, 1964, 1966–69, 1973 and 1978–79.

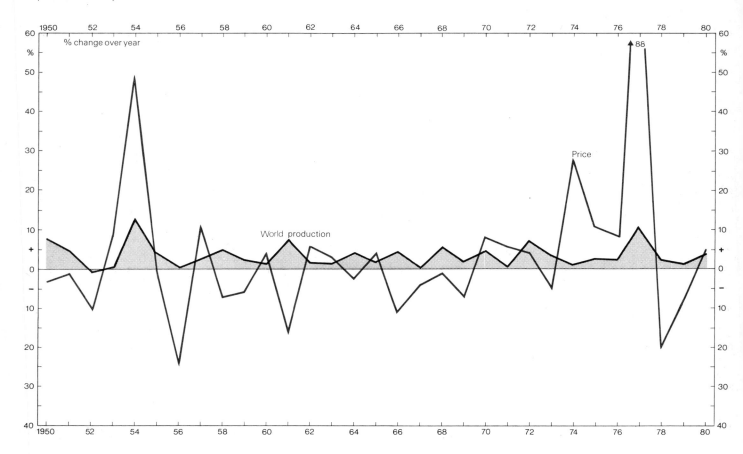

	World production			Price[a]			
	Tonnes (000)	Index 1970 = 100	% change over year	$ per tonne	Index 1970 = 100	% change over year	
1950	710	53.2	7.7	1 146	114	−3	1950
1951	742	55.6	4.5	1 133	112	−1	1951
1952	736	55.1	−0.9	1 025	102	−10	1952
1953	737	55.2	0.2	1 116	110	9	1953
1954	827	62.0	12.2	1 660	164	49	1954
1955	861	64.5	4.1	1 656	164	0	1955
1956	864	64.7	0.3	1 265	125	−24	1956
1957	888	66.5	2.8	1 409	140	11	1957
1958	931	69.8	4.9	1 312	130	−7	1958
1959	951	71.3	2.2	1 239	123	−6	1959
1960	966	72.4	1.5	1 287	128	4	1960
1961	1 038	77.8	7.5	1 076	107	−16	1961
1962	1 056	79.2	1.7	1 140	113	6	1962
1963	1 071	80.3	1.4	1 171	116	3	1963
1964	1 116	83.6	4.2	1 142	113	−2	1964
1965	1 134	85.0	1.7	1 190	118	4	1965
1966	1 184	88.8	4.4	1 065	105	−11	1966
1967	1 188	89.0	0.3	1 023	101	−4	1967
1968	1 252	93.8	5.4	1 014	100	−1	1968
1969	1 277	95.7	2.0	939	93	−7	1969
1970	1 334	100.0	4.5	1 010	100	8	1970
1971	1 344	100.7	0.7	1 074	106	6	1971
1972	1 444	108.2	7.4	1 118	111	4	1972
1973	1 492	111.8	3.3	1 065	105	−5	1973
1974	1 505	112.8	0.9	1 367	135	28	1974
1975	1 548	116.0	2.9	1 517	150	11	1975
1976	1 586	118.9	2.5	1 638	162	8	1976
1977	1 748	131.0	10.2	3 082	305	88	1977
1978	1 793	134.4	2.6	2 456	243	−20	1978
1979	1 814	135.9	1.2	2 258	224	−8	1979
1980	1 886	141.3	4.0	2 363	234	5	1980

[a]Sri Lanka/India (US wholesale price)

Tin

There was comparatively little change in the level of world production over the 30-year period. The level increased at a low rate of growth for 1950–56, 1964–68 and 1976–80; there were main increases in production for 1960 (recovery), 1966 and 1978, with falls in 1957–58, 1963, 1969, 1973 and 1975. The price of tin increased mainly in 1951, 1955–56, 1959, 1961, 1964–65, 1969–70, 1972–74 and 1977–80; there were falls in the price for 1950, 1952–54, 1957–58, 1960, 1966–68, 1971 and 1975.

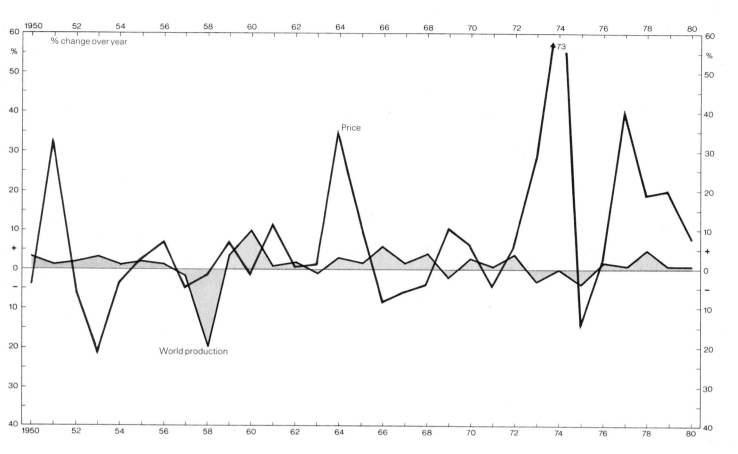

	World production[a]			Price[b]			
	Tonnes (000)	Index 1970 = 100	% change over year	$ per tonne	Index 1970 = 100	% change over year	
1950	177	81	3	2 105	54.8	−3.8	1950
1951	179	82	1	2 804	72.9	33.2	1951
1952	183	84	2	2 654	69.0	−5.3	1952
1953	189	87	3	2 099	54.6	−20.9	1953
1954	190	87	1	2 030	52.8	−3.3	1954
1955	194	89	2	2 083	54.2	2.6	1955
1956	196	90	1	2 227	57.9	6.9	1956
1957	193	89	−2	2 125	55.3	−4.6	1957
1958	155	71	−20	2 094	54.5	−1.5	1958
1959	161	74	4	2 249	58.5	7.4	1959
1960	177	81	10	2 233	58.1	−0.7	1960
1961	178	82	1	2 493	64.9	11.6	1961
1962	182	84	2	2 524	65.7	1.2	1962
1963	181	83	−1	2 573	66.9	1.9	1963
1964	187	86	3	3 479	90.5	35.2	1964
1965	191	88	2	3 887	101.1	11.7	1965
1966	202	93	6	3 580	93.1	−7.9	1966
1967	207	95	2	3 386	88.1	−5.4	1967
1968	215	99	4	3 258	84.7	−3.8	1968
1969	210	97	−2	3 609	93.9	10.8	1969
1970	217	100	3	3 845	100.0	6.5	1970
1971	220	101	1	3 686	95.9	−4.1	1971
1972	229	105	4	3 915	101.8	6.2	1972
1973	221	102	−3	5 053	131.4	29.1	1973
1974	221	102	0	8 721	226.8	72.6	1974
1975	211	97	−4	7 498	195.0	−14.0	1975
1976	215	99	2	7 703	200.3	2.7	1976
1977	216	99	1	10 858	282.4	41.0	1977
1978	228	105	5	13 009	338.4	19.8	1978
1979	229	106	1	15 723	408.9	20.9	1979
1980	232	107	1	17 077	444.2	8.6	1980

[a]Metal content of ores and concentrates   [b]United States (wholesale price)

Tobacco

The main periods of expansion in world production were 1950–51, 1953–56, 1959–60, 1962–64, 1967, 1972, 1974, 1976 and 1978; there were falls in production for 1952, 1957–58, 1961, 1965, 1968–69, 1971, 1977 and 1979–80. The price of tobacco increased mainly in 1950–51, 1956–59, 1961, 1964, 1966, 1968–69, 1972–75 and 1977–80; there were falls in the price for 1952–53, 1955, 1960, 1963, 1965 and 1971. The price rise in 1973–74 was low compared to that for most other commodities.

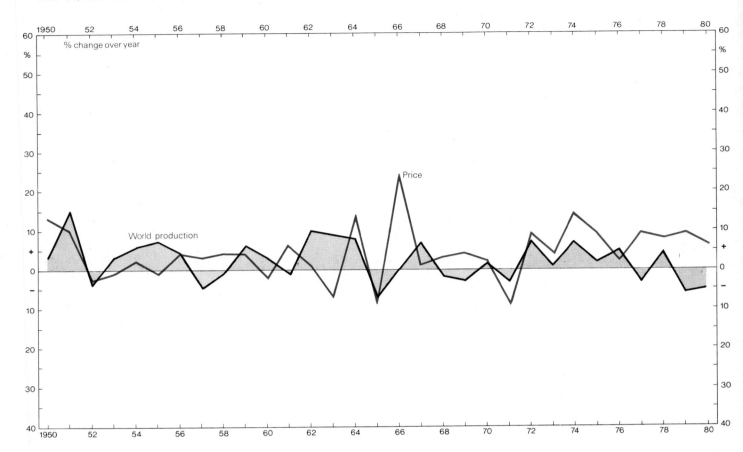

	World production			Price[a]			
	Tonnes (000)	Index 1970 = 100	% change over year	$ per tonne	Index 1970 = 100	% change over year	
1950	2 802	60	3	1 056	59.4	13	1950
1951	3 224	69	15	1 160	65.3	10	1951
1952	3 102	66	−4	1 125	63.3	−3	1952
1953	3 200	68	3	1 117	62.8	−1	1953
1954	3 403	72	6	1 142	64.3	2	1954
1955	3 630	77	7	1 135	63.9	−1	1955
1956	3 761	80	4	1 177	66.2	4	1956
1957	3 568	76	−5	1 210	68.1	3	1957
1958	3 546	76	−1	1 254	70.6	4	1958
1959	3 742	80	6	1 307	73.6	4	1959
1960	3 854	82	3	1 283	72.2	−2	1960
1961	3 803	81	−1	1 356	76.3	6	1961
1962	4 190	89	10	1 371	77.2	1	1962
1963	4 570	97	9	1 279	72.0	−7	1963
1964	4 948	105	8	1 443	81.2	13	1964
1965	4 622	98	−7	1 312	73.8	−9	1965
1966	4 607	98	0	1 620	91.2	23	1966
1967	4 910	105	7	1 630	91.7	1	1967
1968	4 791	102	−2	1 673	94.1	3	1968
1969	4 647	99	−3	1 744	98.2	4	1969
1970	4 696	100	1	1 777	100.0	2	1970
1971	4 563	97	−3	1 620	91.2	−9	1971
1972	4 891	104	7	1 764	99.3	9	1972
1973	4 964	106	1	1 842	103.6	4	1973
1974	5 317	113	7	2 106	118.5	14	1974
1975	5 442	116	2	2 288	128.7	9	1975
1976	5 692	121	5	2 332	131.2	2	1976
1977	5 541	118	−3	2 537	142.7	9	1977
1978	5 743	122	4	2 735	153.9	8	1978
1979	5 399	115	−6	2 971	167.2	9	1979
1980	5 129	109	−5	3 144	176.9	6	1980

[a]United States (wholesale price)

Wheat

The main periods of expansion in world production were 1950–52, 1955–56, 1958, 1962, 1964, 1966, 1968, 1971, 1973, 1976, 1978 and 1980; there were falls in production or comparatively low growth for 1953–54, 1957, 1959–61, 1963, 1965, 1967, 1969–70, 1972, 1974–75, 1977 and 1979. The wheat price rose mainly in 1951–52, 1957–58, 1961–62, 1964, 1966, 1972–74 and 1978–80; there were falls in the price for 1950, 1953–56, 1959, 1963, 1965, 1967–70 and 1975–77.

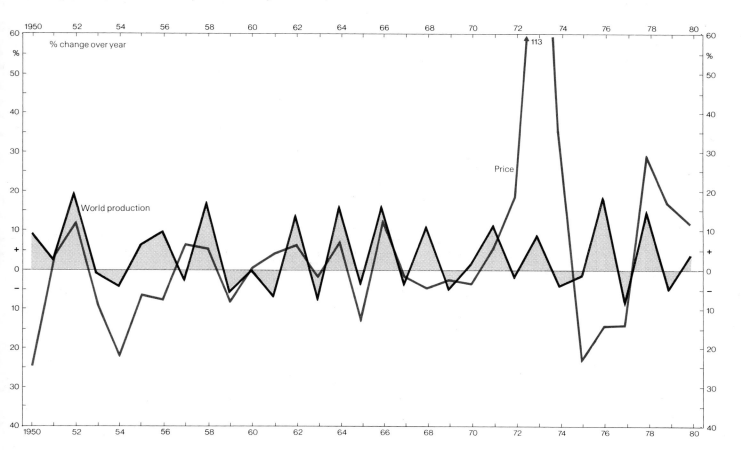

	World production			Price[a]			
	Tonnes (million)	Index 1970 = 100	% change over year	$ per tonne	Index 1970 = 100	% change over year	
1950	168.3	52.6	9.1	77	141	−25	1950
1951	172.8	53.9	2.6	79	145	3	1951
1952	206.6	64.5	19.6	89	162	12	1952
1953	205.2	64.1	−0.7	80	147	−9	1953
1954	196.3	61.3	−4.3	63	115	−22	1954
1955	208.2	65.0	6.1	58	107	−7	1955
1956	228.3	71.3	9.6	54	98	−8	1956
1957	222.7	69.5	−2.4	57	104	6	1957
1958	259.5	81.0	16.5	60	109	5	1958
1959	245.5	76.6	−5.4	55	100	−8	1959
1960	244.9	76.5	−0.2	55	100	0	1960
1961	229.5	71.7	−6.3	57	104	4	1961
1962	260.3	81.3	13.4	61	111	6	1962
1963	240.9	75.2	−7.5	60	109	−2	1963
1964	278.6	87.0	15.7	64	117	7	1964
1965	269.0	84.0	−3.4	56	102	−13	1965
1966	311.8	97.4	15.9	63	115	12	1966
1967	300.7	93.9	−3.6	62	113	−2	1967
1968	333.4	104.1	10.9	58	107	−5	1968
1969	316.4	98.8	−5.1	57	104	−3	1969
1970	320.3	100.0	1.2	55	100	−4	1970
1971	356.3	111.2	11.2	58	105	5	1971
1972	349.4	109.1	−1.9	68	124	18	1972
1973	378.9	118.3	8.5	145	264	113	1973
1974	364.4	113.8	−3.8	195	357	35	1974
1975	360.1	112.4	−1.2	148	270	−24	1975
1976	425.3	132.8	18.1	126	230	−15	1976
1977	391.4	122.2	−8.0	107	195	−15	1977
1978	449.4	140.3	14.8	136	249	28	1978
1979	429.1	134.0	−4.5	158	288	16	1979
1980	444.7	138.8	3.6	175	320	11	1980

[a]Australia (wholesale price); converted from US dollars per bushel price

Wool

The main periods of expansion in world production were 1952, 1955–56, 1958–59, 1965–69, 1975 and 1979–80; there were falls in production or a low rate of increase for 1950–51, 1953–54, 1957, 1960, 1962, 1964–65, 1968, 1970–74 and 1976–78. The price of wool rose mainly in 1950–51, 1953, 1956–57, 1963, 1966 (recovery), 1972–73, 1977 and 1979–80; there were falls in the price for 1952, 1954–55, 1958, 1960, 1964–65, 1967–71 and 1974–75.

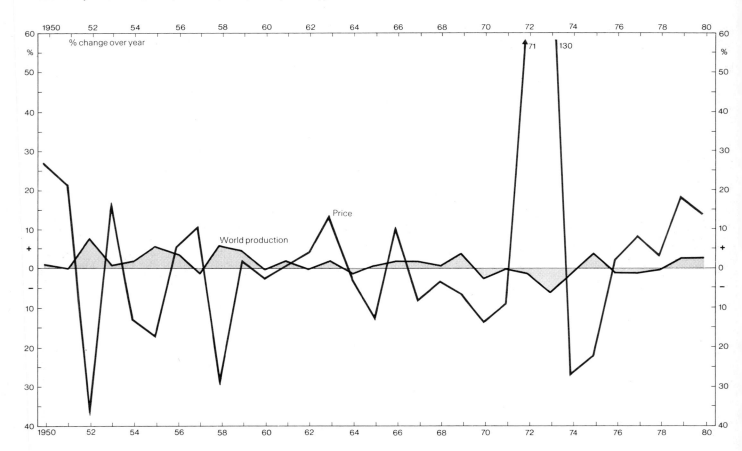

	World production[a]			Price[b]			
	Tonnes (million)	Index 1970 = 100	% change over year	$ per tonne	Index 1970 = 100	% change over year	
1950	1.93	68	1	4202.7	222.3	27.1	1950
1951	1.93	68	0	5105.5	270.1	21.5	1951
1952	2.09	74	8	3245.9	171.7	−36.4	1952
1953	2.11	74	1	3775.8	199.7	16.3	1953
1954	2.16	76	2	3294.8	174.3	−12.7	1954
1955	2.28	80	6	2747.0	145.3	−16.6	1955
1956	2.37	83	4	2901.3	153.5	5.6	1956
1957	2.35	83	−1	3215.1	170.1	10.8	1957
1958	2.49	88	6	2286.6	121.0	−28.9	1958
1959	2.61	92	5	2332.9	123.4	2.0	1959
1960	2.60	91	0	2281.4	120.7	−2.2	1960
1961	2.65	93	2	2304.6	121.9	1.0	1961
1962	2.64	93	0	2404.9	127.2	4.4	1962
1963	2.68	94	2	2739.2	144.9	13.9	1963
1964	2.66	93	−1	2696.4	142.6	−1.6	1964
1965	2.67	94	1	2366.9	125.2	−12.2	1965
1966	2.73	96	2	2607.2	137.9	10.2	1966
1967	2.77	97	2	2396.8	126.8	−8.1	1967
1968	2.80	98	1	2325.7	123.0	−3.0	1968
1969	2.89	102	4	2172.7	114.9	−6.6	1969
1970	2.84	100	−2	1890.5	100.0	−13.0	1970
1971	2.84	100	0	1722.5	91.1	−8.9	1971
1972	2.80	99	−1	2937.4	155.4	70.5	1972
1973	2.64	93	−6	6740.7	356.6	129.5	1973
1974	2.60	91	−1	4951.7	261.9	−26.5	1974
1975	2.71	95	4	3857.8	204.1	−22.1	1975
1976	2.67	94	−1	3959.9	209.5	2.6	1976
1977	2.66	93	−1	4283.1	226.6	8.2	1977
1978	2.67	94	0	4416.2	233.6	3.1	1978
1979	2.74	96	3	5225.2	276.4	18.3	1979
1980	2.82	99	3	5962.0	315.4	14.1	1980

[a]Greasy wool   [b]Australia/New Zealand 64s (UK wholesale price)

Zinc

The main periods of expansion in world production were 1950–52, 1955–56, 1960–62, 1964–70, 1972–73, 1977 and 1979; there were falls in production or low rates of growth for 1954, 1958–59, 1971, 1974–76, 1978 and 1980. There was a period of comparatively stable growth during the 1960s. The zinc price increased mainly in 1950–51, 1955–56, 1959–60, 1963–65, 1969–70, 1972–75 and 1979; there were falls in the price for 1952–54, 1957–58, 1961, 1967–68 and 1976–78.

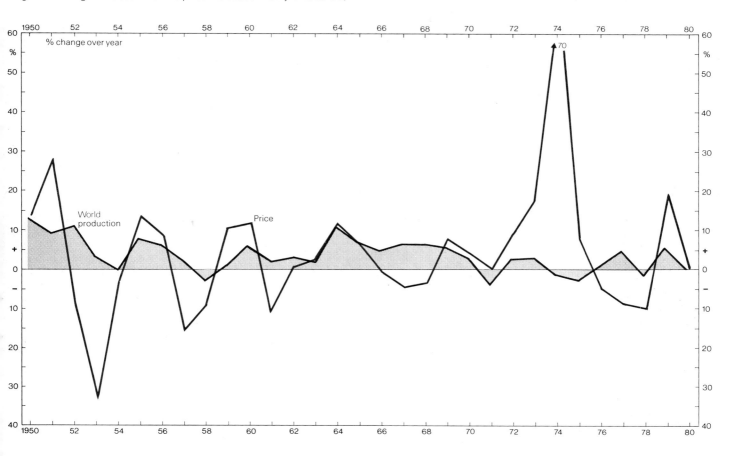

	World production[a]			Price[b]			
	Tonnes (000)	Index 1970 = 100	% change over year	$ per tonne	Index 1970 = 100	% change over year	
1950	2197	40	13	322	92	14	1950
1951	2391	43	9	413	118	28	1951
1952	2658	48	11	375	107	−9	1952
1953	2726	49	3	254	73	−32	1953
1954	2732	49	0	247	70	−3	1954
1955	2954	53	8	282	81	14	1955
1956	3133	57	6	308	88	9	1956
1957	3187	58	2	262	75	−15	1957
1958	3106	56	−3	238	68	−9	1958
1959	3134	57	1	264	75	11	1959
1960	3332	60	6	297	85	12	1960
1961	3409	62	2	266	76	−10	1961
1962	3524	64	3	267	76	1	1962
1963	3585	65	2	276	79	3	1963
1964	3964	72	11	310	88	12	1964
1965	4249	77	7	331	94	7	1965
1966	4445	80	5	331	94	0	1966
1967	4758	86	7	317	91	−4	1967
1968	5091	92	7	309	88	−3	1968
1969	5380	97	6	335	96	9	1969
1970	5529	100	3	351	100	5	1970
1971	5332	96	−4	355	101	1	1971
1972	5489	99	3	390	111	10	1972
1973	5660	102	3	465	133	19	1973
1974	5598	101	−1	789	225	70	1974
1975	5478	99	−2	858	245	9	1975
1976	5526	100	1	827	236	−4	1976
1977	5805	105	5	761	217	−8	1977
1978	5759	104	−1	694	198	−9	1978
1979	6125	111	6	833	238	20	1979
1980	6128	111	0	840	240	1	1980

[a]Metal content of ores and concentrates   [b]United States (wholesale price)

Technical appendix

The analysis of fluctuations

It is not usually clear from a series of the actual levels for an economic item just where any fluctuations begin and end; this is mainly because there is generally an underlying growth trend. In order to isolate the fluctuations it is usual to adopt one of two main methods: either to isolate the trend and show the figures as % variation above or below the trend, or to show the % changes from one year to another.

Showing the % variation above or below the trend has some advantage when concentrating on the actual peaks or troughs of any cycle; the peak is usually near the same time in the % variation as in the original series. When showing the % change over the previous year the peak of that series is not at the same point as the peak in the original series, it always precedes it. This can be seen from the following chart of a theoretical sine basis curve (Chart 1), indicating both the % change over year and the % variation around a trend.

The peaks in the original series used and in the % variation around the trend are at 1952–53, 1962–63 and 1972–73, and the bottom of the trough is at 1957–58, 1967–68 and 1977–78. The % change over year reaches a high point at 1950, 1960, 1970 and 1980 – at the point of greatest expansion; that is, the % change over year shows more clearly the periods of expansion and conversely the periods of recession. The % change over year is zero both when the original series reaches a peak and when it reaches the bottom of a trough. The series for % change over year moves about 2 years ahead of the original series; when it is positive (above the zero line) the item is increasing and when it is negative (below the zero line) the item is falling.

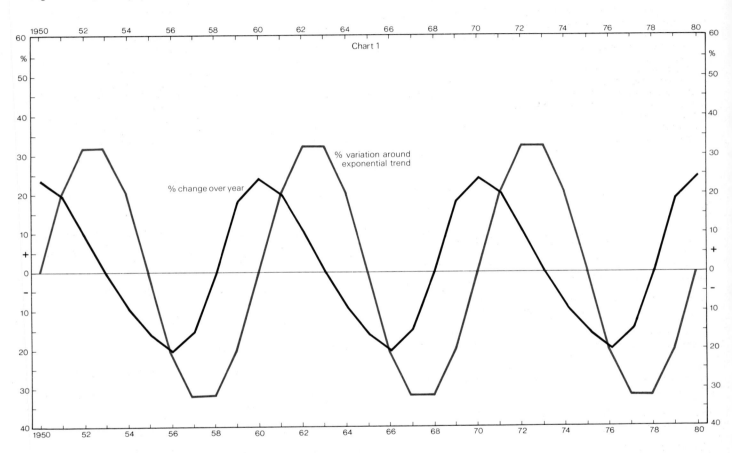

An actual example is shown in Chart 2, being the % change over year and the % variation around an exponential trend for US fixed investment. The tendency for the % change over year to move ahead of the original series can be seen for 1965–66, 1972–74 and 1977–79.

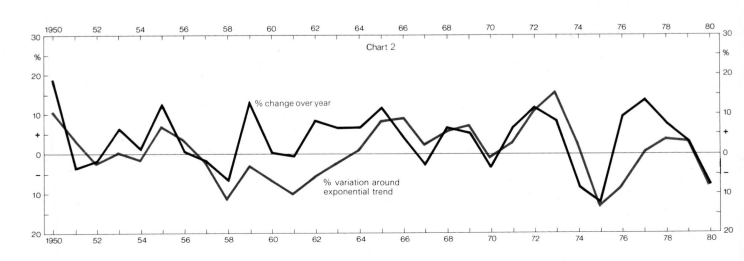

190

Technical appendix

Using the % change over year, in addition to showing more clearly the periods of expansion and recession, also has the practical advantage of being easy to use. It is possible for the reader to add the % change over year for additional years simply by dividing the figure for each year by the previous year's figure; it would be more difficult to add to a series of % variations around a trend, since the trend would itself nearly always change with additional years.

Finally it may be noted, when using a series of % change over year, that a zig-zag appearance – a marked change from one year to the next – encountered particularly in commodity series, means growth then consolidation when the % change stays above zero, and means a swing from a good year to a bad one when the % change moves below zero. In commodities the pattern of high production and low price swinging to low production and high price is often encountered.

Technical footnote. The % change over year is a discrete form of a first differential, and the mathematics of differentials applies. Following is an extract from The Economist publication 'The World Measurement Guide' (page 179), which outlines the general mathematics:
'Over the period of a business cycle, the rate of growth is positive during expansion, and accelerating during the early stages of recovery; then the rate of growth falls and is small or negative during recession. In terms of calculus, where dy/dt is the first differential ('rate of change') and d^2y/dy^2 is the second differential ('rate of acceleration'), the changes in these rates are indicated in the following diagram (of a sine curve):

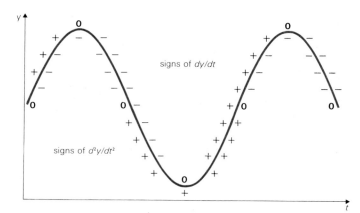

That is, the first differential is positive (there is positive growth) during recovery from a trough; the second differential is at first positive (the rate of growth is increasing), then as recovery continues a 'point of inflexion' is reached at which the second differential becomes zero (the rate of growth, while still positive, begins to slacken); at a peak the first differential becomes zero (the rate of growth changes from positive to negative), while the second differential is still negative; the rate of fall then increases until another point of inflexion is reached (when the second differential is zero), when the rate of fall begins to slow down, becoming zero at the bottom of the trough'.

Definition of terms

% change over year the percentage change for the item concerned in the amount for the year specified over that for the previous year

Gross domestic product total product for the country, in quantity terms (at constant prices)

Consumers expenditure current spending by households on goods and services, in quantity terms (at constant prices)

Government expenditure current spending by all forms of government, including local, in quantity terms (at constant prices)

Fixed investment gross fixed capital investment or formation, in quantity terms (at constant prices). Excludes stock (inventory) investment

Stock investment increase or reduction in the value of stocks held, in quantity terms (at constant prices)

Exports the quantity of exports of goods only

Imports the quantity of imports of goods only

Unemployment the number of people unemployed; the precise definition varies according to country

Industrial production general index of industrial production, usually excluding construction

Coal production index based on quantity produced in terms of weight

Electricity production index based on quantity produced in terms of kilowatt hours

Steel production index based on quantity produced of crude steel in terms of weight

Cement production index based on quantity produced in terms of weight

Sulphuric acid production index based on quantity produced in terms of weight of 100% H_2SO_4

Passenger car production index based on number of cars produced

Ships built index based on ships completed in terms of gross tons

Unit value actual value as recorded for an item in export or import statistics

Wholesale prices actual price or general index of prices at a pre-retail level of distribution

Consumer prices general index of prices at the retail level

Wages general index of wage rates or earnings

Shipping freight rates general index of the value of freight rates

Corporate profits total value of corporate profits, in value terms (at current prices)

Share prices general index of industrial share prices

Money stock notes and coin in circulation, and liabilities on demand deposits to the domestic sector by the banking sector (narrow definition). Figures refer to the position at the end of the calendar year

International reserves gold, foreign exchange, SDRs and the IMF fund reserve position; gold is valued at SDR 35 per troy ounce. Figures refer to the position at the end of the calendar year

Interest rate call, short-term or Treasury bill rate

Commodity price in general, a representative price for the commodity; prices have been standardised to be in terms of $ (US dollars) per tonne or, for gold and silver, per troy ounce.